A History of the British Labour Party

British Studies Series

General Editor JEREMY BLACK

Alan Booth **The British Economy in the Twentieth Century**

Glenn Burgess **British Political Thought, 1500–1660: The Politics of the Post-Reformation**

John Charmley **A History of Conservative Politics since 1830 (2nd edn)**

David Childs **Britain since 1939 (2nd edn)**

John Davis **A History of Britain, 1885–1939**

David Dutton **A History of the Liberal Party since 1900 (2nd edn)**

David Eastwood **Government and Community in the English Provinces, 1700–1870**

Philip Edwards **The Making of the Modern English State, 1460–1660**

W. H. Fraser **A History of British Trade Unionism, 1700–1998**

John Garrard **Democratisation in Britain: Elites, Civil Society and Reform since 1800**

Brian Hill **The Early Parties and Politics in Britain, 1688–1832**

Katrina Honeyman **Women, Gender and Industrialisation in England, 1700–1870**

Kevin Jefferys **Retreat from New Jerusalem: British Politics, 1951–1964**

Kevin Jefferys **Sport and Politics in Modern Britain: The Road to 2012**

T. A. Jenkins **The Liberal Ascendancy, 1830–1886**

David Loades **Power in Tudor England**

Ian Machin **The Rise of Democracy in Britain, 1830–1918**

Allan I. Macinnes **The British Revolution, 1629–1660**

Alexander Murdoch **British History, 1660–1832: National Identity and Local Culture**

Anthony Musson and W. M. Ormrod **The Evolution of English Justice: Law, Politics and Society in the Fourteenth Century**

Murray G. H. Pittock **Inventing and Resisting Britain: Cultural Identities in Britain and Ireland, 1685–1789**

Nick Smart **The National Government, 1931–40**

Howard Temperley **Britain and America since Independence**

Andrew Thorpe **A History of the British Labour Party (4th edn)**

Michael J. Turner **Britain's International Role 1970–1991**

British Studies Series

Series Standing Order ISBN 978–0–333–71691–5 hardcover
Series Standing Order ISBN 978–0–333–69332–2 paperback
(*outside North America only*)

You can receive future titles in this series as they are published by placing a standing order. Please contact your bookseller or, in the case of difficulty, write to us at the address below with your name and address, the title of the series and the ISBN quoted above.

Customer Services Department, Macmillan Distribution Ltd, Houndmills, Basingstoke, Hampshire, RG21 6XS, UK

A History of the British Labour Party

Fourth Edition

Andrew Thorpe

palgrave

First published 2015 by
PALGRAVE

Palgrave in the UK is an imprint of Macmillan Publishers Limited, registered in England, company number 785998, of 4 Crinan Street, London, N1 9XW.

Palgrave Macmillan in the US is a division of St Martin's Press LLC, 175 Fifth Avenue, New York, NY 10010.

Palgrave is a global imprint of the above companies and is represented throughout the world.

Palgrave® and Macmillan® are registered trademarks in the United States, the United Kingdom, Europe and other countries.

ISBN 978–1–137–40983–6 hardback
ISBN 978–1–137–40982–9 paperback

This book is printed on paper suitable for recycling and made from fully managed and sustained forest sources. Logging, pulping and manufacturing processes are expected to conform to the environmental regulations of the country of origin.

A catalogue record for this book is available from the British Library.

A catalog record for this book is available from the Library of Congress.

Typeset by MPS Limited, Chennai, India.

Printed in China

For Rhodri Thorpe

Contents

Acknowledgements

Once again, I have to thank my publishers for suggesting that I should produce a new edition of this book. Certainly, enough has happened since 2008 to justify a reappraisal. The main tranche of new material comes in Chapter 13, on the period since 2007, but I have also made significant revisions to Chapter 12, and have taken the opportunity to review the whole text, making changes where appropriate. I have also revised the Introduction and Conclusion, and have updated the bibliography and appendices.

I am delighted to record my thanks to my successive editors at Palgrave, but in the case of this edition particularly Sonya Barker, Rachel Bridgewater, Felicity Noble, Jenna Steventon and Clarissa Sutherland, for all their help, patience and understanding. I completed this edition while Dean of the College of Humanities at the University of Exeter, and must thank my colleagues in the Dean's Office – Sue Tait, Laura Newberry, Kerrie Brealy and Isobel England – for their support, which has allowed me to sustain my research activity alongside a major managerial role. My academic debts are shown in the bibliography, but I should make special mention of two excellent historians who are sadly no longer with us: both Nina Fishman and Duncan Tanner were huge influences on me and on many others, and they are greatly missed. The participants in the informal, but very serious, Exeter–Bristol labour history seminars have been a great source of ideas and support: thanks go to Laura Beers, Dean Blackburn, Richard Jobson, James Parker, Hugh Pemberton, Simon Peplow, David Thackeray, Richard Toye and Mark Wickham-Jones, in particular. Sincere thanks are due once more to my parents, Chris and Shirley Thorpe, for all their ongoing support, and also to Roger Fisk, Andy Jay, Catherine Laughton, Phil Telford and Sally Thorpe. Life would be a lot drabber without Sue and Rhodri, and I thank them for helping me to live a full, and fun, life.

Abbreviations

AEU	Amalgamated Engineering Union
ASBO	anti-social behaviour order
ASE	Amalgamated Society of Engineers
ASRS	Amalgamated Society of Railway Servants
AUEW	Amalgamated Union of Engineering Workers
BL	British Leyland
BSP	British Socialist Party
CBI	Confederation of British Industries
CLP	Constituency Labour Party
CLPD	Campaign for Labour Party Democracy
CND	Campaign for Nuclear Disarmament
CPGB	Communist Party of Great Britain
DEA	Department of Economic Affairs
DETR	Department of the Environment, Transport and the Regions
EAC	Economic Advisory Council
EC	European Community
EEC	European Economic Community
EFTA	European Free Trade Area
ERM	Exchange Rate Mechanism
EU	European Union
GATT	General Agreement on Tariffs and Trade
GDP	gross domestic product
GFTU	General Federation of Trade Unions
GLC	Greater London Council
GMB	General Municipal and Boilermakers' Union
GMWU	General and Municipal Workers' Union
ILP	Independent Labour Party
IMF	International Monetary Fund
IRA	Irish Republican Army
LPYS	Labour Party Young Socialists
LRC	Labour Representation Committee

MEP	Member of the European Parliament
MFGB	Miners' Federation of Great Britain
Mintech	Ministry of Technology
NATO	North Atlantic Treaty Organization
NCL	National Council of Labour
NEB	National Enterprise Board
NEC	National Executive Committee
NHS	National Health Service
NJC	National Joint Council
NLWM	National Left Wing Movement
NPF	National Policy Forum
NTWF	National Transport Workers' Federation
NUM	National Union of Mineworkers
NUPE	National Union of Public Employees
NUR	National Union of Railwaymen
NUWSS	National Union of Women's Suffrage Societies
ODPM	Office of the Deputy Prime Minister
OMOV	one member, one vote
PFI	private finance initiative
PLP	Parliamentary Labour Party
PSBR	public sector borrowing requirement
R&D	research and development
RMT	National Union of Rail, Maritime and Transport Workers
SDF	Social Democratic Federation
SDP	Social Democratic Party
SERPS	state earnings-related pensions scheme
SLP	Socialist Labour Party
SNP	Scottish National Party
SSIP	Society for Socialist Inquiry and Propaganda
SSLP	Scargill's Socialist Labour Party
TGWU	Transport and General Workers' Union
TUC	Trades Union Congress
UDC	Union of Democratic Control
UKIP	UK Independence Party
VAT	value added tax
WEC	War Emergency Workers' National Committee
WMD	weapons of mass destruction

Introduction

When the Labour Party was formed (as the Labour Representation Committee, LRC) in 1900, its prospects were unclear. Yet it survived, and, by the early 1920s, it had eclipsed the Liberal Party as the main opposition to the Conservatives. Periods in government followed, but they were often punctuated by long periods in opposition, and even – in the 1930s, 1950s and 1980s – predictions of demise. Such predictions proved unfounded, however, and 1997 marked the first of three successive general election victories. Even defeat in 2010 was met with a sense that the circumstances had been exceptional and that it had taken a Conservative–Liberal Democrat Coalition to put Labour out of office. And although Labour's experience of government at national level was episodic for much of its first 110 years, its dominance of the British left since the early 1920s has been close to total. Rivals have come and gone, but no organization has been able to mount anything like a credible and sustained threat to Labour's pre-eminent position on the progressive side of British politics. By studying it, we can learn a lot, not just about the party itself but also about British politics, and indeed society, more generally.

Before 1945, Labour was unable to win a parliamentary majority. The LRC elected two MPs at the general election of 1900, and 29 at that of 1906, after which it changed its name. Although the party continued to develop down to the outbreak of the First World War in 1914, it was still not a major party; indeed, the Irish Nationalists won about twice as many seats as Labour at the two general elections of 1910. Labour participated in wartime Coalition governments from 1915 onwards, but in 1918 adopted a new constitution which made it more independent of the Liberals and, having withdrawn from the Lloyd George Coalition, won 57 seats at that year's post-war general election. In 1922 it became the main Opposition party, with 142 seats, and Ramsay MacDonald was elected the party's first 'leader'. Rapid progress

1

followed, with Labour forming minority governments in 1924 and 1929. However, the first lasted only nine months, while the second, battered by economic slump and political difficulties, collapsed in August 1931. MacDonald formed a 'National' government with Conservative and Liberal support, which went on to trounce Labour at the polls. During the 1930s there was limited recovery, but a further election was lost in 1935, and Labour would almost certainly have been defeated at the next election as well had not the Second World War intervened. In 1940, however, the National government fell and was replaced by a Coalition under Winston Churchill, in which Labour had more than a fair share of ministerial posts. As in 1914–18, war suited Labour very well, and the party's fortunes improved markedly in the next few years.

At the first post-war election in 1945, Clement Attlee led Labour to a landslide victory, and his government went on to implement significant reforms. In 1951, however, Labour was defeated, and, after further defeats in 1955 and 1959, was eventually out of office for 13 years, leading to considerable debate as to whether Labour would ever win again. However, it returned to power under Harold Wilson in 1964 and was re-elected by a very healthy margin in 1966. By 1970, though, Wilson's government was widely perceived to have failed, and Labour was consigned once again to opposition. Rather fortuitously, perhaps, Labour returned as a minority government in February 1974, and that October was re-elected with a tiny overall majority. A difficult term in office, first under Wilson and then under James Callaghan, ended in defeat, and the victory of the Conservatives under Margaret Thatcher in 1979 ushered in a long period of opposition.

The general election of 1979 was to prove the first in a sequence of four successive general election defeats for Labour. In opposition, it tried various strategies, but Michael Foot's efforts ended in heavy defeat in 1983, while Neil Kinnock was defeated conclusively in 1987 and more narrowly in 1992. By the latter year, which saw Kinnock's retirement, a major programme of party reform was under way; under John Smith (1992–94) reform continued, and the Conservative government floundered. When Tony Blair succeeded Smith in 1994, he accelerated the pace of reform, rebranded the party 'New Labour', and went on to win a sweeping victory in 1997. Labour won a further landslide in 2001, and even in 2005, after eight years in office and tarnished by an increasingly unpopular war in Iraq, Blair was able to lead his party to another comfortable majority. When Gordon Brown succeeded Blair in June 2007, it seemed that he could look forward to the future with confidence. However, such confidence proved misplaced, and his inability to lead Labour to victory at the 2010 general election led to the formation of a Conservative–Liberal Coalition under David Cameron. In opposition for the first time in well over a decade, Labour turned to Ed Miliband, although at the time of writing it remained unclear whether he would be able to lead it to victory in 2015.

Naturally, these vicissitudes of electoral and political fortune have led to some wildly varying prognostications as to the party's likely future. In early 1997, the party could point to only five periods in government, totalling fewer than 20 years. Ten years later, it seemed to be ensconced in power, perhaps for years to come. But, of course, there had been hubristic statements about future domination earlier. In the aftermath of Labour's 1929 victory, Herbert Morrison claimed that Labour was 'the miracle of politics' which was looking forward to rolling back the remaining 'bastions of reaction'.[1] In April 1946, backed by a huge Labour majority and with the Conservative opposition under Churchill in disarray, the Labour minister Sir Hartley Shawcross claimed that 'we are the masters at the moment – and not only for the moment, but for a very long time to come'.[2] And Wilson claimed, more than once, that Labour had become 'a natural party of government'.[3] On the other hand, there had been times of real gloom as to the future. Before the First World War, many had questioned the purpose and prospects of the party; in 1908 Ben Tillett had launched a fierce attack on what he saw as the timidity and failure of the parliamentary party.[4] In the aftermath of 1931, there were those who doubted the party's future prospects, and much of the pressure for collaboration with Liberals, Communists and others in the 1930s stemmed from a pessimistic reading of Labour's electoral potential.[5] The defeats of the 1950s led to academics asking the question 'Must Labour lose?'.[6] And the 1970s and 1980s were replete with doomsday-type predictions that Labour was finished, or at least had no serious chance of ever again forming a majority government.[7]

The vicissitudes of Labour's history have obviously contributed to the great fluctuations in its historiography. So too have the political predilections of historians, political scientists and others writing that history. When we add into that the fact that some sources have become available much earlier than others, we can begin to understand why the historiography of the Labour Party is both so rich and so complex. On the first variable, books published in the late 1940s in anticipation of the party's golden jubilee tended to be celebratory in tone, portraying the party's development and success as, to some extent, the inevitable corollaries of democratization.[8] However, even sympathetic accounts emerging in the late 1950s and early 1960s, like Henry Pelling's *Short History* (first published in 1961) offered rather more cautious findings.[9] As the party seemed to move into crisis in the late 1960s, even historians broadly sympathetic to the Labour project began to strike a more pessimistic note.[10] On the other hand, however, it was noticeable that there was a much more upbeat feel to the volumes published around the time of the party's centenary in 2000, reflecting the victory of 1997.[11]

The second variable has been the political outlook of the writers involved. Scholarship on parties of the left is a more complicated business than many people allow. Some historians see their task as studying the Labour Party's past in order to prescribe its future. This construction of politically useable narratives is an important driver of interpretation of Labour's history, and is not without very considerable value, but it is important that it is recognized for what it is. It is usually associated with the Marxist left, and classic works in this tradition include those of Ralph Miliband, John Saville and David Coates. For Ralph Miliband, Labour's commitment to parliamentary democracy meant that it was hopelessly compromised as a vehicle for the achievement of socialism, although he was a lot vaguer on what he thought would be better.[12] Saville offered fiercely critical polemics attacking just about everything that Labour managed to achieve in his lifetime.[13] And Coates, a formidable scholar, has spent more than three decades critiquing Labour's leaders, past and present, from a left standpoint.[14] To the right of Labour, on the other hand, David Marquand and others have attacked the party as a rather unnatural construction which served to divide the 'progressive' left and allowed the Conservatives to dominate twentieth-century

British politics.[15] These tendencies led the editors of one of the centenary volumes published in 2000 to observe that, '[m]easured against absolute standards or the agendas of others, Labour has inevitably been regularly condemned', and they set out instead to 'offer a more positive evaluation ... by judging Labour against its own aims and values, and against what might reasonably have been expected'.[16] This was a refreshing approach: and while historians cannot completely free themselves from their own subjectivities, they can try to guard against them, and control for them.

The quest for a useable past is not only confined to those outside or on the fringes of the party, of course. For example, the narrative of Labour's early 1980s 'extremism' was at least partly a construction by centre-right figures seeking to justify their subsequent political project of 'modernization'.[17] What is most noticeable about these narratives is that they are often ferociously defended when questioned, as could be seen, for example, in the strong criticisms that followed from Roy Hattersley and Gerald Kaufman when Kenneth Morgan's 2007 biography of Foot advanced the notion (also put forward in this volume) that Foot's leadership of the party (1980–83) was not wholly without merit.[18]

The third variable referred to above is the availability of sources. Published sources, like manifestoes, memoirs and the like have always been freely available, as were the most valuable published sources of all, the party's annual conference reports, which included reports of various committees, financial and membership information, and so on. Beyond that, however, material has become available to historians somewhat haphazardly. The party's own national-level archives were opened to researchers in 1960, but listing of them did not begin until 1972, making work on them very difficult.[19] The public records, essential for the periods when Labour was in government, were subjected to a 50-year rule until 1967, and a 30-year rule thereafter, and although in more recent years freedom of information legislation has made it possible to release material earlier, it is still the case that the great bulk of material only becomes available three decades after it was produced. Politicians' diaries, meanwhile, are one of the richest sources available to the political historian, but it is not for the latter to decree the production of such documents, and even where they exist, it is sometimes many years before they become available. Finally, local party records have been very much under-utilized in the past. This is beginning to be rectified, although much remains to be done, both empirically and methodologically.[20]

The shifting historiography can be illustrated by using Ramsay MacDonald as a case study. In 1938, at a time when memories of the 1931 'betrayal' were still fresh and Labour was still stuck in opposition to a National government that most Labourites despised, MacDonald's former parliamentary private secretary, Macneill Weir, published what was to remain for many years the only full-length biography covering MacDonald's whole life.[21] Based on the author's own (rather prejudiced) recollections, conversations with other Labourites who were hardly likely to be sympathetic, and a reading of the available evidence, it was a vitriolic denunciation of the former leader. Naturally, Weir was unable to use party records, and still less government ones; the most 'inside' sources available to him were published memoirs which, at this stage, were pretty uniformly hostile to the ex-premier.[22] Although Lord Elton responded soon afterwards with a pro-MacDonald book covering his life down to 1919, he never completed a volume covering the remainder of his life, and so it was Weir's that became the standard work.[23] The publication, in the 1950s, of further 'insider' accounts, in the form of Hugh Dalton's memoirs and Beatrice Webb's diaries, merely seemed to prove Weir right in his assertions that MacDonald was a vain, rather ineffectual figure whose commitment to the party was tenuous, at least by the later 1920s.[24] However, both Dalton and Webb were unusually antipathetic towards MacDonald even before 1931, and the publication of their recollections further skewed the historical record.

The year 1977 was to see the publication of Marquand's outstanding, and far more favourable, biography of MacDonald.[25] In part, the difference was down to training: Marquand was a graduate in History, whereas Weir had had no such advantage. Politics was also important: Marquand was a right-wing Labour MP who believed that MacDonald's political instincts had been broadly correct, and that it was important to reclaim him for the party, and in particular for its moderate wing. The book was also affected by the context in which Marquand was writing. The struggles of Labour governments in the 1960s and 1970s showed how difficult government could be, and how hard it was to keep the Labour Party united, especially in time of economic difficulty. The parallels with MacDonald's own battles were obvious. In addition, Marquand had access to MacDonald's own extensive collection of papers, as well as the public records and the party archives. All of this offered a much fuller view of the complexities of the problems MacDonald had faced, while his own diaries and letters offered new insights into his own thinking. It was little wonder that Marquand offered a much more sympathetic – though by no means uncritical – view of MacDonald than Weir had done.

This is just one illustration of how Labour Party historiography has developed. It shows how complicated and vexed a project it is to attempt to offer a single-volume history of the party. Nonetheless, historians have a duty to try to put forward such treatments, and to interpret the past for a broader public, as well as to offer an introduction to those students and academics who will (hopefully at least) go on to read much more deeply into the subject; and it is in that spirit that the book is offered. A clear understanding of the Labour Party is a vital component of any attempt to understand twentieth- and twenty-first century Britain more generally.

1 Creation and Early Years, 1900–14

In 1899 the annual Trades Union Congress (TUC) voted by the narrow margin of 546,000 votes to 434,000 to organize a joint conference with socialist and co-operative bodies to discuss Labour representation. The conference met in London on 27 February 1900 and agreed to establish 'a distinct Labour group in Parliament, who shall have their own whips, and agree upon their policy'; to support it financially through affiliation fees; and to elect Ramsay MacDonald, a leading member of the Independent Labour party (ILP), as the secretary of the new organization, which was to be known as the Labour Representation Committee (LRC).[1] After winning 29 seats at the 1906 general election, it was renamed the Labour Party. But by 1914 its successes had not been all that striking, and it faced a somewhat uncertain future.

The central cause of the formation of the LRC was not a major upsurge in socialist sentiment among trade unionists but fears about the unions' legal position. British trade unions had not, traditionally, wanted very radical social change. True, towards the end of the nineteenth century some, such as the Amalgamated Society of Railway Servants (ASRS), had become more interested in aspects of state regulation and collectivism. But on the whole they wanted to be left alone to negotiate with employers on equal terms, the way to achieve 'a fair day's work for a fair day's pay' being through free collective bargaining with employers.

But there was a history of the state placing obstructions in the way of such free collective bargaining, as many trade unionists were only too well aware. Trade unionism had not enjoyed an easy legal existence in the nineteenth century. The Combination Acts of 1799 and 1800, however ineffectual in practice before their repeal in the 1820s, had entered popular memory as repressive legislation aiming to destroy trade unionism. Even after their repeal, the position of unions remained legally dubious. Thus the six Dorset labourers, the so-called Tolpuddle Martyrs, could be convicted of administering illegal oaths and transported as late as 1834. As economic conditions eased and transport and postal services improved around mid-century, though, it did become easier to organize national unions, and their legal position appeared to be secure, with even a degree of picketing being legalized in 1859.

In reality, though, trade union law remained somewhat obscure. Even if no longer considered criminal, unions often found it difficult to obtain legal protection against, say, the embezzlement of funds. The formation of the TUC in 1868 was, in many ways, a defensive measure, taken in anticipation of renewed assaults. Somewhat haltingly, though, the 1870s saw some improvements: in 1871 the Liberal government's Trade Union Act gave legal protection to union funds, while in 1875 and 1876 a Conservative government exempted trade disputes from the laws of conspiracy, made breach of contract a matter for civil rather than criminal action, and legalized peaceful picketing. This was, it seemed, a very satisfactory outcome. Unions could now go about their business unimpeded by legislation or outside interference. With many working-class men possessing the vote after the 1867 Reform Act, the prospect of a further extension in the not too distant future, and two working-class trade unionists, Alexander Macdonald and Thomas Burt, elected to parliament in 1874, it seemed that the unions' position was secure.

At this stage, trade unionism was far from being all pervasive. Even in 1874, a peak year, only about 1,200,000 members were represented at the TUC – by the end of the decade even that figure had halved, as economic recession cut into the membership of all unions and effectively destroyed many of the newer organizations which had sprung up to cater for less skilled workers in the early 1870s.[2] Even the newer unions which survived struggled, while the ASRS, formed in 1871, had the additional handicap that the railway companies refused to recognize it. However, the apparent settlement of the legal position made up for a great deal, and expansion began again in the second half of the 1880s as trade began to pick up. Meanwhile, the 1884 Reform Act enfranchised new groups of working-class men outside urban areas (hence large numbers of coal miners, among others, got the vote for the first time). From then until 1918, around 60 per cent of men had the right to vote at any one time.[3]

It was, paradoxically, the 'new unionism' of the later 1880s and the indirect results of the Reform Act which led to a new challenge to the unions. Historians have long debated what was new about the 'new unionism' and, on the whole, have argued that it was not a great deal. However, the scale of the expansion, and the spectacular victory of the London dockers in their strike of 1889, aroused many fears. The employers were determined not to be caught out again, and from 1890 onwards there was a concerted effort by bodies like the Shipping Federation to weaken the unions' position. The formation of the Engineering Employers' Federation, aiming to counter not a 'new' union but the most respectable of the older ones, the Amalgamated Society of Engineers (ASE), suggested new threats ahead. At the same time, the Conservative Party, under the leadership of Lord Salisbury, was seeking to end years of Liberal ascendancy by appealing to the middle and lower-middle classes, and one way of doing this was to play up the threat of a militant working class and the 'socialism' espoused by a minority of trade unionists. Trade unionism, therefore, provided an admirable target. Lord Halsbury, Lord Chancellor in all the Conservative governments between 1885 and 1905, was an arch-reactionary who appointed anti-union judges with alacrity. During the 1890s, trade union law was increasingly made not by parliament but by the judges, in a series of high-profile and controversial rulings. *Inter alia*, these called into doubt unions' exemption from claims for damages arising out of industrial action, and the right to peaceful picketing.

These factors, then, made the legal position of trade unions look much more dubious than it had been for a long time. Increasingly, they began to look at better methods of mutual support, a fact demonstrated when a minority of unions formed the General Federation of Trade Unions (GFTU) in 1899 as a means of pooling some financial resources. It is in this context, of a renewed and bitter threat to the legal position of trade unions to go about their business freely and without hindrance, that the reasons for the formation of the LRC in 1900 must be sought.

In previous periods there would have been a tendency to rely on the Liberal Party for this kind of political support. In fact, most working-class voters continued to support the Liberal Party up to the First World War. Yet, at the same time, there were doubts about its ability and/or willingness to stand up for trade union interests. The long Liberal ascendancy had now passed; at the 1895 general election the party was heavily defeated, and it looked unlikely to do well at the next election either. In addition, the Liberals had become, in their programmes, more 'faddist' – partly to avoid identification with 'class politics' as they attempted to emphasize other questions – but this was bound to leave at least some trade unionists dissatisfied, especially at a time of increasing threats to the union movement.[4] This combination of unelectability and inattention was merely exacerbated by the fact that local Liberal associations, partly for social and partly for financial reasons, were very reluctant to adopt 'Labour' candidates, the only exceptions being in areas which were so dominated by a single industry that it would have been perverse to put up anyone else; overwhelmingly, these were mining districts. By 1900, a critical mass of trade unionists was more prepared than previously to turn away from – or at least use new means to increase the pressure on – the Liberals if it meant a more secure future for trade unionism.

Other factors are more problematic. There has been much debate on how far the process of industrial change radicalized industrial workers, or forced them into new degrees of class consciousness which then made adherence to an independent working-class party inevitable. Local examples of drastic change during the 1890s can be found – the Leicester footwear industry is one good example.[5] But, in general, things moved more slowly.[6] Most workers 'did not join trade unions and most remained remarkably little affected either by structural changes in the economy, by new legislation, by decreasing regionalisation, by closer supervision or by the introduction of more advanced mechanisation'.[7] Even in the industries at the cutting edge of mechanization, progress was usually slow; for example, in engineering, where the employers won a lengthy lockout in 1897–98, and where there was perhaps greater change than anywhere else, the period up to the First World War did not see a radical transformation.[8] On the other hand, we are not trying to explain a massive breakthrough for working-class politics, just the formation of the LRC as it existed, small and with an uncertain future, in

1900. In that sense, it can be suggested that, while there was not change on such a scale as to *revolutionize* class and production relations, there was *enough* fear of change, and *enough* pressure at certain limited points of the production process, to convince some trade unionists that worse might follow, and that it might thus be sensible to demonstrate that labour had some political, as well as industrial, muscle. While not as important as the desire to protect the legal position of trade unions, therefore, this was a contributory factor to the creation of the LRC.

So far there has been no discussion of socialists. This has not been an accident. The socialist groups which existed in Britain in the 1880s and 1890s were not mere sects, but they were small and sometimes struggling. Their involvement in the formation of the LRC was not decisive, although it helped. It must also be remembered that some socialists had no enthusiasm for the new organization and stayed outside or rapidly left it. Still, it is worth discussing the various socialist groups and socialism briefly, since they were, in time, to play an important role in the new organization.

Britain had been one of the main centres of early socialism, but by 1850 little of this remained. It was not until the 1880s that socialism began to revive. The Democratic Federation, a radical group, came increasingly under the influence of socialists like the upper-middle-class Henry Mayers Hyndman, and was transformed into a Marxist group in 1884. The Social Democratic Federation (SDF) was in many ways a curious body. Hyndman's arrogance and autocratic tendencies made it difficult for many people to work with him. At the same time, his views were as much derived from passionate patriotism and imperialism as from Marxism – he saw socialist transformation as the best way of preserving Britain's world pre-eminence at a time when it was being challenged by the United States and Germany in particular. However, Hyndman was not the SDF; the party claimed a membership which peaked at 10,536 in 1895 (although dues-paying membership was much lower). At grassroots level, members of the SDF played a significant part in putting socialism on the agenda in many parts of the country, especially where it was strongest, in London and Lancashire. A number of younger trade union leaders, such as Tom Mann, Will Thorne and Ben Tillett, were members. And, despite the SDF's reputation for sectarianism, many SDF members did co-operate with members of other socialist groups in campaigns in the 1880s and 1890s; ultimately it affiliated to the LRC in 1900, albeit briefly.

The Socialist League was formed in 1884 as a breakaway from the SDF. It was never more than a few hundred strong, and collapsed in the later 1880s. But it did include the artist and poet William Morris, who wrote a series of utopian works describing what a socialist society could be like. These showed a spiritual side of socialism which was not really to be found with the SDF or the Fabians. Morris offered a vision of a free and equal society, a return to a pre-industrial, pre-urban age. Such idealized medievalism was hopelessly impractical, and its rejection of modernity and conventional morality aroused hostility, among working-class leaders as much as anyone, and gave socialists an image they would long try to play down. Yet at the same time, Morris inspired many, particularly younger, people to work for the movement, presenting a vision of socialism in quasi-religious terms as a heaven on earth.

By contrast, the Fabian Society, formed in 1884, was intensely concerned with the practical. While always a heterogeneous body,[9] the Society was soon dominated by people such as Sidney Webb and George Bernard Shaw, who aimed to influence the existing parties in a 'socialistic' direction. While the Fabians were not as influential as they liked to claim, they did help to stimulate interest and debate, and many of their leading figures, most notably Sidney and Beatrice Webb, were to have a significant role to play in Labour politics in the future.

Relations between these socialists and the trade unions were far from straightforward. The Fabians and the Socialist League had little contact with the unions at all, somewhat predictably given their members' social backgrounds. But in the case of the SDF, things were more complicated. Hyndman, in the early years at least, saw unions as restrictive organizations of skilled workers that were only out for their own members, not the working class as a whole, and would have little to do with them. He has been criticized for this; but trade unions were, after all, very much a minority concern at this time. Even by 1900, only 2,022,000 out of a potential membership of just under 16,000,000 were unionized, which meant that almost 87 per cent of potential members were not in unions.[10] In such circumstances, the view that unions were

an obstruction to working-class unity, concerned with narrow economic gains, and with a mostly elite membership, rather than representative of the interests of the workers as a whole, was at least
plausible. However, it is important not to focus too exclusively on
Hyndman and his acolytes – many SDFers were keen advocates of
trade unionism, as the participation of members like Mann and
Thorne in the 'new unionism' of the late 1880s made clear. The
question of the correct line to take towards the unions remained
one of the most hotly debated issues within the SDF for years
to come.

The formation of the ILP in 1893 was a stronger move in the
direction of co-operation between socialists and trade unionists.
Its leading figure, Keir Hardie, was himself a former miner. While
the ILP always had a strong middle-class element, it also included
significant numbers of workers and trade unionists. Hardie,
elected to parliament in 1892 as MP for West Ham South, was a
keen advocate of the 'Labour Alliance' between trade unionists
and socialists. But he did not get very far at first, and the TUC
effectively excluded him from its proceedings in 1895. It will not
do to see Hardie as the inspired manipulator behind the formation of the LRC; and, for much of the decade, events seemed
to be moving against the ILP. At the 1895 election, Hardie lost
his seat and all the other 27 ILP candidates were also defeated.
However, the commitment of individual ILPers helped push some
unions towards the idea of the LRC, and the ILP did play an
important role in keeping the idea alive in the 1890s.

Why did the appeal of socialism take root in the 1880s and
1890s? Socialism was essentially a reaction against the perceived
arbitrariness of the market.[11] At the least, it demanded sterner
regulations on market forces; at most, their abolition and replacement by a 'better' form of economic and social system. The idea
had little appeal in the mid-nineteenth century, since the market
seemed at that stage to be working, by delivering steadily increasing living standards and a degree of security which, though tiny
by later standards, was a considerable improvement on what had
gone before. However, by the mid-1870s there was a growing perception of economic difficulties, and some people began to look
for an alternative. One such was the proposal for a single tax on
land; it says a great deal that the chief work advocating such a
policy, Henry George's *Progress and Poverty* (1880), rapidly became

a bestseller in Britain. The idea of greater regulation of market forces, linked in some cases to specific socialist demands such as the eight-hour day, also began to have a wider appeal, not least among trade unionists.[12] At the same time, the idea of a larger role for public authorities also appealed to many middle-class people, particularly civil servants like the young Sidney Webb; their status in society would be greatly enhanced, at the expense of capitalists, in a society based on public service rather than the generation of profit. But socialism was not just about controlling markets and other apparently mundane issues. As the work of Morris showed, it also had a strong spiritual appeal, especially to those who, for one reason or another, had begun to reject orthodox religion but who still felt the need for something like it in their lives; hence not just the utopian, 'heaven-on-earth' writings of Morris but also the Labour Church movement, which became relatively strong in the 1890s, and the evangelical preaching style of socialist propagandists like the ILPer Philip Snowden (author of a book published in 1903 entitled *The Christ That Is To Be*). Finally, the retirement of W. E. Gladstone as Liberal leader in 1894 was probably important here, too. He had, in many ways, delivered less than he had seemed to promise in a radical direction, but radicals' faith in him had remained high to the end. Few radicals can have expected as much from his successors at the head of the Liberal Party; certainly none of the latter was ever able to tap into working-class radicalism as effectively. For all these reasons, then, socialism secured a small niche in late nineteenth-century Britain, and appealed to small sections of both the working and middle classes. Crucially, too, it developed potential points of contact with the established labour movement; while most trade unionists did not become socialists, some did, and a larger number heard socialists saying things that they liked from time to time. This meant that a fair number of socialists attended the founding conference of the LRC in 1900, either as trade unionists or as members of socialist organizations.

On the whole, however, the formation of the LRC in 1900 was not the uprising of a class, or the ineluctable and inevitable result of changing production relations or the product of the work of socialists more 'realistic' than Hyndman. It was, primarily, a new chapter in the struggle of the trade union movement for the right to be left alone to negotiate on equal terms with employers and to apply sanctions, such as strike action, where this was deemed necessary. Socialism was not utterly insignificant, but it did not lead the process. The 1900 conference rejected a call from the SDF to base the party upon 'a recognition of the class war'. But, furthermore, it neglected to commit itself to any other form of socialism.[13] The socialists were not as impotent as they might have been, however: as individuals, they were often valued, even by non-socialists, for their dedication and hard work, and it was partly for this reason that the composition of the LRC's executive committee was amended from the proposed 12 trade unionists and six socialists to seven of the former and five of the latter.[14]

The new organization was tiny. The overwhelming majority of the population (between three-quarters and four-fifths) could be described as working class. Yet only around 13 per cent of those who could have been members of unions actually were members. And, even of those, only 17.4 per cent were affiliated to the LRC at its formation: just 41 unions with a total of 353,070 members. About half of those were affiliated through just five unions.[15] Among others, the miners, who could already elect a significant number of MPs under the auspices of the Liberal Party as 'Lib-Labs', stayed outside. And, although the conference elected Ramsay MacDonald, a socialist ILPer, as its secretary, this was not really because of his socialism but because of his reputation as a hard worker and good organizer and, perhaps crucially, because since his marriage he had a solid income through his wife and so could afford to work for nothing.[16]

Thus the LRC was formed in 1900. But it was not very firmly based; there were no guarantees that it would grow, or even remain in existence. That it did so was largely due to the events of the next few years, particularly the continuing legal threats to the unions. But even by 1914 the new organization would still be facing a rather uncertain future and would still be very much a minority taste.

The LRC lacked most of the features normally associated with a political party. It had no programme as such; its machinery was utterly rudimentary. It was not committed in any way to socialist policies. Even among affiliated unions there was often hostility towards co-operation with socialists. For their part, many socialists resented the unions and despaired of their moderation – the SDF voted in 1901 to withdraw from the LRC. Meanwhile, hopes that the Co-operative movement might become involved were dashed; it continued with a broadly Liberal orientation. If anything, therefore, trade union power within the LRC grew. By the end of 1901, the addition of a trades council representative, and the withdrawal of the SDF, meant the unions had 10 of the 13 positions on the executive.

The new organization was faced with a general election almost straight away. The conditions were not promising – the Conservatives were taking advantage of apparent success in the Boer War to give themselves another spell in office. Labour was able to run just 15 candidates, who took a total of 62,698 votes. Two were elected, both in double-member seats: at Merthyr, where Hardie had to face two Liberal opponents, and at Derby, where Richard Bell of the ASRS fought and won in tandem with a single Liberal candidate. All things considered, this was not a bad performance, but it hardly augured major short-term advances.

However, the LRC's affiliates were soon reminded of the original reason for the formation of the committee. In September 1900 the High Court ruled that the ASRS could be held liable for damages arising out of its dispute with the Taff Vale Railway Company in south Wales. This decision was overturned on appeal, but in July 1901 the House of Lords backed the initial judgment. Ultimately, in January 1903, the ASRS was forced to pay damages of £23,000 to the company. Meanwhile, the 1901 case of *Quinn v. Leathem* effectively outlawed boycotts of third parties in a dispute. The Denaby Main and Cadeby Case, started against the Yorkshire Miners' Association in 1903, although eventually won by the union in 1906, tended to reinforce the view that the unions were under serious threat.[17]

All this uncertainty helped to keep the LRC together and moving forward. At the time of the February 1901 conference, the number of unions affiliating had fallen from 41 to 34, and the union-affiliated membership by about 14,000 to just under 339,577. However, the Lords' decision on Taff Vale led to a stream of affiliations – by February 1902, 65 unions were affiliating 455,450 members. The damages case against the ASRS, culminating in the adverse judgment of January 1903, led to a further surge in affiliations, so that by the following month 127 unions and 861,150 members were affiliated. Thus 1902 had seen a rise of 25 per cent over the previous year, and 1903 a staggering

84 per cent increase.[18] This was followed by a rise of 13 per cent in the year to February 1904. At that year's conference, a compulsory levy of a penny per member per year was imposed in order to pay Labour MPs and help with election expenses. This enabled the party to pay its MPs a salary of £200 a year from 1904 onwards, but did result in some disaffiliations of smaller unions and some under-reporting of membership by others.[19] But the committee had come a very long way, thanks largely to the decisions of the courts. By 1906, the main unions outside the Labour Party were in mining: the Miners' Federation of Great Britain (MFGB) and the separate Durham and Northumberland Miners' Associations. Even here, though, it seemed progress was being made, with the Lancashire and Cheshire Miners' Federation affiliating in 1903. Meanwhile, attempts to place the LRC under the direct control of the parliamentary committee of the TUC were thwarted in 1902–03.

At this stage, though, the future of the organization still looked rather hazy. It was not entirely clear how far it would co-operate with other parties, or even with the 11 Lib-Lab MPs. Bell moved steadily towards the Liberals and effectively abandoned the LRC in 1904. During 1902, though, two by-elections showed a degree of Liberal goodwill towards the LRC. At Wakefield, Philip Snowden, a former civil servant who, following a crippling illness, had become a kind of itinerant preacher on behalf of the ILP, was defeated by a Conservative in a straight fight. Although the Liberals, who had withdrawn, made no recommendation as to how their supporters should vote, many of them were impressed with the line Snowden had taken against the Boer War, and backed him all the same.[20] That August, David Shackleton, a textile union official, was elected as MP for Clitheroe in Lancashire; the Liberals, who had held the seat, did not put up a candidate. This victory was a major factor in pushing the textile workers towards affiliation to the LRC, a step they took shortly afterwards.

Two events in 1903 defined the position of the LRC more clearly. The first was the decision of Joseph Chamberlain, the Colonial Secretary, to resign from the cabinet and campaign for protective tariffs. This was significant, because free trade was not, according to labour and radical traditions in Britain, merely one of a number of variations of fiscal policy. It had long been seen as a key radical demand, and during the nineteenth century had become 'the kernel of a new "moral economy" of working-class consumers, supported with great earnestness and an almost religious fervour'.[21] Free trade did not only mean cheap food: it was also seen as the key to other classic tenets of British radicalism, notably international peace, clean government and fair play. Protection had its working-class supporters, of course, but it was an issue that united most socialists and trade unionists.

The other result of Chamberlain's venture was that it gave new point to ongoing efforts to achieve a rapprochement between Labour and the Liberals. The latter had been struggling politically for too long to want to stand on ceremony, and for his part MacDonald was prepared to explore the possibilities of some kind of electoral deal if it meant a bigger share of seats for Labour after the next election. Thus in 1903, MacDonald and the Liberal chief whip, Herbert Gladstone, agreed secretly that, in England and Wales, Liberals would be discouraged from opposing Labour candidates in a number of seats, and that, in return, Labour would restrict its number of candidates elsewhere. Although the agreement was not always easy to enforce, it was to prove a major help to Labour at the next general election.

The fact that such a deal could be struck, and that it was adhered to by both sides, tells us much about Labour in this period. It also helps to demonstrate the domination of a certain outlook at this time. First, there was the essentially limited outlook which has been characterized by some writers as 'labourism'. This point of view, identified especially with the unions, stated that Labour's essential aim was to safeguard workers' rights, by enabling unions to bargain on equal terms with employers, and achieve such – essentially limited – legislation as would improve workers' conditions at work, and, to some extent, away from the workplace. Such claims could be couched in quasi-Gladstonian terms as bringing labour 'into the pale of the constitution'. Labour, in this formulation, was not looking for a revolution, even a peaceful one, but merely a fair deal. While some Liberals felt that this was a dangerous road to go down, many, especially those on the 'progressive' wing of the party, could see little wrong with it, as evidenced by the large number of Liberal candidates who were to pledge themselves at the 1906 election to the full repeal of Taff Vale.

Second, in so far as Labour went beyond this towards socialism, its dominant strain was moderate and, in relation to progressive Liberalism, largely consensual, at least in all but the very
long term. MacDonald was a good example of this outlook. In his
speeches and writings, he stressed the view that Marxism was out
of date, with all its talk of class struggles, capitalist collapse and
revolution. Instead, strongly influenced by German 'Revisionists'
like Eduard Bernstein, with whose work he was well acquainted,
he argued the opposite. Society, far from becoming more straight-
forwardly divided between two main classes, was becoming infinitely more complex. Many workers were becoming increasingly
self-reliant as they became more prosperous, and this was a tendency that other workers should be encouraged to emulate.
For MacDonald, socialism would come about gradually, organi-
cally, from the existing social and economic structures; it would
emerge from the growing success of capitalism. It was thus the
job of socialists to promote this success, to use its fruits to pass
'useful' reforms, to point to continuing areas where action was
needed, and to build upon the workers' developing sense of self-
reliance. In concrete terms, this view meant that there would be
ample scope for co-operation between progressive Liberals and
moderate socialists like himself. Indeed, progressives were moving society towards socialism even if they did not realize or admit
it. In this way, instrumentality combined with ideology to suggest
that the best way forward was in collaboration with progressive
Liberalism. It should come as no surprise, then, that MacDonald
was, at this time, a leading figure in the progressive Rainbow
Circle, a discussion group most of whose members owed some
allegiance to the Liberal Party.

This 'progressive alliance' approach was not without its critics, of course. There were those in Labour politics who took a different view, and who were more influenced by Marxism. People
such as George Lansbury and Fred Jowett argued for more radical changes in the short term, especially in the form of extensive social policy innovations financed from general taxation.
They repeatedly lost the arguments, not least because such policies ran counter to the radical traditions of self-help to which
MacDonald and, indeed, the bulk of the skilled working class
were so wedded. But both aspects of Labour's appeal were important. MacDonald's approach attracted working-class Liberals; yet

the less moralizing, more concrete approach of the dissenters was more appealing to working-class Conservatives, a group for whom the Liberals had little appeal, and so 'Labour's ability to tap into this [Conservative] tradition ... helped create' the 1903 pact.[22]

Between the conclusion of the pact and the 1906 general election, Labour made two more by-election gains. The first came at Woolwich in March 1903, where Will Crooks, unhindered by Liberal opposition, gained the seat from the Conservatives. The second came at Barnard Castle in County Durham in July of the same year. Here, the Labour candidate was Arthur Henderson, who had previously been the Liberal agent in the constituency. Henderson was reluctant to fight at first, particularly as he would face Liberal opposition. However, his union, the Ironfounders, pressed him to stand as an LRC candidate, and he was helped by the fact that the Liberal candidate appeared to come out in favour of protection. Ultimately, he won the seat by a narrow majority, with the Liberal trailing in third place.

Meanwhile, the Conservatives were in increasing difficulties. Finally, in December 1905, A. J. Balfour, the Prime Minister, resigned in the hope that the Liberal leader, Sir Henry Campbell-Bannerman, would be unable to form a government. However, the latter succeeded, and once the government was formed, he dissolved parliament. Polling took place between 11 January and 8 February 1906. The main issue was free trade – other issues, like education and Chinese labour in South Africa, were also of importance, although at a secondary level. This suited the MacDonald–Gladstone Pact very well, since Labour candidates were overwhelmingly in support of free trade. In so far as Labour had a distinct policy, it was the reversal of Taff Vale; but even here, many Liberal candidates, keen to court trade union votes and certainly not keen to defend the judge-made law that the Conservatives had been instrumental in creating, offered pledges of reform. Labour's manifesto was studiously moderate, stressing those aspects of the LRC that were of general appeal: there was no mention of socialism. This did not mean, though, that individual candidates did not mention it and campaign for it; we must beware of attributing too monolithic an outlook to what remained very much a federal organization. But, on the whole, it was a campaign in which points of contact with the Liberals were emphasized.

There were 50 LRC-endorsed candidates in England and Wales, with a further five being endorsed by the Scottish Workers' Representation Committee. Three-fifths of the Labour candidates stood in Lancashire, Yorkshire and the north-east. As well as the five in Scotland, there were only four candidates in the whole of the London area, five in the Midlands and two in Wales. This shows plainly the northern English bias of LRC strength. It was clearly a party rooted in the most heavily unionized areas, the heartlands of the Industrial Revolution. Generally, the MacDonald–Gladstone Pact worked well enough, and enabled many Labour candidates to have a free run against the Conservatives. It was particularly successful in Lancashire, where the Liberals were weak, the Labour movement was relatively strong, there were numerous double-member constituencies which allowed each party to run a candidate, and the threat of tariffs helped to mobilize an unexpectedly strong reaction against the Conservatives in what had been one of their stronger areas. The pact worked less well in places where these factors did not apply, notable examples being Yorkshire and, in particular, Scotland, where official Liberalism would accept no agreement at all. In other parts of the country, the fact that the MFGB was still outside the LRC meant Lib-Lab, rather than LRC, candidatures.[23]

The results were very encouraging for the LRC, although they paled somewhat at the side of the Liberals' achievement in winning almost 400 seats. There were 29 LRC MPs, which increased to 30 as soon as parliament met, with one of the Lib-Labbers taking the Labour whip. Thirteen of them came from the Lancashire area, four from Yorkshire and three from the north-east – in other words, two-thirds of the Labour MPs sat for northern English seats. There were only three MPs from the London area, two from Scotland and one from Wales. Only five seats had been won against Liberal opposition.

In some senses, therefore, this was hardly a great victory; Labour had made a breakthrough, but was heavily dependent on the pact with the Liberals and was very much a sectional party with scarcely any presence at all outside areas of heavy industry and relatively high levels of unionization. Yet, in the immediate aftermath of the 1906 election, a wave of euphoria went through Labour's ranks. Viewed from later standpoints of success, such as the 1920s or the 1940s, it could be seen as the first instalment of the party's inexorable push towards power.[24]

Immediately after the election, the LRC changed its name to the Labour Party. The change to 'party' seemed to signify a new bid for status. But the retention of 'Labour', which was hardly disputed, was also significant. It lacked the foreign and sectarian connotations of 'social democracy'. It could also mean all things to all people, and represented a clear link with manual work. At the same time, MacDonald and others, who hoped ultimately to broaden its appeal, could resort to the formulation that all employees, manual or not, were workers, and hence 'Labour'.

The parliamentary Labour Party (PLP) elected in 1906 was firmly rooted in the working class. About 23 of the MPs were active trade unionists. Yet, 18 described themselves also as socialists, showing the dangers of resorting to too rigid a typology of 'trade unionists' versus 'socialists' in the early Labour Party. In policy terms, most were concerned especially with welfare issues and, particularly, unemployment. On the whole, they were middle-aged and 'respectable'. Most had been Liberals as young men or even, as in the case of Henderson, into early middle age. A significant number were active Nonconformists. On the other hand, only one was a Roman Catholic – a sign of Labour's failure to break into that potentially rich vein of working-class support before the 1920s.[25]

The party did not have a 'leader' as such until 1922. The key position, therefore, was chairman of the PLP, and here, after a tied first ballot, Hardie defeated Shackleton by a single vote. This is usually seen as a poor choice, given that Hardie was a less able organizer than Shackleton. But the former's appeal within the party was broader than that of his rival, and he was, at least, a useful figurehead, behind whom Shackleton (vice chairman), MacDonald (secretary) and Henderson (chief whip) could do business. Later, the chairmanship rotated in turn to Henderson (1908–10) and George Barnes (1910–11). It is perhaps significant that by 1911 Henderson had decided that the party was best led by a moderate socialist, rather than a leading trade unionist.[26]

The first couple of years of the new parliament saw Labour emerge with a by no means discreditable record. There had been fears, for example, that the legislation to sort out the mess created by Taff Vale might not restore the status quo ante.

Campbell-Bannerman, buttressed by the recommendations of a Royal Commission, was keen for a new definition which would leave the unions with greater responsibilities than before. However, a number of Liberal MPs had pledged themselves to the Labour position during the election campaign, and Shackleton was able to use this fact to convince the premier of the need for the acceptance of Labour's demands. This could then be presented as a great victory for the party, and can hardly have harmed it with the trade unions, particularly the MFGB. While the miners stayed outside for the time being, the proportion of TUC members affiliated to the Labour Party rose from 57.4 per cent in 1906 to 66.1 per cent two years later. Labour also played a part in the implementation of other reforms, such as the introduction of school meals, the extension of the scope of workmen's compensation and a slight increase in expenditure on unemployment relief works.

However, bigger projects made much less progress. In 1907 the party put forward its 'Right to Work' Bill, which called on the government to increase expenditure at times of slump in order to offset increased unemployment, but this got nowhere.[27] In the following year, the Minority Report of the Poor Law Commission, written largely by the Fabian Beatrice Webb and the Labour MP George Lansbury, made suggestions for sweeping changes in social policy, including the abolition of the Poor Law and the prevention of poverty through comprehensive social reforms. But, apart from old-age pensions, which were introduced in 1908, this too was largely ignored by the Liberal government. On the whole, the Liberals seem to have seen Labour MPs as a useful gauge of working-class opinion, but little more.

Some Labourites became discontented with the PLP's performance. This disenchantment manifested itself in a number of ways. First, there were efforts to get Labour MPs to act as delegates of the wider party. The MPs, not surprisingly, rejected this view. At the 1907 party conference a compromise was reached: conference would set out the broad lines of policy, but the PLP would retain discretion as to how to follow the policy so laid down. Another point of dispute was the leadership's reluctance to fight by-elections. Although the MacDonald–Gladstone Pact had applied to the 1906 election alone, the basic strategy of trying to avoid conflict with the Liberals remained. Thus Labour left many by-elections uncontested. This galled Labour activists, particularly in areas like west Yorkshire, where the Liberals were neither 'progressive' in their policies nor socially acceptable to Labourites. A spectacular manifestation of these discontents came in July 1907 in the by-election in the west Yorkshire constituency of Colne Valley. Against the strongly expressed hostility of the party leadership, Victor Grayson stood as an independent social-ist candidate and won the seat in a three-cornered fight against Conservative and Liberal candidates. Grayson's candidature, elec-tion and subsequent erratic behaviour as an MP were all worrying to a Labour leadership keen above all to maintain links with the Liberals and to stress their own party's moderation. A further sign of discontent came in 1908, with the publication of Ben Tillett's vitriolic pamphlet *Is the Parliamentary Labour Party a Failure?* Unemployment was rising rapidly and, for Tillett, it was here that the party should make its stand, on moral and political grounds. Yet with the failure of the Right to Work Bill, Labour seemed to have little to say, and to be losing focus as some of its leaders cam-paigned on fringe issues such as temperance and Welsh Church disestablishment. MacDonald pointed out that Labour was still campaigning about unemployment, but could do only a limited amount given its small size.[28] But the dispute did highlight a num-ber of themes which were to be present throughout Labour's history: the conflict between a concentration on parliament and attempts to urge an extra-parliamentary approach in times of cri-sis; questions of prioritization of policies; and the belief that full employment was the key objective of the party.

In any case, Labour was becoming even more union-dominated in this period. TUC membership rose in the first decade of the twentieth century by 38.5 per cent to 1,662,133, and the per-centage of members affiliated to the party also increased. Thus, although from mid-decade the membership of the socialist socie-ties was rising, the unions formed 97.5 per cent of Labour Party membership in 1910 as opposed to 93.9 per cent at the formation of the LRC in 1900.[29] While it would be wrong to read too much into this – many leading trade unionists were socialists – it shows that Tillett's fears of the party's increasing lack of radicalism had some basis in fact.

The single most important development regarding the unions concerned the miners. The MFGB was the largest union in the country, with over half a million members by 1908. But hitherto it had remained committed to a Lib-Lab outlook.[30] However, things were changing. The federation's legal problems had suggested to some the need for a shift; this was facilitated by the death of some staunch Lib-Lab leaders, like Ben Pickard in Yorkshire, and the tireless propaganda work of ILPers in the coalfields.[31] There was a ballot on affiliation in the summer of 1906, but on a turnout of 57 per cent, the miners voted against by 101,714 to 92,222. Majorities in favour in the four areas of greatest membership – south Wales, Yorkshire, Scotland and Lancashire – were not enough to offset massive opposition in the Midlands and most of the smaller coalfields.[32] But so close a result was unlikely to be conclusive, and a further ballot in May 1908 saw a vote of 213,137 to 168,446 in favour of affiliation on a 69 per cent turnout. The coalfields of the Midlands and north Wales opposed affiliation, however; and given that 61 per cent of the membership, overall, had either not voted or opposed the move, it could hardly be claimed that there was a major sea change in the miners' attitudes.[33] That would be reserved for the period after the First World War. But at least the MFGB was now ready to affiliate, which it duly did in 1909. This meant that Labour's trade union membership was now 88 per cent of that of the TUC. The move also meant that 13 Lib-Lab MPs now joined the PLP.[34] In many ways, their political attitudes were not very different from those of the Labour MPs they joined; but clearly the effect was to move the centre of gravity within the Labour Party still further from socialism.

The anti-Labour strain within trade unions remained significant, however. One result of this caused Labour considerable problems from 1909 onwards. In that year, the House of Lords adjudged union contributions to political parties to be illegal. The railwayman who had brought the case, W. V. Osborne, was a staunch trade unionist, but, as a Liberal, opposed union involvement in party politics. The Osborne judgment was clearly a threat to Labour's long-term development. In the short term, many local Labour parties collapsed and Labour candidates at the 1910 elections were often desperately short of money.[35] The party itself coped – it had few paid staff and headquarters were modest and relatively inexpensive to run – but the judgment was obviously a threat to its position and, more broadly, yet another example of legal interference in trade union affairs.

To make matters worse, Labour was soon faced with a general election. The 1906 parliament, with its massive Liberal majority, might have been expected to run until 1912 or 1913, but in 1909, David Lloyd George, who had become Chancellor of the Exchequer when H. H. Asquith had succeeded Campbell-Bannerman as premier the previous year, introduced a radical budget which so antagonized Conservative opinion that the Tory majority in the House of Lords took the unprecedented step of vetoing it. In order to re-establish his mandate, Asquith dissolved parliament. This was hardly a prospect to gladden the Labour heart. Out of ten by-elections fought by official Labour candidates since 1906, eight had been three-cornered fights and Labour had come bottom of the poll in five. Its only gains had come in peculiar circumstances: at Jarrow in 1907 when an Irish Nationalist candidate had taken enough votes from the Liberal candidate to let Labour in, and at Sheffield Attercliffe in 1909 when two rival Conservative candidates had caused enough confusion to allow Labour to steal the seat.

Labour's leaders, therefore, had little inclination to fight on a much broader front than in 1906, even before the Osborne judgment clipped their wings still further. A new deal was done with the Liberals, allowing most Labour MPs a free run against the Conservatives. In a campaign dominated by the radical rhetoric of 'peers against people' and free trade versus protection, Labour had little to say that was distinctive from the Liberals. About 40 of Labour's 78 candidates were victorious, more than in 1906, but a net loss of five seats on its pre-dissolution strength. Significantly, only one of Labour's successful candidates faced Liberal opposition. Overall, the Liberals lost heavily, emerging with 274 seats to the Conservatives' 272. But Labour did not really hold the parliamentary balance of power. There could be no question of them allying with the Conservatives, so they were forced, willy-nilly, to back the Liberals; and, still more significantly, the Liberals had – on paper at least – the greater strength of the 82 Irish Nationalists to back them.

A second election soon followed. The budget was passed, but the government was eager to deal with the House of Lords as well, and could only do so with a fresh electoral mandate. At the December 1910 election, Labour, more strapped than ever by the Osborne judgment, could field only 62 candidates; it emerged with

42 seats. The other parties' positions scarcely changed – the Liberals emerged with the same number of seats as the Conservatives, but were safe in power because of Irish and Labour support.

Labour's position in the period between the end of 1910 and the outbreak of the First World War just over three-and-a-half years later did not suggest that the party was about to make a major leap forward. Performance in by-elections was indifferent; indeed, Labour lost four seats. Three of these were north Midland mining seats where there had been no Liberal candidates in 1910 but where Lib-Labbism remained a potent force. The fact that Labour came third in all three contests was particularly worrying. In eight other seats, Labour put up candidates where it had not done so in December 1910. They all came last. True, Labour's candidates were picking up a fair number of votes, but Labour was clearly a third party, and not yet challenging the Liberals on anything like equal terms. Evidence from local government elections offers a somewhat less bleak picture. In some areas, at least, Labour was capable of gaining votes from the Liberals. In every year between 1909 and 1913 Labour made a net gain of seats, with especially strong performances in 1911 and 1913.[36] But still the image remains of a third party struggling with no great success to establish a greater presence in most parts of the country.

Other developments were more encouraging. The party's performance in parliament improved. The rotating chairmanship had not been a great success, and when Barnes fell ill in 1911 a deal was struck whereby MacDonald retired from the party secretaryship in favour of Henderson and took over the chairmanship from Barnes. This was a development of considerable significance. MacDonald was a man of charisma and style, a fine (if sometimes rather nebulous) orator who had clear electoral appeal. These points are commonplace. What is sometimes forgotten is that he was also a master of organization and strategy and had a relatively coherent ideology. His aim, as stated above, was to stress the points of contact between an evolutionary, consensual form of socialism with, on the one hand, the trade unionists who made up the bulk of the party and, on the other, those 'progressives' who were still in the Liberal Party but who, on many issues, were close to the Labour outlook. In the short term, Labour not only continued to support the Liberals, but also became more professional in parliament.

The concomitant of this was the aim of improving Labour's organization in the country. Here, the period between 1910 and 1914 saw significant developments. The staff at head office was increased, with the appointment of two national organizers. It was agreed in principle to establish a separate Scottish organization. And in London, severe difficulties were overcome finally in May 1914 with the formation of the London Labour Party. Across the country, local trades councils became increasingly Labour dominated.[37] While it would be rash to argue that these changes led inexorably towards the party's post-war progress, they did signify that Labour would be pushing the Liberals for a greater role in the not too distant future.

Labour's consolidation was assisted by two pieces of legislation passed in reaction to the Osborne judgment. The first, in 1911, resulted in the payment to MPs of a salary of £400 a year, which removed a burden from sponsoring organizations (mainly unions) which previously had to find the money for MPs' wages. In retrospect, this can be seen to have removed a potential obstacle to Labour's growth. The second was the Trade Union Act of 1913. Labour grumbled about this, first because it was a long time coming, and second because it did not restore the status quo ante, as the party had wanted. Indeed, it confirmed that unions should not make political donations from their general funds. However, it allowed unions to set up, subject to a membership ballot, a separate political fund, from which contributions could be made to the party. This would be financed by a special 'political levy' from which individuals like Osborne could 'contract out' if they so wished. Many Liberals hoped these complexities would stymie Labour, but, in fact, the Act was to prove a blessing in disguise; the legal position was now clarified in a way that satisfied natural justice; most of the ballots went in favour of establishing political funds, although in some cases by a very narrow margin; and, finally, there was little else that the political fund money could be spent on *except* the Labour Party, giving the latter a firmer base of income and budgeting than ever before. However, union executives often remained reluctant to adopt a very expansive policy of funding, with many 'refusing to finance enough Labour parliamentary candidates to sustain a broad anti-Liberal campaign'.[38]

The clarification of the legal financial relationship between party and unions was especially important given the considerable expansion of trade unionism during this period. TUC-affiliated unions had had 1,200,000 members in 1900. This rose by 37.3 per cent in the next ten years, and then by a further 62.8 per cent between 1910 and 1914, when membership stood at almost 2,700,000.[39] This increased rate of expansion after 1910 was due to three main causes. First, it was a period of trade prosperity. Second, many members were recruited around the time of the major industrial disputes of the period. These included, among others, a short national railway strike in August 1911, which resulted – at last – in the recognition of the rail unions by the railway companies, and a national miners' strike early in 1912. The number of working days lost through disputes soared, peaking at over 40,000,000 in 1912. Many contemporaries suggested that the strikes were caused by revolutionary trade unionism, or syndicalism (see below). This was not the case, although a few strike leaders were influenced by such ideas. In fact, the reasons were much more prosaic, most notably resistance to changing industrial practices and the levelling off of real wages. Indeed, the third cause of the increase in union membership suggested that workers were still thinking in terms of the continuation of the existing social system. Under the National Insurance Act, friendly societies and unions which already ran benefit schemes of their own became 'approved societies' for the administration of the scheme on behalf of the state. This helped to consolidate, and even increase, union membership at the time.

This expansion benefited the Labour Party. Its trade union affiliated membership rose by a third to 1,858,178 between 1910 and 1912. The immediate effect of the 1913 Trade Union Act, of course, was to reduce this figure somewhat, given the 'contracting out' clause. Even so, membership was still over 1.5 million in 1914. But trade unionists were still only a minority of workers.

In particular, the number of women unionized was far less than that of men. But this, and the fact that women were still barred from the parliamentary franchise, should not be taken to mean that the party totally ignored women. Although women were typically treated as second-class members in trade unions, they could not be ignored entirely, as the leaders of the textile and footwear workers' unions found to their cost.[40] Women also played a significant role in the socialist societies. Alongside women prominent at the national level, like Katharine Bruce Glasier, were

women at the grassroots, who could, and often did, play a significant role. For many, socialism was the appeal; for others, Labour
seemed the most likely party to push for women's suffrage.[41] As
pressure grew from women's groups for the vote and for greater
rights in trade unions, so Labour came to take these issues more
seriously. In 1911, when the government introduced a franchise
reform bill which did not include women's suffrage, the Labour
Party conference declared that this, or any similar legislation,
would be unacceptable. This led to greater co-operation between
the Labour Party and the moderate National Union of Women's
Suffrage Societies (NUWSS), and many Liberal women began to
see Labour as the better bet on this issue. Ultimately, the NUWSS
set up a fund to support Labour candidates in by-elections where
there was no pro-suffrage candidate.[42] Labour was at least starting
to make wider connections with women and the organized wom-
en's movement than would have been possible through a narrowly trade union-oriented approach. However, the fact that the
Co-operative movement remained outside the sphere of Labour
politics posed a continuing obstacle to making those links still
closer.

If there were still many workers outside trade unions, and trade
unionists outside the Labour Party, it must also be remembered
that there were significant numbers of socialists who did not
accept the Labour lead. During this period three basic challengers contested the claims of the 'Labour alliance' to be the sole
representative of socialism in Britain: Marxism, syndicalism and
guild socialism.

The Marxist left had fragmented somewhat after the SDF's disaffiliation from the LRC in 1901. In 1903, supporters of Daniel de
Leon's ideas of industrial unionism had broken away to form the
Socialist Labour party (SLP), a small but influential group whose
main strength was on Clydeside. The following year, a group
had broken off to form the Socialist Party of Great Britain. The
SDF (renamed the Social Democratic party in 1907) remained
the most significant force, but made little progress. However, in
1911 left ILPers, including Grayson, led a secession to join the
Social Democrats in a new British Socialist party (BSP). The BSP
hoped to outflank Labour, but although it claimed 40,000 members at the outset, this figure had fallen by two-thirds by 1914. Its
attempt to defeat Labour from without having failed, it applied

for affiliation to the Labour Party, and this was finally accepted in 1916. For its part, the SLP was also in decline by 1914, with a membership of around 300 in 15 branches.[43] In other words, the challenge of orthodox Marxism had been contained, for the time being at least.

The second challenge was that of syndicalism. Syndicalists rejected the state, arguing that full unionization of the work-force and the amalgamation of unions would lead to a revolutionary general strike to overthrow capitalism and replace it with a new order of society based on workers' control. From 1910 onwards a number of trade unionists became influenced by the doctrine, and many of the leaders of the Rhondda coal strike in 1911 were avowed supporters. However, other causes accounted for the strike wave of 1910–14. Meanwhile, union amalgamations were more of an attempt by moderate leaders to increase their hold over the membership than the prelude to a revolutionary general strike. This was certainly true in the case of the merger of the ASRS with other unions to form the National Union of Railwaymen (NUR) in 1912, while the formation in 1914 of the Triple Alliance, whereby the MFGB, NUR and National Transport Workers' Federation (NTWF) pledged to support each other in disputes, was essentially a defensive action.[44]

The third 'threat', guild socialism, originated in the first decade of the century. Despite its occasionally ludicrous medievalism, guild socialism was a serious attempt to marry the syndicalist critique of statism with the Labour critique of syndicalism. It argued that a future socialist society dominated by the state might well be just as undemocratic, even tyrannous, as capitalism; but that, on the other hand, syndicalism alone would not guarantee freedom from industrial tyranny. Accordingly, its leading advocate, the young academic G. D. H. Cole, put forward a model of society in which reformed trade unions, or guilds, would remain to run industry on the basis of democratic workers' control (representing the producers), while the state would remain to represent consumers and guarantee broader liberties. There were all kinds of problems with this concept, of course. In particular, there was the danger of frequent clashes between guilds and state, producers and consumers. Cole argued that in the new spirit of a socialist society such clashes either would not occur or else be easily dealt with, but this was not terribly convincing. Even so, guild social-ism did address problems of power in society which MacDonald and his colleagues tended to ignore or to brush aside. It must be admitted, though, that before 1914 the influence of guild social-ism outside intellectual circles was not very great.[45]

The development of syndicalism and guild socialism did dem-onstrate disquiet with two aspects of the 'socialism' of Labour's leaders. First, there was concern as to the uncritical conception of the state held by many Labour socialists, and in particular by lead-ers like MacDonald. At a time when members of all parties were questioning the unprecedented expansion of the state which was coming with social reform, administrative intervention in indus-trial disputes and war preparation measures (for example, the Official Secrets Act, 1911), it was a sign of health that some social-ists were at least talking about these issues.

Second, there were questions about the way in which Labour's leaders saw a socialist society emerging. The conflicts between MacDonald's mix of ethical socialism and revisionism, on the one hand, and the more interventionist socialists like Lansbury, on the other, remained significant. The former view continued to hold sway, but the fact that the left was looking, albeit rather unsuccessfully, for an alternative suggests that it sensed that there might be problems with the approach. This conflict, in turn, spilled over into electoral policy – if MacDonald was right, then continued co-operation would seem to have a certain logic, but, if a more radical policy was called for, then clearly it would make more sense to attack the Liberals. Indeed, the increasing pressure from grassroots Labourites to run candidates in these years, and the increasing difficulty that the leadership had in stopping such contests with the Liberals, is indicative of a broader debate about the right strategy for the party.

Not surprisingly, then, the question of how far the 'progressive alliance' would have been maintained in the next general election (due, probably, in 1915) has excited some historical debate. It has been argued that Labour would have fought that election as 'a truly independent party of the left and of the trade union move-ment', with anything up to 170 candidates.[46] There is evidence in favour of this argument. The Liberals were in trouble: the tactical advantages of some form of alliance were not, perhaps, as clear to Labour as they had been in 1903 or 1910. The Liberals' social reforming impulse, though not obliterated, had nonetheless been somewhat obscured by issues like Ireland, rearmament, strikes and women's suffrage; and this in turn meant that any alliance would have been harder for the Labour leadership to 'sell' to its increasingly restive followers. Labour's organization was much improved. On the whole, it does seem fair even to say that, given disappointing by-election performances, the mere passage of time made it more assertive.

Yet there are also reasons to doubt whether, ultimately, MacDonald and Henderson would have stuck to their guns. Their bold talk of a broader front may well have been tactical: both to frighten the Liberals into conceding a better deal than last time, and also to appease their own more confrontational supporters. It was one thing to 'talk big' at a time when an election was still some way off; it might have been different if it had meant a real split threatening the imminent election of a protectionist, Unionist, rearming government under the perceivedly extreme Andrew Bonar Law and staffed by some of the very people who had cheered on every piece of anti-union judge-made law since the 1890s. We cannot know for sure, of course: the 1915 election never took place. But it does not seem wholly unlikely that, had matters taken their course, Labour and the Liberals would have renewed their pact for the next election, albeit with Labour probably being given some more seats to fight.[47]

The period between 1900 and the outbreak of war in August 1914 saw Labour establish itself as a force in British politics. But the party was not on the brink of second-party status. The wilder hopes expressed in the aftermath of the 1906 election had not been borne out by events. Yet, to argue that Labour was in some kind of decline also seems wide of the mark. It had developed its organization, forged deeper links with the expanding trade unions and new links with women, and acquired a more polished and effective leadership. However unsteadily, it had begun to establish a few real electoral strongholds. At least, its strength had been consolidated and its position was unlikely to decline. In 1906 Labour had outperformed its potential, gaining position on the back of an anti-Conservative and pro-free trade reaction that took almost everyone by surprise by its magnitude. By 1914 it had not grown very far, but it now had a firmer base. It would not have expanded as far as it ultimately did in so short a space of time had it not been for the First World War, but at least developments to 1914 meant that it was in a position to take advantage of the opportunities which that war was to offer.

2 The Surge to Second-Party Status, 1914–22

The period between 1914 and 1922 saw massive changes on the world stage. In 1914 it had seemed to many that the established order would never change. Eight years later, millions had died in a bloody war, old empires were no more and regimes professing communism and fascism were installed in two of Europe's great states. No major nation had been left unscathed by the conflict. British politics had also been transformed, to the considerable benefit of the Labour Party. In 1914 Labour was still the fourth party in parliament, with just over three dozen MPs and an uncertain future. By 1922 it was the main Opposition party, with 142 MPs, a new constitution and a much-improved organization. The war gave Labour leaders their first experience of ministerial office. The period saw not only tangible electoral and political advances but also a shift from the loose federal structure of the Edwardian era to a much tighter party, closer in many ways to the continental social democratic parties. Many of these changes were directly attributable to the First World War.

Labour's ability to make so much of the opportunities offered by the war was due, mainly, to the party's basic underlying unity during the conflict. It is true that a number of issues did split the party in wartime. The first was entry into the war itself. Labour, as a member of the Second International, was formally committed to opposing a war. On Sunday 2 August, the day the Germans launched a massive offensive in the West, Labour organized a big anti-war demonstration in London's Trafalgar Square. Henderson invited the main institutions in the Labour movement to a meeting on 5 August to discuss the next steps. However, this apparent anti-war unity then collapsed. In fact, some Labourites would have supported the war in any case, but the German violation of Belgian neutrality allowed many more to come over, couching their support for the war in conventional radical terms. When parliament debated the situation on 3 August, the Parliamentary Labour Party (PLP) majority was in favour of a declaration of war on Germany. MacDonald spoke against entry but, realizing his minority position, resigned the same day as PLP chairman, and was replaced by Henderson. The declaration of war followed the next day. Before the end of the month an electoral truce had been agreed, and the party was soon supporting the war effort, even to the extent of putting its organization at the disposal of the military recruiting campaign.

To a large extent, this was a division born of conviction; there was a patriotic surge, and most Labour leaders were unlikely to be immune from it. But it was not just that Labourites wrapped themselves in the flag. Many leaders who were sceptical about the war realized Labour might cause itself great damage by going against the tide of patriotism sweeping the country. The over-whelming view was that the war would be short-lived. For most leading Labourites, including Henderson, the fear was that a critical approach would isolate Labour and leave it vulnerable to charges of defeatism at the general election which would shortly follow an early victory. In addition, there was a more principled argument that Britain (and France) had parliamentary structures which offered at least some possibilities of 'progressive' advance, and that these were therefore worth preserving. The alternative, presented rather hesitatingly by MacDonald, was that Labour should stand on principle, launch a radical critique of pre-war 'secret diplomacy', and so draw in those discontented radical Liberals who were to form the basis of the Union of Democratic Control (UDC); in short, it should steal the radical thunder from the discredited Liberal Party. At first, official party statements tried to paper over the cracks between the two positions, but, as attitudes hardened, Labour's stance became more overtly patri-otic and anti-German.[1]

Even so, the party did not fall apart. One reason for this was the formation of the War Emergency Workers' National Committee (WEC), as a result, ironically, of the meeting called by Henderson for 5 August. Its original purpose was, typically, defensive – to protect working-class living standards against the economic dis-tress and social dislocation which the war was expected to bring. It included representatives of the Labour Party, the TUC and the GFTU, who joined elected and co-opted members under the chairmanship of Henderson and with J. S. Middleton, assistant secretary of the party, as secretary. Members included MacDonald, Sidney Webb, Hyndman, the miners' president Robert Smillie, Mary Macarthur of the National Federation of Women Workers, and Marion Phillips, later to be chief woman officer of the Labour Party. The WEC thus provided a point of contact for a very broad swathe of Labourites who might otherwise have drifted apart.[2]

The WEC could not, of course, prevent all disagreements. One dispute came over compulsory military service, which became an issue later in 1915 as the war dragged on. Conscription was suspect in itself, as a manifestation of the kind of militarism that Britain was supposed to be opposing, but it also raised the spectre of industrial compulsion and an end to the free market in labour which was so important to British unions. It was partly to ward off pressure for conscription that Labour entered so keenly into the recruitment of volunteers. Once in the Asquith cabinet, Henderson was a keen opponent of compulsion. But the government finally introduced conscription in January 1916, and ultimately Henderson decided that it was better to remain in the cabinet and be in a position to resist industrial conscription. The majority in the party took the same view, although a minority of Labour MPs continued to work in close alliance with Liberal rebels in voting against extensions of military conscription to new groups of men.[3]

Further disputes surrounded Labour's entry into the Lloyd George Coalition. As Asquith came under increasing pressure in late 1916, Labour stressed its support for him: on 1 December Henderson described the premier as 'the indispensable man'.[4] On 5 December, probably seeking to demonstrate that he was indeed 'indispensable', Asquith offered the King his resignation. The Conservative leaders decided to support Lloyd George, but the latter clearly needed Labour support, given that the bulk of the Liberal Party would move into opposition if Asquith were ousted, and given the continuing importance of labour questions to the war effort. Ultimately, Labour did join the new government, with Henderson becoming a Minister without Portfolio in the five-man war cabinet. This seemed a startling volte-face. But Henderson, as a loyal member of the cabinet, had had little choice but to back Asquith when the latter had been premier.

Once the change had taken place, though, it was a different story. After all, Asquith had displayed poor judgement, even perversity, in offering his resignation. Labour had little to gain from leaving office, and perhaps much to lose if it did so. Thus on 7 December Henderson and his leading colleagues on the National Executive Committee (NEC) and PLP met Lloyd George. As well as a place for Henderson in the war cabinet, he offered terms better than Asquith had ever conceded: new ministries of Labour and Pensions to be placed under Labour ministers, state control of the coal mines, and a pledge not to introduce industrial conscription. Thus the Labour leaders voted, by a majority, to join the new government.

A further source of dispute came in 1917 with the proposal for a meeting of European socialists at Stockholm. In March 1917 a revolution in Russia overthrew the Tsar, and on 22 April Camille Huysmans, secretary of the Second International, proposed a conference of socialists in the Swedish capital to discuss plans for the future. Peace terms would obviously be on the agenda. The Petrograd Soviet endorsed the appeal in May, but Labour's NEC rejected it because it did not wish to meet with 'enemy' socialists, and proposed a conference of Allied socialists instead. Henderson was then dispatched by Lloyd George to persuade the Russian socialists of the need to stay in the war and to boycott the Stockholm conference. On arriving in Russia, though, Henderson was appalled by the prospects for the Provisional government if steps were not made towards peace, and came to the view that Stockholm would at least show the impotence of the German socialists and the fact that there was no alternative to continuing the fight. On his return he talked the NEC into provisional support for the conference, but it was clear that there would be deep divisions within the movement as a result. However, the war cabinet's position had hardened, and it refused to issue passports to Labourites wishing to attend. Henderson was forced to resign from the war cabinet.[5] In this way, then, he was pushed back towards the party. Paradoxically, a threat to its unity served ultimately to reunite Labour.

In short, a series of crises at the top of the Labour movement were overcome without irreparable damage. This is not to say, though, that there were no divisions at all. 'Super patriots' like Hyndman and the secretary of the GFTU, W. C. Appleton, took the view that everything must be subordinated to the defeat of Germany; on the other hand, revolutionary defeatists like the Marxist John Maclean argued that the war should be turned into a European class war. On the whole, neither strain was strong; Hyndman was forced out of the BSP in 1916 for his views, while the defeatist strain was very weak indeed. Most Labourites took a line similar to that of Henderson and Webb, that the war was 'just', but that the defence of working-class interests should not be forsaken. MacDonald, while critical of the war, 'was no more pre-pared to see Germany win ... than Henderson was'.[6] Other mem-bers of the Labour Party, most notably those in the Independent Labour Party (ILP), did take a stronger anti-war stance, some-times verging on pacifism. But most of these divisions tended to mend as Henderson and others moved towards consideration of a 'just' peace and earlier battles over conscription faded.[7]

Politicians, being in the public eye, had to maintain at least a semblance of consistency. But this applied less as one went further down the movement. Here, it was not unusual for the general swings in the public mood which accompanied Britain's fluctuating fortunes in the war to have a significant impact on attitudes. Thus, in the period 1914–16, the patriotic mood was dominant. In 1917, this waned, as war-weariness grew with increasing casualties and no prospect of an end to the war. But the crises of early 1918, when it seemed that Britain stood on the verge of defeat in the face of renewed German offensives, led to a revival of patriotic sentiment, and as the tables were turned and victory approached in later 1918 this mood reached near fever pitch.[8] Clearly, in other words, many people were not consistent in their views, but responded to changing circum-stances with a combination of patriotism and defensiveness. In this sense, the presence of apparently different tendencies at the top of the Labour movement prevented it from becoming brittle, and kept it responsive to its followers, while the fact that the divisions were often more apparent than real helped to keep the party together.

Labour, then, was able to exploit many of the opportunities offered by the war because of its basic underlying unity. The same could not be said for the Liberals. The most spectacular symbol of Liberal problems, of course, was the split between Asquith and Lloyd George in December 1916. Lloyd George took with him only about a third of the party's MPs; the rest, including most leading Liberals, followed Asquith into opposition.[9] The two sides were to reunite only in 1923, and in the intervening period a series of disputes embittered relations still further. But Liberal decline was about more than leadership jealousies. It was difficult for the party to move forward on policy in wartime. This was less true of the Labour Party where, after a fashion, policies were made by the annual conference and implemented by the NEC and PLP. In the Liberal Party, where the institutional framework was weaker, policy depended much more on the agency of individuals. Here, Lloyd George had been a crucial figure before the war, while the 'New Liberals' had also been significant in keeping the party leaning in a 'progressive' direction. But both Lloyd George and many of the New Liberals were weakened as agents of progressivism by the war and power moved towards more traditional figures, opening up the gap on the left of British politics that Labour had found so elusive in the pre-war years.[10] The split of 1916 merely reinforced this. In addition, Liberal ideology was deeply questioned by the war. The traditional watchwords of most Liberals – 'peace, retrenchment and reform' – were mocked by a bloody and costly war, a massively expanded state (and, between 1914 and 1916, an eightfold increase in public expenditure), the introduction of protective tariffs on luxury imports in 1915, and the clear infringement of individual liberties involved in conscription. All this served massively to weaken the self-confidence and moral force which had been such crucial components of nineteenth-century Liberalism. At the same time, though, the resistance of the Liberals to measures like conscription meant that it was easier than ever for the Conservatives to portray themselves as the truly patriotic party.[11] A more prosaic, but still important, problem the war created for the Liberals was that of finance. Here again, Labour's structure, and the Liberals' lack of it, enabled the newer party to benefit. The Liberals depended heavily on rich men's gifts, many of them donated in the expectation of a mention in the Honours List. After 1916, such people often chose to fund Lloyd George, rather than the party, since he now had the patronage at his disposal. Contributions to Liberal headquarters simply dried up.[12] By contrast, the political levy assured Labour of a significant and growing income at all levels of the party organization.

The impact of franchise reform, which was hastened by the war, is more problematic. Before 1914, only about 60 per cent of men, and no women, had had the parliamentary vote. The 1918 Representation of the People Act, however, enfranchised all men of 21 and above, and most women of 30 and above. It has been argued that Labour had suffered particularly under the old arrangements because they discriminated against the working class; thus the post-1918 electorate was more prone to vote Labour, and, in so far as it did not, it voted for the Conservatives, whose simple patriotic appeals were easier to comprehend than those of the more cerebral Liberals.[13] However, this argument is not terribly convincing. First, the excluded voters were not all working class by any means. Professionals who moved frequently and so lost out under the lengthy residence requirements of the pre-war franchise, commercial travellers, and, perhaps most significantly, young men who lived with their parents were all effectively excluded from the franchise. Even where they were not middle class, they included groups – like domestic servants and soldiers living in barracks – who were hardly natural Labour voters.[14] Second, Liberal appeals to the electorate were not necessarily less populist than their opponents'. It scarcely took an Oxford don to understand such stock Liberal cries as 'the Big Loaf of Free Trade and the Little Loaf of Protection'. Third, it is clear from the evidence of elections in the 1920s that the Liberals did gain some support, at least when united, from the new voters. And, finally, Labour had no 'prior call' on most of the new voters. The latter were a heterogeneous bunch, and they were to be faced, at the end of the war, with a confusing political landscape. What was reasonably clear, at least by 1918, was that the Liberals were the party which had taken Britain into a bloody war that had left scarcely a family in Britain untouched by grief, and that they were divided and doubtful at a time when Labour and the Conservatives were united and self-confident. In that sense, the war must be central to interpretations of Liberal decline.

The war strengthened Labour in other ways, too. It gained experience in office: Henderson served in cabinet as President of the Board of Education (1915–16) and later as Paymaster General under Asquith and as Minister without Portfolio (1916–17) in Lloyd George's small war cabinet. Essentially, he acted in all three posts as an adviser on labour matters. When he was forced out in

August 1917, he was replaced by another Labour man, Barnes. The new ministries of Labour and Pensions went to Labourites, and others served in junior posts. In a sense, the gains were not as great as they might have been, for three of the eight Labourites to serve stayed in the Coalition after Labour withdrew in 1918. Still, the significance of having Labour MPs in ministerial office for the first time can hardly be exaggerated. Labour men had shown that they could fill office, in some cases with distinction.

Labour also profited from the expansion of trade union membership during the war. The economy was soon at full stretch to fuel the war effort; thus employers were more willing to tolerate union membership and indeed government sometimes actively encouraged it as a way of increasing labour discipline. The inflationary pressures of the war, and constantly changing workplace conditions (or fear thereof) in many industries, encouraged workers to join unions as a defence against state and/or employer incursions on real wage levels and established working practices. The result was a near doubling of TUC membership to almost 5.3 million in 1918, with a peak of over 6.5 million the following year.[15]

The Labour Party benefited directly from this. Its trade union membership increased rapidly by 88.3 per cent during the war alone, and more than doubled (to 2,960,409) between 1910 and 1918.[16] With the membership of affiliated socialist societies also increasing, the party was boosted to new heights. The financial implications were very favourable, allowing Henderson to contemplate major reorganization in the latter part of the war.

Furthermore, the war brought to the fore the question of the role of the state in society, in a way which was profoundly helpful to the Labour Party's prospects. The state 'as threat' raised its head in a number of ways. One area, industrial conscription, has already been discussed. This was, perhaps, something of a chimera, although it had no shortage of advocates in the Conservative Party. More realistic was the perceived threat to established working practices and production relations. At first, Asquith had hoped that the war could be won by 'business as usual'. Soon, however, it became clear that labour was at a premium. This led in turn to a series of measures which sought to speed up production by extending the level of state intervention in production relations. Thus, by the Treasury Agreement of March 1915, most of the major unions agreed to concessions which included the suspension of certain established working practices and the dilution of labour, whereby skilled workers' jobs would be done by semi- or unskilled workers, often women. This was followed in May by the first of a number of Munitions of War Acts which made further incursions into what had been considered hitherto to be sacred territory. There was an understanding that the changes would be temporary, but it is worth noting that legislation for the restoration of pre-war practices did not in fact come until 1919. Until then, matters were, understandably, somewhat fraught. Some employers clearly saw an opportunity to remove 'restrictive practices' for good, with the state's help.[17] This led to severe tensions both at the workplace and within the unions – particularly in engineering – where the leaders were often seen as becoming too cosy with government and employers to be reliable. At the same time that unprecedented numbers were joining the unions, therefore, there were severe doubts as to the effectiveness of the established union leadership.

This led to an upsurge in rank-and-file militancy. This should not be overstated – far fewer working days were lost in disputes even in the worst year (1918), than in the calmest year of the immediate pre-war period (1913) – but the number and scale of disputes was far greater than it was to be in the Second World War. A leading role was played in engineering by the shop stewards – ordinary workers elected to act as de facto union officials at workshop level. The shop stewards' movement grew especially in major munitions centres like Clydeside, Sheffield and Manchester. How far this could have been the basis for something more significant is not clear: a national committee was set up but after a peak of activity in the winter of 1917–18 it fell apart, and it must be doubted whether it could have formed the basis of a serious revolutionary movement.[18] Much of the discontent stemmed from craft exclusiveness rather than class consciousness, and some of those who appeared to be potential revolutionaries in late 1917 were probably demanding the trial of the Kaiser a year later. Still, it seems possible that the encroachments made by the state on production relations both fuelled union recruitment and aroused working-class fears of what the state might do if it were to fall into the wrong hands. In that sense, they probably helped draw support to the Labour Party.

The danger of the state being in the wrong hands also played a significant part in pushing the Co-operative movement towards independent political action. Membership of the Co-ops had been increasing steadily, from 1,793,770 in 1901 to 3,054,297 in 1914; by 1919 it was to stand at 4,131,477.[19] Labourite Co-operators had tried to align the movement with the Labour Party before 1914 but without success; the Co-operative movement had not been on the verge of a shift to Labour by 1914. What changed, or at least greatly speeded, matters was the war's demonstration of the state as threat. By 1917, the movement had very real, war-induced grievances. The imposition of excess profits duty on the Co-ops' trading surpluses, the feeling that essential Co-op employees were discriminated against by military service tribunals and discrimination by the Ministry of Food – both in allocation of foodstuffs and in the exclusion of Co-op representatives from local food control committees – all caused great anger. More generally, the 'businessmen in government' air of the Lloyd George Coalition, allied to the debility of the opposition Liberals, suggested that old loyalties must be reviewed. In May 1917 the Co-operative Congress voted by 1979 votes to 201 to set up a political wing, which became known as the Co-operative Representation Committee and later, in 1919, the Co-operative Party. Although a national Labour–Co-operative agreement was not concluded until 1927, the two parties were to form effective alliances in many parts of the country long before then, and the Co-operative Party was to prove a source of great strength to Labour. In addition, the fact that women had most day-to-day contact with the Co-op shops meant that, however tentatively and partially, a link was made between those women and the Labour movement. Labour would be able to pose, through actions and rhetoric, as the party which protected Co-operators, and this helped the development of the party's relationship with the new women voters after 1918. It was crucial in extending Labour's appeal further beyond the workplace and trade unionists.[20]

While showing the threats that the state could pose, however, the war also demonstrated its positive potential, and made more credible and practicable the collectivist policies with which Labour was associated. This was demonstrated in three areas in particular: housing, 'fair shares' and industry. The housing issue made itself felt over the question of rents. At this time, 90 per cent of housing was rented from private landlords. Faced with rising wartime prices, and in some cases at least seeing a chance of profiteering, landlords sought to increase rents. This led, in 1915, to a series of largely spontaneous protests which were then often co-ordinated by local Labour movements, as in Glasgow, where the ILP played a leading role.[21] Ultimately the government was forced to pass legislation fixing working-class rents at pre-war levels. This was significant in that it showed that Labour, more than its rivals, was the party which would defend working-class interests in housing; as with the Co-ops later, it also helped move Labour away from union-based issues and towards areas with some direct appeal to women, in particular. Furthermore, it added credibility to the idea of state action to control market forces which disadvantaged the working class.

Labour also campaigned for 'fair shares', building up a powerful rhetoric which once again attacked unrestricted market forces and profiteering. The main significance of this may have been symbolic: there were few better images for 'fair shares' in twentieth-century Britain than that of the profiteering capitalist growing fat while 'the people' suffered at home and died on the battlefields. The gains were not only rhetorical, though, for some advances were made through pressure on government. Labour pushed hard for high taxation of war profits, rationing, and other controls. Price control from early 1917 led to the stabilization of food prices, while rationing, which came into effect at the start of 1918, ensured a degree of 'fair play'. In taxation, the excess profits duty was imposed in 1915 and reached 80 per cent by 1917. The WEC's 'Conscription of Riches' campaign, which began in 1916, further established Labour's credentials. Since 'fair play' was one of the great traditions of British radicalism, it was clearly to Labour's advantage to push in this direction, and the fact that such policies could be implemented greatly enhanced the party's general credibility.[22]

Collectivism also gained credibility in industry. Rail and coal were taken under state control. Although there was no intention to nationalize them permanently, this showed the miners, in particular, the potential benefits of a shift from private ownership. By the end of the war, there was a widespread feeling that state intervention in industry was one reason for victory.[23]

Labour also gained from its stance on foreign policy. Prior to the outbreak of war this could not have been predicted. Labour had professed to be an internationalist party, but the unions had left foreign policy largely to the 'socialists' in the party leadership, many continental socialists had seen Labour as hopelessly parochial, and some members of the movement had been positively jingoistic. However, Hardie, MacDonald and Snowden, among others, had toed a fairly consistent line over foreign affairs before the war, criticizing the increasing division of Europe into armed camps, favouring rapprochement with Germany, and advocating greater openness in the conduct of foreign policy.[24] Two weeks after war broke out, MacDonald became chairman of a new body, the UDC, which brought together ILPers and radical Liberals critical of Grey's foreign policy. It called for an end to 'secret diplomacy', a negotiated peace, defence of free trade and national self-determination; it later campaigned against conscription. Links between the Labour and Liberal dissidents also flourished in other pressure groups formed later in the war. These bodies were not supported by the Labour Party as such. But they fostered links between people who had been, and might expect to be again, prominent in the Labour Party, and dissenting Liberals who were becoming detached from their party. Many of those involved, such as E. D. Morel and C. P. Trevelyan, later drifted into the ILP and ended up as Labour MPs. The UDC and analogous bodies were, therefore, a crucial conduit of middle-class radicals into the Labour Party.[25]

They were also important, ultimately, in setting the Labour Party's foreign policy agenda. At first, Labour in wartime was more than ever parochial in its concerns.[26] But the party conference of January 1916 set up a committee, which included MacDonald, to look at post-war issues, and the party's new-found prominence in government after December 1916 also encouraged it to think in larger terms. The March 1917 revolution in Russia caused great excitement on the British left. That June, an unofficial Labour convention in Leeds, attended by over 1000 delegates, called for a peace without annexations or indemnities. During his stay in Russia that summer, meanwhile, Henderson saw the threat posed to the nascent regime by the far left Bolsheviks.[27]

All this had two main consequences. First, Labour was pushed towards a wide-ranging statement on foreign policy. When the Bolsheviks seized power that November and published the secret treaties between the Tsarist regime and Britain (among others), new urgency was added, and a special party conference that month adopted a 'Memorandum on War Aims', which essentially accepted UDC policy, including a League of Nations.[28] The result was that many UDCers now saw Labour as the party most likely to fulfil their aims.[29] Second, further urgency was added to the recasting of the Labour Party constitution. This would have happened in any case, given the extension of the franchise which was now planned and the fact that the party was better resourced than ever before. But following his departure from the government, Henderson was able, with Webb, to devote more time to it than might otherwise have been the case. After some wrangling, it was adopted by a party conference in February 1918. The new constitution changed the structure of, and method of election to, the NEC; permitted the establishment of constituency Labour parties (CLPs) with individual membership; and committed Labour, by what became known as 'Clause IV', to a form of socialism for the first time.

While many observers have focused on Clause IV, it was in fact hardly mentioned at all in the debates of the time. Its insertion seems to have been the result of a number of factors: Webb's influence; a fear that otherwise Labour, like the Russian Provisional government, might be unable to compete with the far left in the anticipated leftward swing of working-class opinion; and a desire to mark a clear line of demarcation between Labour and the Liberals. It also served to sweeten the pill, for committed socialists, of a constitution which gave more power than ever to the unions.[30] Its uncontroversial passage was also due to the perceived 'success' of collectivism during the war and, perhaps, to a heightened sense of animosity towards capitalism as a result of wartime profiteering. But the fact that there was little debate about Clause IV does not mean that it was unimportant. Over time, it would become a touchstone of what Labour stood for. In 1959, the party leader, Hugh Gaitskell, would be thwarted in his attempts to get rid of it, and only in the very changed atmosphere of the 1990s would a party leader dare to raise the issue again.

The decision to establish CLPs with individual membership also aroused little real opposition, although there was some union grumbling at the prospect of middle-class recruits taking over. Labour now saw itself appealing broadly, and to garner that appeal it needed both a nationwide organization and a means whereby people who were not members of affiliated organizations (especially unions) could join it. The biggest battles, however, came over the composition of the executive committee.

Until 1917, the executive was composed of 16 members: the treasurer, one individual representing the trades councils, local organizations and women's organizations together, three social-ist societies' representatives and 11 union representatives. Each group nominated and elected its own representatives. But at the 1917 conference, a group of large unions had pushed through a proposal that the party conference as a whole should elect the committee. Given the overwhelming dominance of union votes at conference, this marked a clear shift towards greater union control. Under the first draft of the 1918 constitution, the same method of election – and hence union dominance, at least on paper – would prevail, but the executive's composition would change, with an increase in size to 21 members, comprising 11 trade unionists, five nominees of the local Labour parties, four women and the treasurer.[31] But even this was not enough for many unions. The first party conference of 1918 rejected the proposals, and it was not until the unions were given 13 repre-sentatives – that is, greater power still – that agreement could be reached. In addition, the PLP was given a role in policy making at election times, and stricter disciplinary measures were imposed to ensure greater obedience by Labour MPs.[32] The hegemony of the unions was now clearer than ever; the ILP, whose main functions had been to campaign for the adoption of socialism by Labour and to provide a conduit for individual membership, was faced with an uncertain future.

A further party conference, in June 1918, adopted a new programme, *Labour and the New Social Order,* drafted by Sidney Webb. This programme committed Labour to full employment at decent wages and, failing that, a comprehensive system of ben-efits; nationalization of land, railways, canals, coal and electricity; taxation based on ability to pay, plus a capital levy (wealth tax) to pay off the huge national debt that had been accumulated during the war; and the use of the fruits of prosperity which would fol-low from all this for social reforms in housing, education, health and so on. In many ways this was a radical programme, and can be seen to have formed the basis of Labour policy for the next 30 years. Yet it must also be noted that it was, in many ways, an essentially conservative programme, aiming to preserve the extended wartime state and the increased saliency of working-class demands that the war had brought. It was, in that sense, very much a product of its time; it would soon, in fact, be out of date.

It was also very much a product of Webb. It viewed socialism as an agent of national efficiency. It offered bureaucratic, 'top-down' socialism. What is a little surprising is that Webb's view was so readily accepted at a time when there was debate about the nature of socialism and, in particular, whether it could be brought about by state action alone. Contemporary pluralists like Harold Laski were arguing that the state was just one agent of social change among many. From the Labour point of view, the main critique came from the guild socialists. They had increased their strength during the war, and by 1917 the movement had grounds for optimism. Revolution in Russia seemed to presage a move to the left across the world. In Britain, the expansion of trade unionism was proceeding apace; perhaps all workers would soon be unionized. Further, the rise of the shop stewards' movement suggested that the nature of unions was changing, and augured well for participatory democracy and workers' control. And the 'threat and promise' aspects of the state's performance in wartime seemed to fit, hand in glove, with guild socialist analysis. A National Building Guild was formed and enjoyed early success. Indeed, Webb's inclusion in *Labour and the New Social Order* of a section entitled 'Democratic Control of Industry' can be seen as a concession to this rising strength.[33] But, ultimately, this powerful critique of statism was largely ignored, and this in turn was a major step on the road towards the statism of future Labour governments.[34]

The war ended on 11 November. At a Labour conference three days later it was decided by 2,117,000 votes to 810,000 to leave the Coalition and fight the anticipated general election as a separate party. The minority included a number of Labour ministers; while J. R. Clynes and others abided by the decision, some, like Barnes, chose to abandon Labour rather than the government. But few followed their lead. Meanwhile, it was announced that a general election would be held on Saturday 14 December.

At the election, the voters faced a very unfamiliar political landscape; so did the politicians, the electorate being three times as large as in 1910. Lloyd George and the Conservatives fought as the Coalition that had won the war. It was almost inevitable that they would do well, given the prevalence of patriotism and relief.

Labour put up 361 candidates, far more than ever before, but the result was a massive victory for the Coalition, which took 473 seats with 47.1 per cent of the poll; in addition, 50 'uncouponed' Tory MPs were returned. Labour took only 57 seats and 20.8 per cent of the votes. Given the Irish republican party Sinn Fein's refusal to sit at Westminster, however, Labour emerged as effectively the largest party of opposition, since the Asquithians numbered fewer than two dozen.

The 1918 general election was the first time Labour put up enough candidates to be considered as a player for government, at least in theory. To take a fifth of the votes cast was clearly progress; at the same time, since the turnout was very low, not many more than one in ten of eligible voters had cast their votes for Labour. And to emerge with only 57 seats was worse than anyone had predicted.[35] It doubled its Scottish representation, but only from three to six; in Wales, it was helped by redistribution which gave more seats to the industrial south, and rose from five seats to nine. The position in England was disappointing; it only won eight more seats (42) than it had in December 1910. '[O]nly in the midlands did Labour win seats in distinctly new areas', and this was due in part to the decline of Lib-Labbism.[36] Labour was still to a large extent concentrated in northern England: London, in particular, was a disappointment, only three seats being won. Other than these, and a solitary victory at Wellingborough in Northamptonshire, there was not a single Labour seat south of a line between the Severn estuary and the Wash. Its performance in mining areas was weaker than might be expected given subsequent developments: of the 50 seats with the highest proportion of miners in the male working population, only 24 went to Labour. It also fared badly in most of the big cities, taking only six out of the 87 seats available in the 12 largest provincial centres. While the party often polled well where it did not win, and clearly had avenues of further advance, the 1918 result could not fail to be seen as a disappointment.

The PLP elected in 1918 was somewhat lacklustre.[37] All four of Labour's women candidates had been defeated, so all the 57 MPs were men. Of those 57, 49 had been sponsored by trade unions. No fewer than 25 were nominees of the Miners' Federation of Great Britain (MFGB). The General and Municipal Workers and the Textile Workers had four MPs apiece. A single Co-operator, elected for Kettering, sat with Labour. In contrast, many of Labour's brightest leaders, including MacDonald, Snowden and Henderson, were defeated. This left the party's parliamentary leadership pretty nondescript. The ex-ministers who had remained with Labour were re-elected to parliament but, Clynes aside, they made little impact. J. H. Thomas, first elected in 1910, retained his seat, but was too busy as general secretary of the NUR to consider acting as chairman of the PLP. Henderson was re-elected to parliament at a by-election in August 1919, but, as party secretary, was mainly concerned with party organization, and played little part at Westminster. Almost by default, therefore, the job went to William Adamson, a right-wing Scottish miners' leader of almost legendary dourness. By contrast, Lloyd George's government sparkled with charismatic figures like Winston Churchill, Austen Chamberlain and Lord Birkenhead. These 'supermen', elected with a massive majority and promising social reconstruction at home and pacification abroad, did not make life easy for Labour's parliamentary leadership.

However, Labour's parliamentary strength was but a pale reflection of the strength of the Labour movement as a whole in the period up to mid-1920. During that period, full employment among men was preserved on the back of a rapid comb-out of women from industry and an inflationary boom fuelled by high public expenditure. Employers and government remained, on the whole, favourably disposed towards organized labour, in order to allow the boom to continue and in fear of provoking revolution. The result was that union membership continued to grow: by 1920, almost half of the male, and a quarter of the female, workforce was unionized, a doubling of 'union density' as compared with 1913. (These figures would not be reached again until 1946.)[38] The movement suffered few reverses in industrial disputes. Workers were strong enough to force major reductions in working hours. In January 1919 the miners threatened to strike for a six-hour day, large wage increases and nationalization. Hastily, Lloyd George conceded a Coal Commission under Justice John Sankey, which was composed of three miners, three sympathetic intellectuals, three mine owners and three businessmen. The Commission offered a seven-hour day, and later recommended nationalization, though only on Sankey's casting vote. However, the resolution of the hours issue had taken some of the steam out of the pressure for nationalization, and Lloyd George was able to sidestep it without any immediate industrial conflict. Still, it was a moral victory for the miners. That September, a national railway strike secured improved wages. And early in 1920 an inquiry into dockers' wages and conditions led to the award of better pay, a shorter working week and a national agreement, largely thanks to the advocacy of Ernest Bevin, assistant secretary of the dockers' union.

All this led to demands that union power be used for political ends. The potential of this course was demonstrated in 1920. That May, London dockers refused to allow a ship to sail to Poland until all war materials intended to help the Poles in their war against Soviet Russia were removed. When, in August, the British government seemed to be moving towards direct intervention, a joint meeting of the parliamentary committee of the TUC, the PLP and the NEC warned the government that 'the whole industrial power of the organized workers [would] be used' to prevent this, and set up a Council of Action to monitor the situation.[39] Local councils of action were formed across Britain to prepare for the threatened conflict.

Ultimately, Britain did not intervene in the Russo-Polish War. This suggested that the threat of 'direct action' (as it became known) had been successful. That September, Robert Williams, secretary of the National Transport Workers' Federation (NTWF) and a member of the NEC, advocated the use of direct action to force the government to call an election which, he believed, Labour would win easily. Henderson rejected this view. He told the NEC that '"direct action" propaganda ... ha[d] been definitely harmful' to the party, 'frightening away many voters who were inclined to support Labour'. An election fought on the issue of direct action would play straight into Lloyd George's hands.[40] Meanwhile, party headquarters tried to cool down the local councils of action, which, having been formed, were in many cases itching for a fight. There seems little doubt that Henderson assessed the situation more accurately than Williams. Lloyd George had been reluctant to help the Poles anyway; at most, Labour's stand had strengthened his hand against his more feverish colleagues, notably Churchill.[41]

By this time, in any case, the economic tide had turned. The government had been deliberately slowing down the economy through tax and interest rate increases and spending cuts. Export orders declined. By August 1920 the economy was moving towards 'one of the worst recessions in history', and by May 1921, unemployment would be over 22 per cent, peaking at 2.4 million.[42] The corollary of this was a massive reduction in union bargaining power. Of course, it took some time for the true gravity of the situation to sink in. In October 1920, the miners struck briefly for better pay and a reduction in the price of coal. The strike ended in a draw. It was to be the last time a major conflict did not end in defeat for the unions for many years.

Indeed, it was in the coal industry that the first major battle came. The mines had been taken under public control during the war, with benefits to the miners which included national pay bargaining and wage rates. The government now wanted to be rid of the mines, and brought forward the date for decontrol from August to 31 March 1921. It was clear that this would mean wage cuts in many areas.[43] On the day the mines were decontrolled, therefore, a lockout began. The MFGB appealed to its partners in the Triple Alliance, the railwaymen and transport workers, for support, and it was agreed that they would commence sympathetic strike action on 16 April. However, the leaders of the NUR and NTWF were not over-eager for the fray: there was some feeling that the miners were keener to receive help than to offer it, and both Thomas and Williams realized that strike action in the current economic climate might well damage their own members' interests. When it emerged that the MFGB executive was split, the NUR and NTWF called off their proposed action. In so doing, Thomas earned the undying hatred of many miners, trade unionists and socialists, while Williams was expelled from the recently formed Communist Party. In the annals of Labour history, 15 April 1921 went down as 'Black Friday'. It is difficult to see what else the railwaymen and transport workers could have done, but the result was a lengthy lockout which only ended when the miners were forced back to work on the owners' terms. Two direct results of the debacle were the abolition of the old parliamentary committee of the TUC and its replacement by a larger and more powerful general council, and the establishment, in 1922, of the Transport and General Workers' Union (TGWU) under Bevin, which aimed to be better organized and disciplined than the old Federation. But there was no quick end to the setbacks: in 1922, a lengthy lockout resulted in the defeat of the engineers, one of the strongest and, in recent times, one of the most militant unions.

The collapse of industrial militancy, and the associated collapse of the guild socialist movement, meant that attention returned to parliamentary methods. Here, Labour's performances improved a little from February 1921, when Clynes took over as chairman from Adamson. Matters might have improved further had MacDonald been able to return to Westminster, but when he stood as Labour's candidate in Crooks's old seat of East Woolwich in March 1921, he faced ferocious attacks from his Coalition and Communist opponents, and was defeated by a narrow margin.

Meanwhile, the party organization had been developing steadily. Standing sub-committees on organization and elections, policy and programme, research and publicity, and finance and general purposes had been established. In January 1922 three joint party–TUC departments (research and information, international affairs, and press and publicity) came into being. The new national agent, Egerton Wake, proved more effective than his predecessor, and Labour had 133 full-time constituency agents by 1922. The number of CLPs increased impressively, from 400 in 1919 to 527 in 1922. By 1924, only 19 British territorial constituencies would lack such a body.[44]

It was not all good news. Although some of the constituency women's sections, in particular, did recruit large numbers, individual membership as a whole was somewhat disappointing, and in some places probably non-existent.[45] Where there were no strong trade unions to pay the constituency party's way, parliamentary candidatures were sometimes open to the highest bidder who could show at least a semblance of commitment to the party.[46] In rural areas, Labour was often pitifully weak; if anything it became weaker during the 1920s, following the collapse of agricultural trade unionism in the early part of the decade. Attempts to develop a powerful Labour press at national and local level met with, at best, mixed results, and would continue to do so until the spectacular success of the relaunched *Daily Herald* as a partnership between the TUC and a commercial publisher in 1930.[47] Furthermore, the recession meant that union-affiliated membership of the party fell by about a quarter between 1920 and 1922. While the potentially adverse results of this were offset by increases in affiliation fees, such increases could not go on indefinitely, and the optimism that had characterized the period since 1917 was qualified, at least.[48]

The increasingly illiberal record of the Coalition, on the other hand, was a godsend to Labour. While Clause IV had marked off a line of demarcation between Labour and the Liberals as parties, Labour's instinctive adherence to many of the precepts of liberal or radical politics meant that it was able to draw in the support of many more anti-Conservative voters than hitherto. In foreign policy, Labour emerged gradually as a critic of the perceivedly harsh peace imposed on Germany at Versailles. It also attacked the adventurism which seemed to threaten new conflicts and entanglements, like intervention in Russia and the support for Greece which almost brought Britain and Turkey into conflict at Chanak in 1922. While Labour could hardly be described as a consistently anti-imperialist party, its criticisms of incidents such as the 1919 Amritsar Massacre in India established it in the mainstream of British radicalism. Closer to home, Labour emerged as the major critic of the government's increasingly brutal attempts to suppress the Irish rebellion. And, as the government intruded on free trade with measures like 'safeguarding' and the continuation of wartime tariffs, Labour established its credentials as a defender of one of the canons of the radical tradition. In addition, its attacks on the traffic in honours pursued by the government and its agents set it firmly on the side of 'clean government'. In all these ways, then, Labour was laying claim, with some success, to core Liberal issues, while its advocacy of social reform, increasingly abandoned by the Lloyd George government from 1920 onwards, meant that it was able to consolidate support among groups which felt the promises of 1918 were being betrayed. Although Clause IV had closed off most possibilities of institutional links with the Liberal Party, the Labour Party was continuing to employ a radical rhetoric with considerable resonance in the British political tradition at the same time that it was addressing newly salient issues like housing and unemployment. Increasingly, Labour was able to pose as the champion of public sector housing (construction of which had started in earnest in 1919) and of full employment. The issue of mines nationalization also gave Labour increased purchase among the miners, who were mostly to be staunch Labour supporters from 1922 onwards.

Finally, the government's decision in 1920 to extend unemployment insurance to virtually all manual workers meant that, for the first time, there were actual figures of the number of unemployed. This enabled Labour to speak with authority about the 'victims of capitalism' and, since the number of unemployed did not fall below one million for the rest of the decade and beyond, allowed it a key piece of rhetoric.

By-elections and local government polls were also encouraging. Most of the former were fought, a significant development in itself; the party lost only one seat (East Woolwich) and gained 14. The 1919 local elections saw substantial gains: Labour took control of three counties (Durham, Glamorgan and Monmouthshire) and greatly increased its representation on borough councils nationwide. In London, it increased its representation on the county council from one to 15 in March 1919, and on the borough councils from 46 to 572 that November. A rather flat performance in 1920 was followed by further gains in 1921, when Labour took control of Falkirk, its first major authority in Scotland. The auguries for the next general election, then, seemed bright.

The general election came in November 1922, following the withdrawal of Conservative support from the Lloyd George Coalition. Law, who had retired as Conservative leader on health grounds the previous year, resumed his post and replaced Lloyd George as premier. Having dealt with the tricky question of protection by pledging that there would be no general interference with free trade before a further election, Law could be confident of victory, and in the event his party took 345 seats, and an overall majority of over 70, although with only 38.5 per cent of the votes cast. The Asquithians took 62 seats and the followers of Lloyd George 53. The real sensation, though, was Labour's performance. Fielding 414 candidates, it took 29.3 per cent of the votes cast and emerged with 142 seats. MacDonald and Snowden both returned to parliament, and at the first meeting of the new PLP MacDonald challenged, and narrowly defeated, Clynes to be elected 'leader' of the party. For the first time it could be argued plausibly that Labour was clearly the second party in the state, with a leader who looked like a potential prime minister.

The true scale of the transformation could only be recognized when people looked back across the turmoil of 'peace' and the battlefields of war to the Labour Party of 1914. Then, it had been little more than a trade union pressure group with pretensions, not a serious candidate for power. Lurking in the shadow of the Liberals, it had been marginalized by the salient issues of politics, about which it had had little distinctive to say, and it had been in considerable doubt about where its future lay. By 1922, it had asserted its independence, was clearly the opposition to the Conservatives, had asserted the primacy of parliamentary over other methods of achieving change and felt comfortable with, and had credibility on, the salient political issues. It might very well be that, war or no war, the Liberals would eventually have been supplanted; Britain was by no means alone in enjoying a Liberal Party in serious decline at this time. That the transformation had come about as it had, and at the pace that it had, and that it had benefited the particular type of party that Labour had become by 1918 (and still more, 1922), however, was largely due to the impact and legacy of the First World War.

3   Progress and Collapse, 1922–31

Taken as a whole, the period between 1922 and 1931 was to be one of considerable achievement for the Labour Party. But it was to end in defeat and demoralization. The 1922 election result more than made up for the disappointment of 1918. MacDonald's return to the head of the party brought Labour's most charismatic leader to date back to the fore. The collapse of industrial militancy seemed to leave the field clear for a moderate parliamentary socialism, meshed with a non-radical conception of trade unionism, which seemed to augur well for the kind of party that the leadership wanted. Labour still had a programme of sorts, and could claim that, if only it were given office, it would be able to make significant progress towards a better society.

Labour was still a long way from a parliamentary majority, even so. It had won only 142 of the 615 seats in parliament, and had polled just 29.7 per cent of the votes cast. This vote, further, was concentrated heavily in certain regions and localities. The mining areas were now fairly solid for Labour: of the 50 seats with the heaviest concentration of miners, 44 were now held by the party. On the other hand, only eight of the 20 seats most dominated by textiles returned Labour MPs. The working-class areas of many major cities went to Labour: there were especially striking gains in Glasgow, where Labour took 10 of the 15 seats as opposed to only one in 1918. But elsewhere it failed to break through, winning no seats in Birmingham, Liverpool, Bristol, Hull or Cardiff, and only nine of the 62 in London. Labour won virtually no seats with a substantial middle-class electorate, and in rural areas their performance was lamentable – of the 150 seats in Britain which had at least 15 per cent of their adult male population working in agriculture, Labour won only five. Labour was a party based on the votes of the urban working class in certain towns and cities, along with the miners and a handful of others.[1] While all this meant that Labour had a solid base, it was still a long way from 'replacing' the coalition of support that had made up the old Liberal Party.

MacDonald and his colleagues recognized these problems and sought to overcome them. Three main areas were targeted: the middle class; the remainder of the industrial working class which was so far impervious to Labour's appeal; and the agricultural community. Labour would need to gain significant sections of all three if it was to emulate the old Liberal coalition. To achieve this, organization would be improved, especially in the rural areas; emphasis would be laid on the party's 'national' as opposed to 'class' image; and Labour would proceed cautiously, trying to impress doubters – not least in the working class – of its respectability and fitness to rule.

In the immediate aftermath of the 1922 election, there had seemed no reason to think that the Conservative government would not survive until the middle of the decade. However, the death of Law in May 1923 changed matters. He was succeeded as premier by the Chancellor of the Exchequer, Stanley Baldwin. Baldwin was as keen as the Labour leadership to marginalize the Liberals and establish a relatively straightforward two-party fight between left and right. He was also keen to accommodate Labour within the constitution and, as a less abrasive and partisan figure than Law, he strengthened Labour moderates' position by discrediting ideas of a polarization of politics.[2]

Inadvertently, Baldwin soon helped Labour. In a speech at Plymouth in October 1923 he came out for protection as the solution to continuing high unemployment. Since Law had pledged in 1922 that tariffs would not be introduced, this meant a dissolution of parliament. For Labour, the move was a godsend. For one thing, it allowed the party to fight for the defence of free trade, which remained popular, at least in urban areas and in areas dependent on cheap imports, such as the Lancashire cotton belt, and international trade, such as port towns. The chance to fight a fairly negative campaign against tariffs also meant that Labour could play down the more controversial elements of the 1918 programme, like the capital levy and nationalization.[3]

The outcome of the election was confusing. The Conservatives remained the largest party, but lost almost 100 seats, emerging with 258 MPs. The Liberals, who had reunited in defence of free trade, emerged with 159 members; Labour won 191 seats. Webb had spoken at that year's party conference about the 'inevitability of gradualness', and the election result seemed to bear out that prediction.[4] However, the respective poll shares of the parties had not changed much: Labour edged up from 29.7 to 30.7 per cent; the Liberals rose from 28.8 to 29.7; and the Conservatives fell from 38.5 to 38.0 per cent. Labour remained very much a party of the mining areas plus many – but not all – working-class urban areas. Though it made significant gains in London, winning 22 seats as opposed to nine in 1922, it still took no seats in Birmingham and only managed one in Liverpool. Only one in five eligible voters had voted for the party.

Baldwin did not resign immediately. Instead, he presented a protectionist King's Speech to the House of Commons in January 1924, was defeated, and advised the King to send for MacDonald. The latter had spent the time since the election planning strategy and deciding who should be in his cabinet. That it should be his cabinet, he was in no doubt. He was determined to act just like any other prime minister, to show that he – and his party – were 'fit to govern'. Hence, when he and his ministers arrived at Buckingham Palace to be sworn in, they wore court dress. This made them look ridiculous, and worse, to many on the left, but the main motive was to avoid empty gestures which would only alienate potential support, not least among working-class voters.[5]

MacDonald's 20-strong cabinet included seven trade unionists: three of them were miners, along with one each from the textile workers, ironfounders, railwaymen and the General and Municipal Workers. Only two of the ILPers in the cabinet (John Wheatley and Fred Jowett) could be described as left-wingers. Webb and Lord Olivier were Fabians. Seven members of the cabinet had not been in the Labour Party in 1914: five had been Liberals, who had come to the Labour Party via the UDC; two had been Conservatives, and one of them (Lord Chelmsford, who became First Lord of the Admiralty) still was. The cabinet was dominated by the 'Big Five': MacDonald, who doubled as Foreign Secretary; Snowden, seen as Labour's leading financial expert, who became Chancellor of the Exchequer; Henderson, who became Home Secretary despite MacDonald's apparent efforts to keep him out because, as party secretary, he would be of greater value preparing for the next general election;[6] Thomas, who became Secretary of State for the Colonies; and Clynes, the party's deputy leader, who was made Lord Privy Seal to lead the House of Commons in order to remove some of the pressure from MacDonald. The cabinet did not represent all sections of the movement. Even from a cynically electoral viewpoint it was probably a mistake not to include a woman or a Co-operator. The left was clearly under-represented. And there was a skewing of trade union representation towards the old staple industries.

There was no attempt to form a coalition with the Liberals. Labour wanted to compromise, and so destroy, the Liberal Party; in any case, the Liberals were so afraid of a further general election that they had no alternative, for the time being, but to give general support to the government.[7] Other possible strategies were also ruled out. Some Labourites wanted the government to announce a radical socialist programme, be defeated in the Commons, and then call another election at which, it was believed, the party would win a majority for 'socialism', or at least lay down a marker around which socialists could subsequently muster.[8] This was rejected out of hand by the party leadership, which believed, with reason, that it would simply alienate voters. In any case, it would have been a fight for an undefined vision of 'socialism'; electors wanting to know what a nationalized industry would look like, for example, would have found that Labour had few concrete plans.

That the first Labour government did not achieve much in policy terms was not surprising, given its parliamentary position, whereby the Liberals had only to abstain to allow the Conservatives to defeat it. Benefits were liberalized somewhat, and expenditure on education increased. Wheatley, as Minister of Health, introduced a Housing Act which gave state subsidies to local authorities to build houses for rent, a major achievement which improved the lot of many working-class families over the next few years. Also significant in this field was legislation to protect tenants from eviction, a major issue since rents became 'decontrolled' once a change of tenancy took place. And, in foreign affairs, there was a general reduction of international tension, and a revision of German reparations payments under the Dawes Plan, although progress towards giving the League of

Nations some teeth in the negotiations for the Geneva Protocol fell with the government.

All these things earned some credit with the wider Labour movement. There was more criticism, though, in other areas. The government backed a private members' bill to nationalize the coal industry, but it made little progress towards the Statute Book. Other sectors of the economy identified specifically in *Labour and the New Social Order* fared still worse. Legislation to improve agricultural labourers' wages remained something of a dead letter. No attempt was made to dismantle emergency powers apparatus for dealing with strikes, and indeed the government itself prepared to use this against threatened transport and docks strikes. Finally, there was no radical attempt to deal with unemployment, which remained above one million.

Instead, the government, believing that socialism would emerge from a vibrant, successful capitalism, aimed to restore capitalism to health. The way to do this, it was felt, was to return to the prewar guarantors of prosperity: free trade, the gold standard and a balanced budget, while setting taxation at levels which would not impair industrial efficiency. Therefore, since budgets were now showing a good surplus, Snowden cut tariffs and taxation. He also continued previous governments' policies of aiming to return to the gold standard in 1925. All this has usually been seen as somewhat backward-looking, but most people still believed in such a strategy, and Snowden believed sincerely that it would advance progress towards socialism. Essentially, he saw a sound economy as the key prerequisite of a progressive social policy, as would be the case with most future Labour governments. Finally, since British prosperity was believed to depend upon world prosperity and trade, Labour saw foreign policy as central to the restoration of Britain's economic fortunes.[9]

One aspect of this economic internationalism was the improvement of relations with Soviet Russia, but ultimately this was to be the government's undoing. Over the summer of 1924 there were negotiations for a treaty and a trade agreement, which aroused widespread unease, even among some Labourites. In particular, Liberal qualms about continuing to support the government grew. At the same time, an article by J. R. Campbell in the communist *Workers' Weekly,* calling on troops not to fire on strikers, led to a hasty decision to prosecute him under the Incitement to

Disaffection Act. When, following wider consultations, the cabinet withdrew the prosecution, Labour's opponents claimed that the decision had been taken as a result of far-left pressure on the Labour leadership. In October, MacDonald treated a Liberal motion for the appointment of a committee of inquiry as a matter of confidence. When it was passed, the government resigned and called a general election. In fact, this was merely a pretext. The government had done all that it could. MacDonald himself was worn down by a heavy workload, and demoralized by the allegations of corruption that had surrounded the conferring of a baronetcy on Alexander Grant, his long-time friend and recent benefactor. This was as good a time as any to bow out.[10]

A bitter election campaign followed. Labour was attacked for being a Communist Party in disguise, and Labourites had to try to deal with the accusation that they were conscious agents or unconscious dupes of the extreme left. Scandal and sensation, though, were reserved for the last few days of the campaign, after the *Daily Mail* published a document which was said to be from the Executive Committee of the Communist International, advising British Communists to prepare for revolution. Whatever else it was, this 'Zinoviev Letter' was not the cause of Labour's electoral defeat.[11] The party had been in no position, and had not seriously expected, to win the election even before the letter was published. In the event, Labour lost over 40 seats to emerge with 151 MPs, as against the Conservatives' 412. Even so, the result was, in some ways, a good one for Labour. First, the 1924 government had shown that Labour could run the country, and made a future bid for office more credible, since the party's leaders now had ministerial experience. Second, the Zinoviev Letter episode allowed Labour's leaders to convince many of their followers that the electoral reverse had been based not on the shortcomings of Labour's performance in office or its unacceptably narrow electoral base but on the tricks and deceit of the Conservatives and the 'Establishment'. In other words, a 'fair' fight would see 'the inevitability of gradualness' reassert itself. Third, and most importantly, the Liberals had apparently collapsed, losing more than 100 seats to emerge with only 40 MPs, their poll share falling from 29.7 to 17.8 per cent. Conversely, Labour's poll share actually increased from 30.7 to 33.3 per cent. In so far as the 'Red Scare' had any electoral impact, it seems to have forced Liberal voters to choose between Labour and Conservative; and while most had gone Conservative this time, there was no reason why they should not go Labour next.

But there were more worrying signs, too. Some leading figures had performed indifferently as ministers. MacDonald's own record gave cause for concern: he had tired easily, shown poor judgement and been rather aloof from, and difficult with, colleagues.[12] Second, the party's weakness on policy had emerged. Such distinctive policies as it had, such as the capital levy or nationalization, had been virtually ignored, and there was no sign that even with a majority it would have been much bolder. Despite the stress on the belief that prospering capitalist industry would be the motor force of the transition to socialism, there was a virtual void in terms of industrial policy, while the failure to come up with any kind of policy on unemployment suggested something of a vacuum beneath the rhetoric about the iniquities of capitalism.[13]

Initially, MacDonald's position was weakened. Bevin headed a move to oust him as leader. But, given Henderson's continuing support for MacDonald, Snowden's lack of appeal to trade unionists, and Thomas's unpopularity with the left there was no viable alternative.[14] There were also attempts, again involving Bevin, to get the 1925 party conference to vote that Labour should never again take office without a majority, but these were beaten off.[15] Even so, problems remained. The unions were a source of concern. They had welcomed the first Labour government, but hoped-for legislation on hours and conditions had not been forthcoming, and the apparent readiness of the government to use anti-union emergency powers machinery to smash strikes had increased tensions.

Then, in 1925, the question of 'direct action' re-emerged. That July, the coal owners, forced to charge higher prices for their exports as a result of Britain's return to the gold standard in April, proposed cuts in miners' wages. The TUC threatened an embargo on the transportation of coal, and on 31 July ('Red Friday') the Conservative government announced a nine-month subsidy to maintain wages at their present level. This simply led to overconfidence. When the subsidy ended in May 1926, and the owners locked out the miners until they agreed to work at lower wages, the TUC miscalculated and called a general strike. They believed that Red Friday had shown that the government could be forced into supporting the level of miners' wages. In fact, the government was determined not to repeat the experiment, and had used the nine months to prepare for such an encounter. Accordingly, when the strike began on 4 May, it was met with firm government resistance, and the TUC was forced into unconditional surrender after nine days.

The Labour Party leadership looked on with growing horror as the events of the General Strike unfolded. So far as it was concerned, the strike threatened Labour's claim to be a constitutional party. It marked a low point in union–party communications, as the misgivings of the party leadership were simply ignored.[16] This seemed to confirm a new distance in relations which had been suggested by the TUC's decision to withdraw from the joint departments with the Labour Party in 1925.[17] A major result of the strike, the Trade Disputes Act of 1927, replaced 'contracting out' of the political levy (as established by the 1913 Act) with 'contracting in'. This was a significant threat to Labour, because whereas under the 1913 Act the apathetic worker had been deemed to wish to pay the levy and so paid it, under the 1927 legislation he or she was deemed not to wish to do so, and so did not. Labour tried to arouse nationwide opposition to the legislation, but its protest campaign flopped and the party's income fell by about a third.[18]

Ultimately, these events helped to accelerate Labour's rightward drift. They seemed finally to discredit the idea that direct action could deliver gains that were denied to patient electoral effort. They also pushed the unions, at least at the level of the TUC general council, towards a more compromising stance *vis-à-vis* employers; industrial gradualism came to complement political gradualism. The organizational consolidation which characterized this period also represented a growth in the control that the leadership exerted over the rest of the party. Constituency Labour parties were now a feature of almost all areas of Britain. However, with notable exceptions (such as Woolwich and Derby), individual membership was often low, and active membership lower still.[19] The emphasis on organization emanating from headquarters meant that debate on policy was not encouraged. Even the annual party conference became more and more pliant as the decade progressed.

Closely linked to this was a continuing, and intensifying, marginalization of dissent. This was particularly the case with Communists and with women. The Communist Party of Great Britain (CPGB) had been formed in 1920, and had applied for affiliation to the Labour Party. That application, and another in 1921, had been rejected, but the Communists were difficult to shake off. A 1922 decision to bar Communists as delegates to party conference remained a dead letter, and 38 Communists attended the 1923 event.[20] At the 1922 election a CPGB member, Shapurji Saklatvala, was elected as Labour MP for North Battersea. However, the screw tightened. Some CLPs began to expel Communists unilaterally, and such actions were endorsed by the NEC in October 1923. Following the Campbell Case, the 1924 conference decided that Communists were not eligible to be either candidates for or individual members of the Labour Party. Relations deteriorated further during and after the General Strike, and in 1928 Communists were barred from attending Labour's party conference as trade union delegates. Meanwhile, Labour headquarters had begun to disband CLPs that refused to expel Communists or showed signs of Communist leanings, reconstituting them under keen anti-Communists. Between 1926 and 1928 this happened to no fewer than 26 constituency or borough Labour parties, 15 of them in London. The Communists attempted to work through the disbanded parties via the National Left Wing Movement, set up in September 1926, but its successes, such as they were, were fleeting ones, and by 1928 it was in steep decline. Further attempts to promote the united front, most notably the involvement of some Communists in the Cook–Maxton campaign of 1928 (see below), failed. The move to 'class against class', whereby the Communists came out strongly against Labour, was, in some ways, the logical end of the dispute. It also meant that, for a time, the issue of Labour–Communist relations could be largely ignored by the Labour Party.[21]

The other section of the Labour movement to be consciously marginalized was the women's movement. Before 1914, radical feminism had played a part in Labour politics. The 1912 by-election agreement between Labour and the NUWSS has already been noted. In 1918, the party constitution had provided for separate women's representation on the NEC, the formation of women's sections in the CLPs and an annual women's conference.

All this had led to high expectations among women, but their hopes were soon disappointed. Attempts to achieve a higher status for the women's conference were repeatedly rejected by the NEC, and calls for the women members of the NEC to be elected by women, rather than by the party conference as a whole, were similarly unsuccessful. Issues like birth control were swept under the carpet, despite strong support from the women in the party, partly for fear of alienating voters, especially the Catholics who had begun to come over to Labour in large numbers after the collapse of the Liberal Party and the resolution of the Irish question. Women continued to play an important role in the party, especially at the grassroots, but overall the party slid away from too overt a link with 'women's issues'.[22]

More broadly, the later 1920s saw a degree of ideological stagnation. The 1910s had been a decade of considerable debate about the future of socialism. Yet the alternatives to statism were losing steam by 1922, and Labour intellectuals, like Cole, Laski and R. H. Tawney, moved into a period of reassessment, trying to come to terms with the apparent failure of their pet schemes. Increasingly, such intellectuals could only play a significant role if they accepted and co-operated with the leadership's outlook. Thus they were drawn into mainstream Labour politics, but more for the sake of appearance than for any distinctive contribution they could make. On the one hand, they felt that they could do more within the party than outside it, and preferred a little inside influence to crying in the wilderness; on the other, they seem to have been impressed with Labour's progress and came to believe (or convinced themselves) that MacDonald's strategy might prove successful.

In policy, Labour moved away from specifics. *Labour and the New Social Order* was massively out of date by the mid-1920s. It had been the product of a confident party, issued in a context of relative prosperity, at a time when government was big and when it did not seem outlandish to prioritize working-class demands. What had happened since then, of course, had served to vitiate that programme. The agenda of government had been changed, with inflation being seen as a bigger threat than unemployment by governments from 1920 onwards. High levels of unemployment and disappointing industrial performance were held to rule out some of Labour's most radical and distinctive policies, such as the capital levy.[23] At the same time, some things had not changed enough for Labour to feel able to put forward a radical alternative. Thus it was still possible to argue that if only international problems, like tariffs and war debts and reparations, could be solved, prosperity would return. Thus Labour moved towards a set of policies which sought only limited short-term change at home alongside 'pacification' abroad. The result was the 1928 programme, *Labour and the Nation*. This took almost a year to produce, and it was, in many ways, more comprehensive than *Labour and the New Social Order*. But its very comprehensiveness was its downfall. It was significant that at the 1928 conference Wheatley (who undoubtedly opposed it for other reasons) chose in his speech to attack the lack of prioritization and specificity of the proposals. As he said, what was needed was not a list of ideal policies to be implemented over 50 or a 100 years, but a hard-nosed choice of policies which would be implemented by a single Labour government in a five-year term.[24] This hit the nail on the head: as Tawney, its chief draughtsman, was later to write regretfully, it was 'a glittering forest of Christmas trees, with presents for everyone'.[25] Its vagueness was to be part of the reason why the second Labour government fared so badly.

So why was it adopted? A number of reasons can be identified. First, there was the need to appeal to the 'centre ground' of British politics, since it was clear that Labour needed to pick up new votes if it was be the largest party in parliament, let alone win a majority. Second, the Labour movement was still too fractious to permit a more concrete appeal. A ruthless delineation of a plan for five years in office would, inevitably, have led to discontent and dissension. Third, it seems possible that Labour's leaders did not expect, seriously, to win the next election.[26] The Conservatives did not fare well at by-elections throughout the 1924 parliament, but the swings were not so heavy as to presage electoral disaster; they needed, after all, to lose around 100 seats just to be deprived of a majority at the next election. The Liberals were also reviving from 1926 onwards with the help of Lloyd George's leadership and money, to the extent that some leading Labourites, including Snowden, began to wonder whether some Lib-Lab pact might be necessary.[27] It is also worth bearing in mind that the really heavy tide of Conservative reverses only began in 1928, when the parameters for *Labour and the Nation* had already been set. Had it begun earlier, it is just possible that Labour might have adopted a clearer programme in the keener expectation of victory.

But while all these considerations bore some weight, it is clear that a vague programme suited the party leadership. MacDonald was by now firmly established as leader, but he was also much more than that. His was the prevailing voice in the Labour Party by 1927; he was seen by one well-informed German observer at the time as 'the focus of the mute hopes of a whole class', and even as 'beyond question the outstanding figure of International Socialism'.[28] His view of socialism had always been a consensual one, aiming to break down barriers, not to set them up; and part of this was convincing people that Labour, while envisaging, ultimately, a society that would be very different from the present one, would not make sudden radical changes.

Not everyone was prepared to bite his or her tongue, however. The ILP, long seen as the intellectual wing of the Labour Party, had been somewhat uncertain of its role since 1918. But in the mid-1920s, a section of the party began to emerge as the most significant dissentient group within the Labour Party. In 1926, it elected the Glasgow left-winger James Maxton as its chairman and adopted the radical 'Living Wage' policy. Based on an under-consumptionist analysis, it called for a high-wage economy, in which firms failing to pay the state-set standard would be national-ized. Although there were many different views within the ILP as to what this would mean in practice, it was a useful contribution to a wider debate. However, the proposals were easily defeated at Labour's 1927 conference. The fact that the ILP refused to nomi-nate MacDonald for the Labour treasurership that year, and the increasingly radical rhetoric of Maxton, Wheatley and others, however, played into the Labour leadership's hands, and the brief and unsuccessful Cook–Maxton campaign of 1928 completed the process. Cook–Maxton was not an official ILP campaign. Its manifesto was drafted by a number of ILP leaders, most nota-bly Maxton and Wheatley, the MFGB secretary, A. J. Cook, and a number of leading Communists. The manifesto called for an end to compromise and the launching of a new period of class strug-gle. But the campaign was a dismal failure.[29] Ultimately, it helped no one more than the Labour leadership, which could use the campaign's 'disloyalty' to tarnish the ILP as a whole.

By early 1929, therefore, Labour's leadership's hold was very tight indeed. By then, too, the government had been running out of steam for some time. That spring, Baldwin called an election, basing his appeal on the record of his government: in a conscious attempt to play on fears about 'socialism' and the Liberals' radical programme, the Conservatives fought on the slogan 'Safety First'. However, when the results were declared, Labour had 287 seats to the Conservatives' 260, with the Liberals taking 59. Ostensibly, Labour had made significant gains, and seemed well on the way towards becoming 'national' in its appeal. Only in East Anglia did it gain fewer seats than in 1923, thanks to a Liberal revival based on a farming policy which seemed well suited to the area. In every other region of the country, Labour had never done better in terms of seats gained, doubling its representation in London, the Midlands and Lancashire, for example. Even erstwhile deserts showed significant improvements, with Labour taking six of the 12 seats in Birmingham and four of the 11 in Liverpool. Baldwin, refusing to negotiate with Lloyd George for Liberal support, resigned immediately, and left MacDonald to form his second minority administration.

Understandably, many Labourites were ecstatic. However, the results were not as good as they looked at first sight. The Conservatives had actually received more votes than Labour (38.1 per cent as against 37.1), but Labour's greater concentration of support in certain areas meant that it took more seats. In addition, 1929 was the first general election, and the last until February 1974, at which all three parties put up more than 500 candidates. The result was that 123 Labour MPs were elected with less than 50 per cent of the votes in their constituencies. This might not have mattered had it looked likely that the Liberals would run a large number of candidates next time, but this was not going to happen, because Lloyd George was soon to withdraw most of his financial subsidies to the party organization. A reduction in the number of Liberal candidates – a certainty – and even a small swing of support towards the Conservatives – always likely, and absolutely certain from early 1930 onwards – would be enough to reduce Labour to around 200 seats at the next election.[30]

In forming his government, MacDonald experienced one major setback; he was unable to put Thomas into the Foreign Office once Henderson pushed his own claim, and Thomas became Lord Privy Seal in charge of employment schemes.[31] Although this was not a very promising start, the rest of the cabinet did not pose such difficulties. Snowden, still a popular figure, returned to the Treasury. Clynes became a fairly undistinguished Home Secretary. Seven other members of the 1924 cabinet returned, and there were seven new faces. The veteran George Lansbury came in as First Commissioner of Works, as a sop to the left and as a London face in an otherwise heavily non-metropolitan team. Margaret Bondfield became the first woman cabinet member, as Minister of Labour. Sankey, darling of the miners on the strength of the 1919 coal commission, became Lord Chancellor. Younger men included William Wedgwood Benn, a former Liberal who had only joined Labour in 1927, Arthur Greenwood, A. V. Alexander (the Co-operative Party's leading MP) and William Graham (at 42 the youngest member of the cabinet) who as President of the Board of Trade would be one of the few people to emerge from the government with an enhanced reputation. This was by no means a bad team, and in so far as it included a woman and a Co-operator it was rather more representative than the 1924 cabinet. But the average age of ministers was higher than that of the outgoing cabinet (which itself had been criticized for its ageing appearance); promising younger people, like Herbert Morrison, Sir Oswald Mosley and Hugh Dalton, were not included; and it was even more unrepresentative of the left than the cabinet appointed in 1924.

There was no attempt to bring in the Liberals. There was no need to do so, in fact, because Labour's parliamentary position was reasonably secure, given Baldwin's refusal to negotiate with Lloyd George, and the Liberals' fear of an early election. Even when Lloyd George threatened to withdraw Liberal support, as over the Coal Mines Bill in late 1929 and early 1930, sufficient Liberal MPs were usually prepared to back the government to allow it to survive. Closer links were to be established following the resignation of Mosley from the government in May 1930, leading, in the 1930–31 parliamentary session, to a loose agreement that the Liberals would keep the government in office so long as it carried forward electoral reform legislation.[32]

The government enjoyed some early successes, particularly in foreign policy, but these were soon overshadowed by economic crisis and rising unemployment. In October 1929 the Wall Street Crash compounded a downturn in American industrial production to produce a worldwide slump. In Britain, unemployment, which had stood at 1.1 million when Labour had taken office, exceeded 1.5 million in January 1930 and then rose every month that year, to reach 2.7 million in December. After that, it levelled off a little, but even so the figure of almost 2.8 million in July 1931 was disastrous.

The government did try to solve the problem, but to little effect. It attempted to secure international pacification. It promoted attempts to revise reparations payments (enjoying some success with the Young Plan of late 1929), and to sort out other intergovernmental debts (where less progress was made). It achieved a limited degree of naval disarmament in 1930. And, in May 1931, the League of Nations, encouraged assiduously by Henderson, finally agreed to convene a world disarmament conference for February 1932 (with Henderson as its president, much to MacDonald's chagrin).[33] It also aimed to negotiate a tariff truce at Geneva, although this was less successful, the short-term agreement eventually secured by Graham in late 1930 covering only a few, generally minor, nations.

Labour also sought to encourage the rationalization of industry – that is, the reduction of excess capacity and the consolidation and unification of enterprises in the staple industrial sector. The government was keen not to intervene too far, however, and the bulk of the process was left to industry itself and to the Bankers' Industrial Development Corporation, set up by the Bank of England. Although some schemes were carried out, the results were not startling, and their main short-term effect was to increase unemployment by throwing out 'excess' labour. The government's room for manoeuvre was limited, not just by contemporary inhibitions as to the extent to which state intervention in industry was permissible, but also by the fact that trade unionism was especially concentrated in the staple industries. The government could not go too far against the interests of the unions involved, especially at a time when the party was struggling for financial survival and hence heavily dependent on union goodwill.[34]

Attempts were also made to improve the quality of information available to government. This was done both informally, through consultations with business people and, to a much lesser extent, trade unions, but also in a formal way through the Economic Advisory Council (EAC), set up in February 1930. It was hoped that the EAC, which included representatives of business, unions and academia, would advise ministers on solutions for Britain's economic ills. In fact, it was too unwieldy a body to be effective, and the lack of a firm lead from government meant its discussions were usually too diffuse to be of value. In reality, the time for such a body had been when Labour was in opposition. But its existence then seems not to have been considered; besides, it might have forced the party to take up some definite positions on economic reorganization, and there had been no place for that in the party of the 1920s. An even more academic exercise was the Macmillan committee on finance and industry, which included Bevin and the Liberal economist John Maynard Keynes, among others, but whose proceedings and report have proved to be of far more value to historians than they were to the politicians of the time.

Finally, the government invested limited sums of money in public works, but the jobs created were a drop in the ocean, and such schemes were viewed with extreme scepticism by 'informed' opinion. And this mattered because, above all else, the government did not want to damage business confidence. Crucially, the national budget had to be seen to be balanced; but, with the slump leading to rising expenditure and falling tax revenues, this was difficult to achieve. It is easy, in retrospect, to criticize this position – to argue that balanced budgets were, in fact, deflationary, or to say that confidence did not matter. But such arguments were not widely accepted at the time, even inside the Labour Party. Since gradualism was still the order of the day, anything which would impair the long-term prospects of economic recovery would be fatal. And, because the internationalist argument held that free trade and the gold standard were essential guarantors of co-operation and trade with other countries, Labour was caught in a very difficult position indeed.

The results of all this effort were unimpressive. By late 1930, most of the rationalization schemes were running into the sand, international efforts to promote recovery had produced negligible results, and few had any serious hopes for the EAC. Ministers were publicly rubbishing public works. The government seems to have decided that nothing within the power of human agency could do much good. Essentially, the cabinet sat tight and waited for a trade revival.[35]

Could more have been done? Some people thought so, especially Mosley, who had been appointed to minor office in 1929, with a brief to work with Thomas, Lansbury and another junior minister, Thomas Johnston, on schemes to reduce unemployment. Mosley, Lansbury and Johnston were soon disillusioned with Thomas's ineptitude, however, and by January 1930 they had drawn up a radical set of proposals which became known as the 'Mosley Memorandum'. The Memorandum argued that economic activity should be increased by the inauguration of a big scheme of loan-financed public works; that tariffs and imperial preference should be used to create a largely autarkic imperial trading bloc; and that the size of the labour market should be reduced through an increased school-leaving age and improved retirement pensions. The whole scheme would be implemented by a small emergency cabinet.[36]

In a sense, the scheme had no chance. There was criticism of the fact that it was presented directly to MacDonald, rather than to Thomas; the decision to refer it to a cabinet committee under Snowden ensured its demise. When the committee duly reported against the proposals in May 1930, Mosley resigned and was humiliated in a PLP meeting when he pressed for a vote on the issue. That October he was received warmly by the Labour Party conference, but a motion asking the NEC to look again at his proposals was narrowly defeated. In December, he issued a more radical 'Mosley Manifesto', signed by 17 Labour MPs and Cook, but it made little impact. Mosley abandoned Labour and, in February 1931, formed the New Party with the aid of three other Labour MPs and an Ulster Unionist.[37] A year later, he would be forming the British Union of Fascists.

Could the Mosley proposals have been implemented, and, if so, could they have succeeded? The parliamentary position was one obstacle. Skidelsky has argued that this was just an excuse: the Liberals, having fought the 1929 election on a not dissimilar programme, would have followed a Labour lead.[38] But this is a dubious assumption. The two programmes were different in significant ways, especially tariffs: the Liberals had been elected on a free trade ticket, and could certainly not have been convinced to move en bloc towards protectionism. In addition, even if Lloyd

George had been convinced, his party was so fissile that he would probably not have been able to deliver its votes in parliament. Many of the Liberal MPs elected in 1929 had not favoured Lloyd George's programme even in relatively calm times, and were not going to support anything like it now.[39] There were other objections, too. Attempts by government to raise large loans would almost certainly have pushed up interest rates, at a time when these were already crippling industry. Raising the school-leaving age and improving pensions were both expensive, at a time when all the pressure was to restrict, rather than to expand, government spending. There were administrative difficulties: it was one thing to allocate money to public works schemes but another thing to spend it, since public inquiries were often necessary. The effects on business confidence were not likely to be positive.[40] Finally, it would be difficult to persuade the bulk of Labour MPs, let alone the wider movement, that the tariffs many of them had spent their political lives attacking were now necessary. In sum, then, the Mosley Memorandum was not a lost opportunity. Its chances had been minimal; and it might be argued that, had an attempt been made to implement it, the results would have been much worse than those which ensued from its rejection.

The final attempt to change the government's outlook significantly came in the late summer of 1930. Following Mosley's resignation, a minor reshuffle had sent Thomas to the Dominions Office and brought Christopher Addison, the former Lloyd George Liberal minister, into the cabinet as Minister of Agriculture. The effect of these changes was to strengthen MacDonald's hand in the crucial area of trade policy. For some time the premier had been convinced that tariffs should be tried. In August 1930, a thinly attended cabinet was persuaded by MacDonald and Thomas to defer ratification of Graham's rather feeble tariff truce. However, the likelihood of the government ever getting to the point of imposing tariffs was slim. Resistance would have come at all levels of the Labour movement. For most Labourites, free trade was not just a trade policy but a guarantee of peace, cheap food, a thriving export industry and a corruption-free public life. The free traders within the cabinet soon regrouped, and a meeting in September agreed to push ahead with ratification after all.[41] Tariffs were ruled out for the winter; by the following spring, when the truce expired, the Conservatives had come all out for protection, and Labour was virtually forced to re-entrench itself as a party of free trade.

Labour saw itself as a party of full employment, so to have a Labour government presiding over constantly increasing levels of joblessness was agonizing. The only thing which made the situation at all bearable for Labourites was the notion of 'work or maintenance' – the fact that the government continued to pay unemployment benefit at relatively generous levels, and indeed extended entitlement to such benefits. By early 1931, however, it was clear that a budgetary crisis was looming. The unemployment insurance fund, which was supposed to balance, was in debt to the tune of around £70 million, and the figure was rising. A Royal Commission was set up by Bondfield with an implied brief to propose drastic economies. Most areas of public opinion outside the Labour movement were clamouring for 'economy', and the Conservatives and Liberals took up the theme. On 14 February 1931 a committee on national expenditure was set up following a Liberal motion in the House of Commons, under the chairmanship of Sir George May, head of an insurance company. Although there were two Labour representatives, it was not difficult to predict that substantial cuts in expenditure would be recommended.

In other areas, meanwhile, little in the way of constructive legislation had been achieved. The Coal Mines Act, when eventually passed, could only offer a seven-and-a-half-hour day to miners instead of the promised seven. More successful was Greenwood's Housing Act, which, in offering state subsidies for local authority slum clearance and replacement housing schemes, was to make a major contribution to improving working-class living conditions during the coming years. By early 1931, however, the government was experiencing severe difficulties in passing legislation. Trevelyan's attempt to increase the school-leaving age to 15 was crushed by the House of Lords after being emasculated by Catholic Labour backbenchers who believed that the financial provisions of the measure would force denominational schools into the hands of the local authorities. The presence of leading Nonconformists, like the Wesleyan Methodist Henderson, in the cabinet did little to allay Catholic suspicions here. The results were Trevelyan's resignation from the government and, much more importantly, the loss of much Catholic support at elections throughout the year.[42] (Many Jewish voters had already deserted Labour over the Passfield White Paper, which proposed stringent limitations on Jewish immigration to British-controlled Palestine.) And an attempt to repeal the 1927 Trade Disputes Act was destroyed by Liberal amendments.

By mid-1931 the government was in trouble. The cabinet was ageing, ailing and acrimonious. A reshuffle was required, but MacDonald havered. Some have suggested that he was on the verge of introducing some Liberals into the cabinet,[43] but there is little hard evidence for this, and neither the Liberal Party nor the TUC would have stood for such a move. The TUC, and individual trade unions, had been alienated from the government, not just over the failure to do anything tangible about unemployment but also by the failure to deliver reforms promised in 1929. Textile workers were particularly disaffected by the government-sponsored wage-cutting settlements to their industrial disputes. Radical groups within the PLP moved towards virtual independence, as the New Party departed and a more substantial group of ILPers began to issue their own whips and refuse to accept Labour ones. Party finances were in turmoil, as the effects of the slump and the Trade Disputes Act took hold, and some antagonized unions were refusing to hand over their affiliation fees. In many parts of the country the party organization was crumbling as demoralization spread.[44] And the Conservative Party, itself much divided in the period since 1929, was now reunited under Baldwin on a policy of economy, protection, imperial preference and help to agriculture which promised, if not to end the slump overnight, then at least to do something to protect jobs and expand employment.

It was on to this unpromising scene that the financial crises of 1931 burst.[45] The collapse of the main Austrian bank in May 1931 led to the freezing of assets across Europe, which in turn meant that London became subject to large withdrawals of gold. This threatened Britain's position on the gold standard, and very few people doubted that to leave the gold standard would lead to financial and economic disaster. The reason that this became a political problem was that the British budget was clearly out of balance, with the government doing little to solve the problem. One of the few decisive steps it did take was to pass legislation to rectify 'anomalies' whereby married women, among others, could receive unemployment benefit. This not only saved £3 million, but also alienated many working-class voters in areas like Lancashire where married women made up a substantial part of the workforce.

On 31 July the report of Sir George May's committee on national expenditure was published. It predicted a budget deficit of £120 million. To meet the deficit, it recommended tax increases bringing in £24 million and spending cuts amounting to £96 million, including a 20 per cent cut in unemployment benefit; cuts of up to the same level in public servants' salaries; and more stringent testing of the needs of unemployed persons who had exhausted their insurance benefit entitlement. At first, the cabinet was calm. No statement was issued on the May Report, but it was decided that a committee of five – MacDonald, Snowden, Henderson, Thomas and Graham – would meet on 25 August to discuss the report and prepare a set of suggestions for the full cabinet. However, a run on sterling prompted a series of meetings of the committee in mid-August, and it finally came up with a package of suggestions which were put to the full cabinet on 19 August. Since Snowden had been informed by the Treasury that the likely deficit was now not £120, but £170 million, the economy committee suggested cuts of £78.5 million – less than May had recommended because the economy committee rejected the 20 per cent cut in benefits – and increased taxation to the tune of £88.5 million.

The economy committee's suggestions were, for the most part, accepted by a day-long cabinet meeting on 19 August, but the proposal to transfer responsibility for transitional benefit to local authorities was deleted, leaving a total economy package of £56 million. Most ministers seemed to hope that this would suffice, and that the crisis could be contained. However, when MacDonald and Snowden met Opposition leaders – whose support, given the parliamentary position, was essential – the next day, they were told that even the £78.5 million package was inadequate. That afternoon, MacDonald and Snowden addressed a joint meeting of the NEC and the TUC general council. The latter came out against all cuts. Despite this opposition, however, the cabinet agreed on the evening of Friday 21 August to go ahead with the £56 million package; and no one resigned.

The problem was, of course, that the £56 million package was not large enough to satisfy the Opposition leaders and still less the bankers. MacDonald and Snowden were already aware of this, so next day they recalled their – doubtless somewhat bemused – colleagues and tried to persuade them to increase the level of cuts, but to no avail. Henderson, in particular, now came to the view that Labour should resign rather than place itself at the mercy of the Opposition. The most that the premier could obtain was permission to put a hypothetical question to bankers in New York: would they grant the additional credits needed to preserve the gold standard if there was a 10 per cent cut in unemployment benefit? The answer, that Sunday evening, was that the loan would probably be forthcoming if such a cut were announced. (Some ministers took this, wrongly, as a sign that the bankers were seeking to dictate to the government on the question of benefits, hence the subsequent myth of a 'Bankers' Ramp'.[46]) MacDonald asked his colleagues whether they were prepared to support the cut; of the 20 ministers present, nine (including Henderson, Graham and Clynes) refused to entertain the idea. This was a fatal split, so MacDonald set off to see the King to offer the administration's resignation. At this stage he was still probably thinking in terms of resigning the premiership, but the King, and then the Opposition leaders, realizing that the cuts might be less controversial if introduced by a 'socialist' prime minister, encouraged him to stay on. The result was that MacDonald next day (24 August) formed a National government. Its ten-strong cabinet included Snowden, Thomas and Sankey, plus four Conservatives and two Liberals.

Some Labourites welcomed this development, feeling that with the government dead and buried the party would be able to regroup under new leadership and with a clearer purpose. However, the next six weeks in opposition were a dispiriting time. Defections to MacDonald were gratifyingly few – only about a dozen backbenchers joined what became the 'National Labour Party', and no constituency parties or trade unions followed him, although there were odd local defections. This consolidation was undoubtedly helped by the fact that the party, prodded by the TUC general council, came out in firm opposition to the government and rapidly elected a reluctant Henderson to replace MacDonald as party leader. Labour's new stance against all cuts inevitably raised questions about the political honesty of the ex-ministers, since it rapidly became known that the cabinet as a whole had discussed and agreed to the £56 million package.

This was just a foretaste of things to come. Henderson proved a poor leader, unable to come to terms with the situation, and unwilling to be too radical. He opposed taking too strong a line against MacDonald, whom he still hoped would honour his pledge to return to the party. Labour speakers moved away from specifics, and argued that only 'socialism' could help, yet with little clear idea of what that meant. The National government passed the economy legislation and maintained a parliamentary majority. It soon became clear, in fact, that the government would not collapse, and, indeed, that it was preparing for a general election. By the time parliament was dissolved on 7 October, Labour headquarters was pessimistic, expecting the loss of 100 seats.

Such pessimism was well founded, and the general election campaign was a bitter experience for Labourites. Labour's image was that of a party of depression and unemployment, whereas unemployment had fallen under the National government and the Conservatives' protectionism seemed to offer a chance of combating the worst ravages of the depression. Labour called for the defence of free trade, but it was a policy that had lost popularity sharply in the face of the slump. There was scepticism over Labour's commitment to reverse the benefit cut while balancing the budget, and its pledge to restore the wage cuts as resources allowed was little better than that of the government. The ex-ministers were taken to task for their disingenuous attitude towards the cuts. Many Catholic and Jewish voters were alienated by the late government's policies. It is true, of course, that all kinds of stunts and scares were used against Labour, but these were not in any sense decisive. Labour was beaten because of its recent record in office, because it lacked clear policies, because its leaders had forfeited their credibility and because their opponents were more attractive to a country desperate for economic improvement.

The result was disastrous. Labour gained no new seats and held on to only 46 of those it already held, with unendorsed (mainly ILP) candidates winning six more. The leadership was swept away; old stagers like Henderson, Clynes and Adamson went along with potential future leaders such as Graham, Greenwood, Morrison and Dalton. The only member of the former cabinet to survive was Lansbury; he was joined by Clement Attlee and Sir Stafford Cripps, who had been junior ministers. The new PLP, half of whose members were sponsored by the MFGB, was singularly short of distinction. Arrayed against it were 554 National MPs, 470 of them Conservatives.

Even in terms of votes Labour's performance was dismal. True, its poll share did not fall by nearly so large a proportion as its parliamentary representation, for it took 6.3 million votes (29.3 per cent) as against 8.4 million (37.1 per cent) in 1929. But it would have been complacent to draw much comfort from this fact. First, to lose 21 per cent of the poll share of 1929 was a heavy loss indeed; since the 1867 Reform Act it had been exceeded only by the Liberals, in 1918 and 1924 – hardly encouraging precedents. To lose such a proportion of support in an election when Labour's socialist and trade union bases were so much to the fore was even more worrying. Second, the election had been fought on much more of a two-'party' basis than that of 1929 – Labour candidates had been involved in 359 straight fights as against fewer than 100 in 1929, when extensive Liberal interventions had created almost 450 three-cornered contests.[47] And the large number of unopposed returns (67 – 61 of them National) meant Labour was relieved of a number of inevitable, heavy defeats which would have depressed its poll share below 28 per cent had they all been contested. It takes a peculiar form of optimism, then, to see anything to cheer about in Labour's performance.

The high hopes of 1922, when MacDonald had returned to parliament and assumed the leadership of the party, had been shattered. Three of Labour's dominant and most popular figures during the 1920s had now passed to the other side, replaced by a leadership which was considerably less distinguished. The party's central assumptions of the 1920s – that capitalism was essentially prosperous and that this prosperity could be used as the route towards socialism, and that internationalism could solve what problems remained – seemed to be in tatters. Labour's advance during the 1920s had been spectacular, and its formation of two minority governments had eclipsed the Liberals. But the record of the second government, in particular, showed that Labour had a lot of hard decisions to make. In 1923, Webb had spoken of the 'inevitability of gradualness'. During the 1930s, it was to seem that the only thing inevitable about British politics was Labour's presence on the Opposition benches.

4   Remaking the Party?
1931–39

In the aftermath of the 1931 election, Labour faced a long haul if it was to return to power. By 1939, a further general election had been lost and it seemed highly unlikely that the next one would bring substantially better results. All in all, then, the 1930s was a decade of disappointment. However, developments during the period would help Labour's ultimate return to power.

The immediate position was dire. Labour's parliamentary representation had collapsed to 46, confined to parts of certain coalfields and some of the poorest areas of a few cities. The National government had 554 MPs, and even if, as Labourites often predicted, it broke up early under the weight of its apparent internal contradictions, the Conservatives, with their 470 MPs, would still be in a strong position. The next election would need to produce a swing of 17.5 per cent merely for Labour to return to its 1929 representation of 287 MPs; only a 20 per cent swing would give it a bare overall majority.[1] It is difficult to imagine any set of circumstances in the 1930s which could have provided such a revolution in the party's fortunes.

The party's leadership had been smashed by 1931. Lansbury, by default, became chairman of the PLP, acting as leader in parliament (pending the expected return of Henderson), with Attlee and Cripps joining him in a leftish leadership troika. The gradualist ideology which had dominated Labour's thinking seemed to be in ruins. And, finally, the party's policy was confused, to say the least. The election manifesto had been a call for a return to fundamentals, but its promises had been vague aspirations rather than blueprints for action, and much hard thinking remained to be done.

There were some crumbs of comfort. The 46 seats could be seen as a bedrock. In particular, the mining areas, which as recently as

1918 had not been electing many Labour MPs, were now much more solid than they had been then. There were discrepancies, to be sure – south Wales was more solid than the Yorks, Notts and Derby coalfields which, in turn, produced better returns than County Durham – but even in Durham, two of the 11 seats won in 1929 had been retained, and only a mild swing would be needed at the next election to bring most of the others back. The change in leadership at least cleared out the near-gerontocracy of the 'Big Five', and offered hope of a new, younger leadership in the medium term, which cannot have failed to inspire those who had found preferment so difficult to gain under the MacDonald regime. The lack of policy was not only a problem but also an opportunity. Perhaps it was the chance of fundamental change within the party that encouraged the growth of individual membership at this time. The collapse of the Labour government had also opened the wallets of the unions: after MacDonald's departure, money flooded in, and the party conference agreed to increase affiliation fees, a move it had been resisting for some time.[2] The party's organization remained intact, too. MacDonald's 'National Labour' party was never a significant threat. Labour's base remained essentially firm.

But the question of how to build on that base was a matter of fierce dispute. Some people believed that capitalism was in its death throes, quoting the renewed increase in unemployment, which peaked at around three million late in 1932, to support their apocalyptic rhetoric. This view was found most notably – but not exclusively – within the ILP; Maxton and other leading figures argued that the Labour Party had now become a hindrance to the progress of socialism.[3] A new movement of the left was needed to capture the growing radicalism of the masses. At a special conference in July 1932 the ILP voted by 241 votes to 142 to disaffiliate from Labour. It is easy to understand why a section of the ILP believed that this was a sensible, even necessary, move, but it was ultimately to prove disastrous.[4] Many people left the ILP rather than be forced to abandon Labour.[5] The economic upturn from early 1933 onwards threw doubt on the ILP's apocalyptic rhetoric, while 'co-operation' with the CPGB in 1933–34 saw the ILP asset-stripped of members and property. By 1935, therefore, ILP membership had fallen to less than a third of its level at the time of disaffiliation.[6]

Those ex-ILPers who remained with the Labour Party in 1932 combined with the Society for Socialist Inquiry and Propaganda (SSIP) (established by Cole in June 1931) to form the Socialist League. This aimed to replicate the role of the 'old' ILP within the Labour Party, and be a force for radicalism but not for disloyalty. This was a fine line to tread, and ultimately the League was to fall foul of the party bureaucracy, just as the ILP had.

Paradoxically, the disaffiliation of the ILP strengthened the left within the Labour Party. From the mid-1920s the Labour leadership had been able to deal with the ILP not on the level of ideas, but on that of party management, and at that level the left was always likely to lose. However, such a course could not be pursued with the Socialist League in 1932 for three reasons. First, the League was hardly formed by the time of the 1932 party conference in Leicester, and so could hardly be portrayed as 'a party within a party'. Second, it had been formed by people who were palpably loyal to the Labour Party; had they not been, they would have gone with the ILP. And, finally, the Labour bureaucracy, shaken by crisis and continuing uncertainty and serving a divided leadership itself lacking in self-confidence, was in no position to launch a counter-offensive. The result was that the left scored a number of successes at the 1932 conference, most notably in defeating the NEC to pass resolutions, against the NEC's advice, calling for the nationalization of commercial banks and opposing Labour's taking office again as a minority government.[7]

The ill-tempered delegates at the 1932 Leicester conference dealt a death blow to the second strand of opinion which had emerged from the 1931 crisis. This strand argued that 1931 had been an aberration, that the 'pendulum' of electoral politics would 'swing back', and that therefore the party should stick to the approach set out in *Labour and the Nation* and avoid 'false and ill-considered moves'.[8] The keenest exponent of this line was Henderson. At this point, he was the party's leader, secretary and treasurer; but, paradoxically, his views on the subject carried little weight. Henderson himself spent much of 1932 ill or presiding over the world disarmament conference at Geneva. He had still not managed to find the time or inclination to fight a by-election to secure his return to parliament. He was so out of touch by the time of Leicester that when he spoke for the NEC against a resolution opposing Labour's participation in any future minority government, he was heckled severely.[9] A few days later he resigned the party leadership, to be succeeded by Lansbury. Although he did return to parliament in 1933, remained party secretary until 1934 and was treasurer until his death in 1935, Henderson was now a marginal figure. Surprisingly rapidly, he had become a throwback to a bygone age of Labour politics.[10]

The third clear strategy to emerge from the wreckage was that favoured by the central figures on the TUC general council, such as Bevin and Walter Citrine (general secretary of the TUC), and also by leading moderates such as Dalton. They aimed to bind a future government more closely to the general council, and also to ensure that it had more clearly defined policies to implement once elected. Moves along these lines had started in September 1931, when the general council had voted to revive the moribund National Joint Council (NJC), with an in-built trade union majority over the representatives of the NEC and the PLP. The small size of the post-election PLP helped these plans, as did the fact that it and the NEC were now much more union-dominated than before. The NJC was to become a leading arbiter within the party during the 1930s, a role symbolized by its adoption of the grander title, National Council of Labour (NCL), in 1934. This is not to argue that 'the unions' always got what they wanted; for one thing, 'the unions' were not homogeneous. Still, the NJC/ NCL was to be the forum via which leading trade unionists, in alliance with leading party figures, were able to steer the party generally in directions they liked and away from those that they did not.[11]

Moves on policy had started as early as 1929. Cole's *The Next Ten Years,* published that year, called for radical measures to restructure the economy, with a shift away from staple export industries and towards 'new' industries producing for the less volatile domestic market. On nationalization, Cole argued that ownership was less important than control.[12] Although this work was very largely ignored by MacDonald's government, Cole and others pushed matters forward with the formation of the New Fabian Research Bureau in early 1931 and SSIP some months later. In the immediate aftermath of the government's collapse, a number of policy committees were set up, and these formed the nucleus of similar committees formed after the election. Young economists like Evan Durbin and Hugh Gaitskell were drafted in by Cole and Dalton to work on policy; a quasi-conspiratorial group of City experts sympathetic to Labour, the XYZ Club, advised on financial policy. At first the results were rather piecemeal, but at least there was a recognition of the need for much greater policy planning than had ever been accepted in the 1920s.[13]

Of course, the three categories outlined above were neither watertight compartments nor the whole story. Many people from top to bottom of the party shifted from position to position, or accepted parts of one position and parts of another. Others, perhaps most, continued with the workaday tasks of fundraising, canvassing, voting and attending meetings, without delineating clearly their view of the path the party should take. This confusion became clear during 1932–33 when the party flapped in the wind, first one way, then another. But if any pattern can be detected, it is that the PLP and conference tended to be (rather inchoately) leftish, while the NEC, NJC and policy bodies cleaved much more closely to the Bevin–Citrine–Dalton axis, particularly as it became increasingly clear, from 1933 onwards, that capitalism was not on the verge of collapse.

Labour remained committed to parliamentary methods.[14] The 1933 party conference did pass a motion calling for the organization of a general strike to prevent British participation in a future war, and Labourites talked of the need for a future Labour government to use 'emergency powers' or an Enabling Act to cut through opposition to its policies. But no serious attempts were made to work through rank-and-file movements or to mobilize the masses.[15] In contrast to the 1910s, no alternative means of transformation, such as syndicalism or guild socialism, emerged with any force. The CPGB's membership grew, but not massively, and was still nowhere near the levels that Labour enjoyed. Even at its early 1930s high point, therefore, Labour's swing to the left was piecemeal and qualified; and perhaps, as was to be the case in the early 1980s, the surprising aspect is less that there was a swing to the left, than the fact that it was so shallow, so partial in its effects and so short-lived.

The containment of the swing to the left could be seen in the adoption of the new party programme, *For Socialism and Peace,* by the Southport party conference in October 1934. This replaced *Labour and the Nation.* It differed from the latter in giving a higher priority to nationalization – explicitly, of land, banking, coal, iron and steel, transport, power and water supply. It also called for the setting up of a National Investment Board to plan investments and industrial development. The changes were not as great as they might have been – there was no commitment, for example, to deficit financing. The Socialist League, which saw it as far too moderate, put forward 75 amendments, but all were defeated very heavily.[16]

The reasons for the defeat of the Socialist League in 1934 are not difficult to find. The League itself had not developed far at the grassroots. Its amendments were offered on something of a 'take it or leave it' basis. In addition, by 1934 the League had developed a degree of organization and, since the emergence of Cripps as its leading figure, a higher profile; and so it could be seen as 'a party within a party', which meant that it could be dealt with on a more managerial basis than hitherto.[17] The fact that the Communists were now moving back towards united front policies also damaged the League in this respect.

More general factors also limited the League's appeal. By late 1934, the next general election was starting to loom. This inevitably served to rally the party around its leaders. The success of Morrison in leading Labour to victory in the London County Council elections of March 1934 suggested that practical, reforming moderation might have electoral benefits. The economic upturn apparent from the start of 1933 also affected the party, questioning, if not wholly invalidating, the left's apocalyptic rhetoric, while also, possibly, allowing union leaders to pay more attention to the party as their own organizations' problems began to ease.

In some ways, *For Socialism and Peace* marked a significant change from MacDonaldism. It was definite and full-blooded where *Labour and the Nation* had been vague and anaemic, and was much more strategic and less wishful than the earlier document. At the same time, there were continuities. This was particularly so in its rejection of any agency other than the state in the transformation to and administration of a socialist society. Indeed, in so far as the emphasis was now on planning from the centre, the state assumed a primacy in the party's doctrine which was virtually unchallenged.

Labour socialists had always placed a great burden on the state in their vision of how society would be transformed. Until the 1920s, however, there had always been an alternative, though less

powerful, strain in Labour's thought which pointed to the importance and potential of other agencies. The Webbs, often portrayed as the archetypal statists, had at times accepted that local
government should retain extensive powers and be a major player
in the change.[18] Syndicalism and guild socialism had also stressed
alternative visions, while thinkers like Tawney and, in particular,
Laski had stressed the importance of pluralism in their writings
until the mid-1920s. Even after his turn from guild socialism in
the mid-1920s, Cole was still keen on some form of devolution of
power to workplace councils in nationalized industries.[19]

Yet such calls were heard less frequently thereafter. It is true
that the party conference voted in favour of workers' control in
1932 and 1933 against NEC advice. But these were the last glow-
ings of a dying ember, rather than the sparks to light a new
flame. Over the decade, Labour moved towards Morrison's conception of the 'public corporation', whereby an industry would
be nationalized but then run by a government-appointed board
along essentially business lines. Even the idea that union representatives should sit on the boards – a very different thing from
workers' control – was soon abandoned. The place of the worker,
then, in his or her day-to-day working life would be little different from what it was under private ownership. Similarly, local government's possible role was downplayed; the old idea of a Local
Authorities Enabling Bill, which would have allowed councils far
greater powers to enter into trade and so on, was dropped in the
early 1930s.[20] Labour was on course towards becoming the statist,
centralizing party of the post-war period.

Why? For one thing, the failure of the second Labour government and depression throughout the capitalist world jolted people into new ways of thinking, particularly as the one country
which seemed to be prospering at the time was the USSR, whose
first Five Year Plan (1928–32) seemed to prove the efficacy of
centralized planning. These views were merely reinforced by the
apparent success of later experiments by the Social Democrats
in Sweden and by Labour in New Zealand.[21] 'Planning' became
a vogue word and the idea found its way into party policy with,
for example, the National Investment Board. Clearly implied in
planning, though, was a strong central authority whose edicts
would be fulfilled by a wider nation grateful for the wisdom of its
socialist rulers. Obviously, then, emphasis had to be placed on the

power of the state. In addition, there was greater emphasis than previously on the obstacles that Labour would have to overcome in implementing a socialist programme. MacDonaldite gradualism had assumed that progress could be piecemeal, incrementally gaining support and improving society – more and more people would come over to socialism as they saw its benefits in action. The 1930s offered little comfort for such a view. The fall of the second Labour government was attributed widely to the machinations of international capital, and especially financiers. Far from giving up their advantages voluntarily, it seemed, capitalists would fight tenaciously and ruthlessly in order to cling on to them.[22] The rise of Hitler in Germany in 1933 seemed merely to confirm this view. In such a context, socialists should not footle with minor agencies but must take control of the most powerful – the state – and ensure that the others were in no position to challenge it.

In any case, the position of the other agencies seemed uncertain. Trade unionism now covered fewer than a quarter of all workers.[23] In local government, what had once seemed an inexorable Labour advance was severely interrupted, with heavy losses in 1930 and 1931 and only marginal gains in 1932. While the setbacks would probably only be temporary, they suggested that there was a ceiling to Labour's potential achievement at this level. Put crudely, Labour was likely to gain a majority at Westminster before it gained control of the majority of local authorities. By the mid-1930s, earlier intellectual advocates of pluralism, like Laski, were increasingly statist in their outlook, while younger thinkers like Gaitskell, Durbin and Douglas Jay were expressing 'intellectual scorn' over 'naive and irrelevant' ideas like workers' control.[24] By the mid-1930s, then, Labour was putting its money on the nose of the state. There would be no each-way bets.

In the aftermath of the 1931 election many people might have been tempted to bet that the National government would soon fall apart. If so, they would have lost their stakes, for the government displayed considerable resilience. The resignation of Snowden and the free trade Liberals over protectionism in September 1932 caused little more than a ripple; otherwise, the government plodded along steadily.[25] There were periodic crises – for example, over India and unemployment assistance – but these were overcome without too much difficulty.[26] By the late spring of 1935, the crises were largely past; Baldwin replaced MacDonald as premier and reshuffled the cabinet to give it a rather more appealing look, and it became clear that an election would not be far off. Labour's electoral performance between 1931 and 1935 suggested that it could expect to make some advances. Ten parliamentary seats were gained in by-elections, some on very large swings, and there were heavy local election gains in 1933 and 1934. On the whole, though, the party was merely recovering ground lost in 1930 and 1931: in other areas, it was making few inroads, not least because for most people, though assuredly not all, the government was presiding over generally rising living standards.

In September 1935, the TUC voted in favour of economic sanctions against Italy should it proceed with its threatened invasion of Abyssinia (Ethiopia). It was clear that the party would follow suit. However, some Labourites feared that sanctions would lead to war. Cripps resigned from the NEC, and the pacifist Lord Ponsonby as leader in the Lords, in protest.[27] Lansbury was left in an impossible position. As a pacifist, he could not lead the party along these lines. At the 1935 party conference, he made a well-received speech against sanctions, but the vote went against him by a massive majority. Bevin feared that Lansbury would somehow try to hang on despite the contradictions of his position, and so damage the party's prospects at the now imminent general election. So he made a fierce speech attacking on the leader. Lansbury, finally realizing that the game was up, resigned the following day. The day after that, Italian forces invaded Abyssinia; within three weeks, Baldwin had called a general election for 14 November.

Clearly, Labour's campaign had got off to a difficult start. Lansbury was succeeded by his deputy, Attlee, as a temporary measure pending the return of more senior figures at the election. Attlee had proved a worthy deputy, earning widespread respect within the PLP, and, indeed, leading it during Lansbury's nine-month absence through illness in 1934. But he was hardly a nationally known figure at this time.[28] The government, in addition, was able to play the 'national unity in the face of international crisis' card with alacrity. Yet these factors were not the reason for Labour's defeat: no one could claim seriously that had Italy not invaded Abyssinia and Lansbury not been forced to resign, Labour would have won the election. In truth, the party could never have hoped to make up such a huge margin, and leading Labourites were predicting privately that, at best, the party would win between 200 and 240 seats.[29]

Ultimately, Labour emerged much weaker than that. True, it exceeded its 1929 poll share, taking 38 per cent of the votes cast. But the party did not even manage to triple its pre-dissolution strength of 59 MPs, emerging with only 154 seats. The government took 429 seats, of which the Conservatives claimed 387; the opposition Liberals, with only 161 candidates, could muster just 21. With so few Liberal candidates to split the anti-Labour vote, Labour had needed far more than 38 per cent of the votes in order even to restore its 1929 position with regard to seats. Labour had managed to regain a considerable number of the seats lost in 1931, but its performance was very patchy. In no region did it emulate its 1929 performance; even in industrial south Wales it only won 16 seats as opposed to 22 in 1929. In the relatively prosperous Midlands, the party took only 11 seats as opposed to 35 six years earlier. The party's performance in the south of England was truly lamentable. South of the Severn–Wash line, excepting the London area, there had been two Labour MPs even in 1918; at the 1929 election, 19 had been returned. Now Labour held only two once again, both in Bristol. In addition, the cities where Labour had begun to break through in 1929, like Birmingham and Liverpool, saw little or no progress; in the former, all 12 seats went to the Conservatives, as in 1931. Some seats in depressed areas failed to fall to Labour, presumably because not enough people, even there, could be convinced that Labour had a better alternative to the 'steady as she goes' policy of the National government. Labour was not only failing to take middle-class votes; it was failing even in many areas dominated by manual occupations. Its performance in agricultural areas, where it had made some advances in the 1920s, was now all but hopeless. But at least the PLP was strengthened in quality. Five members of the 1931 cabinet, including Clynes, Morrison and Alexander, were returned, along with a number of former junior ministers, including Dalton and Emanuel Shinwell (who defeated MacDonald at Seaham).

It had been clearly understood that Attlee was a temporary leader, and so a leadership election soon followed. The candidates were Attlee himself, Greenwood and Morrison. In the first ballot, Attlee emerged with 58 votes to Morrison's 44 and Greenwood's 33; in the second, the supporters of Greenwood seem to have swung en bloc to Attlee, who defeated Morrison by 88 votes to 48. This was rather a negative verdict on all three candidates. Greenwood was not unpopular, but he seemed to lack steel, and his freemasonry and heavy drinking aroused suspicion. More significant was the defeat of Morrison. It seems that he suffered from a number of factors: Dalton's counter-productive campaigning on his behalf, his absence from parliament between 1931 and 1935, fears that he would seek to become an all-powerful leader like MacDonald (to whom he had been very close), hostility from the left and certain union leaders (particularly Bevin, who despised him) and fears that he would be over-concerned with London. It is also possible that, at a time when issues of pacifism were to the fore, there were those who feared electing someone who had been a conscientious objector during the war.

'Major Attlee', by contrast, was the antithesis of a charismatic leader in the MacDonald mould; but he was seen as honest, decent and competent, and had earned the respect of the PLP when standing in for the ailing Lansbury during the latter's absences. It may well be, too, that Greenwood's supporters backed him because he would prove, at some future point when Greenwood's stock might have risen somewhat, easier to remove than Morrison might have been. In this, of course, they were to prove somewhat wide of the mark; Attlee's departure was not to come until 1955, by which time Greenwood was dead. At least Greenwood got the deputy leadership, because Morrison, bitterly disappointed, refused to take what he saw – with some justice – as a meaningless consolation prize.[30]

The party Attlee had been elected to lead would make only limited progress for the remainder of the decade. In parliamentary by-elections, the average swing against the Conservatives between the 1935 election and the outbreak of war in September 1939 was just 3.9 per cent, as opposed to 15.8 per cent between 1931 and 1935. As in 1931–35, Labour lost no seats at by-elections; it gained 13. But it also failed to regain five seats it had won in 1929 but lost subsequently. Municipal elections were also disappointing. In November 1935, Labour made tiny overall gains in the English and Welsh boroughs; a year later it made a small net loss of seats. The next two years saw only minor gains. In Scotland,

1936 saw Labour lose control of five of the 19 burghs it had held up to then; by 1938 the figure had only recovered to 14.[31] In short, Labour had reached what appeared to be an electoral plateau by the late 1930s. It is almost impossible to see how Labour could have avoided a further conclusive general election defeat had the Second World War not intervened.

Labour's cause was not helped, electorally, by the growing perception of the likelihood of war. Italy had subjugated Abyssinia by May 1936, by which time Hitler had remilitarized the Rhineland and the generals' rebellion against the Spanish republic had started what was to prove a long and bloody civil war, whose ultimate result was victory for General Franco, assisted by the Germans and Italians. In March 1938 Germany annexed Austria. That September Hitler's claims to the German-speaking Sudetenland area of Czechoslovakia seemed likely to lead to war between Britain and Germany; it was only averted when Britain and France, pursuing the policy of appeasement, conceded most of Hitler's claims at the Munich conference. After an apparent lull, the crisis reached a new stage with the German invasion of the Czech areas of Czechoslovakia in March 1939. Now, Britain and France issued 'guarantees' to a number of states in eastern and central Europe, and somewhat desultory efforts were made to reach an anti-German alliance with the USSR. Ultimately, the Soviet Union tired of this and sought to secure its own position by making a non-aggression pact with Germany; shortly afterwards, on 1 September, Germany invaded Poland, one of the 'guaranteed' states. Britain and France therefore declared war on Germany.

This sequence of events obviously posed problems for Labour. It was a party of peace, which was essential for the 'ordered progress' to which the party was committed. There was also considerable Labour suspicion of the National government. It was pulling the Empire closer together, through imperial preference and so on, than ever before. Might it not use rearmament and conscription, not to preserve peace and the international rule of law through the League of Nations, but to bolster British imperialism?[32] Other members of the party, however, argued that fascism was the main enemy. It destroyed the guarantors of working-class freedom – free trade unionism and social democratic parties – and was also a cruel, vindictive, reactionary force making 'ordered

progress' impossible. Its challenge must, therefore, be met and
defeated, even if this meant accepting rearmament under the
National government.[33]

In the early 1930s, pacifist arguments had appeared powerful within the party. However, pacifism was never as strong as it
seemed. A pacifist resolution at the 1933 Hastings conference had
been passed unanimously but largely for procedural reasons.[34]
The period of fascist aggression in Europe had not really started
yet. And it was still possible at that stage to have hopes of the
world disarmament conference and the Labour and Socialist
International as mechanisms to avoid war. Once these factors
had ceased to apply, as they had by 1935, the pacifists were easily defeated. However, Labour's policy remained somewhat disingenuous. It supported collective security through the League
of Nations, which had itself been strengthened by the USSR's
entry in September 1934. But in parliament the PLP continued
to vote against rearmament, without which collective security
was something of a sham. This position began to be challenged
as the danger of war seemed to increase and the League's weakness over the Italian invasion of Abyssinia in 1935 was felt. In July
1936, Alexander and Dalton led a movement within the PLP to
abstain on, rather than vote against, the arms estimates; about 20
MPs followed their line. A year later, with the Spanish Civil War
in full swing, the PLP voted by 45 to 39 to change the line to one
of abstention.[35] Although there remained a small pacifist section
around Lansbury, most MPs now pressed for rearmament, though
they missed no opportunity to register distrust of the uses to
which the National government might put its increased firepower.

The issue of Spain also created dispute and disunity in
Labour's ranks.[36] Most Labourites were, in theory, fully behind
the Spanish government in its struggle against Franco's 'fascism'. Yet the question of practical action was more vexed. For
some, Spain was a moral crusade against fascism, and this moral
conviction led a number of people, many but not all of them
Communists, to volunteer to fight in Spain for the government
forces. Such people argued that Labour should do everything
in its power to assist the legitimate Spanish government. But in
reality it was not that simple. First, there were broad electoral
considerations. Most British people had little interest in Spain,
and Labour, realizing that it needed to expand its support, not

least among working-class voters, wanted to avoid being dragged into radical causes whose immediate relevance to British workers was debatable. More particularly, there was a very real fear of losing the support of large numbers of Catholic voters. Franco claimed to be the defender of Catholicism against the 'godless' Spanish Republic. Since the early 1920s, Catholics in Britain had come over substantially to Labour, a factor of great significance in advancing the party's position in many major towns and cities, especially in west Lancashire and on Clydeside. Yet Labour's relationship with them remained complex. For one thing, Labour had rather a Protestant image; if the party owed more to Methodism than Marxism, as some of its members liked to claim, then this left the Catholics in an anomalous position, to say the least. The secession of Wheatley from the Labour front bench in the mid-1920s had merely highlighted the under-representation of Catholics in the party leadership. As seen above, the Catholic Church had been alienated by Trevelyan's proposals for its schools, and it seems that many Catholic voters deserted Labour during 1930–31. Around the same time there was talk of trying to set up Catholic trade unions on the continental model. Nothing came of this, but the inevitable result was that Labour remained sensitive to the dangers of losing 'the Catholic vote', not least because Catholics remained under-represented at all levels of the Labour movement. In short, Labour's leadership was worried that to take too firm a stand on behalf of the Spanish Republic might lead to a haemorrhage of Catholic support. Such a haemorrhage would make a Labour government in Britain less likely than ever, and so in turn reduce the chances of Britain pursuing a more vigorous anti-fascist strategy in general. There were challenges to the leadership's line, but, apart from calling for a lifting of the arms embargo and pursuing humanitarian efforts, little was done. Some people moved to the more strident Communist Party in disgust, but it seems that most Labourites were broadly satisfied with the policy.

Spain also raised a wider issue about Labour's line in the 1930s: co-operation with other parties, and with the Communists in particular. From 1933 onwards the CPGB began once again to press for united action. But a proposal for a united front in 1933 was turned down flat by the NEC, and the NJC issued a manifesto, *Democracy versus Dictatorship*, arguing that there was nothing to choose between communism and fascism. The leadership's line was broadly favoured within the party: although some advocated co-operation, the attacks of the 'Class against Class' period had been widely and deeply resented, and trade unionists in particular had been incensed at the CPGB's attempts to form breakaway Communist unions. During 1933–34, the ILP's bitter experience of 'co-operation' with the Communists caused significant numbers of ILPers to return to Labour, bringing with them tales of what many Communists really meant by 'unity'. However, matters did not rest there. The seventh world congress of the Communist International in the summer of 1935 unfurled the policy of uniting all opponents of fascism in a 'popular front'. The CPGB began to act in a conciliatory manner towards the Labour party. As a sign of good faith, all but two Communist candidates were withdrawn at the 1935 election, although the fact that one of them, William Gallacher, defeated Adamson at West Fife hardly helped matters. Subsequently, renewed application for affiliation was turned down by the NEC.

The NEC doubtless hoped that this would put an end to the matter, but every crisis in Europe brought renewed calls to reopen the question. By the summer of 1936, some major unions (including the MFGB), around 60 CLPs, and the Socialist League, were all supporting Communist affiliation. That October, the party conference gave the largest vote yet in favour of affiliation, but it was still defeated by a three-to-one majority. Undeterred, the Communists joined with the ILP and Socialist League in talks for a more limited form of unity. The result was the Unity Campaign, which was launched in January 1937.[37] The NEC's response was to disaffiliate the Socialist League and, shortly afterwards, to declare that membership of the League and of the Labour Party were incompatible. That May, League members decided that, rather than face expulsion from the Labour Party, they would dissolve their own organization. The Unity Campaign did result in some interparty co-operation at rank-and-file level, but the 1937 party conference voted heavily against the united front once again.[38]

The issue of cross-party links revived in the autumn of 1938, at the time of the Munich Crisis. A Conservative opponent of Munich, Harold Macmillan, approached Dalton proposing a degree of co-operation, and a number of meetings followed. Attlee, Morrison and Cripps were all sympathetic when sounded,

but the first two were somewhat cautious, foreseeing problems with the trade unions. In the event, the idea foundered,
mainly due to the unwillingness of the former Foreign Secretary,
Anthony Eden, to become involved. Eden had a considerable following among Tory MPs and was clearly crucial to Macmillan's
idea of a '1931 in reverse'; without him, there was little point in
pursuing the idea.[39] 'Unity' with just a handful of malcontents
and mavericks like Macmillan and perceived reactionaries like
Churchill would have been impossible to sell to the Labour movement as a whole, and of dubious value in any case. There was
also, around the same time, a rank-and-file movement towards
a popular front. This found expression in two by-elections: at
Oxford in October, when an independent candidate opposed
to Munich and supported by the local Labour and Liberal parties was defeated narrowly by a Conservative; and at Bridgwater
(Somerset) in November, when the journalist and broadcaster,
Vernon Bartlett, stood as an Independent Progressive candidate (again with Labour and Liberal support) and overturned
a Conservative majority of 10,000.[40] Across parts of Britain, but
particularly areas where Labour was weak, like the south-west,
calls were heard for some kind of an alliance between Labour
and other parties.[41] It was to try to take advantage of this latter movement that Cripps launched his next – and for the time
being terminal – venture in January 1939. He proposed a broad
progressive movement against the National government (though
without the CPGB), on the grounds that the international position was now so serious, and Labour's electoral prospects so weak,
that some alternative must be sought. Deals should be struck
at constituency level, in readiness for the next election, and a
national campaign be launched.[42] The NEC, as expected, vetoed
the proposals, whereon Cripps circulated them to all constituency
Labour parties. When asked to withdraw the document, Cripps
refused and was expelled from the party, along with Trevelyan,
the south Wales MP Aneurin Bevan, and others of his supporters.
The campaign attracted some Labour support but more condemnation, particularly from the unions. The NEC took the opportunity to pay off old scores, expelling a larger number of more
minor figures who had long been a thorn in its side. At that May's
party conference, Cripps's explanation of his actions was poorly
received, and the expulsions were approved by a five-to-one

majority. The proposal for a popular front was even more heavily defeated.[43]

Superficially, Cripps and his supporters had a case, in so far as the international situation was grave and Labour did have little chance of victory at the next election. However, his inability to push Labour onto other courses was utterly predictable. Failure was due, in part, to Cripps himself. His wealth, 'cleverness' and the feeling that he lacked roots in the movement all told heavily against him. Parallels with the Fascist, Mosley, could be, and were, drawn.[44] But personality was not decisive. To most Labourites there seemed to be little advantage in a popular front. The Liberal Party was widely distrusted in Labour circles, and seemed anyway to be in terminal decline; and the Communists, seen by many as part of the deal even despite Cripps's denials, were not insignificant, but had only 18,000 members and were seen as highly unreliable. Alliance would only strengthen untrustworthy and ailing parties at the expense of Labour. In practice, even many of the CLPs which were theoretically in favour of a pact would have baulked at withdrawing their own candidate for a Liberal (or a Communist, for that matter) when it came to an election. Finally, the conduct of the various unity campaigns, but especially that of 1939, offended deeply against the ethos of the Labour movement. It was disloyal: majority decisions, repeatedly reiterated, were being flouted with no less regularity. This kind of behaviour could only mean disunity in the face of the main enemy – the Conservatives –and perhaps lead ultimately to the break-up of the Labour Party. 'Unity', in short, was no short cut to power, and was a recipe for disunity in Labour's ranks. Labour's leadership realized privately that the party's electoral prospects were dim, but at the same time recognized that these could not be improved, and would probably be damaged, by trying to form artificial pacts and alliances with other parties.

The fact that the constituency parties were targeted by Cripps shows, if nothing else, the perception that they had become somewhat more important in the 1930s than they had been in the previous decade. Individual membership more than doubled between 1928 and 1937, at a time when union-affiliated membership of the party was fairly static, so that over the same period individual membership rose from 9.4 to 17.7 per cent of the total membership. A Constituency Parties Movement was formed in

1933 to demand a greater amount of say for such members. The NEC's attempts at suppression failed, and at the 1937 conference that year's party chairman, Dalton, steered through reform against some strong union opposition. First, the size of the NEC was increased from 23 to 25 members (plus the party leader and the treasurer), with an increase in the constituency parties' section from five to seven members. Perhaps more significantly, the method of election for the NEC was changed: instead of being elected by the whole conference, the CLP representatives would now be elected by the CLPs alone.[45] The results of this were not, in the short term, particularly significant (although ironically they were to lead to Dalton's ultimate removal from the NEC in 1952) but the reform succeeded in taking the wind out of the sails of the constituency parties, much as the adoption of Clause IV in 1918 had deflated the ILP.

This period also saw the party develop its programme further. In 1936, detailed plans for the nationalization of coal were adopted. In March 1937, *Labour's Immediate Programme* was published, giving details of the measures a majority Labour government would implement in a single five-year term. It promised planning through a National Investment Board. The Bank of England (but not the commercial banks) would be nationalized; so too would be coal, power and transport. There would be state control over the location of industry. Working conditions would be improved through a 40-hour week and the introduction of holidays with pay. The means test would be abolished. The school-leaving age would be raised to 15 and later 16. Health services would be improved.[46] While much of this reiterated earlier programmes, particularly *For Socialism and Peace,* Labour now had concrete plans for the implementation of most of its policies, whereas earlier programmes had been expressions of wishes rather than plans of campaign. *Labour's Immediate Programme* was to form, essentially, the bedrock of the work of the 1945 Attlee government. At the same time it can be seen as capping the policy-making process: little else was being done about domestic policy before the war.[47] In that sense, it did serve to a certain extent to stifle the debate which remained as necessary as ever to Labour's planning for the future.

The very fact of a detailed programme showing what a Labour government would do in office, buttressed by existing detailed plans for its implementation, was in itself a novelty, perhaps reflecting the greater underlying homogeneity of the Labour Party by this time. The production of a detailed plan of campaign meant that one of the main criticisms that had been levelled at *Labour and the Nation* in 1928 had been met. Transported ten years ahead, the delegates who had applauded that programme would also have been surprised at specific aspects of Labour policy: in particular, planning, regional policy and the signs of limited influence from Keynesian ideas. In other senses, though, Labour's position had not changed all that radically. It remained, and indeed had become more committed to being, a statist party which conceived of socialism in almost exclusively 'top-down' terms. The plan would be drawn up in London, and implemented from London, with perhaps a nod towards the dreaming spires of Oxford. True, it would take into account regional differences – hence regional policy – but this would all be defined at the centre, and implemented through Westminster and Whitehall, with local government coming in only as an agency of central government. Industries would be 'nationalized', to be run by boards appointed by the minister in London, meeting in London. Even the more diluted forms of worker participation retreated further from view as the 1930s wore on.

In addition, in so far as Labour was becoming more Keynesian, it was, paradoxically, allowing the basic premise of the socialism of MacDonald and Snowden to make a comeback. In his *Politics of Democratic Socialism,* written in 1939 although not published until the following year, one of the party's leading young intellectuals, Evan Durbin, argued that while '[t]he capitalist economy [was] ossified, restrictionist and unjust', it was 'expanding and stable', and that it could provide 'a most substantial rate of expansion'.[48] In other words, capitalism's economic growth would be the basis of the development of a socialist society. Durbin did, of course, see much more clearly than MacDonald and Snowden the need for substantial reforms of the economy within capitalism, but he still predicated his strategy on economic growth under capitalism. 'Planning' and Keynesianism would, hopefully, avert such crises as the one that had toppled them; but it remained open to question whether this would in fact prove to be the case. This is not to say, of course, that anyone else in the party, least of all on the left, had any clearer ideas on this point.

By the time Durbin's book was published, however, Britain was at war, and a new phase in the party's history was opening. The 1930s had witnessed a limited revival and consolidation after the disasters of 1929–31. The party's organization had held good, while rising individual membership pointed to a widening appeal in the country, and trade union affiliated membership was also rising from 1935 onwards. However, continuing union stickiness about increasing affiliation fees left the party shorter of cash than it would have liked, and by 1939 it was facing serious financial worries, which in turn were severely hampering its campaigning plans ahead of the general election expected for the autumn of that year. Meanwhile, election results after 1935 were largely disappointing, reflecting continuing distrust and the party's failure to wholly break out of images of being unduly connected with trade unions and the unemployed. This left Labour remote from power, but not perhaps as remote as it might have been had it succumbed to the seductive rhetoric of 'co-operation' with other parties. In its foreign policy, Labour emerged from a long period of confusion to become, by late 1938, a staunch opponent of appeasement, although a small section of the party's membership remained outright pacifist and a much larger number remained very deeply uneasy about any prospect of Britain going to war, especially under such a bitter political opponent as the National government. At home, the party's policies were better worked out than ever before. But they were also increasingly centralizing and statist, with few proposals which offered real empowerment to ordinary people in their own lives. By the end of the decade, the centre right was very clearly in the ascendant, partly because, to some extent understandably, the left had spent so much of the decade concentrating on the international situation and advancing various 'fronts'. The Second World War which they had hoped to prevent was, paradoxically, to provide Labour with a massive boost to its fortunes.

5   The Impact of the Second World War, 1939–45

If the First World War had hastened Labour's progress in becoming Britain's second party, then the Second World War undoubtedly speeded the party's opportunity of competing with the Conservatives on equal, or even superior, terms. In 1939 Labour looked like losing yet another general election. Six years later it was to win a landslide victory and form its first majority government.

The outbreak of the Second World War found Labour rather less divided on the justice of the conflict and the need for British intervention than had been the case in 1914. Following the German invasion of Poland on 1 September, Labour's leadership remained united, and Greenwood – acting leader for much of 1939 due to Attlee's absence through illness – did his and his party's reputation much good by appearing, in the Commons debates, keener than Chamberlain on an early declaration of war. The great majority of Labour MPs supported the leadership, although with a not insignificant group of about 20 MPs, including pacifists and supporters of a negotiated peace, dissenting.[1] Labour refused Chamberlain's half-hearted offer of a Coalition, but accepted an electoral truce shortly after the war broke out.

The reasons for Labour's greater unity in 1939 than in 1914 are not hard to fathom. The nature of the enemy was much clearer. In 1914, Germany had not been a democracy, but it had had a large Social Democratic party (SPD), much admired by the British left, and the question of how far the war had been caused by German aggression had been, at the very least, debatable. By 1939, however, the nature of Hitler's regime was a matter of little debate: it had banned the SPD and imprisoned its leaders, crushed free trade unionism, carried out policies of racial discrimination and persecution which appalled the British left, and, at least since 1936, pursued an apparently insatiable policy of expansionism. The nature of the expected war was also different; with defence planners expecting massive aerial bombardment of the British mainland to begin as soon as war commenced, this was, for many people, no time for debate, but for action. Finally, the nature of the party itself had changed. Since 1914, it had become more centralized and more disciplined. Dissent had been increasingly marginalized, while 'disruptive' elements like the ILP had been forced out of the party altogether. Thus Labour's response to the outbreak of war, on the whole, was one of unity in the face of a common – and commonly despised – enemy. Even here, it should be noted that party members were not unanimous. Some Labourites continued to question the party's support for the war; and greater numbers expressed concern when the leadership was slow to declare what its 'peace aims' were. Thus, although the majority of the party remained united behind the war effort, the first winter of the conflict – the co-called 'phoney war' – did see some tensions.

However, the period also saw a number of quite favourable developments. Leading members of the front bench were appointed to liaise officially with specific ministers, refreshing the governmental experience of 1929–31 with ministers such as Greenwood, Alexander and Dalton.[2] The problem of the leadership, which had brewed during Attlee's absence, was resolved in November when Greenwood, Dalton and Morrison, who had all been nominated against the leader in the annual PLP elections, refused to go forward to election (though rather reluctantly, in Morrison's case).[3] The electoral truce held firm, despite protests from some unions and constituency parties, and Labour candidates at by-elections trounced anti-war candidates. There was renewed thought on policy, with the policy committee deciding in February 1940 that a comprehensive new statement of Labour's aims should be prepared; the result, *Labour's Home Policy* (April 1940) stressed the opportunities presented by the new situation and 'provided the rhetorical framework for later war programmes'.[4] And the readmission of Bevan in late 1939, after some pressure from his union, the MFGB, healed some wounds, although Cripps was not to rejoin the party until 1945.[5]

On the other hand, there were anxieties. The electoral truce, and close contacts between the government and opposition front benches, meant that it was sometimes difficult for the PLP to tread the middle line between coalition and outright opposition. The Russo-Finnish War, which began in November 1939 and, because of unexpectedly strong Finnish resistance, lasted until March 1940, also caused problems. After the first flush of enthusiasm for the Five Year Plan, Labour misgivings about the USSR had grown from the mid-1930s onwards. These had intensified massively with the German–Soviet Pact and the consequent Soviet occupation of eastern Poland, and the attack on Finland seemed to many people to be no better than what Hitler was doing: Citrine described it as 'an outburst of savagery' and the NCL condemned Soviet actions.[6] A few fellow-travelling Labourites tried to justify the Soviet action, but their leading figure, D. N. Pritt (a member of the NEC) was expelled from the party in March 1940 as a result of his efforts.[7] The attack on Finland also strengthened the resolve of the NEC to root out supposedly pro-Communist elements. In December 1939 the NEC noted a renewal of Communist activity within the party, and a succession of local parties were disbanded as a result, in the biggest purge since the later 1920s.[8] Opinion against the USSR remained so strong that, when Laski suggested in April 1940 that Labour should consider ways in which Anglo-Soviet relations could be improved, the NEC (of which he was a member) refused even to discuss the idea.[9]

By the time Laski made his suggestion, the difficulties the party faced were leading some of its leaders to consider whether Labour might fare better as part of a coalition, although not under Chamberlain. When British troops were forced into an ignominious evacuation of Norway, the PLP called a debate on the Chamberlain government's general direction of the war. This was held on 7 and 8 May. Initially, the party leadership was reluctant to call a vote on the issue, fearing it would force Conservative backbenchers to back the government and so shore up its position, but events on 7 May, when a number of Conservatives spoke against Chamberlain, changed all that. When the vote took place the next day, the government's majority fell to 81 instead of its normal 200, with some of its usual supporters voting against the government, and others abstaining. This made a reconstruction of the government inevitable. The NEC, meeting in Bournemouth on the eve of the party conference, refused to serve under

Chamberlain, but stated that Labour would be prepared to serve under someone else. Some preferred the Foreign Secretary, Lord Halifax: he was widely respected, and seen as a liberal, consensual figure. The alternative was Churchill, who had returned to the cabinet as First Lord of the Admiralty in September 1939. He was still widely distrusted in Labour circles as an arch-enemy of socialism and trade unionism. But his anti-appeasement credentials were impeccable, he was clearly a fighter, and the German attack on France which commenced on 9 May swung opinion towards him. Thus the party conference voted by 2,413,000 votes to 170,000 against a resolution opposing entry into a new Churchill administration. An official opposition was to be maintained for the sake of parliamentary business, but Labour ensured it was led by safe figures nearing the end of their careers: H. B. Lees-Smith (to December 1941), F. W. Pethick-Lawrence (December 1941 to March 1942) and Greenwood (March 1942 onwards). It would be left to other Labour MPs to offer more stringent criticism.[10]

Labour attained a stronger position in the new government than its parliamentary representation warranted. This was partly because Churchill needed a strong counterbalance against a suspicious Conservative Party. In any case, to have offered ministerial posts to Labour in ratio to its number of MPs would have left the government very lopsided. Most substantially, the need for union co-operation in a total war effort meant that the Labour movement's extra-parliamentary strength had also to be taken into account. Labour took two places in the new, five-strong, war cabinet: Attlee became Lord Privy Seal and chair of the Food and Home Policy Committee, while Greenwood, as Minister without Portfolio, was put in charge of the Production and Economic Policy Committee. Attlee was surprisingly effective in office. In 1943 he became Lord President of the Council and de facto deputy Prime Minister, co-ordinating the home front during Churchill's frequent absences on war business.[11] Greenwood, on the other hand, had little success in office and was effectively sacked in March 1942.

Ernest Bevin, appointed Minister of Labour and National Service in May 1940, was the Labour minister who, ultimately, made the greatest impact. His appointment was a sign both of his own abilities and of the importance of trade unions in wartime. He became an MP for the first time, being succeeded at the

TGWU by his close follower, Arthur Deakin. In October he was promoted to the war cabinet. For a decade or more Bevin had been the most powerful individual in the Labour movement. The Ministry of Labour, meanwhile, had been transformed by war from the Cinderella of government departments into the powerhouse of the war effort, since workers were in short supply, and total war required high levels of production and productivity. During the war, Bevin generally handled manpower problems with an enviable sureness of touch and self-confidence. Although he had draconian powers to coerce labour, he was reluctant to use them, relying instead on persuasion wherever possible.[12] He impressed officials – and Churchill – with his abilities, and further developed his interest in foreign affairs, particularly the German question.[13]

The fourth Labourite to serve in the war cabinet (from November 1942 onwards) was Morrison. After a brief spell as Minister of Supply, he became Home Secretary in October 1940, and retained the position for the duration. An experienced administrator from his time as secretary of the London Labour party, Minister of Transport and leader of the London County Council, he was generally regarded as successful, and remained Attlee's main rival for the leadership.

The other 'Labour' figure to serve at the highest level was Cripps. He had been expelled from the party in 1939, and did not rejoin it until February 1945. However, his left-wing reputation helped persuade Churchill to appoint him Ambassador to the USSR in 1940. He was not notably successful in the post, but his role in forging the Anglo-Soviet Alliance which followed the German invasion of Russia in June 1941 was played up by the press, and he returned to a hero's welcome in January 1942. The following month he joined the war cabinet as Lord Privy Seal. An opinion poll in April 1942 found that if 'anything happened to Mr Churchill', 34 per cent would favour Cripps's succession to the premiership; only Eden, the Foreign Secretary, with 37 per cent, outscored him.[14] His hopes rose in the summer of 1942, when, with the war going badly, Churchill's position seemed to be weakening. However, the British victory at El Alamein that October allowed Churchill to pay off old scores, and Cripps was sacked from the war cabinet. He was to serve as Minister of Aircraft Production for the remainder of the conflict.[15]

Other leading Labour figures also served in office. At ministerial rank outside the war cabinet, Alexander returned to the position of First Lord of the Admiralty that he had held in the 1929 government; Johnston became Secretary of State for Scotland in February 1941 and used his position to push forward a number of valuable reforms, including the development of hydroelectricity in the Highlands;[16] Dalton became Minister for Economic Warfare and then President of the Board of Trade, where he promoted a vigorous regional policy which was of direct assistance to some of Labour's strongest core areas of support;[17] and Sir William Jowitt, who had defected to National Labour in 1931 but rejoined Labour in 1939, held a succession of minor offices. Labour also took more than its fair share of junior posts, with five of those involved – Ellen Wilkinson, George Hall, Tom Williams, James Chuter Ede and Joseph Westwood – later serving in the Attlee cabinet. Finally, a number of Labour's future leaders, like Hugh Gaitskell, Douglas Jay and Harold Wilson, served during the war as temporary civil servants in Whitehall.

Labour derived considerable advantage from this. Its credibility as a governing party, so damaged by the events of 1929–31, was largely restored as its leaders proved their competence and gained, or regained, valuable experience. Policy making was helped by having both senior and junior figures on the 'inside track' of government. And Labour ministers, although constrained by Coalition politics, were able to push through some important schemes of reform, such as Bevin's 1943 Catering Wages Act and Dalton's regional policies. However, the generally favourable view of Whitehall gained at this time by the men who were to lead Labour until 1976 was possibly a handicap to them, perhaps at the time and certainly later. It was not a simple process of their being 'nobbled' by 'the Establishment' – that would be far too crass a formulation. Rather, it was a tendency to see things still more than before from the centre. The 'top-down' approach, admittedly well entrenched even before the war, was still further strengthened; and wartime collaboration between state, employers and unions was taken by many as a model of what might be possible in the future, rather than as an exceptional product of exceptional circumstances.

The roots of the PLP's relative docility during the Attlee governments' tenure are also to be found in these years. As seen above, the official leadership of the Labour opposition was in safe hands. The PLP was not supine: a small group of pacifist MPs continued to exist, and Bevan and Shinwell were among backbenchers who maintained a consistently critical stance towards the government.[18] And although the 'opposition' only divided the House once after May 1940, it did so in February 1943 on an issue – the Beveridge Report – which signalled Labour's distinctive line on welfare, to the party's almost certain benefit at the subsequent election. On the whole, though, the PLP was behind the government and the party leadership.

The war also had a significant impact on trade unionism and this, of course, had major implications for the party. Union density had fallen from 45.2 per cent in 1920 to 22.6 per cent (lower than in 1913) in 1933. Growing prosperity later in the 1930s had led to revival, but even in 1938 membership and density (4,669,186 and 30.5 per cent) were well below the figures for 1920. The number of trade union members affiliated to the Labour Party had fluctuated similarly: standing at 4,317,537 in 1920, it had fallen to 1,857,524 in 1934, followed by a gradual recovery to 2,158,076 in 1938, but then the war led to a massive change. TUC membership soared, rising to a wartime peak of 6,642,317 (40.4 per cent density) in 1943; by 1946 the figure was 7,540,397 (43.0 per cent).[19]

The reasons for this are not difficult to find. As the economy moved on to a full war footing, demand for labour soared. Unemployment, which had stood at 1,471,000 in January 1940, fell to 653,000 a year later, and by December 1941 only 151,000 were out of work, and full employment was maintained for the remainder of the war. Employers' attitudes, naturally, changed. Unions themselves were faced with new challenges which led them to try to recruit more widely: a notable case was the decision of the traditionally all-male Amalgamated Engineering Union (AEU) to admit women in 1943, not through any great conversion to feminism, but through fears that they might otherwise undercut male earnings or be recruited by general unions, potentially weakening the AEU's hold on the industry. Over 100,000 women joined the union in the first year.[20]

In addition, the unions were taken closer to the centre of government and industry than ever before. The state's powers over the workforce were increased to unprecedented levels.

In 1940, Defence Regulation 58A gave the Minister the right to direct labour (something which, as 'industrial conscription', had been bitterly opposed by the Labour movement during the First World War), and Order 1305 banned strikes and lockouts, making all disputes subject to compulsory, binding arbitration. In 1944, Regulation 1AA imposed penalties for agitation and incitement to strike. Dilution of labour and suspension of traditional working practices also took place. However, since Bevin preferred conciliation, and tried to avoid invoking the regulations wherever possible, relatively few workers were 'directed' into specific jobs. Strikes still took place: there were actually more stoppages per year on average than during the First World War, although fewer workers were involved and the disputes were settled more quickly, so that, on average, only a third as many working days were lost per year as in 1914–18. Legal penalties on strikers were used sparingly. The unions' reward was close consultation with government and employers. On the outbreak of war a National Joint Advisory Committee of the Ministry of Labour, with 15 employers and 15 trade unionists, had been established. But Bevin found this ineffective, and appointed a more effective joint Consultative Committee comprising seven representatives from each side and himself in the chair. It met twice a month and monitored events closely.[21] Unions were also represented on regional production committees; and, at factory level, management often consulted closely with shop stewards on how to speed up production. Meanwhile, news censorship of strikes meant that negative images were largely suppressed. All this helped the public image of trade unionism. The party's close identification with the unions had handicapped it in the 1930s, but as the unions grew in prestige, became increasingly respectable and covered wider sections of the population (particularly women), Labour could benefit from the association. High levels of unionization increased the affiliated membership of the party from 2,158,076 in 1938 to 2,510,369 in 1945, and by 1945 Labour's financial position would be stronger than at any previous point in its history.[22]

In the retrospective mythology with which some Conservatives rationalized their 1945 defeat, Labour benefited from the war because its organizers were more likely to be in 'reserved' occupations, and hence in their normal place of residence. Even if there was a grain of truth in this, it underestimated the pressures on the civilian population, and on Labour activists in particular, especially in the early part of the war. The electoral truce and confusion about the role of the party (particularly before the Coalition was formed), longer working hours, war duties in the Home Guard, Air Raid Patrols and so on, and the widespread disruption caused by German air raids, all helped to reduce Labour's individual membership. This had stood at just over 400,000 in 1939, but then fell back to 218,783 in 1942. Thereafter, matters began to improve. People came to terms with their work commitments and were able to negotiate time for party activity, and the end of the major period of German air raids in mid-1941 helped. Then the publication of the Beveridge Report in December 1942, and the PLP's subsequent division of the Commons in its favour, gave Labourites a chance to coalesce around a concrete set of issues. The result was that individual party membership rose to 265,763 in 1944 and 487,047 in 1945 (a new record level). The cancellation of local elections for the duration led to a certain withering of CLP activity, but even so Labour remained more active in cities like Birmingham and Sheffield, which had hitherto had powerful Conservative party machines.[23]

There were improvements in organization at head office. Middleton, who had succeeded Henderson as party secretary in 1934, was finally prised out in 1944 and replaced by the younger and more able Morgan Phillips. Phillips was, in turn, replaced as research secretary by the 30-year-old intellectual Michael Young, erstwhile director of the independent think-tank, Political and Economic Planning. The International Department was finally wrested from the dead hand of William Gillies in 1944, and he was succeeded, the following year, by the former Communist and war veteran, Major Denis Healey. Head office was, partly at least, taking on a fresher, more purposeful air.[24]

A further important consequence of war was the refinement of party policy. Even during the 'phoney war' period the NEC had noted the paucity of specific policy documents in a number of areas. *Labour's Home Policy*, published in April 1940, not only summed up pre-war policy, but also emphasized the need for planning and controls in order to win the war and stressed that such methods would still be needed in peacetime. As Attlee put it, 'the occasion should be seized to lay the foundations of a planned economic system'.[25] It also highlighted the need for social reform as a means of maintaining morale. In early 1941 the party set up a Central Committee on Problems of Post-War Reconstruction, and from this evolved *The Old World and the New Society*, drafted by Laski and published in February 1942. It repeated the message of *Labour's Home Policy*: planning and controls must remain in place. The post-war world must guarantee full employment, social security, reconstruction, a reform of education and the establishment of a national health service.[26] Later that year the Beveridge Report on Social Insurance and Allied Services was published, calling for a comprehensive welfare state. It was met with scepticism, to say the least, by most Conservatives, but the Labour members of the war cabinet pressed for a government commitment to the report. Ultimately, though, the government could only agree to make no pledge for or against legislation on the basis of the report. However, when the matter came up for debate in parliament in February 1943, 97 Labour MPs, led by James Griffiths, voted against the government line, in defiance of the Labour whip. This split actually helped Labour, since it showed plainly which party was more committed to the principles of what was, clearly, an exceptionally popular report.[27] The party supported the Education Act and the introduction of family allowances in 1944. In the same year, the government's White Paper on Employment committed the state to the maintenance of 'a high and stable level of employment'. Unlike Labour's recently published statement, *Full Employment and Financial Policy*, however, it did not commit the government to retaining controls once a full transition to peacetime had been made.[28] The other main development came in December 1944, when, against the advice of the NEC, the party conference voted in favour of a resolution which replaced a vague NEC statement about 'transfer[ring] to the State ... power to direct the policy of our main industries, services and financial institutions' with a definite pledge to effect 'the transfer to public ownership of the land, large-scale building, heavy industry, and all forms of banking, transport and fuel and power'.[29]

How far did Labour move towards more 'consensual' policies in this period? It has been argued that Labour lost many of the features that had made it distinctive in the 1930s: nationalization was played down, while the Beveridge Report and the White Paper on Employment were accepted eagerly as replacements for, or enhancements of, party policy. The party, according to this view, became less interested in physical controls over the economy as a long-term option and moved towards a more 'Keynesian' approach of managing the economy by budgetary and fiscal controls. During the 1940s the Conservatives, for their part, 'were obliged to integrate some of Labour's most important demands into their own philosophy', but they 'were able to do so without too much pain because Labour's demands had largely been cast in a mould of thought provided by the non-socialist intelligentsia between the wars and during World War II'.[30]

This 'consensus' view has come in for strong criticism.[31] Planning and employment policy, for example, were still debated hotly. Labour had spent much of the 1930s talking about the need for planning, by which it meant a combination of nationalization of basic industries and utilities, physical controls, especially (but not by any means solely) over investment and a commitment to full employment. The war resulted in the development of controls, and also saw what can be viewed in retrospect as a kind of proto-nationalization in terms of state control of the mines and railways. It also saw the publication of the White Paper on Employment, as stated above. Crucial differences remained, however, even within the war cabinet itself. For example, Labour saw wartime controls as the start of a permanent process, whereas most Conservatives saw them as something which would not survive the transition to peace. Nationalization was as resolutely opposed by the Tories as it was advocated by Labour. And the phrase about maintaining a 'high and stable level of employment' in the 1944 White Paper was deliberately vague because agreement was elusive on what constituted an acceptable level of unemployment. The TUC, Labour and Beveridge plumped for 3 per cent, whereas the Treasury took the view that 8.5 per cent was the desirable level.[32] Yet a figure of 8.5 per cent would have left well over a million out of work, which would not have been acceptable to Labour. It is true that both parties became somewhat less antagonistic towards Keynesian techniques. But at this stage neither was willing to adopt them as any more than a bolt-on addition to their longstanding economic policies. The most that can be said is that there was a blurring of the lines, and perhaps some acceptance of a mixed economy in theory. But this really does not suggest a consensus, since the nature of the mixture was still very much open to debate.

There were also sharp divisions in other areas. On health, Labour welcomed wartime advances, and its ministers helped to draft the February 1944 White Paper which promised a national health service free at the point of use. But both sides saw it as a consultation document rather than a definitive plan of campaign. The period between then and the end of the war saw the Conservatives retreating from the White Paper and returning to earlier, less comprehensive proposals, while Labour continued to press for its own distinctive policies, such as a salaried medical profession and provision of health centres.[33] In social insurance, too, Labour continued to press its own policies. It was a different story in education, where there was 'a greater degree of party co-operation than [on] any other aspect of wartime policy'.[34] Labour supported the 1944 Education Act, accepting a number of policies which looked to future generations decidedly compromised, such as the failure to push for comprehensive schools at secondary level, the continuation of private education, the failure to set specific dates for the raising of the school-leaving age and the maintenance of fees in direct grant schools. However, to focus on these aspects is to overlook what was gained from the Act. It offered an end to the old system of 'elementary' education: for the first time, all children would receive some secondary education. Further, fees for secondary schooling were abolished. There was a settlement of the thorny question of religious control of schools, which had stymied Labour's earlier attempts to reform the system and cost it much in electoral terms. It is also important not to be anachronistic. Though there was strong support for 'multilateral' (comprehensive) education, many Labourites continued to see selection and grammar schools as positive, in so far as they allowed the brightest working-class children to gain an education as good as that of their 'social betters'. The 1944 Act, then, was seen as a worthwhile and much-needed reform. It might have had imperfections, but they could be rectified at a later date. Better that than to saddle a future Labour government with working on the whole question from scratch. The attitude towards education policy, in other words, was more commonsensical than truly consensual.

It seems difficult, then, to sustain the view that there was a thoroughgoing consensus during the war. Labour retained a distinctive outlook, a fact which is further highlighted when the focus is moved to local government. There, disputes over rate levels, post-war planning, a possible extension of the municipal franchise and the permanence or otherwise of wartime developments like the British Restaurants were commonplace.[35] For their part, the Conservatives, influenced increasingly by the business community from 1944 onwards, were still essentially committed to private enterprise and market forces; that they re-emphasized this during the latter part of the war for fear that a Labour government would nationalize extensively tells its own story.[36]

The approach of the end of the war raised the question of the future of the Coalition. The NEC, in a statement to the December 1944 party conference, declared that there must be an election 'as soon as possible' after the war's end, and that the election must be fought on party lines; there would be no repeat of the 'coupon election' of 1918.[37] This, of course, left the matter of timing open to interpretation; after Germany's surrender in May 1945 there were those who favoured continuing the Coalition until Japan had been defeated. In the event, however, Churchill, himself under some pressure from his party, resigned immediately and was then reappointed as premier of a 'Caretaker' government composed of Conservatives plus a few Liberal Nationals and ostensibly non-party figures. Parliament was dissolved on 5 June, with polling to take place exactly a month later. The votes would be counted on 26 July, to allow time for postal votes from members of the armed forces serving overseas to be sent to Britain.

When the results were declared, there was some surprise at the scale, if not entirely the fact, of the Labour victory. Labour took almost 12 million votes (48.0 per cent of those cast) and emerged with 393 seats, as against the Conservatives and their allies who had only 210. Labour had polled well in all its core areas, but, most strikingly, it ate into what had been, hitherto, more difficult territory. In both the east and west Midlands it smashed through its previous best performance, 1929, to take more than half the seats. It won 84 of the 111 seats in the Greater London area. No fewer than 143 Labour MPs now represented constituencies south of the Severn–Wash line. This all meant a great change in the party's complexion; there was now no region of Great Britain where it did not have at least one MP. Even old Liberal areas like the south-west of England and rural north Wales yielded Labour victories. Labour took ostensibly unlikely seats like Taunton,

Winchester, Wycombe, Great Yarmouth, Dover and Watford. This was truly a national performance, and Labour seemed to have 'arrived' as a party of government.

All sorts of explanation have been advanced for the Labour victory of 1945. Some contemporary Labour explanations suggested that 'gradualness' had been inevitable after all: Labour was simply entering into its inheritance. According to this view, Labour's victory was 'the manifestation not simply of a transitory mood at one general election, but of a genuine and cumulative increase over many years of popular support for Socialist policies', an increase caused by 'the logic of events and the maturing development of circumstance' which had 'shaped the minds of men and women increasingly and inevitably to an understanding of the validity and inevitability of Socialist principles'.[38] Others have argued that 'the People's War' had been important in radicalizing the British people.[39] Yet such arguments rest on dubious assumptions.

In fact, a combination of negative and positive factors was responsible. The Conservatives suffered at the election from being the party that had taken Britain into a long and difficult war. The National governments of the 1930s were now seen as weak and vacillating, even criminally incompetent, in failing to see the true nature of the German threat and make stronger efforts to resist it; it was widely believed that the results of the war could have been achieved more easily at a much lower cost. In addition, five years of full employment, fostered by government action, suggested that the National governments had been cruelly negligent in allowing mass unemployment to remain a feature of British life in the 1930s. There grew up, also, the view that Lloyd George's promises of a better post-war world in 1918 had been thwarted by the selfishness of the Conservative MPs who were his main supporters. These were views which Churchill and the other leaders of the Conservative Party could do little to counter, not least because many members of the Caretaker government had themselves been staunch critics of the National government in the 1930s, and none more so than Churchill himself. Furthermore, while the opinion polls agreed that Churchill had been a fine war leader, there were misgivings about his future intentions, with fears that he was a warmonger and that he was, as his interwar record had sometimes suggested, somewhat unbalanced at times. Perhaps there was a weariness of 'great men'. All this helped Labour.

At the same time, Labour had had a good war. It no longer seemed as sectional as it had in the 1930s; its leaders were now well-known figures who had served effectively in government for five years. Churchill's attacks on Attlee during the campaign were counterproductive and increased the Labour leader's public profile. Labour's policies were more credible and comprehensible than previously, one of its main arguments being the need to develop and extend the measures that had helped to win the war. In addition, socialism and trade unionism had lost much of the opprobrium that had been attached to them before 1939, given the expansion and apparent statesmanship of the unions, and the fact that 'socialism' was not only clearly anti-fascist but also the doctrine which had helped the USSR to heroic resistance against, and later victory over, Nazi Germany. Furthermore, substantial sections of the population favoured further social reform, and believed that Labour was the party most likely to deliver it.

There was, though, no mass radicalization. Many voters undoubtedly remained cynical as to politicians' motives, and of the likelihood of them fulfilling their promises.[40] It is possible to surmise, in fact, that three (partly overlapping) groups of voters were crucial in helping Labour to victory. First, it seems clear that Labour polled a larger proportion of the working-class vote, and over a larger part of the country, than ever before. Here, fear of postwar unemployment was a factor, but there were others, including massively increased levels of unionization and fears about postwar production relations. A distrust of the Conservatives' record on social reform was also important here. Second, many young voters appear to have swung to Labour. To them, unemployment was associated with the Conservative-dominated National governments, rather than the 1929–31 Labour administration. Housing was also an issue which, while of broad significance, pressed particularly hard on young people, and so Labour's past record in local and national government, and its ongoing commitment to council housing, undoubtedly helped it.[41] More broadly, the idealistic aspects of Labour's rhetoric at the 1945 election might also have helped to swing youthful voters. Third, Labour increased its support among middle-class voters, or more particularly lower middle-class voters.[42] This was probably less significant than the rise in working-class support. But social reform might benefit them too; and some sections of the middle class liked Labour's emphasis on a big state, seeing in it opportunities of employment and status. To a certain extent, it might be argued, the Fabians' aim of a middle-class bureaucracy voting for Labour out of self-interest was being achieved.

As with the First World War, it was something of a paradox that Labour, which had always argued that peace was the essential pre-requisite of 'progress', should have done so well out of a long and bloody war. Labour was elected to office in 1945 with arguably its strongest ever team of leaders, and a programme second to none in its history for coherence, prioritization and applicability to the situation in which the country was placed. It now remained to be seen whether that programme could be implemented, and what the results would be, not just for Britain, but for the Labour party itself.

6   The Attlee Governments, 1945–51

The record of the Labour government elected in 1945 was impressive, and set high standards which subsequent Labour administrations would struggle to emulate. At home, it introduced significant social reforms, carried out extensive nationalization and maintained full employment throughout the transition to peace. Abroad, it played a leading role in establishing the system of alliances that dominated the world until the end of the Cold War, and led British withdrawal from India and Palestine. At the same time, though, it can be criticized. Left-wing critics have attacked it for the limitations of its nationalization policies, halting attitude towards redistribution, failure to remodel power relations in British society radically, adherence to the United States in foreign policy and its equivocal position on the Empire.[1] On the other hand, 'new right' critics have launched stinging attacks on what they see as its preference for welfare reform over the need to remodel the industrial base which paid for such changes.[2] Even so, it can still be seen, overall, as Labour's most successful period in office.

In the immediate aftermath of victory there were, once again, moves to replace Attlee with Morrison. However, Attlee's public profile had been boosted during the election campaign, not least by Churchill's backfiring attacks; and the latter's decision to resign immediately and advise the King to send for Attlee pre-empted Morrison's efforts, as Attlee accepted the commission and presented Labour MPs with a fait accompli. In any case, there was little hope for Morrison, who still aroused animosity among other Labour leaders, especially Bevin. Morrison was appointed Lord President of the Council, to act as de facto deputy Prime Minister and co-ordinator of domestic policy. After some hesitation Attlee appointed Dalton as Chancellor of the Exchequer and Bevin as Foreign Secretary.[3] Cripps, the fifth member of the new 'Big

Five' who were to dominate the early years of the government, was appointed President of the Board of Trade; he would play the leading role in industrial and production policy.

Of this 'Big Five', only Morrison had served in the previous Labour cabinet under MacDonald, and then for only five months. There were only four other survivors of that cabinet. Greenwood, now well past his best, became Lord Privy Seal; Alexander returned to the Admiralty; Benn (now Lord Stansgate) went to Air; and Addison, also ennobled, went to the Dominions Office. The left was represented in the new cabinet by Wilkinson (the only woman member) at Education, Bevan at Health and Shinwell at Fuel and Power. There were only six trade unionists in the cabinet; other than Bevin and Bevan they were not particularly significant or forceful figures.

The cabinet was altered in piecemeal fashion over the period between 1945 and the 1950 election, but there was never a thoroughgoing reshuffle. The main changes came in the autumn of what Dalton called the government's *annus horrendous* – 1947.[4] Its self-confidence had been severely shaken by the fuel and food crises and later the convertibility crisis (see below). Cripps wanted to replace Attlee with Bevin, but the plot failed because of lack of support from Morrison, Dalton and Bevin himself. Cripps, regardless, told Attlee that he thought he should resign. Attlee dismissed the suggestion but did appoint Cripps as Minister of Economic Affairs, and set up a new committee of the Big Five plus Addison – now leader in the Lords – to deal with major issues.[5] Cripps was succeeded at the Board of Trade by the 31-year-old Harold Wilson. Then, in November, Dalton inadvertently leaked budget secrets to a journalist, and, after some hesitation on all sides, resigned (he returned to the cabinet the following year in a lesser role).[6] The Treasury passed to Cripps, who thus combined Economic Affairs with the Exchequer.

This powerful team of leaders received strong support from the PLP throughout its term of office. There were occasional problems, as in 1948 when Alfred Edwards, MP for Middlesbrough East, was expelled from the party after attacking the nationalization of steel and the right to strike. Around the same time John Platts-Mills was expelled after a series of attacks on the government and calls for a pro-Soviet foreign policy. But the general tractability of Labour MPs could be seen in the fact that the PLP's standing orders were suspended throughout the life of the 1945 and 1950 parliaments. This loyalty had a number of causes. The suspension of the PLP's standing orders created a comradely atmosphere, in stark contrast to 1929–31 or to some later governments. As Morrison said, parliament 'would be a dull assembly if we overdid discipline', and he hoped that there would be 'a good deal of free speech, even to the extent of disagreeing with Ministers, so long as it [did]n't upset the apple cart'.[7] The Liaison Committee between ministers and backbenchers was more successful than in 1929–31, mainly because the leadership took it more seriously, and Morrison's appointment of 17 policy committees to liaise with individual ministers generally worked well, although the foreign policy committee was a notable exception.[8] In addition, the government did 'produce the goods', going full speed ahead on its manifesto commitments. Two-thirds of Labour MPs were new to parliament, and more than half of these were middle class.[9] Thus a large number of MPs were out to make a career for themselves, and this tended to encourage people towards loyalty. It might also be that middle-class MPs, in a movement which remained, in spirit, very much working class, were feeling their way a little.[10]

A further factor inhibiting fractiousness in the PLP was the unions' strong support for the government.[11] Labour ministers in the 1960s and 1970s would look back almost incredulously at the ease with which union–party relations seemed to have been handled in the 1940s. Strikes and lockouts remained illegal under wartime Order 1305, which was not formally rescinded until 1951. As in wartime, disputes did take place, but fewer days were lost through strikes on average than in the period 1932–38, itself a time of relative calm. This degree of industrial peace was due less to Order 1305 than to the closeness, both personally and in terms of outlook, between ministers and union leaders; the union leaders' sense of involvement in government, both formally and informally; and general contentment with a government which, in contrast to 1929–31, delivered much of what the unions wanted. The 1927 Trade Disputes Act was repealed in 1946; full employment and rising working-class living standards were maintained; and social reform was implemented. The key demands of many individual unions, such as the nationalization of coal mining and railways, were also fulfilled.

Faced with all this, there were few openings for a cogent left-wing challenge to the Attlee administration. The parliamentary left was undoubtedly enervated – as Attlee had intended – by the appointment of Bevan to the cabinet, and Cripps in office was rather different from the Cripps of the previous decade. But, in addition, the left's lack of a coherent and distinctive ideology kept it marginalized. It pushed for further public ownership, and was perhaps decisive in the final determination to go ahead with the nationalization of steel. But it had little else to say, particularly on domestic policy. For example, it did not mount a serious challenge to the public corporation model of nationalization. At first it was more vocal on foreign affairs, but, as will be seen below, the onset of the Cold War had helped to drive the left into more or less grudging support of the main outlines of Bevin's foreign policy by 1949.

Positive perceptions of the government were based, in part, on its ability to handle the economy. Overall economic management was broadly successful. The economic extremes that had followed the First World War were avoided. Unemployment hardly ever exceeded 500,000, except in the wholly exceptional circumstances of February 1947. Indeed, labour shortages were the main problem. Inflation remained under control, helped by a wage freeze between 1948 and 1950. Taxation remained high, but the standard rate of income tax was reduced from 50 to 45 per cent in 1947.

This was all the more remarkable given that it was achieved in a context of severe and continuing exchange and balance of payments problems. The war had cost Britain about a quarter of its total wealth. Overseas investments had been wound down to pay for the war. Even so, Britain had been heavily reliant on the generous provision of Lend-Lease assistance from the USA. Hopes that this might continue for some time were dashed when the end of the war with Japan in August 1945 was followed by the equally abrupt termination of Lend-Lease. A massive crisis loomed, and a British delegation under Keynes set off for Washington to negotiate a loan. Agreement was finally reached in December 1945 on a loan of $3,750,000 from the USA and $1,250,000 from Canada, but the terms were difficult and included making sterling fully convertible by mid-1947.[12]

The loan gave Britain valuable breathing space, allowing the government to push ahead with reforms safe in the knowledge that domestic living standards could be maintained. Without it, imports would have had to be reduced dramatically, with a concomitant decrease in living standards. But, inevitably, when convertibility was introduced in July 1947, the pound collapsed. The result was a sterling crisis and the suspension of convertibility after just five weeks. Ultimately, as seen above, Cripps replaced Dalton as Chancellor. Judged on its own terms, his tenure at the Treasury was the best period of Cripps's varied career. His ascetic lifestyle fitted well with the nation's need to tighten its belt.[13] Even so, the crucial assistance again came, in 1948, from the United States, in the shape of Marshall Aid, which aimed to revive western Europe and see off the Communist 'threat'. Britain received around $2,700,000 to the end of 1950, by which time the position had improved to such an extent that it could announce that it no longer required assistance.[14]

Before then, however, there had been another sterling crisis. During the spring of 1949 the balance of payments position began to take a turn for the worse, and with Cripps absent, ill, three young ministers, all economists – Gaitskell, Wilson and Jay – were forced to recommend devaluation (reluctantly in Wilson's case).[15] Cripps and the cabinet agreed, and on 18 September the pound was devalued from $4.03 to $2.80. This was a sensible move; devaluation was not a national disgrace, simply a recognition of changed realities. But the episode had deeper significance, all the same. Unlike in 1931, the government did not panic, and remained united, while the financial establishment, for its part, was willing to see a Labour government devalue. Wilson's reluctance to devalue would prove to be a signpost for his behaviour when, as Prime Minister in the 1960s, he would again be faced with pressure on sterling. Finally, the crisis showed yet again the fragility of Britain's exchange position and, with it, all that Labour was trying to do. That the government was able, nonetheless, to press ahead with its policies for industry and social reform in such a potentially delicate situation makes its achievements in those areas all the more remarkable.

The 1945 manifesto had promised an extensive round of nationalization: the Bank of England, fuel and power, inland transport and iron and steel would all be taken over by the state with 'fair compensation' paid to the owners, and be run 'efficiently in the interests of consumers, coupled with proper status and conditions

for the workers employed in them'.[16] The Bank of England and
civil aviation were nationalized in 1946; coal, rail, road haulage and
cable and wireless in 1947; and electricity and gas in 1948. Most
of these measures were relatively uncontroversial, although there
was strong Conservative opposition in the House of Commons
over road haulage and gas. Steel, however, was more problematic.
The issue divided the cabinet, with Morrison and others favouring
an interim measure short of full public ownership and some, like
Dalton, favouring postponement. Finally, legislation nationalizing
the industry was passed, against strong Conservative opposition,
with the proviso that it would not come into effect until after the
next general election.[17]

The doubts over steel were due in part to factors like the cool-
ness of the steelworkers' union towards nationalization, and the
fact that it was quite efficiently run in private hands. But ministers' hesitancy seems also to have stemmed from growing doubts
as to the efficacy of nationalization per se, for the nationalization
measures passed by the Attlee governments did pose problems.
Many of the industries were nationalized because of their erstwhile inefficiency; only the state, it was argued, could sustain vital
industries which were unattractive to private investors. This was
particularly the case with coal and rail. But this in turn made a
rod for these industries' and Labour's backs, since they could be
held up, at the time and later, as examples of 'inefficient' 'socialist' industrial policy. Second, the form of nationalization, the public corporation, posed problems. The industries were to be run by
boards which would be appointed by the minister but free from
ministerial interference in day-to-day affairs. But the insistence
that each nationalized board should operate its industry on business lines meant a general lack of co-ordination *between* industries.
Even worse, the industries varied in their administrative arrangements, some being rather less centralized than others and most
adopting different regional coverages.[18] This inevitably led to
problems, and, coming from a government supposedly committed to economic planning, was self-defeating. Furthermore,
there was no attempt to redistribute the balance of power within
industries. No attempt was made at trade union representation
on the boards, let alone workers' control, even though many of
the industries were heavily unionized; that, in the case of coal,
one union spoke for virtually the entire workforce; and that some

people on the left were demanding it.[19] The government does not seem to have taken such proposals seriously, with Cripps speaking witheringly of worker-controlled industry as 'almost impossible' until workers had 'more experience ... of the managerial side of the industry'.[20] If anything, workers *lost* control since negotiations were now still more likely to take place at the centre, remote from the daily life of the worker. On one level this was understandable. Britain was in a tight spot. It needed efficient industry to help the balance of payments, which was in a precarious position (though at the same time the very existence of the crisis meant that it could not have undertaken an extensive modernization of Britain's industrial base even had it been inclined to do so). On a party political level, Labour wanted to prove it was respectable and responsible, rather than to indulge in untried experiments that might backfire. It has also been argued that traditions of trade-union voluntarism would have meant a reluctance of workers to participate, in any case. Yet there was more to it than that. Joint consultative committees during the war had proved effective, with wholehearted workforce and union participation. Some experiments in workers' control could have been tried at regional or even plant level, with the aim of extending them if they proved successful, or abandoning or modifying them if they did not. Instead, the public corporation model carried all before it, and can be seen as having led to poor industrial relations and, after a very brief honeymoon period, lower levels of worker commitment to the principle of nationalization than might otherwise have been achieved.

But, of course, experimentation would have flown in the face of the by now almost all-pervasive Whig interpretation of Labour history; that is, the view that Labour was moving ever onward and upward. Nowhere was this better demonstrated than in the books published in the run-up to the party's fiftieth birthday, such as Cole's *History of the Labour Party from 1914* (1948), the official three-volume extravaganza *The British Labour Party* (1948) and Francis Williams's *Fifty Years' March* (1949). Labour's rise had been inevitable; it would have come about earlier but for the trickery of its opponents, but now, 'Labour was in power with an absolute majority at last'.[21] A second element of this, bearing specifically on nationalization, was the belief that, since 1900, a process of natural selection had been taking place in Labour policy. Thus guild socialism and its critique of statism was a mutant strain of British socialism which had become extinct through its inherent weaknesses, a historical curio, of about as much immediate relevance as Clarion Cycling Clubs or Labour Churches and of considerably less salience than Keir Hardie's cap. The few critics of the public corporation who did emerge could make little headway when they were deemed to be sifting through a ragbag of historical relics.

Labour's line on nationalization meant that a rigid barrier existed *between* the public and private sectors. There was no attempt to practise a mixed economy at micro as well as macro level, with government taking a stake in private companies. Indeed, Labour's attitude towards private industry at this time was generally conciliatory and non-interventionist. Wilson noted that 'this problem of the relationship between Government and private industry is almost a vacuum in Socialist thought', and this should come as no surprise.[22] Labour socialism was predicated on the idea of successful capitalist enterprise as the dynamic force which would bring about a socialist society. Since 1931 Labour had switched away from the somewhat laissez-faire approach of MacDonald and Snowden, but the essential reliance on the private sector remained intact. Most Labourites did not want to nationalize all industries any more than their predecessors had. The Labour government *was* eager, given its balance of payments problems, to encourage greater production and productivity, especially in the export industries. This, and the legacy of wartime and the pre-war period, meant that it talked a lot about planning, but by 1951 Labour had moved a long way even from this.

During the war, Labour had hoped to secure the co-operation of capitalists in an extensive and enduring system of controls of private industry. At the height of the conflict, some civil servants and industrialists had seemed in favour of the idea, but such enthusiasm as there had been waned in the latter part of the war.[23] This opposition to state intervention posed a problem for Labour once it came to power, since the balance of payments position required the full co-operation of all sides of industry, including industrialists. Accordingly, the decision was taken to avoid confrontation. Labour did attempt, especially later in the period, to push industry towards greater levels of employer–workforce consultation, and to establish development councils for various industries. But these depended on industrialists' good will, and by the later 1940s, with a newly self-confident Conservative Party in the wings, there was little pressure on them to conform. Realizing this, Wilson, as President of the Board of Trade, tried to persuade his colleagues of the need for greater coercion, advocating the appointment of government directors on companies' boards, increased controls and nationalization of persistently recalcitrant companies.[24] However, little was done: except for a gradually tapering degree of state control over materials and labour power, policy towards private industry remained largely one of exhortation.

Given the reluctance to intervene in private industry, even to have much to do with the day-to-day management of industries taken into the public sector, planning came to grief. Even during the 1930s, some socialists had doubted the efficacy of physical controls and, during the war, many had been impressed with the potential of the budget as a tool of economic management. As it became clear that only coercion could bring private industry fully into planning, there was a growing tendency to see budgetary methods as a better, more consensual way of proceeding. The unpopularity of controls was also a factor in the move from planning. Rationing and other controls remained long after the war ended; bread rationing was introduced for the first time in 1947. Criticism, fuelled by vigorous Conservative propaganda, soon reached fever pitch, and it was in an attempt to ease these attacks that Wilson held his 'Bonfire of Controls' in November 1948. Another problem which was increasingly recognized was that manpower planning, in particular, involved the direction of labour, which the movement had always resisted.[25] Although new efforts were made in 1947, with the establishment of new planning bodies, it was clear by 1950 that physical controls were being replaced by budgetary methods as the chief means of state economic management. The result of this, of course, was a loss of distinctiveness in policy and a growing perception that there was little to choose between Labour and Conservative economic management.

In social policy, Labour's greatest achievement came in health. The minister responsible, Bevan (at 48 the youngest member of the cabinet in 1945), not only had a reputation as a rebel, but he also had administrative ability and, at this stage of his career, drive. Although a national health service was already on the political agenda, dispute remained as to its exact nature and scope. In late 1945 the cabinet agreed a draft bill to nationalize hospitals, which would be administered by regional boards, taking them out of the control of local authorities and voluntary bodies. However, there were substantial concessions to the medical profession, including the preservation of capitation fees instead of the introduction of salaries for doctors, and the maintenance of private practice and pay-beds in NHS hospitals. The bill passed its second reading in May 1946, but the doctors remained unhappy, and there followed almost two years of wrangling with the British Medical Association which only ended in April 1948 when Bevan announced that there was no question of a move towards a salaried medical profession. The service, free at the point of use, now came formally into operation.[26]

Another legacy of wartime was the pressure that had built up to do something about social security. Here, another Welshman, James Griffiths, Minister of National Insurance, piloted the National Insurance Act through parliament in 1946. Under the Act, people in work paid a flat-rate national insurance contribution, in return for which they (and the wives of male contributors) were eligible for flat-rate pensions, sickness benefit, unemployment benefit and funeral benefit. This was followed in 1948 by the National Assistance Act, which gave financial help to those with no other source of income. To Labourites, this all seemed like a great advance. The universal principle was established, a contrast with the means testing that had characterized the interwar years (although some means testing did in fact remain).[27] Yet criticisms were also made. There was inequity in the treatment of men and women. Rates of benefit were not set at a realistic rate of subsistence.[28] In addition, the principle of flat-rate contributions was regressive, taking a larger percentage of one's income the less one earned. However, Labour was under pressure, not least from working-class voters, to ensure that money was not wasted; and the insurance principle was generally accepted as fair.[29] Finally, Labour's continuing concentration on the world of work meant that minds focused most on unemployment benefits, and here the argument was that in a situation of full employment and labour shortages there was no real problem if benefits were pitched rather low: people would not be out of work for long unless they wanted to be, and if they wanted to be then they should not be supported generously in their idleness.

Labour's record on housing – also Bevan's responsibility – was perceived as less successful. By the end of the war, the situation was grave. Enemy action, lack of repairs during wartime and the virtual cessation of new building for five years had all taken their toll. There was a massive shortage of housing units, while many existing houses had become slums. Many local authorities entered peacetime with high hopes of rapid progress, but these hopes were soon dashed. In Hull, for example, it was estimated that there was a shortfall of 32,000 dwellings, and the corporation aimed to build 5000 in the first post-war year; but due to shortages of materials and labour, and confusion at the centre, the city was able to erect only 1766 permanent and 2457 temporary dwellings by 1950.[30] These failures were symptomatic of the national position. Early problems of a large number of starts but few completions were gradually overcome, but the number of houses built remained unimpressive. Fewer than 200,000 permanent dwellings were completed between 1944 and the end of 1947, and although just over 200,000 were completed in each of the succeeding four years, these figures did not approach the annual average figure of 361,000 dwellings for 1934–38.[31] Labour had promised a great deal more than it delivered, and though it did face severe constraints it might be argued that the commitment of the minister in charge, Bevan, to quality over quantity was a mistake. By 1951 there was an estimated shortfall of over a million housing units.[32] In so far as 79 per cent of the new housing was owned by local authorities, though, the party was clearly adding further to its clientage up and down the country.[33]

In education, Labour was not innovative at all. The 1944 Act had seen to that. At this stage, Labour was by no means against the principle of selection at age 11 which most local authorities had adopted, while an attack on the private sector would have been seen as a diversion from larger concerns facing the administration and would also have gone against the non-confrontational image that the government was trying to portray. The main achievements were the raising of the school-leaving age to 15 in 1947 and a general increase in expenditure. By 1951 the party was moving away from selection and towards comprehensivization, but as a policy for a future, rather than the present, Labour government.

Labour's record in social policy, then, was generally sound, with clear success in the creation of the National Health Service but with more mixed results elsewhere. But Labour had at least set out the parameters of a system of state welfare more extensive than anything previously known in Britain. This system, though it can be criticized, did improve the life chances of most of the population. And, had Labour remained in office after 1951, many of the shortcomings outlined above might have been overcome. However, Labour had created a welfare state without really addressing broader questions about the nature of 'the state'. The war and its aftermath almost doubled the number of civil servants, and the state had taken on new roles in wide areas of the nation's life, but Labour in power did not really address any of the constitutional implications of these developments. Perhaps it also became too complacent about its achievement, which meant that, in later years, it would fail to reflect adequately on areas where improvements were still needed.[34]

The basic premise of mainstream Labourism was that the existing system of parliamentary government, though not perfect, was perfectible. Accordingly, there were some changes, addressing some longstanding Labour grievances. Plural voting was abolished, along with the 12 university seats. There was the first major redistribution of constituencies since 1918, and a boundary commission was set up on a permanent basis to review the situation periodically. The local government franchise, hitherto restricted to ratepayers and their spouses, was now granted to all adults. And in 1949 the delaying powers of the House of Lords were reduced from two years to one. Otherwise, however, little was done. There was no reform of the electoral system (and, it must be admitted, very little demand for it outside the tiny Liberal Party). More surprisingly, perhaps, there was no substantial reform of the House of Lords. Apart from the creation of some new Labour peers, nothing was done to reform its composition (life peerages only came in 1958). One reason for this was the innate constitutional conservatism of Labour's leaders, but another was Labour's ability to work with the 'upper house'. Addison, as leader in the Lords, headed an effective team of Labour peers and was generally able to pass legislation without difficulty. This merely reinforced the view that to take on the Lords when there was little, if any, popular demand for such a move would appear vindictive, small-minded and doctrinaire, distracting the government from more pressing concerns.

The fate of local government was fairly predictable, given the growing statism of Labour over the previous period. Apart from reforming the local government franchise, little was done except to strip authorities of certain functions. G. D. H. Cole's appeals for a renewed emphasis on local authorities, and a new regional tier of government, were ignored.[35] Councils lost their hospitals and, in some cases, their gas and electricity undertakings, to remote regional boards or nationalized industries which owed more loyalty to central than to local government. Furthermore, legislation enacted in 1945 made all local authority loan issues subject to Treasury approval. At the time, there was little resistance to all this. Morrison, one of the few members of the cabinet with recent local government experience, did try to resist the nationalization of hospitals, but without success. Yet in the end it was to matter. Ultimately, local government in many parts of the country – not least where Labour was ensconced in power – was to become enfeebled, enervated and prone to inefficiency and, sometimes, corruption. Turnout in local elections, already falling before the war, fell away further. It would be unfair to blame the 1945–51 government alone for this. But it hastened the process. British 'democracy' became more centralized than ever, at just the time when the functions of the state were expanding. The result was a massive concentration of power at the centre and the increasing inability of elected representatives to oversee the actions of the executive effectively. It also meant that, by the 1980s, local government had become a soft underbelly through which a government of a very different hue could attack much of what Labour had achieved in the immediate post-war period.

The 1945–51 period therefore saw new departures in domestic policy which set up a structure that would remain in place, more or less, for many years to come. The same was true in foreign policy. Here, the main theme of the period, in retrospect, was the development of the Cold War. At first, it was hoped that wartime co-operation between Britain, the USA and the USSR could be continued. But during the latter part of 1945 matters began to deteriorate, and by early 1946 Foreign Office officials were beginning to suggest a less conciliatory line should be taken towards the USSR. Meetings of the tripartite Council of Foreign Ministers became increasingly acrimonious. The Labour left blamed Bevin for this, and claimed that he was either virulently anti-Communist or so much in the hands of his officials that he could not see beyond their blind anti-Soviet prejudice. They favoured the creation of a European 'third force' to stand between the two superpowers.[36] But such a course was never realistic, given that the USSR was clearly committed to enforcing its rule over the countries in its sphere. Bevin was his own man and a fierce realist, and the promulgation of the 'Keep Left' manifesto in March 1947 by his Labour critics was a fairly futile exercise, although it caused a stir at the time.

Deteriorating relations with the USSR and increased warmth between Britain and the USA meant events were moving away from Keep Left. Suspicion of Soviet aims increased rapidly. In 1948, the Communist coup in Czechoslovakia, the creation of the Communist Information Bureau (seen in the west as a successor to the now defunct Communist International), Moscow's break with Marshal Tito in Yugoslavia and the Soviet blockade of Berlin all suggested that the USSR intended to strengthen its grip on its sphere of influence in eastern and central Europe. Anti-Communist feeling was further strengthened by the Communists' victory in China in 1949 and the announcement that the Soviet Union had developed its own atomic weapons. By 1948 many of the Labourites who had been criticizing Bevin were coming to admit that there was now no real prospect of co-operation with the USSR or of wresting eastern Europe from its influence to join a 'third force'.[37]

Meanwhile, relations with the USA improved. At first, there had been very real fears that America would withdraw into isolation, as had happened at the end of the First World War. Relations were not improved by the abrupt termination of Lend-Lease in 1945 and the stringent terms of the American loan agreed in early 1946. It was partly uncertainty about future American intentions that led a small group of cabinet ministers to decide, in January 1947, to develop an independent British nuclear weapons capacity.[38] However, matters soon began to ease with the help of the 'Soviet threat'. When, in February 1947, Bevin told Washington that Britain could no longer aid Greece and Turkey, the Americans agreed to take over those responsibilities. They also accepted the suspension of sterling convertibility that August.

Marshall Aid was warmly welcomed in 1948, and Britain's with-drawal from Palestine in the same year removed a source of ten-sion. And in April 1949, the North Atlantic Treaty Organization (NATO) was formed, for the first time binding Britain and the USA together in a formal peacetime alliance. It guaranteed its member states against external aggression, and was to prove, in the event, the long-term basis of British foreign policy.

By contrast, Labour's attitude towards continental Europe was equivocal. In the interwar period there had been those, particu-larly in France, who had argued for the development of some kind of unity among European states. This had not gone down very well with such British Labourites as had taken any notice.[39] After the war, integrationist ideas were revived. In France, espe-cially, many people saw closer European co-operation as the key to avoiding future wars. The result was the development of the agreements and institutions which were to lead, ultimately, to the Treaty of Rome which set up the European Economic Community (EEC) in 1957. At first, Britain was quite closely involved in these developments. However, the intensification of the process saw gradual British disengagement, so that by 1951 it was reason-ably clear that Britain would stand aside.[40] This has been seen as a tragic mistake, but such a view can be challenged. First, there were diplomatic considerations. Up to 1947, Labour still had hopes of 'Big Three' co-operation; in other words, Britain would be a major power in its own right, and so close co-operation in Europe could only be a distraction. The collapse of such hopes led to an increase in British involvement in 1947–48, but then improved relations with the USA provided a further distraction. Second, there was resistance within the Labour Party itself, both from those who wanted a broader internationalism and from those who were essentially nationalist in outlook and wanted no internationalism at all beyond, perhaps, applauding foreign fra-ternal delegates at Labour Party conferences. Finally, there was a third reason – the Empire/Commonwealth.

In Labour mythology, the withdrawal from India in 1947 and Palestine in 1948 were the first manifestations of a general design to wind up the Empire. The reality was rather different. Labour ministers were committed to the maintenance of Britain's posi-tion as a great power. Though this stance was occasionally ques-tioned, for example, by Dalton (eager, as Chancellor, to cut expenditure), it was never successfully challenged.[41] As the Cold War developed, Labour's fear of communism made it reluctant to give up areas which might then fall under Soviet influence. There also remained questions about whether many of the colonies were 'fit' for self-government or whether, given a British withdrawal, they would collapse into anarchy or white settler tyranny, as seemed to be happening in South Africa with the introduction of apartheid in 1948. Finally, given Britain's straitened economic circumstances, there were hopes that colonial 'development' would provide Britain with increased economic resources. On the other hand, American hostility to the continuation of imperialism of the old kind, criticism from that part of the Labour left which also called for colonial liberation and the dangers of the Empire becoming an economic burden rather than a boon, all pulled in the opposite direction.

These contradictions fed through into policy. At one extreme were India and Palestine. Labour hoped at first that India would continue gradual political development to become a single entity within the Commonwealth. However, a British mission under Cripps in 1946 made little progress, and it became clear that British rule was breaking down rapidly. In March 1947 the decision was taken to withdraw, in order to prevent disaster, and the process was completed that August. Although withdrawal was presented as a victory for common sense, it was followed by massive ethnic conflict which claimed up to a million lives and produced millions of refugees. The ultimate result – partition into a largely Hindu India and a mainly Muslim Pakistan – was the opposite of what the government had wanted.[42] Withdrawal from Palestine the following year was also accompanied by massive violence. Both withdrawals were prompted more by expediency than by principle, and the British left behind many problems which were only 'solved', ultimately, by bloodshed.

The loss of India did not so much presage the end of the Empire as its reorientation towards Africa. Here, there was very little sense of imminent British withdrawal; far from it. Bevin argued that, if the resources of Britain's African colonies could be fully exploited, it might be able to rival the USA as a superpower.[43] There were, therefore, attempts both to 'develop' the colonies as markets and as sources of raw materials, and to increase their dollar-earning potential in the interests of the home country. The results were, first, a series of attempts to locate and extract mineral resources and to propagate new crops, the most spectacular example of which was the fiasco and public humiliation for the government which attended the attempt to grow groundnuts in Tanganyika; and, second, the closer binding together of the sterling area. The latter development was significant especially for the future, since one of Wilson's main arguments against devaluation in the 1960s would be that Britain had a responsibility towards its less-developed partners in that community. Overall, the result was that Britain 'actively and blatantly exploited colonial producers': bulk-buying meant producers were getting less than the world price for their goods, while the terms of trade were deliberately turned in Britain's favour.[44]

If there was no grand design for the Empire, there was no master plan either for one of its legacies: immigration from the 'new Commonwealth', particularly (at this time) the West Indies. In 1948 a number of Jamaicans arrived to look for work in Britain during the period of labour shortage. Eleven Labour MPs demanded an immediate ban on immigration. More generally, many trade unions saw it as a threat to employment prospects and wage levels, and some union branches refused to accept black workers as members. Although, in February 1951, 97 Labour MPs signed a Commons motion demanding racial equality throughout the Commonwealth, the government's attitude remained hesitant. No attempt was made to legislate against racial discrimination.[45] Already, in microcosm, Labour's problems with the issue of race were beginning to emerge. By 1949, Labour's reforming impulse had largely atrophied. The early optimism about domestic and foreign policy had been replaced by a more world-weary air as ministers, many of whom had been in office almost continuously since 1940, became stale, and more likely to want to safeguard existing gains than to take risks in trying to make new ones. Increasingly, attention was turned towards the timing of the next general election, and on 11 January 1950 it was announced that this would take place on 23 February.

Labour had reason to be optimistic. Party organization and finance were in good shape, with individual membership continuing to increase from 487,000 in 1945 to 729,000 in 1949, and union-affiliated membership almost doubling to 4,946,000 over the same period.[46] Its record at by-elections had been formidable, with only low swings to the Conservatives and no seats lost. Some progress had continued to be made in local elections, too, although the loss of overall control of Birmingham, Glasgow and Manchester in 1947, and of Bristol, Leicester, Newcastle and Wolverhampton in 1949 served to warn against complacency.

The 1950 general election campaign was not very inspiring. Labour's manifesto was about consolidation, with proposals for further nationalization confined to sugar, cement and water supply.[47] By and large, the party leadership was prepared to be judged on its record. The Conservatives, meanwhile, had improved their organization greatly, and had also done enough in the presentation of their policies to suggest that they would not, if elected, start to dismantle everything that Labour had done. Labour won the election, but with an overall majority of just five seats, with 315 to the Conservatives' 298. This was not such a bad performance, and with 46.1 per cent of the votes cast, the party was some way ahead of the Conservatives' 43.5 per cent. However, the loss of 78 seats compared with 1945 was disappointing, and the fact that there were only nine Liberals and three 'others' meant that Labour's room for parliamentary manoeuvre was very limited.

Three major factors seem to have pulled Labour back from its 1945 heights. First, some middle-class electors who had voted Labour or abstained in 1945 now voted Conservative. The proportion of non-manual workers voting Labour fell from 28 per cent in 1945 to 23 per cent, a much sharper fall than among manual workers.[48] They might well have been alienated by the government's apparent preference for working-class interests and its specific failings, for example, in not lifting rationing and controls. Labour support among men – where it had had a massive lead over the Conservatives in 1945 – fell significantly, from 55 per cent to 47 (as against a much smaller fall among women, from 47 per cent to 43.5).[49] This suggests, in turn, that explanations which cite militant housewives and resentment from women about rationing as a prime cause of Labour's worse performance are somewhat wide of the mark. Second, and linked to this, the Conservatives had greatly improved their image and organization. Finally, the redistribution of seats carried out in 1949 affected Labour adversely by taking seats from its declining heartlands, especially in inner-city areas, and giving them to the suburban areas which had burgeoned since 1918; on the whole, 'Labour's losses were heaviest in the dormitory areas of the big towns, particularly of London'.[50] Of course, Labour still won. But it was a rather hollow victory. Labour had so little left by way of distinctive policies that a further term of office could not fail to be deflating. And, in addition, the Conservatives now had the scent of blood in their nostrils, and felt confident enough to force the Commons through long sittings which weakened Labour morale as its MPs were left with no choice but to attend. Partly as a result of all this, the government began to fall apart.

This was most noticeable at cabinet level. In October 1950 Cripps, terminally ill, was finally forced to resign as Chancellor. The potential successors were Morrison, Bevan and Gaitskell (at this stage, Minister of Economic Affairs and not a member of the cabinet). Morrison's successes were clearly behind him, and in any case Attlee felt a strong antipathy towards him. Bevan had seniority over Gaitskell in both party and cabinet terms, had a quick mind, and might have proved a success. However, it seems that Attlee doubted his stability, feared the effect on American opinion, and was worried that Bevan's appointment would have antagonized Morrison and the right of the party. In the end, therefore, he chose Gaitskell.[51] Gaitskell was well suited to the post in many ways. A trained economist and junior minister of proven competence, he had been closely involved with Treasury affairs, virtually deputizing for Cripps at various times. However, his appointment antagonized Bevan, who expressed his 'consternation and astonishment' to Attlee; it also upset Wilson, who, though younger and probably not a serious contender himself, had been in cabinet since 1947 and felt threatened by the appointment.[52] Gaitskell's appointment also hemmed Attlee in when he had to choose a successor to the ailing Bevin in March 1951. The premier could not afford to pass over Morrison a second time, given the latter's continuing popularity on the right and centre of the party. Morrison was to be somewhat unlucky as Foreign Secretary, being faced with crises and spy scandals which were not his fault, but even so he lacked his predecessor's 'feel' for foreign affairs and it is difficult to resist the commonly held view that he was not a success in the office.

Less than seven weeks later, a cabinet crisis erupted. The outbreak of the Korean War in June 1950 meant that Britain had to rearm so that it could take part on the side of the United Nations-backed South against Chinese-backed North Korea. In January 1951 a massive rearmament package of £4.7 billion was announced. Bevan opposed it on the grounds that it was simply too much, that such an amount could not be spent (nor was it, in the event).[53] It was also clear that Gaitskell was prepared to sacrifice expenditure in other areas to pay for the programme. In particular, Gaitskell planned to freeze NHS expenditure at £393 million, the figure for 1950–51, by cutting spending on hospitals and saving £20 million by charging for false teeth and spectacles. There followed a period of cabinet wrangling, at the end of which Bevan, Wilson and a junior minister, John Freeman, resigned. Bevan's precise motivations have been much debated. His enemies, then and since, have seen his actions as a self-seeking attempt to re-establish his credentials as a left-winger and as the product of frustrated careerism. These factors were certainly not insignificant.[54] But there were also two substantive issue at stake. The first was the NHS – if a Labour government legitimized charges then the pass would have been sold; the Conservatives, when in office, would be able to cut entitlement to treatment and impose charges while Labour's opposition would be stymied. Second, there was the question of the future direction of the Labour Party. Bevan was not anti-intellectual, far from it. But he had a strong suspicion of Oxford meritocrats like Gaitskell, whose experience of the Labour movement was, he felt, only skin-deep.

The majority of the cabinet backed Gaitskell, however. Loyalty to the leadership was one of the main planks of the Labour movement's ethos, and the leadership was backing the Chancellor very strongly. In retrospect, though, it seems astonishing that some solution could not have been found. The £23 million saving on the NHS was less than half of 1 per cent of the total rearmament package. In short, both Attlee and his deputy, Morrison, failed a crucial test of leadership. Many of their colleagues put personal distaste for Bevan before political realities. It would be impossible for any but the most unreconstructed Gaitskellite to argue that the government was stronger without Bevan than with him. In the end, two of Labour's leading post-war figures – Bevan and Wilson – were replaced in the cabinet by Sir Hartley Shawcross and Alfred Robens. More broadly, the degree of backbiting on both sides showed the extent to which the confidence of 1945 had waned.

In policy terms, too, Labour seemed to have lost its way. The nationalization of iron and steel, carried by the previous parliament, was implemented in February 1951. Rationing and controls continued to be abolished, although not so quickly that they took the powerful rallying cry to 'set the people free' from the Conservatives. But other major measures were not forthcoming. Meanwhile, the pay freeze collapsed and industrial relations became more fraught.

It had been accepted from the start of the 1950 parliament that the next general election could not be long delayed. Ultimately, Attlee chose to hold polling on 25 October 1951, having decided against early 1952 because the King would be on a tour of Africa at that time (in fact he would be dead). Labour's manifesto stood largely on the government's record since 1945. It argued that the party was best placed to maintain peace and full employment, to increase production, to reduce the cost of living and 'to build a just society'. The 'shopping list' of further industries for nationalization, which had characterized the 1950 manifesto, was dropped, and replaced by a vague pledge to take over 'concerns which fail the nation'. Existing policies, such as development councils, would be pushed forward, and there was a promise to 'associate the workers more closely with the administration of public industries and services'. Emphasis continued to be placed on the construction of housing for rent, rather than for sale.[55] But on the whole, the manifesto was a defence of the record of the government and an attempt to contrast it with the perceivedly dark days of Conservative domination between the wars.

Labour attracted 13,948,883 votes at the election, 48.8 per cent of those cast. This has proved to be the party's highest ever percentage of the vote, and no party would gain a higher number of votes until the Conservatives in 1992. But these votes produced only 295 seats, whereas the Conservatives, with 48.0 per cent, took 321. Labour made a net loss of 20 seats at the election, gaining two from the Liberals (both in rural Wales) but losing 22. The average swing against Labour was only 0.9 per cent, but an above average swing was enough to tip marginal seats in Lancashire, the Home Counties and East Anglia towards the Conservatives.[56] In terms of social class, Labour lost further middle-class support but managed to take a higher share of the working-class vote than ever before. Support among women was almost back to the level of 1945, but male support, though reviving from 1950, was still well below the level achieved in 1945.[57] As in the 1930s, the collapse of the Liberal Party (which fielded 109 candidates as against 475 in 1950) worked against the interests of Labour, since those who had voted Liberal in 1950 now split almost two to one in favour of the Conservatives.[58] Still, a national swing of only 1 per cent from the 1951 result would give Labour an overall majority in parliament at the next election, and a 2 per cent swing would give it a majority of around 30, quite enough to last a full term.[59]

For now, though, Labour was back in opposition. It had been in office for all but a couple of months of the past eleven and a half years, six of them on its own. During the period since 1945 it had helped to change the face of Britain at home and abroad. It had taken around 20 per cent of the economy into the public sector, created a National Health Service and made sweeping changes to the social security system, although it had not addressed questions of the nature of the state which were raised by these considerable increases in its functions. It had maintained full employment and, until its last few months in office, kept inflation firmly under control. Abroad, it had, to some extent, muddled through with the Empire, but in deciding to have an independent nuclear weapons capability and playing a leading role in NATO, it had set the parameters for British foreign policy until the end of the Cold War four decades later. There were problems with this legacy, of course. But in the final analysis it would be difficult to argue that this government did not make a significant contribution towards the improvement of the lives of the people who supported it, and indeed of many others. For that alone the Attlee governments deserve most – though not all – the plaudits that Labourites have heaped upon them in the years since 1951. However, they also left flaws in their legacy which, in retrospect, can be seen to have condemned these achievements to at least a questionable future in the longer term.

7   Searching for a New Direction, 1951–64

In the immediate aftermath of the 1951 election, it was widely believed that Labour would be able to regroup in opposition, and that, for all their talk of having changed, the Conservatives under Churchill would soon reveal their true colours. They would seek to undo the Labour government's achievements and, as a result, face nemesis at the next general election. Of course, things turned out rather differently. The Conservatives were to win further elections in 1955 and 1959, each time with a larger majority than before. Labour would not return to office until 1964, and even then only with a tiny parliamentary majority. The period from 1951 proved important for Labour, all the same. It saw the 'bedding in' of the Attlee government's achievements. Widespread affluence gave fresh underpinning to the revisionists' approach, and this in turn set the parameters for many of the policies which Labour would try to implement during the period after 1964. At the same time, though, deep and bitter splits emerged which would cast a shadow over the party long after the 1950s were a remote memory.

Labour's prospects were limited from the outset. The Conservative Party was still committed to private enterprise, but the Conservative government under Churchill accepted that the mixed economy, the welfare state and full employment should not be tampered with too extensively. Here, Labour had fallen victim to its own mythology, for the Conservatives even between the wars had not been so reactionary as Labourites now purported to believe. It was a false view of history to argue, as so many did, that a Tory government necessarily meant depression and deprivation. Similarly, the 'Whig interpretation of Labour history' once again came into play, to the detriment of the party's true interests. The people who saw history as leading ineluctably towards the socialist

141

millennium argued that Labour's progress had only been put on hold in 1951: had the party not gained more votes than any party ever before? It was simply a question of waiting for the pendulum to swing and the 'forward march' would be resumed. But this was too optimistic. The Conservatives would be able to gain cheap popularity for lifting the remaining controls and rationing, and so present themselves as the party of 'freedom' as opposed to that of 'austerity'. Meanwhile, Labour's splits remained and were likely to be as deep in opposition as in office. There was, in addition, no sign of the vigorous leadership that would be necessary if Labour was to regroup swiftly and effectively, with Attlee increasingly a liability but showing little indication of wanting to retire.[1] And, finally, there were few signs that the question of the future direction of British socialism had been or was being resolved. In the event, the years from 1951 to 1955 were to be one of the most dismal periods in the history of the Labour Party. From a position of potential strength, the party sank deeper and deeper into a mire of squabbling, with poor leadership and a lack of clear policy, in the face of an increasingly self-confident Conservative Party.

Despite their small parliamentary majority, the Conservatives were reasonably well set from the beginning. Though Labour led in the polls for much of the period to late 1954, it rarely managed a significant lead after 1952. In by-elections, there was a small swing towards the Conservatives in 1953 and 1954. Increasingly it seemed that, if there were no catastrophic errors of timing, the Conservatives would win the next general election. This is not to say that they did not face problems – in particular, Churchill was ailing badly – but many of the difficulties were hidden from public view. The government's handling of the economy, while open to criticism in retrospect, seemed successful at the time, helped by the demands of post-war rebuilding, favourable terms of trade and a temporary lack of foreign competition in export markets. One area of particular success was housing, where the pledge to build 300,000 houses a year was fulfilled, in sharp contrast to Labour's performance. By 1955 the Conservatives could point to prosperity, and contrast it with the perceived austerity of Labour's time in office. It was in some ways an unfair comparison, but it resonated with the voters. In addition, the Tories' continuation of Labour's scepticism about moves towards greater European integration might well have saved it from an electoral backlash.

But events within the Labour Party also played a part. Once in opposition, Attlee shrank. Now 68 years old, he clung on to the leadership, but largely to ensure that Morrison (now 63), would be too old to succeed him. Given the alienation of Bevan, there seemed to be few other likely contenders. This lack of leadership mattered, because this was a time of considerable division and bitterness within the party. At the 1951 election, Bevan had toed the party line as loyally as anyone. However, left-wing discontent with the leadership grew throughout 1952. One major issue was the question of whether or not western Germany should be rearmed in the face of the 'Soviet threat'. In March 1952, 57 MPs (including Bevan) voted against the measure, instead of abstaining as the whips had demanded. This was seen as a left-wing rebellion, and the PLP's standing orders were reimposed, a sure sign that the relatively harmonious times of the immediate post-war period were a thing of the past.[2] At that autumn's party conference, a degree of organization by the left resulted in a coup, whereby six of the seven CLP places on the NEC were taken by 'Bevanites'. Dalton, a member since the 1920s, was among those to lose his seat. Even though the NEC remained firmly under the control of the moderates who dominated the larger trade union section, the left's caucus tactics and success enraged the rest of the party.[3] Late in 1952 the PLP voted to liquidate separate groups, although this had little real effect in reducing tension.[4]

Even so, Bevan was able to secure re-election to the shadow cabinet in autumn 1952, albeit in last place. It was not to be a long stay, however. Early in 1954 it was decided that the party should vote in favour of German rearmament. In April, therefore, Bevan resigned from the shadow cabinet. However, the impact of this move was reduced when Wilson, the runner-up in the previous autumn's election, took Bevan's place, even though he had been considered a 'Bevanite'. Bevan's standing suffered a further blow that October when he was defeated by a two-to-one majority by Gaitskell for the party treasurership in succession to Greenwood, who had died earlier in the year. Then, in March 1955, Labour accepted that Britain should manufacture the hydrogen bomb. In the Commons vote, Bevan and 62 other Labour MPs abstained, and during the debate many Labour MPs felt that he had insulted Attlee. A few days later, the shadow cabinet voted to withdraw the whip from Bevan, a move confirmed by the PLP by 141 votes to 112. On 30 March, the NEC voted by 15 to 10 to condemn Bevan and warn him as to his future conduct; and, had a general election not been looming, the desire of leading right-wingers like Deakin to have him expelled altogether might have been fulfilled.[5]

The very notion that so eminent a figure as Bevan could be seriously considered for expulsion said a great deal about the deterioration of intra-party relations. The most dramatic manifestation of the deterioration had been seen in the clashes between Bevan and Gaitskell. Bevan, for his part, made little secret of his dislike for his colleague, whom he felt to have no real roots in the movement, who had become Chancellor in 1950 when he, Bevan, had wanted the job, and who had bested him over NHS charges in 1951. When Bevan said in 1954 that it seemed that 'the right kind of leader for the Labour Party is a desiccated calculating machine', it was seen as a swipe at Gaitskell.[6] The right, on the other hand, saw Bevan as over-emotional, even mentally unstable and too much under the influence of his wife, Jennie Lee, and colleagues like Michael Foot.[7] Certainly, it is difficult to avoid the view that Bevan took a certain perverse pleasure in putting himself at odds with the party leadership.

All this might not have been so damaging if it had been part of a general rough and tumble from which policy was emerging. But it was not. There was some debate: 1952, for example, saw the publication of two books which tried to point the future direction of the party. The first was Bevan's *In Place of Fear*. The book sold well, but it was not the great visionary text for which many had hoped. It had some nice autobiographical touches, and was imbued with the author's concern to democratize much of what the last Labour government had achieved; for example, he attacked the boards of nationalized industries as 'a constitutional outrage' because of their lack of accountability, and called for greater industrial democracy.[8] On the whole, however, the book was a disappointment.[9] The second book, *New Fabian Essays*, was edited by Richard Crossman, formerly the leading figure in 'Keep Left'. Among the essayists, the editor and Ian Mikardo represented the left, but most – for example, Anthony Crosland, Denis Healey and Roy Jenkins – were associated with what was becoming known as the 'revisionist' right. The volume was by no means undistinguished, but it was a starting point for a debate which took time to get off the ground rather than an immediate plan of action. Certainly, it seems to have had little impact on the party's lacklustre new programme, *Challenge to Britain,* adopted in 1953.

There is, then, clear evidence that Labour was in some turmoil between 1951 and 1955. However, this is only part of the story, for Labour remained in a strong position, fundamentally. Trade union membership remained high, and continued to expand slowly, thanks to full employment and relaxed state and employer attitudes: union density remained at around 44 per cent, and membership at around eight million, throughout the period between 1951 and 1964.[10] The party's individual membership exceeded a million in 1952 and 1953[11] (though this was almost certainly an inflated figure, and active membership was undoubtedly much lower). Labour was now firmly ensconced in power in local government in many parts of the country. As previously, Labour was being seen as the party which best represented the needs of local authority employees and tenants, and as both these categories expanded this gave it a more and more substantial 'clientage' in local and national elections. This all meant that Labour had a strong base; but it did not necessarily mean that it could win elections.

In April 1955, the octogenarian Churchill was finally persuaded to retire, and was succeeded by Eden, who dissolved parliament almost immediately. Having been ahead in the polls since the start of the year, and having engineered a pre-election boom, Eden had few doubts that he would win. Labour can have had few illusions, either: its policies were dull and uninspiring, its leadership cut a superannuated air at the side of the dashing Eden, and it was clearly divided. Labour's manifesto was based largely on consolidation; apart from a commitment to renationalize road haulage and steel, which had been returned to the private sector by the Conservatives, there was little on public ownership; there were vague nods in the direction of greater industrial democracy; and there were new departures in calls for comprehensive secondary education and equal pay for women.[12] But little else made Labour very distinctive. In a sense this was not surprising: Labour's ageing leadership saw the work of the 1945–51 governments as a pinnacle of achievement, for which they would have settled throughout their long, varied and difficult careers. Their memories included Labour as a weak appendage to Liberalism before 1914, the setbacks and defeats of the interwar years, and the horrors of fascism and war. Like all gerontocracies, the Labour leadership had become somewhat self-satisfied and conservative, and with the left marginalized and rather confused, the unions under little pressure from either government or economic circumstances, and younger, more radical right-wingers having little option but to bide their time, there were few more vigorous or coherent critiques on offer.

The election was one which Labour probably could not have won, although a series of strikes, which led to more public criticism of the unions than at any time since 1940, hardly helped the party. The election results belied the complacency which had followed the 1951 defeat, as the Conservatives became the first party since the 1867 Reform Act to increase their majority after a substantial period in office, winning 344 seats (with 49.7 per cent of the poll), and more than trebling their majority. Labour emerged with only 277 seats (46.4 per cent). The national swing, as in 1951, was only slight. Labour's support among manual workers fell, but only from 63 to 62 per cent, which was still better than in 1945; the Conservatives also polled less well in this area than in 1951, due largely to a slight Liberal revival. Labour's share of the non-manual vote increased marginally.[13] Overall, Labour's support among men increased, but there was a significant fall in its support among women, from 46 to 42.5 per cent.[14] While the result hardly came as a shock, it did signify the need for changes within the party. Leadership, policy and organization would all need attention and, in all probability, alteration.

It was clear that Attlee could not remain for long as leader. He was now 72, and might be 77 by the time of the next election. The deputy leader, Morrison, was 67. The shadow cabinet was also ageing: 5 of the 12 members elected in November 1954 were over 60. Obviously, change was required. When Dalton retired from the front bench he called on his 'fellow veterans' to follow suit.[15] Morrison refused to do so, because he still hoped to succeed Attlee, but most of the others retired. That June's shadow cabinet elections saw the election for the first time of younger people like George Brown and Anthony Greenwood, while Bevan returned. On 7 December, Attlee announced his resignation. He remains Labour's longest-serving leader. His periods as leader in opposition had often seemed rather ineffectual; but in office, surrounded by able colleagues, he had been an effective co-ordinator, successful both in wartime and as post-war premier. His historical reputation might stand even higher if he had retired three or four years earlier.

One of Attlee's main reasons for hanging on for so long had been his desire to block Morrison's succession, for personal and political reasons.[16] As late as 1953, Morrison would have been the obvious successor, but since then the anti-Bevanite majority in the PLP and the unions had become divided between him and Gaitskell. This was not only on account of age, but also because Gaitskell had done a lot to push himself into the affections of the Labour right.[17] His McCarthy-style attack on the left in a speech at Stalybridge in 1952, when he had alleged that one-sixth of party conference delegates were 'Communist or Communist-inspired', had earned him keen attention, especially from the 'Big Three' union leaders, Deakin (TGWU), Will Lawther (Mineworkers) and Tom Williamson (General and Municipal Workers).[18] Since these three unions made up around 40 per cent of the votes at party conference, this was not a bad alliance to strike. Younger, more appealing electorally (or so it was felt) and less complacent in terms of policy, he began to seem a more attractive proposition than Morrison. In 1955, indeed, some of Morrison's friends tried to persuade him not to stand for the leadership, fearing that he would be humiliated.[19] In the event, he was; Gaitskell won an easy victory on the first ballot with 157 votes to Bevan's 70 and Morrison's 40.

The period between Gaitskell's succession to the leadership in December 1955 and mid-1958 was one of some success and many encouraging signs for Labour. First, the Conservatives were in considerable difficulties for much of the period. In October 1955 they were forced to introduce a deflationary mini-budget only months after encouraging a pre-election boom. More serious trouble followed the nationalization of the Suez Canal by the Egyptian government in July 1956. That November, British and French forces invaded Suez; but, with the USA making clear its opposition, Britain had no alternative but to withdraw. In January 1957 Eden resigned as premier, not only on health grounds but also because of the Suez fiasco.

Second, a new spirit of unity emerged at the top of the party. In June 1955 Bevan had been re-elected to the shadow cabinet. In

February 1956 he stood for the deputy leadership, and although he was defeated, the fact that he polled 111 votes against the 141 cast for the widely respected and 'safe' Jim Griffiths was a sign of continuing, and perhaps increasing, popularity. Bevan became shadow Colonial Secretary and acquitted himself well. That October the party conference elected him party treasurer by a narrow margin over Brown. He co-operated closely with Gaitskell over Suez.[20] In November 1956 Bevan came third in the shadow cabinet elections and was appointed shadow Foreign Secretary; by late 1956 Crossman was writing privately of a 'Gaitskell–Bevan axis'.[21] When, at the 1957 party conference, Bevan launched a fierce attack on unilateral nuclear disarmament as 'an emotional spasm', he not only dismayed many of his supporters but also drew himself still closer to the leadership.[22]

This transformation from *enfant terrible* into 'statesman' worried many on the left and some on the right. The reasons for it are complex. Both Bevan and Gaitskell seem to have been sobered by the 1955 defeat, which suggested that luxuriation in internecine conflicts had a price. Gaitskell, after all, was now leader of the party, and had a clearer duty and incentive to seek unity than previously. His election to the leadership seems to have made him more relaxed and self-confident in dealing with his erstwhile adversary. Bevan, for his part, seems to have realized that continued factionalism was pointless, since the Bevanites had lost every issue they had fought. At the end of the day, too, Bevan disliked Conservatives even more than he disliked the party leader. A Gaitskell government might prove much more moderate, overall, than Bevan would really want, but it might just make some real gains for working people. It is also likely that, with the Foreign Office in his sights, Bevan was more inclined to compromise. But there was surely an element of calculation in his behaviour. Labour had a new leader whose position was, for the moment, unassailable. Continued, futile sniping at Gaitskell could have no positive effect. It would simply allow further measures against the left, and give an excuse to the right if Labour lost the next election; many Labourites had already blamed 'Bevanism' for the defeat of 1955. And so, it seems, Bevan decided that he would show loyalty to Gaitskell. Then, if Labour won the next election, he (and, perhaps, some of his supporters) would be appointed to senior positions in government. If, on the other hand, it lost, no one would be able to say that the left had been to blame. The fault would lie with Gaitskell and his line, and the left would be correspondingly strengthened in a renewed struggle for control of the party.[23]

The new leadership was not the only positive development. Policy was also becoming better defined. The hints made towards new directions in *New Fabian Essays* were now consolidated, most notably in Crosland's *The Future of Socialism* (1956). Crosland, an Oxford economist and Labour MP who had lost his seat in 1955, argued that the tools of Keynesian demand management, rather than the ownership of industry, now enabled governments to control the economy and to avoid the old cycle of boom and slump. This, plus the growth of joint-stock companies and the running of firms by salaried managers rather than by owners, meant that capitalism in the classical nineteenth-century sense no longer existed, and that in consequence nationalization was largely a policy of the past. Instead, social justice could and should be pursued by the continuation of post-war policies – a mixed economy, demand management and the welfare state – together with a new radicalism in areas like education to promote greater equality of opportunity. In effect, assured economic growth under capitalism would lead inexorably to the socialist society that he desired. The party certainly did not swallow Crosland's prescriptions whole, but the book was influential and did suggest new directions which chimed in with Gaitskell's thinking. In more concrete terms, Labour issued a number of policy documents, the products of small committees, in the years between 1956 and 1959, which were to lay the basis of party policy into the 1960s.[24]

Attempts were also made to improve party organization. A committee of inquiry appointed to investigate the machine in the aftermath of the 1955 defeat claimed, perhaps with some exaggeration, that it was in poor shape. Wilson, the committee's chairman, said Labour was 'still at the penny-farthing stage in a jet-propelled era'.[25] In particular, he claimed, party headquarters were inefficient, a clear indictment of the secretary, Morgan Phillips, and national agent, Len Williams. In addition, Wilson pointed out that individual membership had begun to fall dramatically, from 1,014,524 in 1952 to 843,356 in 1955. There was also evidence of some constituency, and still more citywide, parties in an advanced state of decrepitude. Glasgow and Liverpool, in particular, were in the hands of right-wing oligarchies which practised 'boss politics' with impunity.[26] At first, it seemed that much would come from the report. A decision was taken to weaken the hold of city parties and devolve more of their power to the constituencies.[27] But few of the report's recommendations came to very much. Phillips and Williams remained *in situ,* with Williams going on to succeed Phillips when the latter retired in 1962. Suggestions to concentrate agents in marginal seats foundered. Party membership continued to fall until 1961, when it was just over 750,000. Thereafter, a change in the minimum number of members each CLP had to affiliate to the national party artificially inflated the figures, but the overall downward trend in actual membership continued pretty well unabated, largely unhindered by a party leadership which was coming to see 'television and political advertising [replacing] the need for campaigning foot-soldiers', and freed from financial worries by heavy funding from the unions, whose membership continued to grow to new record levels.[28] In fact, the main result of the Wilson report was that it got its author noticed in CLPs across the country, for in producing it he had made an extensive national tour, meeting activists and officials and generally acquitting himself well.[29] Thus Wilson's career prospects were boosted, but it is an open question how far the party's organization improved, and headquarters developed a distrust of Wilson that it would never quite overcome.

Meanwhile, the Conservatives recovered strongly from Suez and its aftermath under their charismatic new leader, Harold Macmillan. There was a recession in the winter of 1958–59, with unemployment rising to a post-1947 peak of 620,000, but by July it had fallen to 395,000. And, more generally, a sense of affluence was engendered by the fact that average real wages rose by 7 per cent between January 1956 and June 1959.[30] On the other hand, increasing strike levels meant more public debate about, and criticism of, trade unions, whose links with Labour were very prominent. And, within the Labour Party itself, there were new divisions opening up, most notably the support given by some prominent left-wingers to the Campaign for Nuclear Disarmament (CND), formed in 1958. All this meant that the electoral tide turned towards the Conservatives. In September 1958, only a year after being 19 points behind, they moved ahead in the opinion polls. Macmillan's approval rating was higher than Gaitskell's throughout 1959, and did not fall below 50 per cent after June 1958. After

1957, by-election swings against the Conservatives were generally slight. The borough council elections of May 1959 saw a slump in the Labour vote and a heavy loss of seats.

Thus, although Labour entered the 1959 general election campaign in high spirits, it had little real prospect of forming the next government. With polling set for 8 October, Labour fought a generally effective campaign; in the first TV election, its broadcasts, masterminded by Anthony Wedgwood Benn, were a striking success. The Labour manifesto was based on the policies which had emerged from the three-year policy review (1956–59). The Conservatives were criticized for unemployment and rising prices; the latter had led to a reduction in the real value of benefits, pensions and NHS spending, and Labour pledged to increase these accordingly. Selection in secondary education would be ended, greater protection would be given to consumers and a Welsh Office would be created. On industry, Labour pledged to encourage modernization of private firms, be more sensitive to the needs of public corporations and renationalize steel and road haulage. However, the point was emphasized that Labour had 'no other plans for further nationalization' except in the case of industries which were 'failing the nation', although the possibility was held out of the state buying shares in companies.[31]

Despite a 'socialist' peroration, this was very much a revisionist document. Its basic argument was that Labour was better suited to manage welfare capitalism than were the Conservatives. There was no real sense of radicalism. The problem was whether this was distinctive enough to encourage people to risk a change of government which might upset prosperity, especially since the recent recession had shown that that prosperity could be upset. This is not to argue that a more 'radical' programme would have won the election for Labour, but merely to show how difficult the Conservatives were to beat in 1959. Matters were not helped by Gaitskell's performance in a TV interview when he said that Labour's increased spending plans would not mean increased taxes. In a sense this was true, as Gaitskell saw it: the expenditure would be met over time by economic growth. In the short term, though, tax increases might have been necessary, and people were unconvinced by Gaitskell's explanation, which suggested dishonesty.[32] Again, though, it did not make the difference between victory and defeat.

The fact of Labour's defeat should not have come as a surprise, but the scale of it did. On a national swing of 1.0 per cent, the Conservatives increased their parliamentary representation for the fourth successive election, taking 365 seats with 49.4 per cent of the poll to Labour's 258 (43.8 per cent). Labour lost 28 seats to the Tories, while gaining five in the opposite direction. In some parts of the country it improved its position, but in others it lost seats heavily; in the west Midlands, it lost seven of its 27 seats. Conversely, eastern Lancashire, which had swung so heavily against Labour in 1951, now moved towards the party, and there was a swing of 1.4 per cent to Labour in Scotland.[33] Labour's share of the non-manual vote had fallen from 23 to 21 per cent; similarly, and more noticed at the time, was a fall in its support among manual workers, from 62 to 57 per cent.[34] Support among women had actually increased since 1955, albeit slightly, but among men Labour's share of the poll had fallen from 51 to 47.5 per cent.[35] Age factors were also seen as significant: voters in their twenties, who had split five to four in favour of Labour in 1955, were now almost evenly divided, while it seems that Labour's pensions proposals, plus the ageing of a cohort who were more likely to support Labour, meant a shift in the votes of those aged 65 and over in favour of Labour.[36]

Labour's third successive defeat, each by a wider margin, led to a great deal of fuss among the commentators. In a book entitled *Must Labour Lose?*, Mark Abrams and Richard Rose argued that Labour faced a serious problem, in so far as a large section of the working class no longer saw itself as working class, and that this process of 'embourgoisement' was loosening the ties between Labour and its core support. Increasingly, Labour was being seen as an outdated party representing 'the poor' at a time when 'many workers, regardless of their politics, no longer see themselves as working class'.[37] Some of the evidence presented suggested hostility towards nationalization in particular. Even worse, young people were alienated from Labour in large numbers. It was pointed out that for the party to take office at the next election would require a larger swing than at any previous post-war election. Labour was in trouble.[38]

How accurate was this picture? It is easy to see why it seemed persuasive in the aftermath of yet another electoral defeat for the Labour Party. But other surveys, published later, contested it.

A 1963–64 study of Luton, a town dominated by the motor industry, found that, despite affluence, there was 'no evidence of any
shift in [working-class] political loyalties away from the Labour
party'.[39] Where there was a shift, it argued, was in the reason why
such voters supported Labour. It was now less of an expression of
class solidarity and more of an 'instrumental' position; that is, the
workers concerned saw the Labour Party and trade unionism as
the most likely routes to material betterment.[40] This did offer the
possibility of future disillusionment, of course, but the idea that
Labour was in secular decline was not to be taken too seriously.
On the whole, it seems that the picture of Labour in decline due
to broad sociological factors was overdone. It is also worth reiter-
ating the underlying strength of Labour's position in the 1950s;
the party was polling very well, and losing elections by relatively
narrow margins. Part of the problem was that comparisons were
being made with the number of votes gained in 1951, when, due
to an unusually low number of Liberal candidates, an exceptional proportion of the vote had gone to the two main parties.
The swings of 1955 and 1959 were both very low, yet affluence was
expanding significantly. What is surprising, given the general perception of Conservative success in economic management, therefore, is less Labour's failure than its success in retaining so much
support. And the Conservatives' share of the manual vote had also
been falling from 1951 onwards: from 34 per cent in 1951 to 32 in
1955 and 30 in 1959. While this was partly due to the revival of the
Liberals, it hardly suggested that the working class was abandoning Labour in droves for the Conservatives.[41]

In retrospect, it seems clear that the basic cause of Labour's
defeat in 1959 was that enough voters continued to believe that
the Conservatives were and would remain successful in government. The fact that Labour did worse than in 1955 could probably be attributed to short-term factors, such as the uninspiring
nature of Labour's message, doubts about Gaitskell, and perhaps
some feeling in the Midlands, in particular, that the Conservatives
would be better placed to 'deal with' issues of race and immigration which, following 'race riots' in Notting Hill and Nottingham
the previous year, were beginning to achieve a certain electoral
saliency. But this was not the message which the leadership took
on board, partly because it raised awkward questions about its
own performance.

It was easier to subscribe instead to the view that radical changes were needed within the Labour Party to enable it to win in the future. The example of the German SPD, which was repudiating Marxism and giving itself a 'softer', less stridently working-class image at this time, culminating in the Bad Godesberg conference of November 1959, was seen by some as a good example to fol-low.[42] The extent of the panic which gripped sections of the party at this time is difficult to credit, in retrospect. But Gaitskell had to find a scapegoat if he was to shore up his position.

This was particularly so since traditional Labour scapegoats were conspicuous by their absence. The unions were so vital to Gaitskell's intra-party position that he could not offend them. Bevan's tactics since 1955 made it difficult to blame the left, and given the fact that the old right-wing dominance among union leaders was beginning to crumble, with, for example, the succes-sion of the left-wing Frank Cousins to lead the TGWU in 1956, the leadership could not afford to be too rude about the left in any case. The media had not been unusually biased. The Soviets had not graced the campaign with correspondence, nor had the bankers deigned to construct a ramp. So the scapegoat found was a small passage in the Labour constitution, drafted in 1918 by Sidney Webb, ritually ignored by every leader since, and virtu-ally unknown to the mass of the population, a passage whose only effective function was to reassure the idealists in the party's ranks that sitting through tedious meetings and tramping around can-vassing for often undesirable and egocentric candidates at elec-tion times was contributing in some small way to the achievement of a fairer and better society. Gaitskell's failure made him take up Labour theology by challenging Clause IV.

There were some who wanted to go further than that. The leader's close ally, Jay, publicly questioned the union link, and proposed significant limits to further nationalization; in private, he wanted to go further on both issues, and to consider both changing the party's name and working more closely with the Liberals.[43] There is no evidence that Gaitskell wanted to go so far, but his close association with people who were expressing such views was hardly likely to endear his proposal to drop Clause IV to the Labour movement at large. After a fierce debate at the 1959 party conference, it was decided that the existing Clause IV would be retained, though supplemented by new statements of principle drawn up by the NEC.[44]

This whole episode throws Gaitskell's leadership abilities into question. Perhaps it was not a bad idea, in the abstract, to get rid of Clause IV. If it had not already been in the constitution, certainly, Labour would not have chosen to insert it in 1959. It had been adopted in 1918 for essentially short-term reasons, and had never formed the touchstone of Labour's policy. But although the party had never proposed nationalization of 'every pub and garage', as Gaitskell put it, for many socialists it was a question of faith, and for others, a matter of nostalgia for an older and supposedly purer form of Labour politics.[45] As Wilson was to show, it would prove possible to lead a modernizing and moderate Labour Party with Clause IV still in place. More broadly, Gaitskell's 'smart set' followers who, for example, disliked Wilson because he was 'such a common little man', aroused suspicion, as had Mosley in the 1920s or Cripps in the 1930s.[46] Where, asked some Labourites, were their Labour roots, their shop floor experience? Where would they be in a few years' time? This was unfair, in many ways. But people feared, understandably, that the Labour Party would be hijacked in the interests of vocal middle-class groups, which were at best indifferent to many working-class concerns. Labour might even end up like the late-Victorian Liberal Party which the LRC had been set up to counter. At the same time, though, Gaitskell's opponents had no particularly coherent alternative to offer. The successful defence of Clause IV was seen as a victory. In the sense that it prevented the right wing of the party from doing something, it was. But the left's outlook remained simply that the party should be moving faster and further. According to this view, there was no need to engage in a meaningful debate about the party's future strategy. It was enough simply to block the right. But this would not necessarily take the party very much further towards the socialist society to which the left aspired.

Bevan had played an essentially conciliatory role in the crisis. He might still have challenged Gaitskell at a later stage, but he died of cancer in July 1960. Even so, Gaitskell's position remained under pressure. First, that September's party conference narrowly passed a resolution in favour of unilateral nuclear disarmament. Gaitskell pledged to 'fight and fight and fight again to save the

Party we love', which impressed his admirers but raised questions for others – by no means all on the left – about his leadership, particularly his ability to unite the party.[47] This was all the more regrettable in that Gaitskell had done a great deal, between 1955 and 1959, to assuage lingering fears that he was a splitter. It was in this context that he faced a challenge for the party leadership at the start of the new parliamentary session in November 1960. The political position of the challenger, Wilson, was not easy to define. He had attained something of a 'left' reputation for resigning with Bevan in 1951, but had to some extent dissipated this by taking Bevan's place in the shadow cabinet in 1954. However, his performance as shadow Chancellor since 1955 had established his reputation as a formidable parliamentary performer, as he had scourged successive Tory Chancellors. He had little chance of defeating Gaitskell in 1960, but his performance, taking 81 votes to the leader's 166, was far from a humiliation, and suggested that he might be a future contender for the leadership. But it also aroused great short-term and long-term hostility from the leader's supporters.[48]

All this drama was being played out against the backdrop of continuing success for the Macmillan government, as economic indicators remained favourable, and the Conservatives remained ahead in the polls until late 1961. But things then began to change. Economic growth slowed down. Inflation rose, unemployment edged upwards and the government's attempts to control public sector wages and salaries through the 'pay pause' of July 1961 suggested continuing Tory antipathy towards the public sector. Slipping behind in the polls in July 1962, Macmillan sacked a third of his cabinet on the 'Night of the Long Knives'. This was intended to demonstrate firmness and resolution, but looked more like panic.

Within the Labour Party, meanwhile, a status quo was reached on the issues that had split the party over the past two years. Gaitskell's victory over Wilson, in this sense, marked something of a watershed. The Clause IV compromise held good, and the issue receded once more. At the 1961 conference, the vote on unilateral nuclear disarmament was reversed after powerful lobbying by Gaitskellites in the Campaign for Democratic Socialism, whose chairman was William Rodgers, secretary of the Fabian Society. When the left-winger, Anthony Greenwood, challenged for the leadership in November 1961, he took only 59 votes to the leader's 171, a significantly worse performance than that of Wilson the previous year. Barbara Castle's attempt to wrest the deputy leadership from Brown (who had succeeded Bevan) was equally unsuccessful, and Brown was able to defeat a similar challenge from Wilson in 1962. In the latter year, Gaitskell's attack on Macmillan's attempt to take Britain into the EEC (formed in 1957) astonished and appalled many of his usual supporters, but was cheered by many on the left, which was, on the whole, strongly opposed to entry.[49] By taking this line, and perhaps even more by so publicly repudiating so many of his leading supporters, Gaitskell strengthened his position within the party as a whole. Some people believed his line was opportunistic, but there was more to it than that. Joining the six-state EEC could be seen as counter to, rather than a demonstration of, Labour's 'internationalism'; there were fears that the Commonwealth, of which there were high hopes in the first flush of African decolonization, might have to be sacrificed, and that the hard-won relationship with the USA might also be lost. And there were concerns about further dividing the world into power blocs. This is not to say that straightforward xenophobia did not play its part for many Labourites. But to dismiss the arguments against entry in such terms is simplistic.

By the end of 1962, then, Gaitskell's position was apparently strong, and the party was well ahead in the polls. That year a strong Liberal revival had allowed Labour to gain three seats from the Conservatives at by-elections, and there was little sign that Macmillan could pull his party round. There were real hopes that a Labour government under Gaitskell might follow the next election.

But it was not to be. In January 1963 Gaitskell died suddenly from a rare disease at the age of 56. Around him was to develop a mythology not unlike that which was soon to envelop another 'lost leader', US President John F. Kennedy. Gaitskell had many qualities: a good brain for economics, the power to inspire those with whom he was in agreement and much personal charm. The one general election he fought as Labour leader was probably unwinnable, and by 1962 he did seem to have overcome many problems and secured his leadership. However, he was at times too impatient and intolerant of honest dissent for his own, or the party's, good. He had led the party, at times, in an over-combative manner. His revisionist view of socialism, finally, meant that he would have had little idea of how to tackle affairs when the economic going became tougher. There is nothing in his record to suggest that a Gaitskell government elected in 1964 would have been any more successful than the Wilson administration that eventually came to power: it must be a moot point whether Gaitskell could even have won in 1964. But Wilson, like Kennedy's successor in the USA, Lyndon Johnson, was to suffer in comparison with a predecessor whose acolytes remained powerful and whose faults were quickly forgotten in an outpouring of grief at an untimely death.

Gaitskell's death threw the party into something of a panic. A general election was due by late 1964, and might come earlier; a new leader would not have long to establish himself. Three men stood for the leadership. Wilson, who could count on the support of the left plus a substantial number of MPs who had been impressed by his parliamentary performances, was the youngest, at 47, but the only one with cabinet experience. The two candidates who were more acceptable to the Gaitskellites were Brown (49), and James Callaghan (51, and a member of the shadow cabinet since 1951). Both had been junior ministers in the last Labour government. In the first ballot, Callaghan took only 41 votes, compared with 88 for Brown and 115 for Wilson, and was eliminated. In the run-off, Wilson beat Brown by 144 votes to 103. Both candidates were seen as having their flaws: Wilson was distrusted by many for his alleged slipperiness and his apparent changes of line during the 1950s, not to mention his opposition to Gaitskell in 1960; Brown was seen by some as too unstable (a condition not helped by heavy drinking), and too combative in internal party affairs. Wilson was seen as more likely to heal rifts, but at the same time the shadow cabinet had voted heavily in favour of his opponent.[50]

In reality, Wilson, the 'man of the left', shared most of the assumptions of the revisionists. He saw a 'fairer' society being funded by the fruits of economic growth. Clause IV was simply there to placate party activists: he had no time for further extensive nationalization. Where he perhaps differed was in his expectation that a greater degree of intervention would be needed to secure higher levels of growth. Frequent visits to the USSR in the 1950s had convinced him of the merits of centralized economic planning and the application of science to industry. To some extent, he was a technocrat and meritocrat, and it was on those grounds that he sought to base his appeal. This was a change of emphasis rather than of content in Labour's message. At the party conference at Scarborough in October 1963, he made a thrilling speech, stressing the need for 'democratic planning' for the new Britain that was going to be 'forged in the white heat' of scientific revolution.[51]

Between January and April 1964 Wilson returned to the attack with a series of speeches in which he combined emphasis on socialism being about science and economic growth – an adaptation of the revisionist message – with knockabout rhetoric attacking aristocrats and 'upper-class accents' to appease the inverted snobbery of his followers.[52] This rhetoric, like the other aspects of his reinvented image – pipe-smoking, brown sauce and Huddersfield Town Football Club – marked a sharp and probably conscious contrast to the perhaps rather elitist image of his predecessor.

The government continued to face difficulties. The economy slowed down, prices and unemployment rose, and there was an increasing perception, much fostered by Wilson, that Britain was falling behind its competitors. The French veto on British entry to the EEC in January 1963, and the Profumo scandal that summer, severely dented Macmillan's image. Finally, in October 1963, he resigned. His successor was the Earl of Home, who relinquished his title so that he could return to the Commons as Sir Alec Douglas-Home. This suited Wilson very well: at a time when he was trying to portray the Tories as being out of date, it helped that their new leader was an aristocrat who claimed to use matchsticks to do calculations. Home delayed the election until the last possible moment, allowing the Chancellor, Reginald Maudling, to engineer a long pre-election boom. Labour's poll lead, which had stood at 20 points in June 1963, was pegged back to only 3 points by September 1964.

Labour fought the general election of October 1964 on the basis of revisionism given a significant twist in the direction of Wilsonian state planning and a more *dirigiste* approach to industrial modernization. There were no pledges to extend nationalization beyond the renationalization of iron and steel, although greater co-ordination of the public sector in industry was promised.

Efforts would be made to stabilize prices and reform taxation. Social services would be improved. Secondary schools would be comprehensivized, the school-leaving age would be raised and there would be 'a massive expansion in higher, further and university education'. On immigration, Labour promised not only to restrict entry but also to introduce legislation outlawing racial discrimination. Foreign aid would be increased. In defence policy, Labour would re-examine Britain's commitments, but despite rhetorical attacks on the government's nuclear weapons policy there were no pledges to disarm. Overall, Labour was, it claimed, 'offering Britain a new way of life that will stir our hearts, rekindle an authentic patriotic faith in our future, and enable our country to re-establish itself as a stable force in the world today for progress, peace, and justice'.[53]

It was clear throughout the campaign that the result would be a close one. Ultimately, Labour emerged with 317 seats to the Conservatives' 304, and a working majority of just five. A national swing of 3.5 per cent left Labour with 44.1 per cent of the poll, as opposed to 43.4 for the Tories and 11.2 for the Liberals. Labour support had risen among both manual and non-manual workers (in the former case, from 57 to 64 per cent).[54] Far from representing further class dealignment, as Abrams and Rose had implied, the 1964 election has been described as marking 'a peak in relative class voting'.[55] Doubtless this reflected growing disillusionment with the Conservatives' ability to continue increasing working-class living standards on the scale experienced in the 1950s, as well as, perhaps, some response to Wilson's often rather crude working-class rhetoric during the campaign and the months that had preceded it. In terms of gender, a more complex picture emerged, with the proportion of women voting Labour actually falling from 43 to 39.5 per cent.[56] This failure to attract women voters in large enough numbers was increasingly commented on around the time; many saw it as a symptom of the party's continuing reliance on masculine appeal and trade union imagery and ethos.[57] Labour lost five seats; it gained 61, two from the Liberals, the rest from the Conservatives. The gains were spread fairly evenly across the country, but there were regional variations in the swing, with the west Midlands, in particular, providing only a very low swing to Labour (although even here there were gains). This could be attributed not only to affluence but also to some white working-class voters switching from Labour because they saw it as a pro-immigrant party; in three of the five seats that Labour lost nationally, '[i]mmigration played some part'.[58] Still, even these sombre facts could not prevent Labour feeling euphoric at its return to office after so long a period in opposition.

In the immediate aftermath of the 1951 election, few would have predicted that Labour would not return to office for 13 years. But assumptions about the Conservatives, based on their perceived performance in government during the interwar period, had proved erroneous. After 1951 the Conservatives had not launched a frontal assault on the achievements of the Attlee governments, but had presided over a period of economic growth and rising living standards. Still worse, once in opposition, Labour had become bitterly divided. In reality, a period of reassessment after 11 years in office had been inevitable, but the bitterness which accompanied it was not, and for that, all concerned must bear a share of the responsibility. Such a long period of opposition should at least have been used to redefine Labour's future strategy and to reorientate its ideology after the first tranche of 'socialism' had been implemented. But despite some advances on policy, Labour's outlook remained largely founded upon the assumption that capitalism would continue to produce the goods, but that it would continue do so in such a way as to arouse calls for reform that only Labour could satisfy. Revisionism was not a new departure but an adaptation of the old belief in inevitable progress clothed in pseudo-Keynesian language. Wilson, it is true, had helped to add a new technocratic, scientific gloss; but in reality all still depended on the ability of the system Labour purported to despise to give it the wherewithal to finance the society it claimed to want. The problem would be that, during the period that was about to open up, British capitalism was to begin to falter.

8   Wilson in Power, 1964–70

The Labour governments elected in 1964 and 1966 have not been remembered with great affection. Even before the defeat of 1970 they had become a byword for failure and demoralization, broken promises and dashed hopes, not just for Labourites but for a large section of the wider population. This condemnation has been questioned by many historians, but popular memory does not accord these governments a high reputation.[1] And it is safe to say that many of the problems faced by Labour in these years were ones which were to continue to cause it difficulty long after the political events of the 1960s had faded from view.

The new government's parliamentary position was, to say the least, difficult, since the election had given it an overall majority of just five, and a seat was lost at an early by-election. From then onwards, however, Labour lost no more seats. With the Conservative opposition in disarray, Labour had a good year in 1965, implementing many of its policies and promulgating the National Plan that September. Wilson was able to taunt Home's successor, Edward Heath, with threats of an early dissolution. With the economic indicators favourable, and fresh from a resounding victory in a marginal seat in Hull, Wilson called an election for 31 March 1966.

Labour began the campaign eight points ahead in the polls, and that lead was scarcely dented before polling day. The essential appeal was to trust; unlike the Conservatives in recent years, Labour had shown its competence in office. Labour could argue that it would have achieved more had it not been for the difficult parliamentary position and the situation it had inherited from the previous government. Controversial issues which were seen as vote losers, like the unions, Europe and nationalization, were scarcely mentioned.[2] The results were impressive: Labour took 48.0 per cent of the vote to the Conservatives' 41.4 and the Liberals' 8.6, and won 364 seats to their 253 and 12 respectively. Labour had an overall majority of 97. On a swing of 3.5 per cent, it had made a net gain of 48 seats. The electorate was still highly class defined in its voting patterns; indeed, Labour had taken its highest ever share, 69 per cent, of the manual workers' vote, while also taking more than a quarter of the non-manual vote for the first time since 1945.[3] Both men and women had increased their support for Labour substantially, which was an encouraging sign.[4] Little was heard now of 'embourgeoisement' and 'affluence', at least as factors damaging Labour's prospects. Freed from the major constraint which had appeared to face it – its small majority – it was hoped that Labour would be able really to press ahead with its policies.

In part, the improvement in Labour's performance in 1966 could be attributed to the able team of leaders that had come to office in 1964. Although only three of the 23-strong cabinet had previous experience at that level, ten others had served as junior ministers under Attlee. The cabinet included 13 graduates (and was, incidentally, the least working-class Labour cabinet yet). Inevitably, it had a strong 'Gaitskellite' feel, but Wilson strengthened his own position by bringing in people who had not been elected to the shadow cabinet the previous year, like Crossman, Castle and – in an attempt to emulate the success of Bevin in the 1945 government – Frank Cousins of the TGWU. Wilson's main rivals, Callaghan and Brown, were appointed to the Treasury and the new Department of Economic Affairs (DEA) respectively, which militated against the formation of a Callaghan–Brown axis to threaten his position. Patrick Gordon Walker became Foreign Secretary (despite his having lost his seat at the general election), Healey Defence Secretary, and Griffiths the first Secretary of State for Wales. Promising figures appointed to junior office included Crosland, Benn and Roy Jenkins, while Peter Shore, who had been largely responsible for many of Labour's recent policy statements, became Wilson's parliamentary private secretary.

The changes that took place at the top level over the next five-and-a-half years were made for a variety of reasons. Some were made from choice, with Wilson particularly keen to promote talent and remove time-servers, especially if it enhanced the youthful image of his cabinet. Other alterations were forced on Wilson, but he did retain a penchant for making a virtue of necessity, and there was sufficient talent available for him to make even enforced changes look like beneficial developments.

The first adjustment in the cabinet was forced on Wilson, after Gordon Walker sought to return to parliament by fighting a by-election at Leyton in east London. He was defeated and now had no alternative but to resign. Michael Stewart replaced him as Foreign Secretary and was in turn replaced at Education by Crosland. This was something of a humiliation for Labour, but the loss of Gordon Walker was not really a major blow, and it might well be that Wilson was able to work better with Stewart.

A more positive change came in December 1965 when, in readiness for the expected election, Wilson carried out a limited reshuffle which removed some dead wood and brought in talented younger people like Jenkins, who became Home Secretary at the age of 45. Other older figures were removed after the 1966 election. However, alterations continued to be forced on Wilson. Cousins, unhappy as a minister, and opposed to the government's pay policies, resigned in July 1966. But Cousins had proved somewhat ineffectual, and the opportunity was taken to bring in Benn, one of the brightest young prospects in the party and a Wilson loyalist, as Minister of Technology. Wilson was compelled to reshuffle his ministers again when the effective abandonment of the National Plan in the summer of 1966 meant that Brown had to be moved from the DEA: he switched jobs with Stewart and went to the Foreign Office. Another enforced switch came in November 1967, when the devaluation of sterling left Callaghan with little credibility as Chancellor. He switched posts with the Home Secretary, Jenkins, who was now very much the government's rising star. In March 1968 Brown's frequent threats to resign finally bore fruit, and Stewart returned to the Foreign Office in his place. The following month saw a major reshuffle, which included the promotion of Castle from Transport to become First Secretary, in charge of the Department of Employment and Productivity. After that there were fewer changes, and none affecting the leading figures in the government.

In many cases, these moves reflected the failure of many of Labour's leading figures in office. Jenkins was one of the few leading ministers who had enhanced his reputation by 1970. However, the number of personnel shifts should not mask the fact that there was great political continuity; on the whole, the cabinet was mainly of the right and centre of the party, and even those left-wingers who were included could hardly be described as extremely committed to 'left' causes; furthermore, people like Castle and Crossman were forced to support Wilson for fear of his being succeeded by someone less in sympathy with the left, like Callaghan, Brown or, latterly, Jenkins. The outlook of the cabinet remained essentially revisionist. Wilson, further, was able to shore up his own position by a policy of divide and rule, by being prepared to move ministers between jobs on a fairly regular basis, and through the sheer good fortune that his critics were rarely united, not least on whom they would like to see succeeding Wilson should he be ousted. In short, Wilson's position remained more secure than might have been expected, given the fluctuating fortunes that Labour experienced in this period. Wilson himself did not always fully recognize this fact, though, and spent considerable time and energy seeking out disloyalty, 'leaks' and the like. This nervousness, which for some people seemed to shade into paranoia, was one of the least attractive and most self-destructive aspects of Wilson's leadership; but he had always been a controversial figure, and his opponents' intrigues were by no means entirely the product of a vivid imagination.

Any account of the government's fortunes must begin with the economy. Labour's 1964 manifesto combined revisionism with the vigorous application of new technology to industry and, in particular, 'Socialist planning'. Only in this way could full employment, faster growth, 'a sensible distribution of industry throughout the country', control of inflation and a cure to Britain's balance of payments problems be achieved.[5] Once in power, the government set up the DEA under Brown, charged with formulating a National Plan to promote faster growth. Cousins was brought in to head a new Ministry of Technology ('Mintech'), which was charged with co-ordinating research and development (R&D) and with increasing the application of new technology in industry generally.[6]

Almost as soon as it began, however, the government faced a major crisis. On taking office, Wilson, Callaghan and Brown were told by civil servants that the trade deficit for 1964 would be £800 million, far worse than the Labour leadership had expected. The three ministers had to choose between devaluation and some form of import controls. Wilson took the lead against devaluation, and a temporary 15 per cent tariff on manufactures and semi-manufactures was imposed. This decision was taken in defiance of the General Agreement on Tariffs and Trade (GATT) and Britain's responsibilities to the European Free Trade Area (EFTA), but it did steady the markets and lead to a marked fall in the level of imports.[7] It seemed that the problem might have been solved.[8]

But a further crisis followed in July 1965, and was met with more austere economic policies. The real difficulty was that, in terms of the respective strength of the British and American economies, the pound was overvalued against the dollar. Even so, in the immediate aftermath of the 1966 election, the decision not to devalue was re-endorsed, this time by the whole cabinet. That July a major sterling crisis was sparked by fears about the government's unity and the efficacy of its prices and incomes policies. There were now many supporters of devaluation, including Brown, who saw the issue as a way of ousting Wilson and taking over the premiership. But on 17 July the cabinet voted by 17 to 6 against devaluation, and the following day agreed a severely deflationary programme to calm the markets.[9] It worked, at the cost of higher taxes, spending cuts and a statutory six-month income freeze.[10] Once again, though, the benefits proved temporary, and in November 1967 the government was finally forced to devalue from $2.80 to $2.40. Another austerity package accompanied this decision, and at length had the desired effect, but at great political cost. Wilson's credibility was dealt a huge blow.

In retrospect, the failure to devalue earlier has become one of the stoutest sticks with which to beat this government and, indeed, Wilson himself. In the end, devaluation 'worked'; in concert with other policies it led to a rectification of the trade balance to such an extent that there was a £700 million trade *surplus* by 1970.[11] Devaluation in 1967 was, according to this view, 'three years and £1500 million of borrowed money too late'.[12] The results for the rest of the government's economic strategy, as will be seen, appeared to have been highly damaging. Wilson's anti-devaluation stance has made him the target of strong criticism ever since: on this reading, the exchange rate had been allowed to become an obsession, a fetish, a political virility symbol. To read some accounts, one would think that Wilson needed the $2.80 rate to have any sense of self-worth at all.

Yet this is all too simplistic. It is, after all, easy to be wise after the event. Wilson thought that he had good reasons to avoid devaluation. The Treasury feared that devaluation might lead to inflation, and inflation was something Labour had pledged to avoid. There were fears that British devaluation might lead to a round of competitive devaluations throughout the world, with concomitant worsening of international relations. Past experiences of devaluations had not been politically happy for Labour: the issue had helped to destroy one Labour government in 1931 and rocked another in 1949. Wilson did not want Labour to be seen as the party that could not maintain the value of sterling. Then there was the old radical belief, with which Wilson's boyhood hero, Philip Snowden, would have concurred, that devaluation would hit hardest those who had managed to save a little and who lived on low incomes; that it was the duty of government to maintain the value of money in the interests not of financiers but of 'ordinary people'. There were also international implications: many poorer countries (particularly, but not exclusively, in the Commonwealth) still held their balances in sterling and would be hard hit by any devaluation. This in turn showed another side of the argument – that devaluation would signal an end to the world role which Wilson still felt was important for Britain to sustain. And, of course, the choice was not between devaluation and a tight fiscal stance: as Crossman, by that time an avid devaluer, admitted privately during the 1966 crisis, 'the scale of the package [of spending cuts] required to float the pound was not very different from that required to save it'.[13] It must also be noted that Wilson had, perforce, backed himself into a corner. Since 1964 he had had to reassure the markets by stressing that devaluation would not take place; panic would set in the moment he said anything else.[14] The final problem followed from this. Maintaining the parity became identified as Wilson's personal policy. This not only meant problems for Wilson once the parity was abandoned, but also made problems for cabinet colleagues who wanted to devalue. By 1966, at the latest, supporting devaluation meant supporting someone else for the premiership, and that 'someone else' was Brown. And there were not many in the cabinet who, by 1966, wanted Wilson to go if it meant Brown replacing him. In short, there was probably no alternative but to try to the utmost to preserve the parity and, ultimately, be forced into devaluation. But it was a game the government could not win. Only a rapid improvement in Britain's economic performance would have squared the circle.

It seems likely that one of the main reasons why Wilson was reluctant to devalue was that he genuinely believed that his government's policies would strengthen the economy significantly.[15] But there was the catch. Long-term stabilization depended on high rates of growth, yet the government's attempts to promote those higher growth rates were stymied by the recurrent exchange crises. Thomas Balogh, who became Wilson's economic adviser, had written in 1963 that Britain could 'create economic dynamism only by a consciously contrived expansion based on the selective encouragement of investment and technological innovation'.[16] It was to this end that the DEA, Mintech and, later, the Industrial Reconstruction Corporation were created. The DEA's National Plan, published in September 1965, aimed at a 25 per cent increase in GDP between 1964 and 1970, which meant an annual growth rate of 3.8 per cent.[17] This was very ambitious; growth even in the generally favourable conditions of 1951 to 1964 had only averaged 2.9 per cent a year, and many of those favourable conditions were now disappearing rapidly.[18] Even before the Plan was published, contractionary measures taken in the light of the 1965 sterling crisis were calling it into question; and it was not given adequate preparation, prioritization or administrative back-up to survive further shocks. In the summer of 1966, as stated above, the Plan was abandoned; the DEA was finally abolished in 1969. The whole affair had been something of a fiasco, although, given the context, it is difficult to see how any plan simply imposed from the centre could have succeeded.[19] In the event, the average annual growth rate between 1964 and 1970 was 2.2 per cent, exactly the same as between 1924 and 1937, a period most ministers would have regarded with a shudder.[20]

Part of the National Plan which did survive, however, was the desire to retain full employment while controlling inflation. By later standards, neither rose to massive levels. The period until about 1966 can be seen as a continuation of the full employment trends of the post-war period. However, there was an upward trend from then onwards: in the period 1964–66 the average annual rate was 1.6 per cent, whereas the rate for 1966–70 was

2.5 per cent. In January 1970 unemployment stood at 628,000. While these rates were still relatively low, the increase scarcely added credibility to Labour's claim to be the party of full employment.[21]

But it was the control of inflation that caused more immediate problems for the government. On taking office in 1964, it took advantage of the TUC's goodwill to get the latter's agreement to a joint Statement on Productivity, Prices and Incomes. A National Board for Prices and Incomes was set up in February 1965. However, wages and inflation continued to rise. In April 1965 the TUC agreed to a voluntary incomes policy which set a 'norm' for increases of between 3 and 3.5 per cent, but inflation increased to 4.7 per cent that year.[22] Then, in May 1966, a seamen's strike blew the agreement apart, and following that July's sterling crisis the government announced a pay freeze to operate until the end of the year, despite TUC opposition. The level of inflation fell in both 1966 and 1967, but the end of the freeze saw further upward pressure on wages. This, combined with the 1967 devaluation and general inflationary trends in all western economies, led to a renewed increase in inflation, which reached 4.7 per cent in 1968 and 5.4 per cent in 1969. It is not surprising that inflation was the most-mentioned issue in Conservative candidates' election addresses at the 1970 election.[23]

The problem was that wages were the only area where the government felt it could take effective counter-inflationary measures. This in turn implied the need for some action to deal with trade union powers, a 'need' made more urgent, so it seemed, by the rash of 'unofficial' strikes that had followed the increasing decentralization of wage bargaining from industry-wide to plant level during the decade.[24] In 1968, the government-appointed Donovan Commission on trade unions reported broadly in favour of the status quo. However, Wilson and most of his cabinet colleagues wanted some action to deal with what was becoming a major issue. Accordingly, Castle's White Paper *In Place of Strife* (January 1969) envisaged sweeping changes in the relationship between unions and the state. Some of these were anathema to the unions: for example, the Secretary of State would have the power to order a 28-day 'conciliation pause' before a strike could commence; strike ballots could be demanded by the Secretary of State; and there would be penal sanctions, culminating in imprisonment, for breaches of these rules. There was a more positive side: employers would be compelled to recognize unions, and the appointment of worker-directors would be encouraged.[25] However, these concessions did not impress the unions, which remained deeply suspicious of worker participation in management, and did not see mandatory recognition as a burning issue at a time when levels of unionization were still rising steadily. So union attention was concentrated on the penal, restrictive aspects of the proposals.

The result was fairly predictable. Strong opposition, led by Callaghan, emerged within the cabinet itself, and the wider party was very hostile. In March 1969, almost 100 Labour MPs voted against the proposals or abstained, and the NEC declared its opposition. That June, after almost six months of bitter dispute, the White Paper was withdrawn. Instead, the TUC signed a 'solemn and binding undertaking' covering unofficial strikes and inter-union disputes, which amounted, in fact, to little more than a face-saving exercise for the government. The whole episode had left Wilson and Castle severely damaged. Wilson's approval rating, of just 26 per dent, was worse than that of any other premier since polling began. It can be argued, of course, that the ultimate results of the rejection of *In Place of Strife* were to be disastrous for the unions, but that was not as clear in 1969 as it was to be with post-1980s hindsight.

These policy failures put severe constraints, in turn, on the government's industrial policy. The mixed economy was maintained in virtually the same balance as had existed before 1964, the only exception being the renationalization of iron and steel in 1967. Some efforts were made to galvanize the public sector, and there were productivity gains during the 1960s, although it is hard to see how far these were due to Labour's policies; in any event, the improvement did not last into the 1970s, and much of the gain came from redundancies.[26] In the meantime, little was done to address the problems thrown up by the Morrisonian public corporation. There was no real effort to produce closer integration of the nationalized industries. Workforce commitment was not encouraged by the fact that, under the government's various incomes policies, wage increases in nationalized industries were easier to limit than in the private sector. Nothing was done to increase worker participation. It was possible for the government to argue that the unions were not much interested in the idea, but in fact some workers and union leaders were coming round to it.[27] A more open-minded policy from government at this stage might have restored workers' faith in nationalization, and given it a new, more positive image with which to face the last third of the century. As it was, an opportunity was missed or, perhaps more accurately, scarcely seen.

What ministers did see was the need to revamp the private sector and, in particular, manufacturing. To this end, Labour set out to improve government support for the application of science and technology to industry and to use regional policy to redistribute industry more evenly across the whole country. The agent for the execution of the former aspiration was Mintech. The initial idea was that it would shift R&D expenditure from military to civil purposes. In this, it had some success; one estimate suggests that, by 1969, government expenditure on civil R&D was greater than on military R&D for the first time since the war. From 1966, when Benn succeeded Cousins, the scope and profile of Mintech gradually increased, as it absorbed the Ministry of Aviation, much of the DEA, and certain functions of the Board of Trade to become 'one of the first "superministries"'.[28] Mintech oversaw numerous mergers in a decade which saw more company amalgamations than any since the 1920s.[29] However, it was not all success. It was still difficult to get industry to apply R&D developments, as conservatism still ran deep. The expansion of the ministry inevitably meant it lost some of its cutting edge as a pioneer of new technology. It is open to question whether the mergers it encouraged really benefited the economy or consumers.[30] Yet it was a pity that Wilson had raised such high expectations in 1964; judged by that standard, Mintech tended to be seen as something of a failure, but in all probability it did as much as could have been reasonably expected, and deserves to be remembered as one of the government's more successful initiatives, especially given the restrictive nature of macroeconomic policy for much of the period.

The Wilson governments also wanted to use regional policy to end the drift of industry towards the south and build up 'declining economies' elsewhere in Britain.[31] This was motivated by a humanitarian desire to avoid a repetition of the interwar experience of the depressed areas, by a political desire to improve employment prospects in these predominantly Labour areas, and to make macroeconomic management more straightforward.

Macmillan had already made a start here, and, in real terms, there was a 16-fold increase in regional expenditure between 1962 and 1970. This included new planning machinery; the creation, in 1966, of five development areas (covering almost half of Britain); and subsidies to employers taking on new workers in the development areas. There were significant effects on employment, and the period between 1963 and 1970 has been seen as marking 'the most prolonged, most intensive, and most successful attack ever launched on regional problems in Britain'.[32]

Overall, though, Labour's economic experiences were not particularly positive. Despite some valuable achievements and a slight increase in productivity, the series of austerity packages necessitated by the recurrent sterling crises militated against greater success.[33] Inflation and unemployment proved difficult to control. Given this background, life was always going to be hard for the government in social policy, since it was committed to the revisionist view that a healthy, growing economy was the prerequisite of social reform.

Given the constraints, we should perhaps be more surprised at what the government was able to do, than condemnatory of what it failed to achieve, in social policy. In education, Labour's main aims were to comprehensivize secondary schooling, to raise the school-leaving age from 15 to 16, and to expand further and higher education. There was some success in moving towards these goals. The ongoing elimination of selection was accelerated by Crosland's 1965 circular asking local education authorities to draw up plans for comprehensivization. By 1970, about a third of secondary pupils in England and Wales were in comprehensives, a tenfold increase over 1964.[34] However, nothing was done about the independent sector, so the degree of 'democratization' was limited. And, as comprehensives came under fierce attack in the 1970s, Labour was to be labelled, unfairly, as the party which favoured 'levelling down' in education. The other areas of significant achievement came in the higher education sector. Here, Labour implemented existing Whitehall plans to establish polytechnics and increase the number of universities. By 1967, 29 polytechnics were being set up.[35] The government's other significant achievement was the establishment of the Open University, using distance-learning methods to offer higher education to those who had missed out earlier in life. As a whole, expenditure on education rose by between 6 and 7 per cent a year under Labour.[36] Problems still remained, nevertheless, and the postponement of the raising of the school-leaving age to 16 in 1968 due to spending cuts was a severe blow.[37]

A still more mixed picture emerged in housing. In numerical terms, there was great achievement: the period from 1965 to 1970 saw just over two million new dwellings built, and a net increase in the housing stock of 1.3 million.[38] In no other five-year period since 1918 have so many new homes been built as in 1965–69.[39] Almost half the new building was council housing for rent, built with financial assistance from central government. But the type of council housing built at this time was often rather cheap and nasty, with much of the high-rise and high-density housing erected proving to be poorly constructed and unpopular with tenants. Social and extended family networks were disrupted by rehousing, a fact which led to increased strain on social services and hence public expenditure as older, informal support networks were ruptured. Labour's achievements were equivocal, and in retrospect many would see its policies as leading to significant social problems.

In other areas of social policy, Labour continued to act as the guardian of the welfare state, but at the same time was forced by economic circumstances into some unpalatable decisions. Spending on health and social services grew, and poorer families in particular benefited from increases in pensions and family allowance and the introduction of rate rebates. On the whole, however, the results of this extra expenditure were not startling.[40] A particular embarrassment was the decision, in 1968, to reintroduce prescription charges, which had been abolished on Labour's return to office in 1964.

Other reforms tended to give the government a more liberal image. The abolition of capital punishment in 1965, the legalization of abortion and male homosexuality (for those over 21) in 1967 and the easing of divorce in 1969 were all creditable achievements; while introduced as private members' bills, the government effectively supported their passage by granting the necessary parliamentary time. However, some Labour voters were unhappy with these changes, and Labour was finding itself caught between the desire to do 'the decent thing' on the one hand, and the beliefs of a substantial section of its supporters on the other. It

tended to suggest to many people, among them significant numbers of Labour voters, that the party was 'soft' on crime and irres-
olute on important matters of personal morality.

The Attlee government had left Labour a lot to live up to in
the field of domestic policy, and the same was true in the field
of foreign affairs. At the 1964 election, Labour attacked the
Conservatives for having let the country down, but there were few
concrete proposals, other than to set up a Ministry of Overseas
Development and promote increased Commonwealth trade; and,
once elected, Labour found its options to be very limited, and
was increasingly constrained by the difficult economic position.
Wilson had no doubts about the importance of sustaining Britain's
world role, stating on one memorable occasion that Britain's fron-
tiers were on the Himalayas.[41] His Foreign Secretaries, Gordon
Walker, Stewart and Brown, were all right-wingers, keen on the
EEC; Gordon Walker and Stewart were also pretty lightweight, and
even Brown found it hard to assert himself as Foreign Secretary
against Wilson. Healey, Defence Secretary throughout the period,
had worked closely with Bevin in the later 1940s as international
secretary at party headquarters, and was very much a NATO man.
In personal terms, then, Labour brought expertise into office.
In terms of policy, continued adherence to a world role and the
Atlantic alliance could be expected, while the issue of Europe
was likely to arise at some point. The left, on the other hand,
remained marginal to external policy throughout the Wilson
years.

Thus Britain remained strongly committed to NATO and the
USA. This made for some controversy, because American forces
were involved in bitter fighting in Vietnam, supporting the South
against the Communist North. In September 1965, Wilson made
a secret deal with US President Lyndon B. Johnson promising
tacit British support for the American position in Vietnam, and
the maintenance of Britain's existing international commitments,
in return for American support for the current sterling exchange
rate with the dollar. But the Americans had wanted more:
British arms or, preferably, troops to help with the war effort.
Britain's need for US support, not just over sterling but also in
its own Asian difficulties in regard to the Malaysian–Indonesian
Confrontation of 1963–66, might have impelled Wilson towards
accepting Johnson's position. However, despite his regard for

'LBJ', he wanted to avoid intervention, which he saw as potentially hugely damaging. Ultimately, this stance can be seen as highly successful: as Young puts it, 'Wilson's willingness to criticise the USA at certain points, his refusal to become actively involved and his attempts to mediate a settlement helped to keep domestic opposition manageable and avoided a costly war'.[42]

Cost was a major issue. Britain's existing overseas commitments were becoming increasingly difficult to sustain. The February 1966 Defence White Paper stressed Britain's world role, but pared away at expenditure, which meant that it was increasingly difficult even to pretend that the commitments could be fulfilled.[43] The deflation package of July 1966 forced Britain to give up even this halfway house, and large spending cuts were made. Following devaluation in 1967, it was decided that British forces would be withdrawn from east of Suez by the end of 1971. But this arose from economic necessity, not principle. The true colour of government attitudes could be seen in the retention of Britain's nuclear weaponry and its continued loyalty to NATO.

The Commonwealth also posed problems for Labour. The party was pledged to continue decolonization, which had proceeded apace and, compared with other European states, with relative ease since the late 1950s. Unluckily for the Labour government, the easy period soon ended. In Rhodesia (Zimbabwe), a white minority was adamant that there should not be black majority rule on independence, but Labour refused to grant independence without majority rule. The resulting stalemate ended dramatically in November 1965 when the white Rhodesians under Ian Smith unilaterally declared their independence. Inconclusive talks followed, but the problem could not be resolved. Rhodesia's action was illegal, and sanctions were imposed. But the latter proved ineffective. There was considerable criticism of the British government, but it is difficult to see what else could have been done: military intervention would have had no public support in Britain, might have been fruitless and would almost certainly have spelt political nemesis for Labour. The question was left to drag on for many years to come. Problems in handling the Nigerian civil war later in the decade also posed serious challenges to, and aroused considerable criticism of, the government. In addition, overseas aid was an early casualty of the continuing demands for public expenditure cuts, and the proportion of GDP spent on it actually fell between 1964 and 1970. The Ministry of Overseas Development, set up with high hopes in 1964, was rapidly downgraded. All this aroused left-wing criticism and seems to have turned some vocal young activists against the Labour Party, or at least against its leadership.[44]

The other contentious area in foreign policy was the question of entry into the EEC. The party was split on the issue, as it had been in 1961. While there were ardent supporters of entry, like Brown and Jenkins, there were many who were sceptical, and on the whole it would seem there were more firm opponents than clear supporters of entry. This was not really a 'left–right' split. It would be true to say that, on the left, few advocates of entry could be found, but there was no corresponding unity in favour in the centre or on the right of the party.[45] Thus people like Jay and Shore, neither of them 'left-wingers', opposed entry. If anything, Wilson was neither pro- nor anti-, but he did see the issue's destructive potential. The solution was, in the short term only, brilliant. In 1967, Britain applied for entry, but knowing that the French President, de Gaulle, was certain to veto it. In this way, the issue was shunted into a siding; pro-Europeans were appeased because the effort had been made, while the antis were relieved that it had come to nothing. But the issue would not go away for ever; even in the medium term there would be a problem when de Gaulle departed the scene and a future Conservative government then reapplied.

At the 1970 election, Labour's manifesto would claim that the government's 'fundamental and historic changes in Britain's defence and foreign policy ha[d] given Britain a more credible and realistic position in world affairs than we ever enjoyed under the last Tory administration'.[46] In fact, the government's foreign policy had not been as purposeful, as skilfully directed or as successful as that of the 1945–51 administration. Instead, problems had been met with vacillation and procrastination. And in many areas – Vietnam, Rhodesia, nuclear weapons – the failure to take a stronger line, however understandable, had alienated many, particularly younger, people from Labour altogether, and made many people within the Labour Party far more critical of its leadership. Neither in terms of world affairs nor of party management, therefore, was the government's legacy in this area a happy one.

The 1964–70 government did not, then, live up to the reputation of the Attlee administration in terms of economic management, social policy or foreign affairs. But this was not all. For Wilson also faced other problems, in issues which had scarcely disturbed Attlee and his colleagues. Six areas stood out in particular: the reform of government, Scottish and Welsh nationalism, Northern Ireland, race, gender and youth.

The question of constitutional reform had hardly bothered the 1940s government. But by the 1960s there was growing interest in the nature and powers of government and, in particular, a growing tendency to see administrative problems as one cause of low economic growth rates. The Wilson government set out to deal with a number of aspects of the question. One answer was the creation of five new ministries in 1964. But these had mixed experiences. As seen above, the most important, the DEA, was scrapped in 1969. By then, the Ministry of Land and Natural Resources had already been abolished. Overseas Development, though it survived, was downgraded in 1967. Thus, only two of the new ministries, Mintech and the Welsh Office, survived fully. An attempt to reform the House of Lords foundered in April 1969, a victim of an alliance between the Conservative right, which wanted no change, and the Labour left, which wanted abolition and nothing less. An attempt to reform and modernize the civil service on the basis of the 1968 Fulton Report came to very little. The Redcliffe-Maud committee, set up to look at the functions and boundaries of local authorities, made radical proposals, but its suggestion of eight regional authorities was not adopted by the government; and the sclerosis of local government continued, even despite the plans to redraw boundaries and reallocate functions which resulted, ultimately, in the 1972 Local Government Act. While Wilson's governments did not substantially reduce the functions of local government, they had no real conception of the need to revitalize it, and in so far as they saw any need for the 'modernization' of local government it was more in the context of the desire to promote faster economic growth than in terms of strengthening democracy and participation.[47] Centralization continued, if only by default.

Increasingly, though, there was resistance to centralization. This began to be expressed especially through growing support for Scottish and Welsh nationalism, which emerged during the 1960s as 'new' issues on the British political agenda, and ones with which the Labour Party was ill equipped to deal. Labour had had a paper commitment to Scottish home rule from the 1920s, but in

1958 this had been quietly extinguished, a logical step given the party's commitment to centralization and statism, and the apparent political weakness of nationalism.[48] Labour's commitment to Welsh nationalism had been, if anything, even weaker. Yet the Welsh nationalist party, Plaid Cymru, had made steady progress during the 1950s, taking 3.1 per cent of the vote in Wales in 1955 and 5.2 per cent in 1959. It fell back a little in 1964, but Wilson's creation of the Welsh Office with its own Secretary of State was, in part at least, aimed to reduce this threat in what was one of Labour's strongest areas of support. However, the gesture did little to assuage nationalist discontent; and in Scotland, too, support for nationalism began to grow. At the 1966 election, though electing no MPs, Plaid took 4.3 per cent and the SNP 5.0 per cent of their respective nations' votes. In July 1966, Plaid gained Carmarthen from Labour at a by-election, and subsequently slashed Labour's majorities at West Rhondda and Caerphilly. The nationalists also began to make an impact in Scotland, gaining Hamilton from Labour in November 1967, averaging around 25 per cent in the other three seats they fought during the lifetime of the 1966 parliament, and making gains in local elections.[49] While few Labourites yet saw devolution as necessary, the government did appoint a constitutional commission under Lord Crowther to study the problem, and also tried to alleviate some nationalist concerns by passing the Welsh Language Act in 1967.[50] However, all this came a little late in the day, and as economic problems mounted, so too did support for the nationalist parties, particularly as unemployment was higher in Wales and Scotland than in most of England. The nationalist backlash in safe Labour areas also represented resentment at virtual one-party rule, with its attendant complacency and, at times, corruption, in many parts of Wales and Scotland.[51] At the 1970 general election both parties polled over 10 per cent of the votes in their respective nations, and it is hard to avoid the conclusion that Labour's centralizing tendencies had helped to raise problems which were soon to cause the party significant difficulties.

Problems with Northern Ireland were less of Labour's making. The 1921 settlement had separated Ireland into the Irish Free State (later the Irish Republic) and Northern Ireland, which remained part of the United Kingdom, electing 12 Westminster MPs, but also with its own parliament at Stormont. The Stormont regime was Protestant dominated, and Catholics had suffered much discrimination. In the 1960s, Catholic civil rights groups became increasingly vocal, and in 1969 there was a Protestant backlash; that summer saw a series of riots and clashes, and in August the Home Secretary, Callaghan, deployed British troops in order to keep the peace. The situation stabilized for a while, and the government, and Callaghan, took credit for what seemed to have been a successful operation.[52] However, even before the 1970 election, the situation had begun to deteriorate once more, and in 1972 Heath's government would dissolve Stormont and impose direct rule from London. So far as Labour was concerned, the short-term results were quite favourable: its defence of Catholics against perceivedly oppressive Protestants boosted its image on the left and, possibly, helped to win back some support among British Catholic voters who had been alienated by the legalization of abortion. The imposition of direct rule by the Conservatives in 1972 would lead the Ulster Unionists to cease taking the Conservative whip; had they not broken with Heath at this point, the February 1974 general election would have given the Tories more seats than Labour, although not an overall majority. But in the longer term, the upsurge in violence in Northern Ireland, and its extension to mainland Britain through Irish Republican Army (IRA) bombing campaigns, meant renewed emphasis on an issue – law and order – where the Conservatives were perceived as stronger than Labour by most voters, and would also add to the perceived crisis of governability in the UK which would, ultimately, damage Labour so severely in the 1970s. In the longer term, therefore, the eruption of Ulster was to help the Conservatives to the detriment of the Labour Party.[53]

Race and immigration was another issue which broke on to the political agenda in the 1960s, and again it was one with which Labour struggled to deal. Labour had long been committed to the right of Commonwealth citizens to settle in Britain, and had claimed to be in favour of racial equality. The restrictive immigration legislation of 1962 had faced strong Labour opposition. However, because immigrants settled mostly in working-class areas, there were fears of a backlash among Labour's traditional supporters, and such concerns seemed to be borne out at the 1964 election when Gordon Walker was defeated at Smethwick, a west Midland constituency with a relatively high immigrant population, by a Conservative candidate whose campaign relied heavily on racism. The favourable reaction of some working-class people to Enoch Powell's major anti-immigration speech of April 1968 tended to intensify concerns that Labour was in a difficult position on this issue. Crossman had acknowledged after Smethwick that 'immigration c[ould] be the biggest potential vote-loser for the Labour Party', and such concerns were married to fears of the effects for members of ethnic minorities if there was a strong white backlash; at the same time, though, openly racist attitudes survived in the party and the trade union movement.[54] The Labour leadership deplored such views, wanted to pursue liberal policies as far as it could, and also recognized that it was the most likely beneficiary of ethnic minority votes.[55] Its response, therefore, was to try a balancing act. In 1965, it tightened immigration controls, while passing a Race Relations Act outlawing racial discrimination and establishing a Race Relations Board. There was much less balance about the Commonwealth Immigrants Act, rushed through in 1968 in order to prevent the entry of large numbers of Asians who were being expelled from Kenya and who held British passports. This discriminated clearly on grounds of race, since it gave preference for immigration to those with at least one white grandparent over those with none at all, and was described in *The Times* as 'probably the most shameful measure that Labour [MPs] have ever been asked by their whips to support'.[56] The issue was not really resolved: in trying to placate white voters, Labour had upset many ethnic minority voters, and the fact that it was not until 1987 that a non-white Labour MP was elected hardly did much to draw in this growing section of the British population.[57] At the same time, it did not go as far as some white voters wanted. The real problem, though, was that there were no easy answers for Labour in this area.

The same was true with issues of gender. Labour, for all its protestations, had never really prioritised women's specific concerns. At times, as in the period immediately before the First World War, it had forged alliances with women's groups, and the 1918 constitution had set up separate women's sections in CLPs, reserved four NEC places for women and established a separate women's conference. But the conference and the women's sections were largely ignored when it came to decision making within the party, while the four women on the NEC were elected not by women but by the whole party conference. By the 1930s, ambitious women like Barbara Betts (later Castle) were deliberately bypassing the women's organization, realizing how marginal it was. Between the wars, Labour resisted family allowances on the grounds that they would threaten the principle of the 'family wage', and a Labour government had withdrawn married women's rights to unemployment benefit. During and after the Second World War, Labour ministers had resisted women's demands for equal pay with men. Because, on the whole, the women's movement had been quite weak since the 1920s, these lines had not faced too much opposition. But the 1960s saw the women's movement become more vocal and influential than at any time since the First World War. Although Wilson had some personal commitment to equality, he did not feel he could go too far towards it. True, Castle was promoted higher than any previous woman cabinet minister, and two women sat together in cabinet for the first time in 1968 when Judith Hart joined her as Paymaster General. In 1970 an Equal Pay Act was passed. But having one or two women in the cabinet was rather a token victory, and the Equal Pay Act, due to come into effect only in 1975, looked like cynical electioneering. Most women did not suddenly become radical feminists, but some who might have come into the Labour Party now turned their backs on it in favour of the women's movement or far-left groups, while others, who did stay with Labour, became more critical of the leadership.

The 1960s was also a decade when youth came more clearly on to the political agenda. But here again the party was slow to respond and, when did, it was often in a discouraging manner. The growth of youth culture, with roots in the 1930s but really blossoming from the 1950s, had left the party cold; there was little attempt even to understand modern movements and feelings among young people. The party's youth movement, Young Socialists, had been disbanded for ultra-leftism in 1965 and re-organized as the Labour Party Young Socialists, with most of its (already limited) powers removed. At constituency and ward level, LPYS members were more likely to encounter suspicion and hostility than encouragement – except at election times when, unsurprisingly, their commitment to canvassing and committee room work meant a temporary reprieve. In addition to these perennial problems, the youth organization began to crumble as the government struggled, the number of branches halving between 1962 and 1969. Government policies did little to stem the growing alienation of young people from the party. Youth protest movements offended party leaders and many stalwart Labour voters. The reduction of the voting age from 21 to 18 in 1969 was less a principled commitment to young people than a piece of gerrymandering based on the assumption that young people were more likely to vote Labour than Conservative. Here again, then, the political agenda was being amended in ways that did not at all suit the Labour Party.

At the same time, many of the old signs of Labour vitality were beginning to fade. Union membership was still expanding. But the unions were strongest in the very industries that were in decline: the National Union of Mineworkers fell from 586,000 members to 279,000 between 1960 and 1970, while in the same period the NUR shrank from 334,000 to 198,000. Government pay policies and attempts at union reform loosened, perhaps permanently, the commitment of many trade unionists to supporting the Labour Party.[58] The Co-operative movement was losing its old vitality, too: greater prosperity, more consumer choice and a rationalization programme all made its shops less central to working-class life than they had been in earlier times, while membership of the Co-operative Women's Guild in 1971 was little more than half of what it had been in 1960.[59]

This decline was reflected, to some extent, by a fall in the Labour Party's individual membership. The official figure fell from 830,116 in 1964 to 680,191 in 1970, a drop of over 15 per cent in just six years.[60] While the significance of this should not be exaggerated, there was undoubtedly a sharp decrease; and both figures were overstated, reflecting the arcane rules for CLP affiliation to the national party. There were external factors involved, such as the '"privatization" of lifestyles',[61] but many people did seem to be falling out with and from the party, some to join the new far-left groups which began to emerge in the period, more to join no party at all. Those who remained were often more rebellious than they had been in earlier periods, and this, allied with growing trade union discontent, meant that the NEC suffered no fewer than 12 defeats on major issues at party conferences in the late 1960s.[62] The CLPs were now, on the whole, well to the left of the party leadership, a trend that was to continue into the 1980s.

During the 1966 parliament, electoral trends were generally very unfavourable towards Labour. As late as February 1967 Labour had been 11 points ahead in the polls, but by that December, it trailed by 17 points: by May 1968 it was 28 points behind. That month, Labour fared catastrophically in the local elections. Among other setbacks, it lost control of Sheffield for the first time since 1932. In parliamentary by-elections, meanwhile, it lost 15 seats between 1966 and 1969.

The Conservatives were still 11 points ahead in the polls in December 1969, but by then the worst crises were past. Jenkins's austerity measures were beginning to bear fruit in improved balance of payments figures, while Wilson's reputation seemed to be recovering remarkably. And there were still widespread doubts about Heath, the Conservative leader, especially as his party seemed to be moving towards a more radical free-market approach. Thus, the early months of 1970 saw some Labour recovery, and Wilson, enjoying a seven-point lead in the polls, dissolved parliament on 29 May 1970. Labour issued a 'safety first' manifesto and asked the voters to trust it. All in all, it seemed, Labour would win the election.

But, on a significantly lower turnout than in 1966, it was defeated. The announcement, two days before polling, of an unexpected balance of payments deficit did not help Labour's cause; it can hardly have been decisive, but it probably helped remind people of the travails of recent years, which was just what Wilson had been trying to avoid. Whatever the reason, enough voters turned to the Conservatives, or abstained, to put Heath in power.[63] Labour made a net loss of 58 seats on a swing of 4.7 per cent, the greatest since 1945: in parts of the Midlands, and in east Lancashire, there were even heavier shifts against Labour. The party performed better in the rest of the north and in Scotland, but in the south outside inner London its performance was weak. Support among men fell more heavily than among women, and while its share of the non-manual vote scarcely declined at all, it suffered a huge loss of manual workers' support, from 69 per cent in 1966 to 58 per cent (only slightly higher than in 1959).[64] This shift is explicable less in terms of 'class dealignment' as such than in terms of policy failure on the part of the government: a significant number of workers, perhaps more 'instrumental' in their voting than previously, felt they had had enough of incomes policies and restrictions, and wanted a change because they felt they could do better economically out of a Conservative government than a Labour one.

Labour, then, was back in opposition. The gap between the leadership, on the one hand, and the unions and party membership, on the other, was wide, and, some thought, unbridgeable. There were worrying signs of a leakage of traditional Labour support. The government's revisionist strategy of seeking a more socialist society through economic growth under capitalism had come to little, because the economy had refused to grow as required, even despite the special efforts that had been expended on it. 'New' issues were posing serious moral and political dilemmas for the party. It was not a happy situation, and in the immediate aftermath of defeat it was unclear how it could be resolved.

9   Labour in Crisis? 1970–79

Labour's loss of office in both 1931 and 1951 had been followed by long periods in opposition, and the same was to be true after 1979. By contrast, the party had to wait less than four years after its 1970 setback to resume control of government. The years between 1970 and 1974 proved a period of intense activity, as economic crisis intensified and the Labour movement sought to reinvigorate itself. Policies were reworked; positions were changed. But the cost of the resulting radicalization of party policy was increasing tension within the party, the sowing of some of the seeds of the split which led to the formation of the Social Democratic Party (SDP) in 1981, and a general intensification of doubt both inside and outside the party as to the route it should now take. All these developments were then exacerbated by the five years of Labour government between 1974 and 1979. Shedding party policies left and centre – if not right – and reeling from a concatenation of economic crises and severe challenges to traditional Labour politics, the party ultimately succumbed to conclusive defeat at the general election of 1979. The roots of many of the problems which were then to consign Labour to 18 years of opposition were to be found in this period.

The Heath government presided over troubled times. Unemployment grew, peaking at 929,000 in January 1972. Inflation rose to an annual average of 8.6 per cent for 1971–73. Keynesians had assumed that there was a trade-off between inflation and unemployment, but now the economy seemed to be in the grip of 'stagflation', where both rose together. External pressures, like the quadrupling of oil prices by Middle Eastern states in 1973, fuelled inflation further. All this led to greater wage militancy on the part of workers, and a further deterioration in industrial relations. Working days lost through strikes averaged just under 4 million per annum between 1965 and 1969; between 1971 and 1973 the figure was almost 15 million, with 24 million days being lost

185

in 1972 alone. When this was linked to the ongoing conflict in Northern Ireland, it seemed to many that the United Kingdom was becoming ungovernable, and that, for the first time since the war, capitalism was in crisis. This crisis was reflected by developments inside the Labour Party. Revisionism, already under pressure, lost credibility still further; if socialism was all about an egalitarian distribution of the surplus produced by a growing capitalism, how could it respond to a situation in which capitalism was manifestly in trouble? As early as 1962, Crosland had pointed out that a *deus ex machina*, in the form of entry to 'Europe', 'may' well be needed to solve the problem of low growth.[1] By 1970, this 'may' was becoming a 'must' for much of the revisionist right. And it was also combined, increasingly, with strong advocacy of another panacea: 'a prices and incomes policy' to control inflation.[2] The problem with both these solutions, however, was that they aroused the hostility of the bulk of the Labour movement, and particularly of the trade unions. The bankruptcy of revisionism at a time of economic crisis, in short, was leading to the break-up of the historic alliance between the unions and the party's right wing, just as surely as that alliance had cracked under the pressure of economic crisis between 1929 and 1931. Here were the roots of both the party's leftward swing in the later 1970s, and the isolation of the right among whose consequences was to be the formation of the SDP. The other basic element in the beginnings of the swing to the left was the perception that the Wilson governments had failed. Many people across the party were disappointed; some felt betrayed. There was a strong feeling that next time it must be different. Many people in the party began to work even more seriously for new policies and strategies for a future Labour administration.

Given the extent of change in this period, it might be thought surprising that Wilson remained leader. But he was still seen as a great electoral asset, and was canny enough to see off potential threats.[3] Jenkins's election as deputy leader in succession to Brown in 1970 suggested he was the obvious alternative, but there was no attempt to overthrow Wilson in his favour. With Jenkins as shadow Chancellor, Callaghan as shadow Home Secretary and Healey promoted to shadow Foreign Secretary, the leadership was still in centre-right hands. True, Michael Foot, seen by many as the spiritual heir to Bevan, was elected to the shadow cabinet in

1970, and Benn now emerged as a fervent opponent of entry to the EEC, an advocate of much greater state intervention in industry, and possessor of a new, more populist image. But the right also continued to throw up new stars, such as Shirley Williams, who became one of the most popular figures in the PLP and who served as shadow Home Secretary in 1972–73. Indeed, since it was almost impossible for a CLP to deselect its MP, the PLP remained to a large extent insulated from the leftish pressures in the wider party, and since it alone elected the party leader and shadow cabinet, the party leadership was always likely to remain in cautious hands.[4] The realization of this problem led, in 1973, to the formation of the Campaign for Labour Party Democracy (CLPD), which aimed, *inter alia,* to enfranchise the wider party in the election of the party leader.[5] The NEC, elected annually at party conference, was a different matter altogether; and, after 1970, the left became far more significant. The NEC had always been more prominent when Labour had been in opposition than in office, but now there were conscious efforts to enhance its status at a time when its balance was tilting leftwards. One sign of this was the extensive work done on policy formulation.[6]

To some extent the leftward shift of the NEC reflected a degree of trade union radicalization. This was partly due to disillusionment with the Wilson governments, and anger at *In Place of Strife,* but rising inflation and unemployment also increased militancy. Some of the leading unions, like the TGWU and the Amalgamated Union of Engineering Workers (AUEW), elected more combative leaders, moving matters still further from the days when a bloc of right-wing unions and their leaders had made the party safe for social democracy. The self-marginalization of a section of the party's social democratic right was part cause and part effect of these developments. Thus the party conference, at length, moved still further away from the PLP and its leadership, inflicting regular defeats on the latter and, in 1973, adopting a programme about which Wilson and his colleagues had grave reservations. In addition, strike activity increased. The miners' strikes of 1972 and 1974 both led Heath to declare a state of emergency, and resulted in power cuts. There were overtime bans by train drivers and power workers, among others. Some of these disputes were accompanied by a degree of violence and the use of flying pickets, bussed in from other areas to close down secondary targets. As in other periods, the party leadership felt distinctly uneasy about all this, but could do little to stop it.

But the forces operating on union–party relations were not all divisive in their effects. While the balance was shifting left-wards, many unions remained willing to back the leadership. And Heath himself helped push unions and party back together. Two things particularly antagonized the unions. The first was the 1971 Industrial Relations Act, a massive statute which aimed to provide a comprehensive legal framework for trade unionism. The Act, which included numerous intrusions on unions' powers, backed by penal sanctions, aroused massive union and Labour hostility. Legal actions under the Act, and the imprisonment of the 'Pentonville Five' in July 1972 for breaking an order of the National Industrial Relations Court, led the TUC to demand nothing less than total repeal. Labour accepted this position with alacrity. Second, growing government pressure to restrict wage increases, culminating in the enactment of a statutory wages pol-icy in 1972, further antagonized the unions. The result was that, as early as the end of 1971, the TUC and the Labour Party were 'in closer alliance than at any time since 1967'.[7]

Union leaders were hostile to pay restraint on the lines imple-mented by Heath but, nonetheless, many of them, like Jack Jones of the TGWU, did see the need to bring inflation under control. The result was a revival of the concept of the 'social wage'; pay restraint would be accepted but only in return for social reforms beneficial to union members. The result of this was the 'Social Contract', adopted as party and TUC policy in 1973. While its details remained vague, it helped to cement still further the renewed bonds between unions and party, and it suggested, if nothing else, that Labour had at least some idea of how to deal with what was rapidly becoming the dominant issue in British politics.

The most radical manifestation of Labour's leftward shift came in the field of economic policy. At one stage almost 50 policy committees were at work under the aegis of the NEC, and the end result of their endeavours was *Labour's Programme 1973*, which was approved by that year's party conference.[8] The programme committed Labour to price controls; to the Social Contract; to increased pensions; to renegotiation of the terms of entry to the EEC; and to the restoration of free col-lective bargaining and repeal of the Industrial Relations Act.

Industrial democracy would be extended. A National Enterprise Board (NEB) would buy into individual firms (thus marking the abandonment of the sector-by-sector approach favoured by the party hitherto), and make planning agreements with companies to ensure greater control over their actions. It would also take control of 'twenty-five of our largest manufacturers' at an early stage.[9] The NEC had been split on this last issue, with moderates led by Callaghan, Healey and Williams vocal in their opposition.[10] Wilson had reserved his position, but at the party conference he came out against it, suggesting that it might be ignored in the drafting of the next election manifesto.[11] This aroused considerable left-wing ire.[12] But the programme as a whole was passed, committing Labour to a more radical package of concrete economic proposals than ever before.

The debates on economic policy were bitter, but paled beside the problems posed to the party by the issue of entry to the EEC. The arch-Europhile Heath revived Britain's application and completed negotiations for entry in June 1971. In January 1973 Britain became a member of an enlarged, nine-member EEC. Labour remained split. For some, like Jenkins and Rodgers, it remained axiomatic that Britain must be a member of the EEC on almost any terms. But opposition was hardening. The old considerations against entry (see Chapter 7) still held good for many. They were supplemented by the growing desire of some on the left to see the imposition of import controls – which were incompatible with EEC membership – as a way of bolstering British industry against increasing import penetration.[13] The 1970 party conference almost passed a resolution opposing entry on principle, but matters eased somewhat once Heath had agreed terms; it could now be argued that the issue of principle was academic, and Labour could, instead, unite very largely in criticism of the terms agreed to by the government.[14] This was the line Wilson took, and it gave him ample ammunition for attacks on the government, which meant his stock rose with the left. But Jenkins and his followers were infuriated by anything less than wholehearted acceptance, and in the Commons vote on entry in October 1971, 69 Labour MPs (including Jenkins, Williams, Rodgers, David Owen and Dick Taverne) voted with the government, while a further 20 (including Crosland) abstained.[15] Jenkins, seen as the leader of the revolt, came in for strong criticism, and narrowly beat off Foot's challenge in that year's deputy leadership election. However, matters did not rest there. Benn, party chairman for 1971–72, had come round to the idea that a referendum should be held on entry. At first the idea had attracted little support, but soon people began to see its value as a way of avoiding a permanent split in the party. Jenkins and his colleagues were staunchly against the idea, ostensibly on constitutional grounds, but probably also fearing that a referendum would result in a vote against membership. In March 1972, Wilson came out in favour of the idea, and the shadow cabinet supported him by a narrow majority. As a result, Jenkins resigned the deputy leadership, and Owen, Harold Lever and George Thomson resigned from the front bench.[16] But there was no major party split and, all in all, Wilson managed to keep the party more or less together, if not united. In October 1973, Jenkins, his position in the party much diminished, re-entered the shadow cabinet on Wilson's terms. For the time being, the EEC issue was under control. But that control had been bought at the cost, first, of fudging over the splits in the party, and, second, of increasing the siege mentality of a section of the party's right wing.

Jenkins rejoined the shadow cabinet just in time, for Heath's government was running into what would turn out to be terminal difficulties. After a series of embarrassing policy U-turns, the Conservatives opted to face down the miners, who were demanding a large pay increase as the price for ending an overtime ban. Emergency fuel-saving measures, such as a reduced speed limit on the roads and a three-day working week, were introduced from 31 December 1973. When the miners voted overwhelmingly for strike action to start on 10 February, Heath decided to dissolve parliament and fight an election on what he believed would be the winning slogan of 'Who rules Britain?' His optimism was matched by Labour pessimism, for earlier poll leads had dissipated and the Gallup poll for January 1974 put the Conservatives two points ahead. No seats had been gained from the Conservatives at a by-election since May 1971, while Labour had lost Rochdale to the Liberals in October 1972, Lincoln to the erstwhile Jenkinsite Taverne (now standing as 'Democratic Labour') in March 1973 and a seat in Glasgow to the SNP that November. Since it would be an election in which issues of union power would be central, it was hardly surprising that Labour's expectations were not altogether rosy.[17]

However, the Conservatives were also under pressure: the three-day week was just the latest in a long string of states of emergency, the government had backtracked on a number of its 1970 pledges, and inflation and unemployment were both rising. Labour's share of the vote fell by almost six points to 37.2 per cent, but the Conservatives fared even worse, their share plummeting from 46.4 to just 37.9 per cent. The beneficiaries of the partial collapse of the 'two-party' vote were the minor parties: the Liberals more than doubled their poll share to 19.3 per cent, while the SNP's performance in terms of the Scottish vote was scarcely less spectacular. In terms of seats, though, the electoral system played the trick of 1929 and 1951; it gave the party with the second-largest number of votes the largest number of seats. Labour emerged with 301 MPs, and the Conservatives with 297. Thus, for the first time since 1929, a general election had produced a parliament in which no party had an overall majority: the balance was held by the 37 'others', who included 14 Liberals, 12 Northern Ireland MPs (one of whom was broadly in sympathy with Labour), two independent Labourites, seven Scottish Nationalists and two Plaid Cymru representatives.

It would, therefore, be something of a misnomer to describe the February 1974 election as a Labour victory. The party had made a net gain of 13 seats, but its fall in the share of the popular vote suggested that it was not massively loved by the electorate. The party's main gains came in the west Midlands, where it captured nine more seats than in 1970, and in western Lancashire, where its net representation rose by five.

Under the circumstances, Heath tried to stay in office. He appealed to Jeremy Thorpe, the Liberal leader, to form some kind of coalition. However, the Conservatives were clearly discredited, and Thorpe was under pressure from radical elements in his own party to have nothing to do with any such arrangement. To the surprise of no one, the talks soon proved fruitless, and the failure of Heath's attempts to attract Thorpe meant that, on 4 March, Wilson was invited to form his third administration.

Wilson's cabinet was full of experience, and contained few surprises. Healey became Chancellor, Callaghan Foreign Secretary and, in a clear sign of his diminished standing, Jenkins returned to the Home Office. Other prominent members of the social democratic right included Crosland and Williams (at the newly created Department of Prices and Consumer Protection). But the left was also well represented, and took some crucial posts. Benn went to Industry. Foot became Employment Secretary, a position involving close dealings with the unions, particularly on the Social Contract. Castle went to a major role at Health and Social Security. It would be facile to call this a 'left-wing cabinet', but in no other Labour government have so many important portfolios been handed to the left.

Obviously, a further general election could not be long delayed. For the next six months, there was something of a return to 1964–66, with Wilson and his colleagues manoeuvring to provide themselves with a suitable base from which to launch an appeal for a stronger position. They ended the coal dispute swiftly, reaching a settlement favourable to the miners on 6 March, and repealed the Industrial Relations Act. A move was made towards a more progressive taxation regime as value added tax (VAT) was reduced and income tax increased. And council house rents, which the Conservatives had intended to increase considerably, were frozen. Longer-term policies included the start of the renegotiation of British terms of entry to the EEC and a flood of White Papers in the summer on industry, pensions, land and devolution. With Labour slightly ahead in the polls, an election was called for 10 October.

The election campaign was, once again, lacklustre. There was never much doubt that Labour would win, but the polls overpredicted its support and, in the event, the result was rather disappointing: Labour took 39.2 per cent of the votes, the Conservatives 35.8 per cent and the Liberals fell back a little to 18.3 per cent. Plaid Cymru's share of the Welsh vote was static, but the SNP made further advances, to register a 30.4 per cent share of the Scottish vote, more than the Conservatives. All this translated into an overall Labour majority of just three: it took 319 seats, while the Conservatives had 277 and the other parties totalled 39. The seats of Taverne and another Labour rebel, Eddie Milne at Blyth, had been regained, at least. The parliamentary position was going to be difficult. However, it was a little more secure than it appeared at first sight, because Labour had a hefty lead over the Conservatives, and the plethora of other groups – many of them with axes to grind against the Tories – made it unlikely that all opposition MPs would be able to find an issue around which to unite. Labour had made further gains, especially in the west Midlands, but the lower than average swing in key marginals meant it took fewer seats than it might have expected on a national swing of 2.2 per cent.[18]

A new poll soon followed: the referendum on the EEC. Labour had started to renegotiate Britain's terms of entry shortly after its return to office. It was clear, however, that the party remained deeply split, and that the division ran right up the party to the cabinet room. Accordingly, it was decided that, following a 1932 National government precedent, there would be an 'agreement to differ': on this issue alone, ministers would be relieved from the normal obligations of collective responsibility, whereby they were supposed to speak with one voice, although the government's official line would be to support continued membership. To many, this seemed to plumb new depths of Wilsonian cynicism, but, if the party was to be kept together, it was hard to see what else could have been done. By March 1975 the negotiations were complete, and a referendum was set for 5 June. The renegotiated terms came in for considerable criticism, with the left in particular feeling that they were 'very far short' of what party policy demanded. They only passed through parliament with opposition support, as a total of 145 Labour MPs, including seven cabinet ministers, voted against.[19] On 26 April, a special party conference rejected the terms by a two-to-one majority.[20] The referendum campaign itself was a strange spectacle, with people like Heath, Jenkins and Thorpe united in the 'Yes' campaign and Foot, Benn and Enoch Powell in the 'No' lobby. Wilson and Callaghan posed as somewhat reluctant supporters of the deal they had negotiated. The result showed a two-to-one majority in favour of continued membership on the new terms. This seemed to settle the matter.[21] Of course, the issue did not go away for long, but in the immediate aftermath Wilson took the opportunity to downgrade the referendum's main advocate, Benn, whose radical policies at Industry had become increasingly embarrassing to the premier. He was switched with the loyalist figure of Eric Varley, erstwhile Energy Secretary. Benn decided against resignation on the grounds that he would have more leverage for the causes in which he believed if he remained within the cabinet.[22]

This whole affair – the 'successful' outcome of the referendum, and the marginalization of Benn – was to prove one of Wilson's greatest coups. In fact, with one exception, it was also his last. The final act came, with characteristic theatre, on 16 March 1976 when, to almost universal surprise, he announced that he would resign the leadership as soon as the party had elected a succes-sor.[23] This move gave rise to considerable speculation, but the explanation was prosaic enough. Wilson was 60, and felt stale. He felt a debt to his wife, who had married an Oxford don but then spent three decades in the public spotlight she hated. Finally, and perhaps most of all, there was Wilson's ordinariness, surely his best feature. Civil servants retired at 60. Politicians should do the same, not amble on into their dotage. It may be, as well, that he feared he was already losing some of his mental powers.[24] And so he went. One of the few people to be informed in advance was Callaghan, in order to allow him to prepare for the leadership election: this was a notable sign of the extent to which relations between the two men had improved.[25]

Ultimately, there were six candidates in that election. Callaghan was the centrist figure, sceptical of the enthusiasms of the left and the social democratic right, close to the unions both in style and substance, and with more experience of high office than any of his rivals. Healey, the other centre-right candidate, was handi-capped by perceptions that he was over-combative and likely to split the party, and the fact that he was Chancellor at a time of seri-ous economic problems. Crosland and Jenkins, from the social democratic right, were both now rather marginal figures. From the left came Foot, whose ministerial record – especially in deal-ing with the unions – had surprised and impressed many with his leadership potential, and Benn, for whom this was, generally, not the case. The first ballot of the PLP gave Foot 90 votes, Callaghan 84, Jenkins 56, Benn 37, Healey 30 and Crosland a derisory 17. Jenkins, Benn and Crosland withdrew before the second ballot, in which Callaghan took 141 votes against 133 for Foot and 38 for Healey. The final run-off, on 5 April, saw Callaghan pick up most of Healey's votes to emerge as leader with 176 votes to Foot's 137.[26] Foot's consolation came later in the year, when he defeated Williams for the deputy leadership following Edward Short's resignation.

Callaghan, ironically, was five years older than the man he succeeded, as Wilson was wryly to point out. Youthful links to

Keep Left in the 1940s were now a distant memory, but his wide experience of government meant that he was well known and widely respected in Whitehall, where his innately cautious instincts chimed in with those of senior civil servants, many of whom called him the 'foxy old peasant'.[27] For all that, Callaghan instilled a new sense of purpose and drive to an administration which, under Wilson, had been drifting. Callaghan made few changes to the cabinet, other than replacing some ageing Wilson retainers like Willie Ross and paying off old scores by sacking Castle. Callaghan's one-time disciple, Crosland, became Foreign Secretary. Finally, Foot moved from Employment to take a more synoptic role as Lord President of the Council. Callaghan also tried to establish decent relations with Benn, although without offering him a change of post. Clearly, the new premier was trying to pull the team together and re-establish a sense of common purpose. In this, he was surprisingly successful, and his cabinet was to prove happier than Wilson's.[28] But it would be on his ability to deal with the trade unions that he would be judged; this was supposedly his special area of competence. How well he would fare remained to be seen.

As stated above, one of Callaghan's first acts was to try to improve relations with Benn. In a sense, he was on easy ground, for the radical industrial policy favoured by the latter was by now well off the agenda. Benn's appointment as Industry Secretary had seemed to suggest that the 1973 policy would be carried out, but the private sector and senior civil servants had made little secret of their misgivings, which made Wilson and other leading ministers less keen than ever to give Benn his head. Therefore the August 1974 White Paper dropped or diluted the more coercive elements of the 1973 programme, with planning agreements, in particular, becoming voluntary.[29] Wilson also moved to reassure worried industrialists, giving delegates of the Confederation of British Industries (CBI) 'two draft letters, one to himself and a reply to it', which could be published to demonstrate the government's essential soundness.[30] This looks, and was, pretty shabby. However, simply to condemn Wilson and others who took a similarly sceptical view of the party's radical industrial policy as Treasury-minded obscurantists, while emotionally pleasing, is inadequate. The basic outlook of the leading figures in the party remained based on the premise that, for 'progress' to occur, there had to be economic growth, and this meant preserving business confidence. Second, the policies were not as well worked out as their advocates liked to suggest.[31] All sorts of questions remained unanswered, although, to be fair, more could have been done had the party leadership entered willingly into a real debate instead of simply trying to block. Third, the unions were worried by certain aspects of the proposals, especially on industrial democracy: some on voluntarist grounds, others because they wanted union officials to be most closely involved whereas Benn was keener on 'real' shop floor militants.[32] Finally, Benn's tactics and approach, stumping the country making radical speeches, enamoured him to the left but aroused considerable distrust both inside and outside the Labour movement, and not least within the cabinet itself.[33]

Thus the tide had already receded a long way by the time the Industry Bill was published in January 1975. The bill was still further from the 1973 proposals than the White Paper had been, and Varley's succession to Industry was another step in the same direction.[34] In November 1975 the NEB came into existence, but with very limited powers and a 'safe' chairman, Sir Donald Ryder. Essentially it became a device for propping up 'lame ducks'.[35] The only planning agreement ever reached with a private firm was with Chrysler, the car manufacturer, which was bailed out to save jobs; and, in any case, the agreement was breached in 1978 when Chrysler sold its British operation to the French firm, Peugeot.[36] The NEB did have some successes, creating new high-tech companies and revitalizing the ailing Ferranti electronics company, but, overall, industrial intervention remained, as under Heath, 'primarily defensive and reactive, rescuing losers rather than picking winners'.[37]

A number of nationalizations were carried out in these years. In part, these were in key areas of the economy with good long-term prospects, like the creation of the British National Oil Corporation in 1976 and British Aerospace in 1977.[38] But public attention and debate focused much more on the nationalization of the ailing car manufacturer British Leyland (BL) and of the virtually moribund shipbuilding industry, whose collapse would have had disastrous employment implications in a number of already depressed areas like Tyneside and Northern Ireland. There were some productivity gains in the public sector as a whole in the period and, under Callaghan, efforts were made to introduce greater market discipline and appoint senior managers more willing to challenge established working practices.[39] But these actions did little to offset prevailing negative public perceptions of nationalized industries. Those employed by the latter, meanwhile, often felt undervalued, and in particular resented the way in which their industries' dependence on government subsidies meant they always tended to bear the brunt of incomes policies. Nationalization was widely deemed to have failed by the 1970s, and Labour's failure to implement its 1973 policies meant the party lost what would prove to be its last chance for at least two generations to show public ownership in a more favourable light.

Callaghan thus inherited a fairly 'safe' industrial policy. But the wider economic position remained anything but secure. Inflation, caused by internal and external factors, had averaged 9.2 per cent, easily the highest since the war, in 1973. It exceeded 19 per cent by December 1974, and peaked at 26.9 per cent in August 1975. When Wilson resigned it was still 21.1 per cent. One consequence of this was increased wage militancy on the part of trade unions.[40] Labour had tried to anticipate the problem by its adoption of the Social Contract, but although the Wilson government did pass a series of reforms favourable to unions and workers, such as the Employment Protection Act, wage settlements continued to be very high. This in turn fuelled inflation further, while public expenditure and the budget deficit rose. The end results were severe balance of payments difficulties and, eventually, a sterling crisis.[41]

Healey's policy options in the face of this were limited. Import controls, supported by the left, were ruled out by EEC membership; in any case, free trade sentiment within the party remained strong. Healey's solution was deflation. In April 1975 he cut expenditure and increased taxation, in effect abandoning Keynesianism by putting the conquest of inflation before the maintenance of a 'high and stable' level of employment.[42] Meanwhile, there were signs that union leaders were themselves becoming worried by high levels of inflation. Jones, for example, was fearful that, if something were not done to control it, there might be serious political destabilization, possibly culminating in an extreme right-wing *coup d'état*.[43] Finally, in July 1975, after considerable effort by Wilson, Healey, Foot, Jones and Hugh Scanlon of the AUEW, it was agreed that there should be a £6 per week ceiling to wage increases, and a freeze for those earning more than £8500 a year. But there was opposition: the TUC general council approved it only narrowly, left-wing MPs voted against it in parliament and even Scanlon's own union came out against it.[44] When the policy expired in August 1976 it was replaced by a still tighter limit of the lower of 5 per cent or £4 per week.[45] The average level of wage settlements did fall from 26 per cent in 1975 to 15 per cent in 1976 and 10 per cent in 1977, but how far this was due to the incomes policy remains a point of dispute: rising unemployment was perhaps more significant.[46] The annual rate of inflation also fell back from its August 1975 peak of 26.9 per cent to 12.9 per cent in July 1976 (although the rate then edged upwards again to peak at 17.7 per cent the following June). However, sterling remained under severe pressure. Over the summer, loans had to be secured from other central banks to prop it up. At first, Healey was determined to avoid an appeal to the International Monetary Fund (IMF), but by September he felt he had no alternative.[47] The cabinet remained to be persuaded.

The cabinet which had to deal with the crisis had just been reshuffled, following Jenkins's resignation to become President of the European Commission. Three new faces (Rodgers, Roy Hattersley and Stanley Orme) had been brought in; overall, almost half the members of the cabinet were in new jobs, and thus, to an extent, preoccupied with other things as the crisis broke. On 28 September Callaghan made a stern speech to the party conference in which he told delegates that 'we have been living on borrowed time', and failing to face up to realities: governments, he said, could no longer 'spend [their] way out of recession'. Such policies only led to inflation, which 'hit hardest those least able to stand [it]'. The key thing was to reduce labour costs and so make British industry more competitive.[48] There were parallels with the agenda that Snowden had outlined in 1931: the fear of inflation, the view that higher unemployment would follow inaction on the part of government, the belief that 'progress' could only come through competitive capitalist industry in Britain, and also the warning that the working class was not coterminous with the strongest sections of the trade union movement. Even so, the parallels were finite. Callaghan was a good deal more self-confident than MacDonald had been: the upper echelons of the party now felt thoroughly at home with bankers, civil servants and financial crises. There was also a conscious sense that there must be no repetition of the events of 1931: Benn even circulated copies of the minutes of the 1931 cabinet, as a warning.[49] That, at least, was one option which must not be followed.

MacDonald's government had felt itself under great pressure to make a quick decision, but Callaghan was much more relaxed in this respect. The IMF demanded £5000 million of cuts in public expenditure. Wisely, the premier decided not to declare his own position, even though he was clear in his own mind that the loan must be secured.[50] The application for a loan of $3900 million was made on 29 September. Representatives of the IMF arrived in London on 1 November, but Callaghan kept them waiting and talks only opened on 19 November. The premier tried alternative approaches to Germany and the USA, but these failed.[51] Only on 23 November did the cabinet begin to discuss the matter in earnest. While Healey and Edmund Dell (Trade) wanted to secure the loan at all costs, and a group of about nine ministers was prepared simply to follow a Callaghan lead, there was, initially, strong resistance from both the left and the social democratic right around Crosland.[52]

Callaghan allowed ministers to range freely over the issues in cabinet. But neither the social democrats nor the left could convince their colleagues of an alternative, and the two groups themselves began to disintegrate.[53] This all made Healey's position stronger, and eventually it became safe for Callaghan to back the Chancellor. Once he had declared his position, resistance collapsed. On 2 December Crosland told the cabinet that he was 'absolutely unconvinced by the economic arguments', since in theory Britain could afford to run a still bigger budget deficit, but added that it was his duty to support Callaghan.[54] The problem with Crosland's objection, as Healey later pointed out, was that this was a question of confidence, not an academic seminar.[55] At the end of the day, Crosland had done what those who were to claim his mantle a few years later were not willing to do: he had subordinated his views to the Labour ethos of collective responsibility and loyalty to majority decisions. But in a sense it was a last gasp of such loyalty from the social democratic right, for, as Benn later wrote, 'I think the death of the social democratic wing of the party occurred in that cabinet, when Tony Crosland said at one stage: it is mad but we have no alternative'.[56] At the 2 December cabinet, 18 ministers supported the proposals, and while the six left-wingers were still critical, only Orme seems to have considered resignation.[57] The union leaders were squared, and a cut of £1500 million in the public sector borrowing requirement (PSBR) for 1977–78 was announced, based on the sale of British Petroleum assets plus expenditure cuts of £1000 million in each of the next two years.[58] It was much less than the IMF had originally wanted.[59]

In so far as the crisis was surmounted without a single resignation, and with cuts much lower than the IMF had originally proposed, it is hard to see how Callaghan could have handled it better. But it could also be seen as a watershed for the government. It marked an end to the expansive view of public expenditure that had marked its first months in office. It drew a line under a particular application of Keynesian policies and the idea that the conquest of unemployment was government's first responsibility. It also marked a clear end to any lingering hopes that this would be a radical reforming administration. In addition, it held longer-term significance for the development of the Labour Party. First, Callaghan's rhetorical renunciation of 1970s Keynesianism could be read as inadvertently legitimizing the anti-Keynesian, monetarist critique of the new Conservative leader, Margaret Thatcher. Further, the gap in Labour's economic thinking which had been covered by Keynesianism since the 1940s was embarrassingly re-exposed. The crisis also highlighted further the ideological confusion and self-isolation of the social democratic right within the party. Further, the defeat of the left seemed, even at the time, only to postpone a further round of infighting. Finally, the crisis killed the Social Contract. Wage restraint would have to be maintained, given the strategy that the government had adopted, but restrictions on public expenditure would make it difficult to deliver the 'social goods' and, still more significantly, the full employment commitment which had been central to the Contract.

Ironically, the PSBR estimate provided by the Treasury had been, in the event, 'grossly overestimated', and so in fact the loan had not really been necessary at all.[60] Healey only ever had to draw on half of it, and was able to introduce a reflationary budget in April 1978. The IMF had received its money back in full by the time Labour left office in 1979.[61] Indeed, economic conditions became calmer after the crisis, helped by recovery from the

1974–76 recession. The incomes policy for 1976–77 held fairly steady, and in August 1977 Stage III, with a 10 per cent maximum limit, was agreed with the unions, to run until July 1978.[62] Inflation had fallen to 7.4 per cent by June 1978, and even unemployment fell back from a peak of 1,522,500 in the third quarter of 1977 to stand at 1,306,300 in the last quarter of 1978. A period of crisis, it seemed, had given way to one which had at least some semblance of tranquillity.

Such economic conditions were hardly conducive to a very effective social policy, however. Growth was supposed to pay for social reform, and, in the main, the government's achievements were confined to continuing with as much expenditure as could be achieved without upsetting the fragile economic situation. While there had been some talk of redistributive taxation, this did not really happen. There were some innovations, like the introduction of the state earnings-related pensions scheme (SERPS), improvements in old-age pensions and child benefits, a freeze on council house rents and subsidies of some foodstuffs; many of these were part of the Social Contract. But real expenditure on personal social services fell dramatically in 1977–78, and towards the end of the government's life there was increasing talk of the need to 'target' benefits, raising the spectre of the means test once again.[63] In some areas, too, Labour faced increasing resistance: thus in education the process of comprehensivization slowed down in the face of resistance, supported by the courts, from recalcitrant local education authorities. The net results of the government's policies were, not surprisingly, minor, and in some cases they merely stored up trouble for the future.

Labour's performance was also hindered by its parliamentary position. By April 1976 its overall majority had disappeared; that July, two MPs defected to form the Scottish Labour Party; and subsequent by-election losses meant further problems. However, these were not as great as they might have been. The high number of 'third party' MPs meant that, although it had no overall majority, Labour still had many more MPs than the Conservatives, who were even more unattractive to the Liberals under Thatcher than they had been under Heath, and who remained suspicious (as the party of the Union) in the eyes of the nationalist parties. Labour was able to placate the ten-strong Ulster unionists with the promise of a review of Northern Ireland's representation at

Westminster (which was ultimately increased from 12 to 17 members), and by the government's tough anti-terrorist policy, which included the draconian Prevention of Terrorism Act (1974) and a military-based approach to the IRA. Relations with the Liberals warmed further in March 1977 with the formation of the Lib-Lab Pact. The new Liberal leader, David Steel, was keen to avoid an election, partly because he was new to the job, and partly because of the scandal surrounding his predecessor, Thorpe, who had been forced to resign when it was revealed that he faced charges of conspiracy to murder a male model with whom he was alleged to have had an affair. The pact was certainly not a coalition; its main terms were consultation on economic policy, direct elections to the European parliament and devolution for Scotland and Wales, and Labour 'simply undert[ook] to do what it had anyway intended to do and desist from what it could not do'.[64] The pact was orchestrated on the Labour side by Foot, who was emerging as the government's chief 'fixer'.[65] Liberal criticisms finally forced Steel to abandon it in August 1978 but, even then, the ongoing Thorpe case and the Liberals' poor standing in the polls made them reluctant to bring the government down.[66]

Relations with the Scottish and Welsh Nationalists proved rather more challenging because both parties were clear on the price of their co-operation; devolution for Scotland and Wales. In October 1974 the SNP had won 11 seats with 30.4 per cent of the Scottish poll and Plaid Cymru three seats with 10.8 per cent of the votes cast in Wales. This meant that Labour, which had been pre-eminent in both countries since 1945, had to take notice of nationalist feeling; and its parliamentary position meant that it had to take direct notice of the nationalist parties. In November 1975 a White Paper offered each country an elected assembly. The Welsh one would have fewer powers than the Scottish, but even the latter would not be able to raise revenue or have much say in economic affairs, and the Secretaries of State would retain wide powers of veto. The Nationalists accepted these proposals as better than nothing, and the Devolution Bill passed its second reading in December 1976.[67] However, the defeat of a guillotine motion, essential to speed the passage of the bill, in February 1977, spelt its demise. Twenty-two Labour MPs voted against the motion and 15 abstained.[68] In November 1977, separate bills were introduced for Scotland and Wales, and these became law in July

1978 subject to referenda.[69] However, an amendment introduced by a Labour backbencher meant that, in order to be enacted, the Acts had to receive the support of at least 40 per cent of the total electorates in Scotland and Wales.[70] This made Welsh devolution highly unlikely; the position in Scotland was cloudier. Still, the passage of the legislation had kept the nationalist parties close to the government, and their loyalty was assured at least until the referenda had been held on 1 March 1979.

While devolution was more prominent in the 1970s than in the 1960s, the reverse was true of foreign and defence policy. With the Vietnam War over, debates within the party were somewhat muted: left-wing grumbles about possession of nuclear weapons and membership of NATO cut little ice with ministers keen to maintain the Atlantic Alliance and, in particular, retain American goodwill at a time of economic stress. All three Foreign Secretaries – Callaghan, Crosland (who died suddenly in February 1977) and the inexperienced David Owen (appointed to keep the seat warm for Healey)[71] – were from the right of the party. There were few new initiatives, the main development being the decision, taken in secret, to press ahead with the modernization of Britain's nuclear weapons in the Chevaline programme. That this went against conference votes in 1972 and 1973 in favour of unilateral nuclear disarmament worried the ministers involved not a jot.[72]

By mid-1978, though, ministers seemed to have less cause for worry than they had had for some time. The parliamentary position looked reasonably secure, austerity was giving way to a degree of reflation and unemployment and inflation seemed to be under control. Electorally, the party's record was less impressive, with by-elections still showing swings against Labour, but even here only one seat was lost in 1978. Similarly there had been recovery in the opinion polls: from being 20 points behind the Conservatives in May 1977, Labour recovered so that the two parties were neck and neck that December, and it edged into a four-point lead in August 1978. In that same month, Stage IV of the incomes policy specified a 5 per cent limit to pay increases, with a promise of a return to free collective bargaining – now being demanded strongly by many trade unionists – in early 1979.[73] The new limit was clearly nonsensical, given that the TUC refused to back it, and given the fact that pay settlements at that point were breaking even the

10 per cent limit of Stage III. But most observers felt that the new pay policy was not intended seriously; rather, given the apparently favourable electoral signs, it was seen as a piece of pre-election window dressing.

But Callaghan and Foot had their doubts about an autumn election. Party officials believed it would only produce another minority Labour government, and for Callaghan, who was 'sick to death' of deals and compromises, this was an unappealing prospect.[74] An early election would also mean the loss of legislation which was currently going through parliament, not least that on devolution. Thus Callaghan and Foot decided to gamble. If they got through the winter, and broadly enforced the 5 per cent pay policy, they would be able to go to the country the following spring as the party that could work with the unions and control inflation.[75] The announcement that there would be no election was greeted with almost universal surprise. The Labour movement was especially shocked, since it was now clear that Stage IV was not a piece of electoral window dressing but a policy which the government aimed to implement, a fact which even right-wingers like Dell found scarcely credible.[76]

Indeed, the 5 per cent policy was doomed from the start. In the private sector, the figure was often ignored: Ford awarded its workforce 17 per cent, and the government's attempts to impose sanctions against the company for its breach of the policy were defeated in parliament with the help of left-wing Labour MPs. This, in turn, encouraged lorry drivers, who went on strike claiming a 30 per cent rise.[77] The government still had more leverage in the public sector, where pay policies had already bitten hard and effected cuts in real wages for many workers.[78] But now, the National Union of Public Employees (NUPE), which represented some of the lowest-paid local authority workers, demanded a 40 per cent increase for its members in January 1979. Various groups of workers struck or started overtime bans. Since groups like dustmen were involved, there was considerable public inconvenience and some threat to public health, much sensationalized by the press.[79] The government was totally wrong-footed. In cabinet, Callaghan became little short of hysterical, suggesting that 'what was happening in this country was a threat to democratic society'.[80] In public, he tried to brazen it out, but this backfired on him when, trying to play the world statesman, he returned from a summit in sunny Guadeloupe on 10 January to be asked what he intended to do about the 'mounting chaos' in which the country found itself. His reply – 'I don't think that other people in the world would share the view that there is mounting chaos' – was rapidly transformed into the screaming tabloid headline 'CRISIS? WHAT CRISIS?'[81] Eventually, a settlement was reached, with immediate pay increases plus the establishment of a Comparability Commission to report by August and suggest 'just' wages. In the end, wage settlements for 1978–79 were higher than they had been in the previous year.[82] The political costs of all this were horrendous. Labour, and Callaghan in particular, had lost their reputation for being able to 'handle' the unions. As late as November 1978 Labour had been five points ahead in the polls; three months later it trailed by 20 points. Callaghan's approval rating collapsed. What became known as the 'Winter of Discontent' could have been largely avoided had Callaghan played safe and called an election in October 1978. But he had gambled; and he had lost.

The denouement was fairly rapid. On 1 March the Scottish and Welsh referenda on devolution were held. In Wales, the result was a conclusive 'No', with only 11.9 per cent of the electorate voting in favour. In Scotland, however, the result was closer. The 'Yes' vote amounted to 32.8 per cent, the 'No' to 30.8 per cent and 36.4 per cent did not vote. A majority of those voting had supported the measure, but because the figure did not reach 40 per cent of the total electorate, the legislation, like that for Wales, had to be repealed. The nationalist parties were incensed and, seeing their opportunity, the Conservatives put down a motion of no confidence in the government on 28 March. Labour tried to cobble a majority together, but in vain, and the motion was passed by a single vote. Next day an election was called for 3 May.

Labour's campaign got off to an acrimonious start when Callaghan vetoed the inclusion of House of Lords abolition in the manifesto, angering the NEC and many party activists in the process.[83] Labour faced a severe struggle in the election. The Conservatives were confident, and boosted by highly professional advertising. Labour's manifesto promised to reduce inflation, increase government control of industry, build more houses and improve pensions. It was not, for all the Conservatives' efforts to portray it as such, a notably radical document; it could hardly be claimed that Labour lost in 1979 because its manifesto was 'too left-wing'.

On a swing of 5.2 per cent – the largest since 1945 – Labour lost 51 seats, all to the Conservatives, while regaining five seats from the minor parties. The party lost particularly heavily in the south-east, the Midlands and the north-west of England. But it maintained or improved its position in most of northern England, in Wales and in Scotland. Labour particularly lost support among skilled workers, only 42 per cent of whom voted Labour (as opposed to 49 per cent in October 1974 and 55.4 per cent in 1970).[84] But the plain fact was that Labour had lost support in all sectors of the population and in most geographical areas. And the main reason for this seems to have been the party's perceived failure in government: before the winter of 1978–79 enough people might have been willing to give Labour the benefit of the doubt, but the events of that winter put paid to that. The 1979 election was more of a negative verdict on Labour's performance in office than a positive endorsement of what was to become known as 'Thatcherism'.

The Labour governments of 1974–79 are usually seen as having failed. Conservative propaganda at the time, and for years afterwards, made much use of images of the period as reasons for people not to vote Labour. They suggested that it was a time of economic mayhem, characterized by high inflation, high unemployment, and numerous, and often bitter, strikes. Government efforts to get the economy moving were, on this reading, counterproductive at best; and in any case, for most of the time, the administration simply drifted from crisis to crisis, ducking the issues.

From the left, other criticisms would be added, such as the government's failure to carry out the party's radical industrial policy or, more generally, to promote greater equality. Since the later 1960s, the Labour Party outside parliament had been shifting, quite strongly, towards the left. Many CLPs were now well away from the kind of approach that the government had favoured. They felt let down and angry. In addition, the left now had a programme, based on the autarkic proposals of the 1973 *Programme*, which was, ostensibly at least, more plausible than most of the programmes previously put forward by the left. The record of the Wilson and Callaghan governments in the 1960s and 1970s suggested to many party activists that a new departure must be made; never again must there be governments like these.

Certainly, there is something in such criticisms. Yet the record of the 1974–79 governments must be seen in a wider context. They faced worse economic problems than any government since the Second World War, problems which were more the result of world developments – especially the increase in oil prices – and the incompetence of the previous Conservative government than of Labour's own failings. They had had to face those difficulties with either a tiny, or no, parliamentary majority. Serious problems which might have smashed the party to pieces, like the EEC and the IMF crisis, had been overcome without too much short-term damage. The 1976 financial crisis, in particular, had shown Callaghan's political mastery, and at least until the autumn of 1978 he proved a much better premier than many observers had expected. Inflation fell dramatically after 1975. Unemployment fluctuated, and was high by post-war standards, but was not heading out of control as it was to do under the first Thatcher government. Finally, it should be remembered that governments in other industrialized countries were experiencing similar difficulties: Callaghan's colleagues at the Guadeloupe summit – the American Democrat Carter, the French Gaullist Giscard d'Estaing, and the German Social Democrat Schmidt – were all out of office, and their parties blamed for the crises of the 1970s, within a relatively short period of time. It is perhaps worth noting that Thatcher was to leave office in 1990 with inflation, unemployment, public spending (in real terms), homelessness, dependency and crime rates all higher than they had been when Labour had left office in 'failure' eleven-and-a-half years earlier.[85]

Yet for all that, it would be facile to deny that, in 1979, many people both inside and outside the Labour Party were angry with the government's record. The trade unions were antagonized by extended periods of pay restraint which had brought them, ultimately, few of the benefits promised by the Social Contract: many, particularly among skilled workers, responded by voting Conservative in 1979, while their leaders were preparing, in some cases, to take their revenge on Callaghan and Healey. Second, the left was angered by its own impotence, and determined that in future a radical plan of campaign like the 1973 *Programme* should not be discarded as soon as Labour returned to office. Third, the social democratic right was increasingly isolated, disillusioned and disaffected with the failure of revisionism, the party's lack of commitment to the EEC and the increasing stridency of the unions and the left within the party. Finally, Labour now stood in opposition to a premier whose declared aim was to undo much of what it had achieved in government since 1945. It was very unclear, in the immediate aftermath of the 1979 election, what all this would portend; but no one in the Labour Party seriously expected a quiet life in opposition.

10   Down and Out? 1979–87

The appointment of Margaret Thatcher to the premiership on 4 May 1979 was to prove an event of enormous significance for the British Labour Party. It did not seem so to everyone at the time: many, Conservatives as well as Labourites, were prepared to write her off as a flash in the pan, and suggested that her government would soon be out of office. However, by 1982 it was reasonably clear that Labour, at least, would not be able to do the ousting, especially since the breakaway of a section of its right wing to form the Social Democratic Party in March 1981. At the 1983 general election, Labour was trounced, and, despite vigorous efforts by its new leader, Neil Kinnock, it did little to dent the Conservatives' ascendancy in 1987, either. There was much talk of Labour being finished as a party of government. Its electoral strength in its old heartlands in northern England, Scotland and Wales meant that it would not disappear, but many observers thought that its prospects of emerging from the political margins were slight, and Callaghan's description of the 1979 election as 'a sea-change in politics' would come to be seen as being amply justified.[1]

As in the aftermath of 1931, there were various views of the direction Labour should now take. The left argued that defeat, disappointment and economic crisis demanded a more full-blooded policy.[2] As if to symbolize this demand, Benn announced that he would not be standing in the shadow cabinet elections. Meanwhile, the left called for constitutional changes within the party to ensure that there would be no more 'betrayals', insisting, in particular, on mandatory reselection of MPs, election of the leader by an electoral college comprising all elements of the party, and drafting of the election manifesto by the NEC alone.[3] There was also strong union criticism of Labour's recent record. Pay policies, the failure of the Social Contract, and the Labour leadership's attitude towards the unions in the 'Winter of

Discontent' had all stirred up hostility. While many trade unionists at all levels remained loyal to the leadership, the experience
of the 1970s governments had moved trade unionism's centre
of gravity leftwards.[4] This was not the case with the party leadership, however. Its reaction was not unlike that of Henderson to
the debacle of 1931. They felt, as Callaghan later put it, that '[t]
he Labour Government of 1974 to 1979 had no reason to feel
ashamed, and much to be proud of'.[5] If Labour continued along
its present lines, and waited for more favourable circumstances, it
would soon return to office. But other opponents of the left saw
this view as too complacent. In particular, Jenkins, in a televised
lecture in November 1979, came close to advocating the formation of a new 'centre party'.[6] However, he still had more than a
year left in Brussels, and the lecture was more of a marker than a
call to arms.[7]

But economic and political circumstances made it difficult
for the party leadership to maintain its stand-pat line. Renewed
world recession hit Britain late in 1979 and lasted into 1982.
Its effects were ferocious; more than 5000 factories were closed
between 1979 and 1982.[8] In May 1979, when Conservative election posters had blared out that 'Labour Isn't Working', unemployment had stood at 1,299,000; by October 1981 it had more
than doubled. There was negative economic growth in both 1980
and 1981. Inflation more than doubled to peak at 21.9 per cent
in May 1980. In such circumstances, the left's hand within the
Labour Party was strengthened. So deep a recession so soon after
the last one suggested that capitalism might well be on the verge
of collapse. It was, it seemed, no time to be tinkering with a system that was about to fall apart. And all this was reinforced by
the performance of the Thatcher government. Thatcher gloried
in the 'free market' and hated 'socialism', which she defined very
broadly to include Labour, the trade unions, nationalized industries, the welfare state, high levels of public expenditure, council housing, Labour local authorities, high direct taxation, the
redistribution of wealth downwards, and full employment. What
unfolded was a fundamental attack on much that Labourites
held dear, and on practically all the work of Labour governments
since 1945. The results of all this were, first, a feeling that, in
the face of a 'reactionary' government, Labour could not afford
to prevaricate; and, second, the belief of many Labourites that

the government's policies would be so unpopular that electors would be now more willing to listen to arguments in favour of a 'socialist' alternative.

Callaghan clung on to the leadership in order to avoid charges of desertion, to try to secure a Healey succession and to keep the party from moving leftwards. But the party moved leftwards all the same.[9] In October 1979, the party conference voted in favour of mandatory reselection of MPs, and for a resolution calling on the NEC to submit proposals to the 1980 conference as to how 'the NEC alone' would draw up the final version of the election manifesto. A resolution for an electoral college was defeated in 1979, but passed in 1980, although even then no majority could be found for any concrete form of electoral college, and it was decided that a special conference early in 1981 should settle the matter. However, the NEC's proposals for its having the decisive voice in the drafting of the manifesto were lost by a narrow margin. There was a vote of 5,042,000 votes to 2,097,000 to withdraw from the European Community (EC), and a vote in favour of unilateral nuclear disarmament; but a motion stating that 'the safety of the British people ... will be best served by multilateral disarmament in the nuclear and conventional fields' was also passed, and a resolution calling for withdrawal from NATO was heavily defeated.[10]

The defeat of the proposal for the manifesto was clearly a defeat for the left, but the electoral college and mandatory reselection were victories. Why did these changes come about? In part it was due to the general factors mentioned earlier. Groups campaigning for the changes were also significant. The CLPD was certainly important in raising consciousness and concentrating party members' minds on a few key issues, but its significance should not be exaggerated. It was able to mobilize support on these issues, but it could not have swung the party to the left by itself. The unions were the key to conference majorities, and some leading union figures were bitterly angered by the record of recent Labour governments, and were looking, at least to a certain extent, to 'pay back' Callaghan and his colleagues. With a general election some years away, they now had the perfect opportunity to do so, as it seemed, without too much long-term damage to the party. But this was a tactical manoeuvre, more a fit of pique than a real swing to the left. In addition, most ordinary trade union members did not suddenly become supporters of the left.[11] At the 1980 conference – in many ways the high point of Labour radicalism in this period – the left's margins of victory were very narrow indeed: 50.7 per cent to 49.3 per cent on the electoral college, and 53.2 per cent to 46.8 per cent on reselection. And, of course, the manifesto proposal did not go through at all. In other words, even at this stage, the left was advancing on a knife edge rather than triumphantly carrying all before it.

Just 12 days after the 1980 conference closed, Callaghan announced his resignation. Since the constitution of the electoral college had still to be decided, his successor would be elected by the PLP only, and the leader's action was attacked bitterly by the left as a pre-emptive strike to install Healey as leader while there was still time.[12] This may have been a little unfair, since Callaghan, at 68, was keen to retire, but he probably felt some mischievous pleasure in upsetting his left-wing critics.[13] Benn considered standing against Healey, but was dissuaded by his allies, partly on principle and partly because he would clearly not fare well if the PLP was the electorate.[14] Shore and John Silkin came forward, but while both were capable figures with some experience of high office, neither seemed likely to defeat Healey. The only candidate likely to stop the latter, in fact, was Foot, and he was eventually persuaded to stand by left-wing MPs and union leaders. Neil Kinnock, a young Welsh MP, acted as his campaign organizer. On 3 November, the first ballot gave Healey 112 votes, Foot 83, Silkin 38 and Shore 32, and in the run-off Foot took the leadership by 139 votes to 129.[15] Healey became deputy leader.

The result was so close that it is important not to 'over-explain' it – had half a dozen MPs switched, Healey would have become leader. Indeed, it seems that a number who had already decided to defect to a new party (discussions for the formation of which were by now well under) voted for Foot on the grounds that, if he won, the breakaway party could be portrayed as more 'necessary' as a barrier to the 'left'.[16] Even so, Foot had many qualities which appealed to Labour MPs. His left-wing reputation suggested he might be able to get on better with the wider party than the 'Establishment' figure of Healey. He had proved himself an able and loyal minister, and a good conciliator, in the most recent period of Labour government; union leaders, who had worked with him closely, had found him impressive.[17] Healey, meanwhile,

had alienated many usually moderate trade unionists, had not cultivated support and was seen as a bully, a divisive figure who would
only intensify existing splits.[18] In short, Foot's election did not
mark any great swing to the left in the PLP. This was borne out
by the subsequent shadow cabinet elections, where all the existing
members who stood were re-elected, and Owen (who had refused
to stand) and Callaghan were replaced by Kinnock and the right-
wing Gerald Kaufman. Significantly, Benn failed to gain election,
his 88 votes placing him just behind Kinnock (90).

The special conference on the electoral college took place
on 24 January 1981. Six versions were on offer, but in the end it
boiled down to a choice between the proposal of David Basnett,
leader of the General and Municipal Workers' Union (GMWU)
for a college wherein the PLP would have 50 per cent of the votes
and the unions and CLPs 25 per cent each, and the left's favoured
option, of 40 per cent for the unions and 30 per cent each for the
PLP and CLPs. That the latter succeeded was thanks to the position taken up by the right-wing AUEW, whose delegation, man-
dated not to support any proposal giving the PLP less than 51 per
cent of the votes, abstained on the final vote. Had it supported
Basnett's proposal, the latter would have triumphed: as it was,
the 40/30/30 mix scraped through. For the first time, Labour
was committed to electing its leader on the basis of a party-wide
franchise.[19]

On the same day, Jenkins finally returned to Britain. Within
24 hours, he, Owen, Williams and Rodgers – 'the Gang of Four' –
issued their 'Limehouse Declaration', stating that the 'calami-
tous outcome' of the special conference 'demand[ed] a new start
in British politics'. It fell short, at this stage, of launching a new
party, but it did establish a Council for Social Democracy, 'half in
and half out of the Labour Party'.[20] Foot tried to persuade Owen,
Williams and Rodgers to remain, but to no avail. On 26 March,
the SDP was formally established. News that members could
pay their subscriptions by credit card excited deep scorn from
Labourites still mired in the 1940s when it came to party organization, but did not put off the thousands who flocked to join in the
first week. At first, only ten MPs followed Owen and Rodgers, but
by the time of the dissolution of parliament in 1983 there were
to be 30, 27 of whom had been elected as Labour MPs in 1979.[21]
Other noteworthy recruits included George Brown.

Why did people defect? Some, like Jenkins, had departed from many of their earlier positions and wanted to strengthen the 'radical centre' – in Jenkins's case, in close alliance with the Liberals. Others, like Owen, were keen on a new radicalism, free from the unions and the block vote. Most felt that Labour was moving too far to the left to be a viable alternative to a government they deplored. Some had their careers in mind; those facing deselection by their CLPs saw the SDP as a life raft. The issues of the EC and defence were also important, the former for Williams, the latter for Owen. But the formation of the SDP was also a reflection of the deeper trends already traced in previous chapters, namely the apparent bankruptcy of revisionism and the consequent self-isolation of a section of the revisionist right within the party.

However, most of Labour's right wing did *not* join the new party. Jenkins, Owen, Williams and Rodgers went; but Healey, Hattersley, Kaufman and John Smith stayed, even when some on the left would have been delighted to see them go.[22] The defections tended to be heavily localized: eight of those who left were MPs in the London area, four in the north-east, and three in Liverpool, where the local party had swung heavily to the left. By contrast, '[t]he overwhelming view in Scotland's right-wing Labour establishment was in favour of staying and fighting'.[23] So why did so many right-wingers 'stay and fight'? Many calculated that their career prospects would still be better in the Labour Party than in the SDP, which might prove to be (as it did) a flash in the pan. But careerism was probably not the main consideration. More important was ethos, an almost tribal loyalty to the Labourism, whereby one did not go home and sulk if one lost a round of the fight, but fought on until victory could be achieved. In addition, MPs with union links were reluctant to break them. Finally, though, there was also a calculation being made about the medium- and longer-term direction of the party. For Owen and his colleagues, it was axiomatic that Labour had swung violently to the left and would not swing back. Others made a more sober and, as it proved, sounder judgement. For in retrospect what is most striking about Labour's 'swing to the left' at this time is not its extent but its limitations. For example, neither reselection nor the electoral college gave enormous powers to left-wing 'activists': in most cases, they strengthened the union block vote which, for most of Labour's history, had been close to the party leadership and the PLP in outlook and would be again. The extension of the franchise for electing the leader was hardly revolutionary – the Liberals had done it in the 1970s, after all. And even when the left could get its way in conference – as it could not, significantly enough, on the manifesto issue – it was often by a very narrow majority.

At first, though, the SDP seemed successful. In December 1980 the Gallup poll had given Labour 47 per cent, the Conservatives 35 per cent and the Liberals 14 per cent. A year later, it suggested the Liberal–SDP Alliance had 50 per cent support against 23 per cent each for Labour and Conservative. At the Warrington by-election, in July 1981, Jenkins, for the SDP, slashed Labour's majority from over 10,000 to 1750. That November, Williams won the 'safe' Conservative seat of Crosby, and Jenkins himself was returned to the Commons when he took Glasgow Hillhead from the Conservatives in March 1982.

Much of this success was gained at the expense of Labour, whose prospects were hardly helped by Benn's decision, in April 1981, to challenge Healey for the deputy leadership. Benn, who had returned to the shadow cabinet when Rodgers had defected to the SDP, believed sincerely that the new machinery of the electoral college should be tested, and so bedded into the party's consciousness; but there was a feeling, shared by some on the left, that his move was opportunistic and selfish.[24] There followed almost six months of campaigning, marred by severe bitterness on both sides and well-publicized episodes of thuggishness as Healey was barracked by left-wingers at some of his meetings. The main significance of the contest came when a number of 'left' Labour MPs, including Kinnock, announced that they would not support Benn, but would vote for Silkin and then abstain should he be eliminated. When the voting took place that September, Silkin was eliminated on the first ballot, and in the run-off Healey defeated Benn by a margin of less than 1 per cent. Benn had trounced Healey among the CLPs, but Healey had taken around two-thirds of the votes in the other two sections. The action of the Silkinite MPs had been enough to tip the balance: had even a proportion of them voted for Benn, the latter would have emerged victorious.[25] The Bennite left was furious, but Kinnock and his colleagues had a stout defence. The party had been plunged into six months of civil war at a time when it faced an unprecedented challenge from the SDP and when the Thatcher government was wreaking havoc with much that Labour held dear, all in the cause of Benn's quest for an essentially meaningless post. The contest was also counterproductive for Benn and the 'hard' left which supported him, because the 1981 conference marked a clear end to the left's advance within the party. Five left-wingers failed to gain re-election to the NEC; the party treasurership was also lost. The left majority on the NEC was thus shattered, and a new alliance of centrist and 'soft left' now began a process that would end in them recovering full control of the party. True, Benn and Heffer retained the chairs of the NEC's important Home Policy and Organization committees respectively, but it began to look as though they were living on borrowed time.

Any hopes of a Labour recovery once the deputy leadership imbroglio was over were illusory, however. On 2 April 1982 the military regime in Argentina invaded the British colony of the Falkland Islands in the South Atlantic. The government dispatched a Task Force to recapture them, a feat finally achieved on 14 June. Thatcher's government undoubtedly gained popularity during the conflict. Foot's line was to support the government, on the grounds that Britain should not allow a quasi-fascist regime the prestige of a victory, especially when that would involve taking the Falkland Islanders, against their will, under the Argentinian flag. Some Labourites were more critical, but to little effect other than to make the party seem split at a time of perceived national crisis.[26] The Falklands issue rallied support to the Conservatives, whose poll rating improved from 31 per cent in April to 46 per cent in July, by which time they had a 19 point lead over Labour. Nevertheless, the 'Falklands factor' probably only gave the Tories a short-term boost: in the longer term the more significant developments were tax cuts in 1982 and the economic upturn which began early in the same year. Labour did not lose the 1983 election because of the Falklands War.[27]

A continuing problem for Labour at this time was its image of factionalism and 'extremism', the most publicized manifestation of which, by early 1982, was Militant Tendency. Militant was an entryist, Trotskyite organization, which sought to radicalize Labour from within and use it as a means for fomenting revolution in Britain. Since it had started with its entryist tactics in the 1960s, it had had some success, and by the early 1980s some members of Militant were securing adoption as Labour parliamentary candidates. With a substantial budget and organization, it was clearly 'a party within a party', and as such was in breach of Labour's constitution. Its membership rose from 1800 in 1979 to 3500 in late 1982. Even so, the overwhelming majority of CLPs were not influenced by Militant, and Militant candidates for the NEC never came anywhere near being elected.[28] Pressure to deal with Militant grew, particularly (but not only) from the right, but was initially resisted. Militant argued that it was no more of a party within a party than right-wing organizations like the Labour Solidarity Campaign (whose members included people like Shore and Hattersley).[29] The Tendency's only function, they argued, was to publish and sell the newspaper, *Militant*. Even if they were dubious as to how far this was really the case, many Labour left-wingers were still reluctant to act, fearing (with a degree of justification, as it turned out) that banning Militant would be the start of a 'witch-hunt' which would end in a general assault on the left.[30] It was a fear that Foot shared, initially at least.[31] The new NEC elected in 1981 set up an inquiry, and on its recommendation the 1982 conference established a register of approved groups.[32] The 1982 NEC elections, meanwhile, gave further gains to the right, and in the aftermath of the conference Benn and Heffer were removed from the chairs of the Home Policy and Organization committees.[33] Militant was proscribed in December 1982, and in February 1983 the NEC decided by 19 votes to 9 to expel the five members of *Militant*'s editorial board from the Labour Party.[34] There, for the moment, the matter rested, not least because it was becoming clear that a general election was looming on the horizon.

Electoral trends had been moving in contradictory directions. Labour performed poorly at the May 1982 local elections, held at the height of the Falklands War. But that October a right-wing candidate, John Spellar, gained Birmingham Northfield from the Conservatives against the odds and despite a big and scurrilous Alliance campaign. The Gallup poll for December put Labour only seven points behind the Conservatives and 12 points ahead of the Alliance. It was not wholly obvious at this point that Labour under Foot was necessarily heading for a conclusive electoral defeat. However, these buds of promise were soon frozen to death by the chill wind of events in Bermondsey, where in a by-election in February 1983 Labour's perceivedly hard-left and gay

candidate, Peter Tatchell, was defeated after a bitter and homo-
phobic campaign in what had been a safe Labour seat. Worse still,
Foot's handling of the Tatchell candidature – he had initially dis-
owned him, then retracted – aroused criticism from practically all
sides of the party.

There had been various moves against Foot's leadership during
1982, with a number of leading right-wingers and 'soft left' figures
making noises behind the scenes.[35] These soon became much
louder. In early February, just as the campaign in Bermondsey
was going wrong, the Australian Labor Party ousted its ageing
leader, Bill Hayden, in favour of the more dynamic and telegenic
Bob Hawke: Hawke went on to win the general election that followed on 5 March.[36] With polls suggesting that Labour would
be on equal terms with the Conservatives if Healey were leader,
it was not surprising that pressure built up for a change. Foot
seems to have considered resignation, but decided ultimately to
await the result of the pending by-election in the Labour marginal of Darlington, and this was tacitly accepted by his critics as
a litmus test of his leadership.[37] Perhaps Healey could have forced
the issue, but he seems to have been reluctant to act 'disloyally',
and doubtless realized that to oust an unwilling Foot might reunite the soft left with the Bennites and so give him a truly awful
inheritance.[38] But, against all the odds, Labour managed to hold
Darlington on 24 March with an increased majority. Any realistic
chance of removing Foot had been lost.

Foot's survival cheered the Conservatives. Thatcher dithered
over whether to call an early election, but finally did so after
favourable local election results on 5 May. The first opinion poll
of the campaign showed the Conservatives with 46 per cent support against Labour's 31 and the Alliance's 21. It looked, as Foot
later put it, as though Labour 'had a well-nigh insurmountable
task ahead'.[39]

Labour's performance at the 1983 general election has become
a byword for inefficiency and incompetence. The manifesto was
rushed out before it had been fine-tuned, perhaps with the con-
nivance of right-wingers who wanted to be able to blame a 'left-
wing' document for the inevitable defeat.[40] It was not short of
policy proposals, including the reduction of unemployment
to 'below a million' within five years by a huge increase in public expenditure. There would be a five-year economic plan, the

promotion of industrial democracy and a start to the renation-alization of the few industries which had so far been privatized. Social benefits and expenditure on education would be increased. There were also promises to end sexual and racial discrimina-tion. A Labour government would pull Britain out of the EC. On defence, the manifesto was a mess; there had to be a fudge because few of the party's leaders agreed with party policy, which called for unilateral nuclear disarmament. Accordingly, the mani-festo came up with the nonsensical formula that 'Unilateralism and multilateralism must go hand in hand if either is to suc-ceed'.[41] The document gave numerous other hostages to fortune. During the campaign Labour speakers spent most of their time trying to explain it away or paper over the cracks, a process not helped by interventions from Callaghan and Wilson attacking the party's defence policy. In addition, organization and propa-ganda were poor, to say the least, while Foot was a liability, look-ing uncomfortable on TV, rambling when interviewed and lacking presence. His tendency to hark back to past battles delighted those in the know, but baffled many, especially the young. Beside Thatcher he looked amateurish and lacked credibility.[42] Realizing this, Labour strategists tried increasingly to portray an image of a collective leadership, in contrast to Thatcher's autocratic image, but to little effect.

But Labour did not lose in 1983 because of Foot. The party would have been divided, and the economy recovering, whoever had been leader. In reality it was an election that Labour could not have won. If Healey had become leader in 1980, things might have been even worse; for then there would have been a right-wing leader leading a party with a strong and united left, and Healey would have appeared under siege. Under Foot, on the other hand, the left split between 'hard' and 'soft', so forging the soft-left/centrist alliance which was to dominate the party for years to come. Foot's record as party leader was not as bad as the conventional wisdom would have us believe, but there was nothing in his locker to bring about a miracle in 1983.

The results were devastating. No poll published after 5 June gave the Conservatives anything less than a 17-point lead; indeed, five of the last 16 polls published suggested that the Alliance would take more votes than Labour. In the event, Labour emerged with only 209 seats, by far its worst performance since

1935, and 27.6 per cent of the votes, its lowest share since 1918 (when it had put up far fewer candidates). In terms of votes cast per candidate it was the party's worst showing ever. A record 119 deposits were forfeited, and three ex-cabinet ministers, including Benn, were defeated.[43] The Alliance almost pipped Labour into second place in terms of votes, taking 25.4 per cent, but emerged with only 23 MPs, of whom only six were SDPers. Labour had lost particularly heavily in London, the wider south-east, eastern Lancashire, West Yorkshire and the east Midlands. Outside Greater London, Labour held only three of the 182 seats south of the Severn–Wash line, as against 31 seats in October 1974 and 42 in 1966. Worse still, in this area in particular, Labour had been beaten into a bad third place behind the Alliance in numerous constituencies. Labour attracted the support of just 38 per cent of skilled workers, only slightly ahead of the Conservatives' 35 per cent, while its share of the non-manual vote fell to 17 per cent, its lowest since the war.[44] While Labour's heartlands remained reasonably solid, the party was obviously a long way from power, and in terms of the popular vote it seemed an open question as to whether Labour could see off the Alliance threat. Clearly, something needed to be done to restore the party's fortunes.

The most obvious, indeed inevitable, change to make was in the leadership. There was no conceivable reason for Foot to stay on. Assured that some big unions, including the TGWU, would support his favoured successor, Kinnock, Foot made it known that he would resign once the electoral college had chosen a new leader at that autumn's party conference.[45] Healey stepped aside, having no desire to emulate Morrison's 1955 humiliation, and it soon emerged that the main choice was between Kinnock and Hattersley. Hattersley had strong support from the right, and was more experienced than Kinnock, who had been an MP for only 13 years and had little front-bench experience. But Kinnock could still get the support of much of the left, certainly in preference to Hattersley; had some appeal to the centre and even the right because of his hostility towards the Benn candidature of 1981; and was younger and appeared more telegenic at a time when memories of Foot meant such things seemed to matter more than ever. With Benn out of parliament and thus ineligible to stand, the standard bearers of the hard left were Eric Heffer for the leadership and Michael Meacher as deputy.

By the time conference was convened on 2 October it was widely expected, given what unions, CLPs and MPs were known to have decided, that Kinnock would win the leadership and Hattersley be elected as his deputy, forming the so-called 'dream ticket' balancing left and right. The hard left argued that a real balance would have been Kinnock–Meacher, but Kinnock was much keener to work with Hattersley, a message that got across to the broader party.[46] In the event, Kinnock won just over 70 per cent of the votes for the leadership, with Hattersley taking a shade under 20 per cent and Heffer and Shore being unable to poll 10 per cent between them. Kinnock had the support of three-quarters of the union vote, more than nine-tenths of the CLPs, and just under half of the MPs. Hattersley went on to win the deputy leadership by a scarcely less impressive margin, taking around 66 per cent of the votes. Interestingly, the CLPs, so often seen at this time as the hotbeds of the hard left, not only voted overwhelmingly in favour of Kinnock rather than Heffer but also went, by a narrow majority, in favour of Hattersley over Meacher.[47] This suggested, first, that the party had not been as left-wing between 1979 and 1983 as has often been claimed, and also that the scale of the 1983 defeat had shocked some party members into loosening their links with the hard left. The result also meant that Kinnock had a clearer mandate from party activists than any previous leader. Paradoxically, this fact would allow him, in the end, to push the party further to the right, in terms of policy and organization, than any leader since Gaitskell. The electoral college, designed as a guarantor for the left, was ultimately to be a weapon with which to beat it.

When Kinnock took over the leadership there were high hopes for the future. Although the next election would need to produce 117 new seats for Labour on a bigger swing than at any election since 1945, many Labourites believed, in the first flush of enthusiasm for the 'dream ticket', that it might just be possible.

But, of course, it was not. Economic indicators, volatile between 1979 and 1983, were much steadier between 1983 and 1987, helped by favourable world trends. While unemployment continued to rise until 1986, it increased more slowly than in the earlier period, and its heaviest impact tended to be in areas where Labour was already strong. Most of the other economic indicators were favourable. GDP grew by 27 per cent between 1981 and 1988, inflation remained relatively low and revenue from North Sea Oil and privatization allowed the government to continue planning cuts in direct taxation.[48] Considerable and, according to many sources, intensifying deprivation remained in much of Britain, but for those in work this was, on the whole, a period of relative prosperity and, in contrast to most of the period since the later 1960s, general optimism. This did not mean that people were suddenly 'converted' to Thatcherite 'values',[49] but it did mean that Labour had a very real problem in attracting new voters, especially as the Alliance was still seen as a viable alternative.

The Conservatives also gained some popularity for their frontal attack on many of the keystones of Labourism. Trade unionism had been a mixed blessing to Labour before the Second World War, not only a source of strength but also an easy target for Tory attacks. This had changed dramatically in the 1940s, but increasingly adverse comment from the mid-1950s onwards had begun to cause new problems for the party. The failure of Wilson and later Callaghan to 'tame' the unions was merely a prelude to a much more sustained attack under Thatcher, who was able to use rapidly rising unemployment (especially in manufacturing) to weaken the movement. Second, there was much employer, and not a little public, support for a legislative attack on union rights. Thatcher's government chose to advance, not by one huge and unworkable statute like Heath's Industrial Relations Act, but by a series of measures over a number of years. The Employment Acts of 1980 and 1982 limited the right to picket, placed strict restrictions on closed shops and allowed unions to be sued for damages, in effect repealing the 1906 Act. Five further Acts between 1984 and 1990 ate away further at unions' legal immunities, imposed ballots for strikes and political funds and abolished the pre-entry closed shop. Deregulation – effectively sweeping away the workers' protection that had been built up over the years – was also carried on apace, so that after the 1989 Employment Act had been passed it was legal for women to work in coal mines (although the question was largely academic by then since there were hardly any coal mines left).[50] As a result of all this, union membership fell from an all-time peak of 13,498,000 in 1979 to 11,337,000 in 1983, 10,475,000 in 1987 and 9,585,000 in 1991, by which time union density, at 34.4 per cent, was at its lowest since 1940.[51] This all had a number of effects for Labour. First, it held financial implications for the party, although the worst effects were vitiated by increases in affiliation fees. Second, it made union leaders keener than ever to get rid of the Conservative government under which they were faring so badly, and so they became more responsive to those who claimed that they had a reasonable strategy for achieving this, and increasingly keen to back them. Ultimately, too, it was to make the unions – and hence the party – keener on the EC once it became apparent that the latter might be able to restore some of the rights that workers and unions had lost.

Trade unions were not the only Labour sacred cows to come under attack, of course. The nationalized industries were largely privatized during the Thatcher regime. Privatization proved in many ways a popular policy; the period from 1983 to 1987 saw the government build on earlier, more limited operations with a whole series of high-profile sell-offs. Because the shares were available in small quantities and also under-priced, large numbers of people could buy them, often to sell on for a short-term windfall profit. It said a lot for the essential failure of the public corporation model that there was so little effective (or ineffective, come to that) resistance from either the workers in, or the customers of, these industries at the time.

Local government also came under sustained attack. Here, Labour had built a very solid base for itself over the years. The Conservatives recognized this and resolved to do something about it. In an attempt to curb local authority expenditure, the government introduced rate-capping (which allowed ministers to set limits to the level of local taxation an authority could raise) and, later, the community charge, or 'poll tax' (a flat-rate levy), one of whose aims was to ensure that 'wasteful' Labour councils would have to set a high charge to everyone, and so be ousted. Central government also removed functions from local authority control. The first sign of this was the sale of council houses to their tenants at a discount, in an attempt to increase owner occupation. This proved to be a popular policy; it also seemed to reduce Labour's clientage. Local education authorities lost control over some schools as a result of the 'opting out' procedures introduced in 1988. And local government functions were increasingly delegated to unelected 'quangos' set up by central government bodies.

Thus Kinnock inherited a party which was in difficulties, not least from a self-confident government determined to eat away at Labour's vitals. His aim was, from the outset, to regain power for Labour. This meant a continuation of the party's shift to the right, which had begun at the 1981 conference. Economic trends further weakened the hard left's case. By the mid-1980s, it was again credible for Labour's leaders to talk about the need to manage prosperity better: what was needed was not radical change, but a more egalitarian distribution of the surplus which capitalism was once again producing. Surprisingly rapidly after its apparent demise, revisionism was back on the agenda. At the same time, the hard left was increasingly blamed for the scale, and sometimes for the fact, of the 1983 defeat. In some ways, of course, this was too sweeping. First, many of the most unpopular policies in 1983 had not been the sole preserve of the hard left, but had been based on prejudices shared broadly by Labourites. The case of council house sales is a good example. Labour could have encouraged such sales, and used the receipts to build new council housing. Such a scheme had been considered, in fact, by the last Labour government, but rejected, showing the extent to which paternalism lingered on in the mainstream of the Labour movement.[52] And when people did apply to buy from Labour councils under the Conservatives' legislation after 1979, those councils often treated them as second-class tenants, refusing to carry out any repairs except those they were statutorily obliged to execute, and trying every possible delaying tactic to prevent the sales.[53] As a result, Labour managed to look unsympathetic to some of its core voters. Other policies which were more exclusively associated with the left were not necessarily unpopular. Unilateral nuclear disarmament and withdrawal from the EC, for example, fared poorly in opinion polls, but a strong case could have been made for each in the early 1980s, on strategic and economic grounds. The real problem was that the left failed to discipline itself sufficiently to work out the policies and explain them fully, resorting too frequently to the easier option of sloganizing. The Labour left, as so often, proved itself better at criticizing the party leadership than at taking an opportunity to provide a lead itself. Its rigid adherence to the precepts of the 1973 economic programme also showed its failure to accept that there could be change and development in policy without betrayal.[54] The failure of the left to make a credible case, the growing perception of 'left' policies as being unpopular, the scale of the 1983 defeat, the imprimatur of the electoral college and the easing economic situation all combined to lubricate Kinnock's subsequent efforts to move Labour back to a more centrist position.

Two problems largely overshadowed Kinnock's first two years in the post, however. One was the miner's strike which began in April 1984 and lasted for almost a year.[55] The NUM executive, under its president, Arthur Scargill, refused to hold a strike ballot, and as a result some miners, mainly in Nottinghamshire, refused to come out. Attempts to persuade them to do so by picketing were met by a firm, and at times heavy-handed, police response, and violence ensued. Relations between Scargill and the Labour leadership broke down completely, since the latter was critical of the failure to hold a ballot and felt it could not afford to be associated with violence, a position which led to its failing, on the whole, to argue the economic case against pit closures or even challenge obvious police excesses. Of course, the position was not made easier for Kinnock by the fact that the working miners were overwhelmingly Labour voters. As in 1926, major industrial conflict made it difficult for the Labour leadership to satisfy anyone. Kinnock only spoke on the dispute once in parliament, and party headquarters were dissuaded from issuing propaganda on the coal question.[56] But the strike's long duration, and its emotiveness for most Labourites, meant the issue could not just be brushed aside.

In March 1985 the miners were forced back to work; for them, the whole affair had been a catastrophe. Its impact on the Labour Party, however, was not so clear-cut. In the short term, it was a disaster. It suggested Labour was split, portrayed its new leader in a poor light, and emphasized issues, like law and order and industrial efficiency, with which the Conservatives were usually perceived as being best able to cope. It also split the NUM with the formation of a breakaway union, the Union of Democratic Mineworkers, in Nottinghamshire. Finally, in so far as it saw the beginning of the virtual cessation of deep mining in Britain, it represented the end of the road for what had been, since 1922 at least, one of the key constituents of Labour's electoral strength. In the longer term, though, the strike was of great benefit to the Labour leadership. For it was the industrial counterpart to the

1983 election defeat. Like the latter, it could be used by the leadership as an object lesson in the dangers of 'leftism' and the need for moderation and caution.[57]

The other major problem Kinnock faced was Militant. The 1983 party conference confirmed the expulsion of the paper's editorial board by a three-to-one majority. Soon some local parties were following this lead by expelling members, while LPYS's budget was cut drastically.[58] The next two years saw a general hardening of opinion against the hard left in general and Militant in particular. Evidence that the Tendency was a revolutionary party within a party grew. Meanwhile, the conduct of certain Labour local authorities was causing adverse media comment and threatening Labour's chances of portraying itself as a responsible party of government. The most spectacular example came in Liverpool. In 1985 the City Council, which was strongly influenced by Militant members such as the Council deputy leader, Derek Hatton, employed tactics of brinkmanship in an attempt to obtain more government money for the city. This culminated in September 1985 with the council issuing redundancy notices to all its 31,000 employees, as a way of showing what it believed to be the logical conclusion of Conservative policies.[59] But this was a step too far. Many union leaders and members were appalled at what they saw as playing with people's livelihoods. Other councils, after all, had managed without such demonstrations despite being in a similar position to Liverpool. Crucially, Militant had offended against a key part of the Labour ethos, security of employment. Kinnock, who had a keen nose for that ethos, took his chance to strike at Militant at the 1985 party conference. He made a strong attack on Liverpool Council's conduct in his keynote speech, which was well received by the majority.[60] His approval rating in the polls soared. A group of leading trade unionists who visited Liverpool on behalf of the NEC reported very unfavourably on the performance of the Council and on the state of Liverpool Labour Party, and a subsequent NEC inquiry found 'very serious and deep-seated problems', including widespread evidence of patronage and intimidation. In February 1986 the district Labour Party was suspended. There followed a lengthy process of expulsions, and by 1987 Militant was on the run.[61]

By now the hard left was utterly alienated from Kinnock, but other elements in the party were also having doubts about his leadership qualities. There was a growing feeling, exploited by the media, that he lacked experience and administrative ability. His past could always be trawled by the media for a quotation to show him either as a left-winger or as a hypocrite who would say anything to gain votes. His parliamentary performance continued to be indifferent, and began to be compared unfavourably with that of the shadow spokesman on Trade and Industry, John Smith, a Scottish lawyer who had spent seven months in the cabinet as Trade Secretary in 1978–79, and who gave the Conservatives far more worries over the Westland scandal in early 1986. With the polls showing Labour behind the Alliance, although ahead of the Conservatives, in early 1986, there were grumblings about Kinnock's leadership.[62] No rival emerged to challenge him, however, and this meant that, by the time of the next general election in June 1987, he had been able to push through something of a transformation within the party, in the fields of both organization and policy.

From 1985 onwards, Kinnock developed the leader's office into an alternative party organization. Charles Clarke (in charge of his private office) and Peter Mandelson (party communications director) were crucial in developing a new emphasis on packaging and presentation, in reaction to the perceived failings of the 1983 campaign.[63] Party representatives were smartened up, and Labour became much more media-friendly. More than that, it was now a question of following the leadership because there seemed to be no viable alternative on offer. The leader's office exploited this: helped by a collaborative shadow cabinet, an increasingly united NEC and the perceived proximity of the next general election, it ensured that the 1986 party conference bore no small resemblance to a leadership rally. However, Kinnock's opinion poll rating had slumped again by the end of the year, and was not to recover substantially before the election.

These years also saw changes in party policy. The aim was, essentially, to make policy more 'popular', more credible (there had been widespread disbelief, for example, in Labour's 1983 promise to reduce unemployment to below one million), and more congenial to the views of the shadow cabinet. The ensuing shift to the right was buttressed by, even predicated upon, the 'boom' conditions which were clearly prevailing by the end of 1985. At the same time, change was rather piecemeal. One of

the reasons for the emphasis on better presentation was a realization by party strategists that the transitional state of policy made
it unwise to rely too heavily on detail in that area. In 1987, the
manifesto would be 'full of compromise and ambiguity'.[64] Plans
to remove US nuclear bases from Britain were omitted, for
example, but the party remained committed to unilateralism.
Withdrawal from the EC was dropped, but this simply meant that
the party had little to say on Europe at all. The recently privatized gas and telecommunications industries would be taken into
'social ownership', but there was little clarity as to what this would
mean in practice. The plan to reduce unemployment was scaled
down; now the party only pledged a reduction of a million over
two years, but even then it carried little conviction. Large-scale
increases in public expenditure, particularly on welfare, were
also suggested, but with little real notion of how to pay for them,
which allowed plenty of opportunities for the Conservatives to
attack them as being 'uncosted'.[65] In short, the policy changes
in the run-up to the 1987 general election showed that making
policy more 'moderate' did not necessarily make it any more
coherent.

There was, nevertheless, great optimism among Labour strategists when Thatcher announced on 11 May 1987 that there would
be an election in a month's time.[66] But such feelings had more
heart than head about them. The European elections of 1984
had seen Labour advance somewhat from its dismal 1979 showing, but still left the Conservatives some way ahead. By-elections
had seen the Conservatives lose four of the nine seats they had
defended, but only one of these had gone to Labour, which had
itself lost a seat to the Alliance in February 1987. As late as March
1987 Labour was in third place behind the Alliance in the polls.
Thus by the time the election was called, it was less a question of
whether Labour could win, but whether it could hold on to second place – in terms of votes, if not seats – in the face of what
appeared to be a strong Alliance challenge. Considering the state
of its manifesto, Labour fought a good campaign, which focused
particularly on its leader, and for a time the Conservative high
command was worried. But its spending plans were savaged by
the Conservatives as being likely to lead to massive tax increases, a
charge to which Labour did not have a clear response.

For all its professional campaigning, Labour increased its poll
share only by 3.2 points to 30.8 per cent, and managed a net gain

over 1983 of only 20 seats, emerging with 229 MPs. The party's main advances came in the east Midlands, Scotland, Wales and Yorkshire; the image of an electoral 'two nations' scenario was intensified by the fact that it actually lost three seats in the south-east and still held only three seats south of the Severn–Wash line outside London. Had the rules for forfeiture of deposits not been changed since 1983, 94 Labour deposits would have been lost, scarcely fewer than in 1983, and well in excess of the party's previous worst (35 in 1929). Labour was still in third place behind the Alliance in more than 200 seats. It failed to improve its position significantly among non-manual workers, while among skilled workers only 36 per cent supported Labour, whereas 40 per cent voted Conservative.[67] Whatever else Labour had achieved in 1987, it had not built a strong base from which to challenge the Conservative ascendancy next time; to win such an election Labour still needed a swing larger than any achieved by either party at a post-war general election.

In the aftermath of defeat, many commentators expressed the view that Labour was probably finished in its present form: that the affluence and embourgeoisement of a section of the working class, particularly skilled workers in the south and Midlands, and the shrinking of the working class overall, had made the party unelectable. This argument was not without its flaws.[68] In particular, it might have been useful to ask why the party was failing to get so many of what might be thought of as its 'natural' voters – young people, members of ethnic minorities and the poor – to the polls at all. But the class dealignment argument carried almost all before it for the time being. The 'logical' corollary was that Labour should move further towards the 'centre ground' of politics. The alternative sometimes touted at the time – that it should form an electoral pact with the Alliance – received little support within the party and, in any case, lost what little force it had once the Alliance began to tear itself apart in the attempt to merge the SDP with the Liberals, although the idea of a 'progressive alliance' did not go away.[69] Labour certainly appeared to face a very uncertain future in the aftermath of its third successive general election defeat.

11   Modernization and New Labour, 1987–97

In the aftermath of the 1987 defeat, Labour supporters could have been forgiven for feeling depressed. After eight years, a government which most of them found politically and morally repugnant had been re-elected, while Labour, after four difficult transformative years, had fared little better than it had under Foot in 1983. It would be another decade before Labour would finally return to office under Tony Blair, in 1997. But Labour's fortunes were improving for much of the intervening period, and although the 1992 election was to end in a further defeat, Labour was at least once again looking like a real contender for power. This was to be a period when conditions would start to turn in Labour's favour, and when an increasingly self-conscious project of 'modernization' would culminate in the creation of the 'New Labour' brand which was to accompany Blair's election to the leadership in 1994.

Modernization had, of course, begun before the 1987 election, but Kinnock and his colleagues presented defeat at the polls as indicating that the pace of change needed to increase. In July 1987, Kinnock announced the establishment of seven 'policy review' groups which would report to the 1989 party conference. The results were broadly as intended. On the economy, Labour moved still further away from nationalization, stressing the need for market disciplines and a government sympathetic to business and willing to create an environment in which it could prosper. This meant, in turn, that Labour ruled out large increases in taxation. Smith, who took over as shadow Chancellor in 1987, embarked on a round of meetings with City and business leaders in which he was at pains to emphasize Labour's 'respectability', while Margaret Beckett, appointed shadow Chief Secretary to the Treasury in 1989, belied her one-time hard-left reputation by stressing what became known as 'Beckett's Law': the need to avoid new spending commitments and use the formulation that expenditure would only rise 'as resources allowed'.[1] This was, in short, a return to the notion, generally dominant in the party's history, that socialism (although the word was by now rarely used, and would not appear in the 1992 manifesto) would emerge from the redistribution of a growing surplus produced by an increasingly prosperous capitalism. This view, in turn, remained tenable because it did seem, at least until the end of the 1980s, that the economy was still growing significantly; and even after the economy began to move into recession in 1989, the view was still defended, on the grounds that government errors, rather than something inherent in capitalism, had been to blame for the end of prosperity.

In other areas, too, there were changes. Occasionally these were innovative, as with the pledges to introduce a national minimum wage and to create a Ministry for Women.[2] But generally the trend was towards policy becoming more 'moderate'. First, policy on the EC was modified. With withdrawal seeming increasingly a lost cause, and Thatcher's continuing rhetorical opposition to greater integration leaving a gap in the political market, Labour became warmer towards Europe. The process was helped along in 1988 when the President of the European Commission, Jacques Delors, impressed delegates at the Trades Union Congress with a speech which emphasized the social policy and workers' protection aspects of the EC. By the time of the 1992 general election, Labour would be standing firmly as a pro-'European' party.[3] Second, there were changes in industrial relations policy. Previously, Labour had pledged to repeal all the Conservatives' anti-union legislation, but now, even many trade union leaders saw that, paradoxically, the Conservatives' policies had prevented unions from doing things which made them unpopular with the wider public; here Blair, as Employment spokesman, played an important role in shifting Labour's position.[4] On welfare, Labour tried to adapt to changing times by moving away from the 'paternalism and bureaucracy' which had so characterized its policies in the past, but the vexed issues of targeted benefits and unification of the tax and benefits systems were left to one side.[5] Finally, the party ditched its commitment to unilateral nuclear disarmament, a step made easier by developments in the outside world, first with the prospect of real progress in disarmament talks between the superpowers, and later with the collapse of the Soviet bloc in 1989–91.

The policy review took policy out of party politics for two years. This allowed Kinnock to concentrate on organization and image. A number of developments took place which aimed to increase the power of the party centre, and, still more, the leader, at the expense of Labour's traditional structures. The party conference became more and more of a rubber-stamping talkshop, where delegates came to applaud rather than to debate. The NEC and shadow cabinet became still more Kinnockite. Potential areas of dissent were marginalized, be they local councillors, women's groups or ethnic minority groups campaigning for Black Sections. Some awkward individuals were removed from the party, often on rather flimsy evidence. CLPs' powers were reduced as the NEC took greater powers over candidate selection and, in 1991, instituted a national membership scheme whose initial results were at best disappointing.[6] There were yet more reforms of the youth movement, which ultimately eliminated most far-left influence, but which also failed to galvanize large numbers of young people to join the party.

All this led, ultimately, to a left-wing reaction. In March 1988, Benn – who since his return to parliament at a by-election in 1984 had been a marginal figure – and Heffer announced their candidatures for the leadership and deputy leadership respectively. A six-month campaign followed, but they had no chance of success. At the October 1988 party conference Kinnock easily beat off Benn's challenge, taking almost 89 per cent of the votes. Even Hattersley, who faced a second challenger in the combative figure of shadow cabinet Employment spokesman, John Prescott, took two-thirds of the votes for deputy leader, whereas Prescott took just under 24 per cent and Heffer just under 10. Only 38 MPs voted for Benn; still more depressing for him was the fact that only 119 of the 600-plus CLPs did so.[7] This showed the marginalization of the hard left, the extent to which Kinnock had established a firm hold over the party at all levels, and the way in which memories of the 1979–83 period could still be used against the left and to emphasize the need for loyalty to the leadership. The perils of disloyalty were clearly seen when Prescott was punished for standing against Hattersley by being demoted to Transport (being replaced at Employment by Blair). But, in truth, there had been an air of futility about the whole affair. The ageing Benn and Heffer seemed in many ways like throwbacks to a bygone era.[8] There was, in any case, little of substance behind their campaign. The parallels with the Cook–Maxton campaign 60 years earlier are striking. Both were left-wing attempts to resist the increasingly accommodationist stance of a moderate leadership which seemed to be carrying all before it; both were, in a sense, profoundly irrelevant to the contemporary situation; and both were doomed to fail, not least because they almost totally failed to excite trade union enthusiasm. Neither made much impact on ordinary party members or MPs who were hoping for victory at the next election and who knew the penalties for crossing an increasingly powerful party leadership. And, of course, both were counterproductive, since they highlighted the weakness of the left and gave the ruling oligarchy ample opportunity to re-emphasize the dangers of division and the value of loyalty. The only concrete result of each was to reinforce the leadership they despised and to ease the rightward path of that leadership.

By 1989, then, Kinnock's hegemony within the party was virtually complete. It was buttressed by Labour's improving electoral performance. In March 1989 Labour won the Mid Staffordshire by-election from the Conservatives on a 21 per cent swing.[9] That May there were gains in the local elections, and the following month Labour won 45 seats in the Euro-elections, more than the Conservatives, although on a very low turnout. By April 1990 Labour had a 28-point lead in the polls. However, this was a 'soft' lead, based on the unpopularity of the government, and of Thatcher in particular. Rising inflation and interest rates severely dented the Conservatives' claims of economic competence. Thatcher's devotion to the flat-rate poll tax to replace the rates as a way of funding local government weakened her position further. When, in November 1990, the deputy Prime Minister, Sir Geoffrey Howe, resigned in protest at her anti-EC stance, it was the signal for the malcontents to act. Michael Heseltine challenged her for the party leadership, and after she failed to win enough votes to fend off a second ballot, she was persuaded to withdraw, to be succeeded ultimately by the Chancellor of the Exchequer, John Major.

Labour had been looking forward to fighting Thatcher at the next election, believing she could now be portrayed as out of touch and dictatorial. Major seemed a more conciliatory figure; his first actions were to bring Heseltine back into the cabinet and announce that the poll tax would be abolished. There was some sense of a fresh start, and a feeling widely expressed was that Major should be given a chance. The recession continued, but talk of economic recovery being on the way did not seem wholly ludicrous, and the run-up to the 1992 election saw inflation back below 5 per cent, income tax cuts and a massive stimulus to public expenditure. From December 1991 the Conservatives had a slight edge in the polls, and Labour was still trailing on leadership and economic competence, which would obviously be crucial issues.[10] Still, despite all this, Labour had high hopes of victory in the election which was finally called for 9 April 1992.

Labour's campaign was again highly professional. As in 1987, Kinnock figured largely. However, things did not go as well as planned. Labour's 'shadow budget' seemed rather pompous and unnecessary, and allowed the Conservatives to focus on taxation, where Labour was still rather vulnerable. There were serious disagreements between Kinnock and Smith.[11] The party's celebratory Sheffield rally, held, perversely enough, a week before polling, did the party little good and might even have damaged its prospects.[12] Then, in the last week of the campaign, Kinnock struck a strangely ambivalent note about electoral reform. All in all, it had not been as good a campaign as it should have been, and led to subsequent calls to put the publicity agents and advertisers under closer political control.[13]

On the night of 9 April three exit polls suggested that there would be a hung parliament, but in the event the Conservatives won an overall majority of 21, with 336 seats and 41.9 per cent of the poll, as opposed to Labour's 271 and 34.4 per cent. The overall swing to Labour was only 2.1 per cent, producing a net gain of 42 seats, especially in the west Midlands, the north-west and the London area, and it increased its non-London representation south of the Severn–Wash line from three to ten, although this was still well short of pre-1979 levels.[14] Under the pre-1985 rules, it would still have forfeited 65 deposits, and its share of the total poll was lower than in 1979. It would still take a further 2.3 per cent swing to Labour to make it the largest party, and a 4.1 per cent swing to give it an overall majority.[15] Three elections on from the 1979 defeat, Labour was still not in a particularly strong psephological position from which to launch its next election campaign.

The reasons for the result have been much debated. There was some feeling that an inept campaign had cost Labour victory, but this seems unlikely.[16] In all probability, it was an election that Labour could not have won. The Conservatives had got rid of their two biggest handicaps, Thatcher and the poll tax. They could point with some degree of credibility to the start of economic recovery. At such a time, enough people, having just come through recession and with 'memories' of past Labour governments, were not willing to risk a change, particularly to a party which had changed so rapidly and under a leader who was still not altogether trusted. The 1987 election result had left Labour with a mountain to climb; ultimately it did not have the resources to achieve the feat.

Labour's defeat led to the resignation of a devastated Kinnock. After almost nine years of hard graft, he had really expected to become Prime Minister in 1992. As it was, he had to face the reality that the next election would be four or five years away. The idea of a further stretch of opposition did not appeal to him. He also blamed himself, to some extent, for Labour's defeat.[17] And, in any case, it was clear that the poor relations he now had with Smith and others in the leadership would make any attempt to retain the leadership untenable.[18] Having taken Labour as far as he thought he could, therefore, Kinnock announced shortly after the election that he would be resigning as leader and that Hattersley would resign as deputy at the same time. In order to expedite matters, the leadership election would not have to wait until the party conference in the autumn, but would take place in June.

Verdicts on Kinnock's leadership have been mixed. The case for him would state that he pulled the party back from the brink of disaster in 1983 to the brink of office in 1992; that he saw off the challenge of the Alliance; that he got rid of Militant and marginalized the hard left; and that, part cause and part effect of all this, he made considerable progress in modernizing the party's policy and organization, and so made it possible for future leaders to continue the process and make Labour a party fit to face the challenges of the 1990s and beyond. It was certainly the case that he had faced huge challenges from many directions, and that he had had little luck. Then again, he had not always been a great electoral asset: there must, for example, be questions as to how it was that a leader elected to boost the party's fortunes by running ahead of it in the polls actually managed to trail behind it so often, particularly after 1987. Further, the policies Kinnock was instrumental in pushing through were and remain open to question. For example, he largely reverted to earlier Labour ideas, especially in the commitment to achieving a 'fairer' society through economic growth; and this maxim had tripped up MacDonald, Crosland, Wilson and others in the past. Little attention was paid to devolving power to the people: to a larger extent than is sometimes recognized, Kinnock's Labour Party remained pretty uncritical of the nature of the state and its power. Party members also grumbled that he had downgraded the party's democracy, and it was certainly true that the leadership had levels of power within the party as a whole by 1992 that were probably unprecedented in the party's history. Ultimately, however, Kinnock handed over a party with much better prospects than the one he had inherited in 1983; and, to that extent, the verdict on his leadership must be broadly positive.

It was clear even before Kinnock's announcement that John Smith would be his successor, although Kinnock himself would have preferred Bryan Gould.[19] The leader of one of the biggest unions, John Edmonds of the General Municipal and Boilermakers' Union (GMB), came out for the shadow Chancellor at an early stage.[20] Smith's credentials were excellent. He had served in Callaghan's cabinet in 1978–79, making him the only current party leader to have such high-ranking experience. Despite being a right-winger, he had – along with most of the Scottish right within the party – demonstrated his loyalty to Labour by having nothing to do with the SDP in 1981–82. In opposition, he had been one of Labour's most effective performers, as seen over Westland in 1986. He fitted Labour's perceived need for a leader with 'bottom', his background and legal training giving him an air of gravitas that Kinnock had never quite managed to pull off. At 53, he seemed to be at the height of his powers; fears over his health (he had had a serious heart attack in 1988) had been assuaged by a new, healthier regimen.

Indeed, Smith's claims were so strong that some people called for his election as leader to be unopposed.[21] This was not entirely idle chatter and spin by Smith's people: since the Benn–Heffer challenge of 1988, the rules had been changed so that any candidate needed the support of 20 per cent of Labour's MPs before they could stand, effectively ruling out left-wingers like the former Greater London Council leader Ken Livingstone.[22] However, Gould was able to get sufficient PLP support to enable him to run. In 1987 Gould had been attacked by some as an undesirable media manipulator, and as too smooth by half. But now he emerged to fight Smith from the left. Gould based his campaign in particular on a critique of the European Exchange Rate Mechanism (ERM), of which Smith was a staunch supporter. Gould's objections stemmed at least in part from his New Zealand roots, but there was more to it than that. He believed fervently that fixed exchange rates would debar a British Labour government from pursuing the kind of Keynesian measures which, he believed, were necessary to ensure full employment and social justice.[23] Although scarcely, in itself, much more than a tepid reassertion of Keynesian priorities, Gould's campaign was latched onto by some with a leftish reputation: David Blunkett, darling of the municipal Labour left in the 1980s, ran his campaign. However, he was a less convincing candidate than Smith, lacking the latter's experience in senior positions and widespread backing within the party; and his scarcely veiled hostility to the EU sat ill with a party that, since 1983, had moved steadily in a pro-European direction. Gould soon recognized that he had no chance of victory, but continued with the fight because he believed an unopposed election would be undesirable, and to stake out an alternative to what he saw as Smith's unquestioning pro-Europeanism.[24]

The final result in July 1992 was nothing short of a rout. Smith was supported by 91 per cent of the electoral college, taking 97.7 per cent of the CLP votes and 96.2 per cent of the union votes; Gould did a little better among MPs, but even here Smith took 77.3 per cent.[25] Gould was also defeated in the ballot for the deputy leadership; Margaret Beckett, Smith's own preferred candidate and one whose own one-time hard-left credentials gave an impression of political as well as gender balance, won by a safe margin. Gould was elected to the shadow cabinet, but resigned within a few months, and thereafter criticized Smith's pro-Europeanism from the back benches before finally bowing out of British politics in early 1994 to return to academia in his native New Zealand.[26]

Smith's inheritance was made considerably easier by the problems that began to dog the Major government from a very early stage. First, economic recovery was slower to show tangible benefits than had been expected. At the 1992 election, Conservative talk of 'the green shoots of recovery' had not appeared incredible. But unemployment continued to nudge upwards for the rest of the year, and into the first quarter of 1993; indeed, it did not fall below pre-election levels until 1994.[27] And, unlike the recession of the early 1980s, this one was hitting middle-class families – core Conservative voters – to a significant extent. Second, the government – elected on a pledge to reduce taxes, and attacking Labour as a 'tax and spend' party – found that it needed to increase existing taxes, and introduce new ones, in order to balance the nation's books. Third, from a very early stage the government was rocked by scandals or, as the phenomenon soon became known, 'sleaze'. This took two forms. There was the kind of thing beloved by the tabloids, centring on sexual activity; and there were also more complex issues, such as dishonesty and rank corruption, which the broadsheet press pursued with great tenacity. One such was the scandal about illegal arms sales to Iraq, which emerged that November.[28]

But the most spectacular example of apparent government ineptitude came on 'Black Wednesday', 16 September 1992. The ERM was already creaking, and the pound – overvalued against the German Mark when Britain had entered – came under massive speculative pressure on the markets. Major was intent on keeping Britain within the ERM, however, and drastic steps were taken to do this, including raising interest rates from 10 to first 12 and then 15 per cent and spending up to £10 billion in an ultimately doomed attempt to achieve this objective. For the Conservatives the result was devastating. They lost the reputation they had built up over the past decade, however tendentiously, for economic competence. The day shook the morale of all who depended on low interest rates, be they business people or mortgage holders. And the whole affair opened up wounds within the Conservative Party over Europe which were to prove impossible for Major to heal.

Against such a background, Smith's early months as leader were none too difficult. He was able, for example, to humiliate a discomfited government front bench in the Commons debate about Black Wednesday. More substantially, he also sought to heal rifts within the party that had developed under Kinnock. He responded to increasing criticism of 'spin doctors' by distancing himself from Kinnock's tactics in this area and, in particular, making it clear to Mandelson that he was no longer at the centre of Labour politics. The Shadow Communications Agency was abolished; Mandelson, now MP for Hartlepool, was allowed more time with his constituents.[29] This served Smith well in bringing him goodwill from those, not least on the left of the party, who had become exasperated at the party's privileging of style over substance. But it also enabled him to avoid any major inquest into the 1992 defeat. After all, Smith had himself been closely involved with Labour's strategy before 1992, and particularly, as shadow Chancellor, involved with the party's new attempts to reassure and seduce business. Smith was happy to continue, and indeed accelerate, the shift back to the old line that a fairer society had to be paid for by economic growth, as opposed to the 'tax and spend' option that the fairness could come before, and even without, the dynamic economy. And the basis of a dynamic economy had to be low inflation; growth, in short, must be sustainable, not of the 'boom and bust' variety produced by the Conservatives in the 1980s.

Smith's stolid image, and his criticism of 'spin' under Kinnock, made him somewhat unpopular with many would-be Labour 'modernizers'.[30] But his leadership was not the period of inertia often implied by such critics. Any understanding of Smith's strategy must recognize the situation in which Labour found itself. It had lost four successive general elections, and had not polled more than 40 per cent of the votes cast since 1970. In the past, Labour had committed itself heavily to policies while in opposition; and many of these had subsequently proved to be hostages to fortune. Recent experiences, and not least Smith's shadow budget during the 1992 campaign, had suggested that such a strategy should be avoided in future. In addition, there *was* no short cut to office. The Conservatives' overall majority of 21 was small, but was theoretically large enough to afford them a full parliamentary term. Some suggested that a deal should be done with the Liberal Democrats, promising electoral reform in return for support against the Conservatives. But while Smith was not religiously wedded to the existing electoral system, such a deal might only have served to split both Labour and the Liberal Democrats, while not ousting the Conservatives. Smith might have been 'playing the long game', but in retrospect it seems clear that his strategy of waiting and allowing the Conservatives every opportunity to tear themselves apart would have paid dividends had he lived to fight the next general election campaign.[31]

Second, Smith was not a conservative on party policy. To be sure, he believed that Kinnock's policy review had settled many issues for the foreseeable future, and felt that to reopen such questions and try to push Labour even further to the right would have been counterproductive. But he could see that the party needed to move further in some areas of policy. Accordingly, on the fiftieth anniversary of the publication of the Beveridge Report, in December 1992, he announced the establishment of a Commission on Social Justice, under the auspices of the leftish Institute for Public Policy Research, to be chaired by Sir Gordon Borrie. The Commission's members were academics, pressure group leaders and business people. Significantly, it included David Marquand, academic biographer of Ramsay MacDonald and one-time Labour defector to the SDP, who was now a Liberal Democrat but who would, ultimately, return to the Labour Party.[32] The Commission set about looking at how the economy and the welfare state could be modernized. While many of its prescriptions were later overtaken by Blair's launch of 'New Labour' shortly before it reported in October 1994, it did, nevertheless, show how Labour was continuing, under Smith, to seek to modernize its policy approach.

Two other major changes during Smith's brief leadership centred on the October 1993 party conference. The most significant of these was the adoption of the policy of all-women shortlists for parliamentary candidatures in half of all vacant Labour-held and marginal seats. During the 1980s, a number of pressure groups had emerged which sought the adoption of more female candidates, given the continuing lamentably low number of women MPs. The 1991 and 1992 party conferences had already agreed a quota system, whereby a proportion of positions at all levels of the party, from the NEC downwards, were to be reserved for women, and left vacant if no women came forward to fill them. Now the principle was extended to parliamentary candidatures. All-women shortlists, although criticized by some, did enable more women candidates to be adopted for winnable seats.[33] This positive discrimination would be declared unlawful by an industrial relations tribunal in January 1996; but, by then, a large number of women candidates had been adopted, and the benefits were garnered at the 1997 election when record numbers of women were elected to parliament.[34]

The second change at the 1993 conference was the adoption of 'one member, one vote' (OMOV) for candidate selection. In future there would be no electoral college for such selections: all members' votes would be of equal value. This was not a new proposal; Kinnock had tried to introduce it as long ago as 1984. But he had been defeated then by a combination of trade unionists who resented the diminution in their powers that was involved, and constituency activists who were unhappy at enfranchising passive non-attending members.[35] In 1989 Kinnock had managed to establish the principle of electoral colleges to choose candidates: trade unions were to have not more than 40 per cent of the votes, and OMOV was to apply to the rest of the party membership. But one of Smith's pledges in seeking the leadership had been to reduce the significance of the union block vote, and OMOV was a good place to start the process. This was something of a gamble. Many union leaders, including Edmonds, remained hostile.[36] Smith realized that his credibility was at stake, and told his private office staff that he would resign as leader if defeated.[37] But considerable leadership arm-twisting of the unions ensured that Smith won the vote. In addition, the make-up of the electoral college to elect the party leader was changed, from the 40:30:30 ratio in favour of the trade unions adopted in 1981 to an even union/CLP/PLP split. It was also agreed that plans would be laid for reducing the general voting power of the unions at conference.[38] Finally, the conference agreed that there need be no candidate reselection in the case of MPs who gained at least two-thirds of the nominations.[39] Even here, therefore, the legacy of the early 1980s swing to the left was being eroded.

Another change was the establishment of a National Policy Forum (NPF). This had first been suggested in 1990, as a body of 150–200 members representing all elements of the party, who would be able to discuss policy development away from the frantic media attention of the party conference. The forum had not been set up by 1992, but once Smith became leader, new emphasis was placed upon it, and his first party conference as leader established it as a body of 81 members. Its first meeting was held in May 1993. The NPF's main role at that meeting was to discuss a document drawn up by shadow ministers, which hardly suggested grassroots empowerment, and it remained 'a shadowy body which raised suspicions amongst party members' and which had 'little real power'.[40] That said, it remained to be seen what potential it might have in the future. But perhaps the most immediate significance of the NPF was that its existence meant that the annual party conference could be even more of a propaganda rally, and even less of a serious exchange of views, than hitherto.[41]

By this time, though, critics who pointed out such problems were very much in the minority; and their position was further weakened by the fact that Labour performed well throughout 1993 and into 1994. In the opinion polls, it was ahead of the Conservatives all through 1993: in an average of all polls, its rating never fell below 41 per cent (August), nor its lead over the Conservatives below 9 per cent. There was no change in the first five months of 1994; the Conservatives remained seemingly rooted on around 26 per cent, whereas Labour varied only between 47 and 49 per cent. At the local elections on 5 May 1994, Labour polled over 40 per cent of the votes cast, and the Conservatives suffered huge losses.[42]

Just a week later, on 12 May, Smith died from a massive heart attack, at the age of 55. His death was utterly unexpected; he had made a good recovery from his earlier attack, and had seemed to be in good health. Parallels were drawn with the party's sudden loss of Gaitskell more than 30 years earlier.[43] Some of the tributes paid to Smith seem, in retrospect, to have been somewhat excessive. He was widely seen as personally impressive, a man of integrity and a formidable Commons performer; his achievements at the 1993 party conference were important, and he might well have made an effective Prime Minister. He had his critics, all the same. Modernizers felt that he was a brake on modernization at just the point when the process begun under Kinnock needed to be completed. As Opposition leader, he was probably not as effective as many had hoped, and certainly seemed uninspiring at times. Although it is hard to believe, given the scale of the problems that were to dog the Conservatives up to 1997, that he would have failed to lead Labour to victory at the next election, how he might have fared as Prime Minister really is impossible to say, and in death, Smith would become the repository of frus-trated hopes for those who recoiled from Blair and New Labour. But recently one of his former colleagues, Jack Straw, has gone on record as expressing concern that Smith's unwillingness to consider new ideas (which was commented upon at the time) as well as his occasionally bad temper and his heavy drinking (which were much less remarked) 'would have made it difficult for him had he become prime minister'. It is difficult to be sure; Blair's view was that the drinking, while sometimes on a large scale, was always done at appropriate times.[44] The moderation on policy could be seen as being as much about uniting the party as it was about an aversion to change per se. Perhaps the safest conclusion is that Smith was a capable politician who had the potential to be an effective premier, but that questions must remain.

In the immediate aftermath of Smith's death, however, the focus was less on the next general election than on the question of who would be elected to succeed him as party leader. It was decided that the electoral college process could not be completed in less than ten weeks, which meant that Beckett would have to act as leader until 21 July. In that period, the European elections were to be held, on 9 June. Those elections saw Labour perform exceptionally well, taking 44.2 per cent of the votes cast and win-ning 60 of the 87 seats (a net gain of 15); the Conservatives, with 27.9 per cent, only managed to elect 18 MEPs. It was clear that whoever succeeded Smith would enter into a very promising inheritance.

There was a frenzy of media speculation as to who Smith's successor would be. Robin Cook, who had been close to both Kinnock and Smith and who had proved effective as a shadow minister, was touted as a soft-left candidate, but he chose not to stand. A more promising prospect who also, ultimately, stood aside was Gordon Brown. Brown was already regarded as a politician of considerable weight and ability. First elected to the Commons in 1983, he had soon caught the attention of the party leadership. He was appointed to the front bench in 1985, and was elected to the shadow cabinet two years later. He served as Smith's deputy in the shadow Treasury team, and made a big impact while stand-ing in as shadow Chancellor following Smith's 1988 heart attack. Although he was close to Smith, Kinnock also had a high regard for him. The PLP took the same view, and he topped the shadow cabinet polls in 1988 and 1989. In the autumn of the latter year, Kinnock promoted him to shadow the Department of Trade and Industry. When Brown again topped the shadow cabinet poll in the aftermath of the 1992 election, Smith rewarded him with appointment as shadow Chancellor. The extremely hardworking Brown seemed well on track to succeed Smith in the fullness of time.[45] Although a 'modernizer', he also had a real feel for, and some sympathy with, the longer-standing traditions of the Labour movement, and had, indeed, published an excellent biography of Maxton in 1986.[46]

By 1994 it was clear, however, that Brown would have to fight hard to beat another of the 1983 intake, Tony Blair. Blair's background was seen as unconventional in Labour terms: his father had aspired to be a Conservative MP, and Blair had not taken much interest in politics as a student at Oxford. However, as a young barrister in the 1970s he had gradually emerged as a right-ist figure in London Labour politics, and had gone on to stand in the hopeless seat of Beaconsfield at a 1982 by-election. He had then proceeded to secure the nomination for the safe seat of Sedgefield in Durham for the 1983 election. At Westminster, he was soon seen as a rising star, being promoted to the front bench in 1984 after only seven months in parliament.[47] After the 1987 election, he joined Brown and Beckett under Smith in argu-ably the most formidable shadow Treasury team in British his-tory.[48] His star continued to wax after the 1992 election, when Smith made him shadow Home Secretary. Throughout this period, Blair and Brown had remained close political colleagues. But their friendship was to take a severe blow in the immediate aftermath of Smith's death. Up to that point, Brown appears to have believed that he was the senior partner; Blair had done lit-tle to disabuse him. Brown's friends have even suggested that the two men had made a pact not to split the 'modernizer' vote in a future leadership election, and that it was understood that Brown and not Blair had the first claim to run as the 'modernizing' candidate.[49]

In the event, however, Blair, and not Brown, was to run in the election and succeed Smith. Part of the reason for this was that Brown was wrong-footed by Smith's sudden death, which 'shat-tered' the shadow Chancellor.[50] Blair, by contrast, had not been close to Smith, whom he had seen as a brake on modernization.

Blair was therefore quick to declare his candidacy, and Labour modernizers, who were keener on getting a modernizer elected as party leader than in who that modernizer was, came to see Blair as the better bet to beat off rivals less keen on their 'project'.[51] They might also have calculated that Blair, as a southern Englishman with a young family, would play better to 'middle England' than the perceivedly dour Scottish bachelor, Brown.

There was a further factor, too. In the two years since the general election, Blair's profile and popularity had soared. While there were still those who regarded him with suspicion, as being 'too smooth by half', his tough stance on crime – an area where the Conservatives' traditional strength was coming increasingly into question – had made him popular with many in the party, and with the media and the wider electorate. Brown, on the other hand, had lost popularity as a result of his strong support for the ERM and his refusal to countenance extensive new spending pledges.[52] In 1992 he had seemed unstoppable, gaining election to the NEC for the first time and coming well ahead of Blair; but a year later he had only just managed to retain his place, and had come behind Blair in the poll.[53]

The Blair bandwagon, therefore, was rolling even before Smith's funeral, despite the fact that campaigning was not supposed to start until after that event. Union leaders and newspapers, ably 'spun' by Mandelson and others, were quick to declare for the shadow Home Secretary. By the time Blair and Brown dined together to discuss the issue on 31 May, Blair was in no mood to withdraw. Brown therefore had no choice other than to back off or risk opening up divisions among the modernizers, possibly allowing someone else less in tune with the 'project' to succeed to the leadership.[54] He took the former course. However, the results were to be longstanding: his relationship with Blair never recovered its former closeness, and his view of Mandelson – who, he believed, had betrayed him – was soured for years to come.[55] The very nature of Blair's elimination of Brown created problems for the next Labour government three years before it was formed.

At the side of all this, the actual leadership election was a pale affair. Beckett and Prescott both stood against Blair, but with little if any hope of success. Beckett's campaign, like her tenure as acting leader, was rather lacklustre. It did not work in her favour, under the circumstances, that many had perceived her to be rather unsupportive of Smith in the 1993 conference controversies over OMOV. This was, perhaps, a little unfair. If Smith had been forced to resign, then she would have become acting leader, and having reserved her position on the issue would have made it easier for her to reconcile the rival factions.[56] But it was the perception of disloyalty that counted. It was also remembered against her, by both left and right, that she had travelled a long way to the right very quickly. Prescott, for his part, was something of an enigma. He had never been part of the hard left; views of him as a leftist owed more to his working-class roots and the party's shift to the right than they did to political reality. Indeed, high-profile attacks on the 'spin doctors' following the 1992 election defeat masked the extent of his support for the modernizing project. Although his status and prestige had increased since his 1988 deputy leadership challenge, he was deemed to lack Blair's broad appeal, and some expressed doubts as to his ability. Given such unconvincing opposition, it was hardly surprising that Blair won a comfortable victory, taking 57 per cent of the electoral college vote, as against 24.1 per cent for Prescott and 18.9 per cent for Beckett. In each section of the college, Blair took more than half the votes cast.[57] Prescott won the ballot for deputy leader.

At the age of 41, Blair was the youngest leader in the party's history. He was quick to turn this to his advantage. One of the key themes of his leadership campaign had been the need for 'national renewal'; he would soon be talking of the need to reinvent Britain as 'a young country'.[58] Amid all the talk of renewal, however, there was a great deal from the old upon which he could build. He had been fortunate in his inheritance, and not for the last time. Thanks to Kinnock, and to wider circumstances, the left was largely insignificant. Militant trade unionism, which had caused Kinnock such problems in 1984–85, seemed to be a thing of the past.[59] OMOV had been accepted, the bloc vote was in the process of reform, and the party's policies were, in historic Labour terms, very much those of the right. It was not only nationalization that was a distant memory: so too were tax and spend, and Keynesian economics. Furthermore, Labour was well ahead in the opinion polls, and had just enjoyed considerable success in the European elections against a Conservative government which, at times, seemed unable to put a foot right.

Major's troubles had continued and intensified. Ironically, the economy was now performing quite well; by mid-1994 recession was increasingly a memory as unemployment fell and inflation and interest rates remained low. But the Conservative Party was increasingly split over Europe. Sleaze continued to be a major problem. A cabinet reshuffle in July 1994 failed to have the galvanizing effect hoped for. By early August, one opinion poll was showing Labour 33 per cent ahead of the Conservatives. Shortly afterwards, a massive increase in the already substantial salary of the head of privatized British Gas, Cedric Browne, was used by Labour and others to attack 'fat cats' in industry, and to suggest that it was only the rich who were benefiting from Conservative policies.

Polling evidence suggested that most voters saw the Conservatives as, at best, incompetent. It was Blair's good fortune to inherit this situation, but his task to exploit and deepen it. The first element was to play the Conservatives at their own game of competence in office. Labour began even more to play down its own distinctive policies in order to offer voters a very clear and simple choice on the matter of competence, as will be seen below. This was clearly intended to maximize points of contact with voters who had supported the Conservatives in 1992 but who now seemed likely to defect.

Such a strategy, of course, carried the danger that Labour would look so like the Conservatives that it would fail to win over such voters or, even worse, that its own core support would start to abandon it. Labour countered this danger in two ways. First, it claimed boldly that the issue was competence; it would form a better government than Major's flailing and failing administration. Second, Blair launched a vigorous rhetorical campaign. At the October 1994 party conference, the slogan 'New Labour, New Britain' was unveiled; and Blair, in his keynote speech, drew on his own communitarian and modernizing views to portray Labour as something very different from the incompetent, complacent and sleazy Conservatives, promising 'a project of national renewal' to create 'a nation with pride in itself – a thriving community, rich in economic prosperity, secure in social justice, confident in political change; a land in which our children can bring up their children with a future to look forward to'.[60] This messianic message was clearly intended to convey a sense that

Labour – or 'New Labour' – stood for something very different from the Conservatives, even if, in concrete terms, it was often difficult to see what that was. In some ways, Blair was here adopting the kind of strategy used by Thatcher in the late 1970s in opposition to Labour, in arguing for a moral change in British life, without specifying very far what such a change would comprise. Like Thatcher then, too, he was largely able to succeed in scoring off a government that was now becoming discredited.

Symbolic proof of New Labour's 'success' came shortly afterwards. In his 1994 conference speech, Blair had stated that Labour needed to change with a changing world in order to remain relevant: the party must not become 'a historical monument' and, in particular, it needed 'a clear, up-to-date statement of … objects and objectives'.[61] It was clear from this that Blair was preparing an assault on Clause IV of the party's constitution, something that Jack Straw and others had been urging for some time.[62] Although earlier in the year Blair had felt that the issue was not worth raising, he and Mandelson were now convinced by the party's private polling that 'fear of the unknown' was still hindering Labour's progress among its target voters.[63] In March 1995 a new version of Clause IV was approved by the NEC, and at the end of the following month a special party conference approved it. The new clause gained the support of 65 per cent of the party's members, including 90 per cent of CLPs and 54.6 per cent of trade unions.[64] Those unions which opposed the change, like the TGWU and Unison, had not balloted their members, as Blair's supporters were quick to point out.[65] In 1959, Gaitskell's attack on Clause IV had come to grief and severely weakened his position: 36 years later, Blair's attempt to change it had received overwhelming support and made his position as leader more secure than ever.

Why did Blair succeed here in particular and, more generally, in pursuing what seemed like a very right-wing strategy in Labour terms? First, he was a new leader, elected by an overwhelming majority only a few months earlier, and there was a general election no more than two years away. To have gone against him here would have been a major boost to the Conservatives. Indeed, Blair appears to have said that he would resign if the vote went against him, at least once it was clear that he was not going to lose.[66] Under such circumstances Labourites had to think very hard before opposing him; there was great desire to win the next election, and little desire at all to renew infighting or have the party portrayed as 'unleadable'. Indeed, in launching Blair on a nationwide tour, meeting countless party activists, the campaign for the new Clause IV had real public relations benefits for the leader.[67] The NEC, at Blair's urging, released funds so that CLPs could ballot their members; the result was 90 per cent support for the planned change. This was due in no small part to the members who had joined since Blair's accession to the leadership, itself testament to the leader's own magnetic appeal. In 1959, by contrast, Gaitskell was not a new leader, but one who had just lost a general election that many Labourites had expected, however unrealistically in retrospect, to win.

Second, Blair had the support of the rest of the party leadership. Ten years earlier, people like Cook, Beckett and Blunkett would have come out against the change, but they had moved a long way to the right since then and could, in any case, see which way the wind was blowing. If they had opposed Blair at this stage, they would have been defeated, and their political futures would have looked doubtful, to say the least. Meanwhile, Prescott had been persuaded by Blair of the need for change, and was publicly linked with the campaign for a new Clause IV from an early stage in the process.[68]

This meant, third, that public resistance to the change was left to somewhat ineffectual elements from the party's lower ranks. Thirty-two Labour MEPs published a statement against the change. But no one cared about MEPs; indeed, they found it so difficult to get a platform for their views that, in the end, they had to resort to publication in the pro-Conservative *Daily Telegraph*, which hardly put them in a favourable light with the rest of the party.[69] Barbara Castle, one of the leaders of resistance to Gaitskell in 1959, criticized, but no one was going to take such a veteran figure very seriously against the party leader. Arthur Scargill, for his part, attacked the move fiercely, and headed a rump of leftists in resisting the change.[70] But this was merely playing into the leadership's hands. Scargill had become an embarrassment long before 'New Labour'. He was the epitome of a 1970s-style militant trade unionism from which Labour had long wished to distance itself. His union, the NUM, once one of the strongholds of Labour politics, was now a mere shadow of the powerful organization that he had inherited in 1982. New Labour strategists were delighted to see Scargill emerge as an open critic of the leadership, reckoning that every piece of invective heaped on Blair was worth thousands of votes in 'Middle England'. That the left had to rely on so discredited and by now marginal a figure merely showed its weakness. It came as little surprise when Scargill departed in May 1996 to form the Socialist Labour party (SLP); it was, perhaps, even less of a shock that so few other Labour leftists followed him, or that the party was unable to garner any significant electoral support, or that it was soon, itself, riven with splits and attacks on Scargill's own allegedly autocratic leadership style.[71] In December 2005, after almost a decade, its membership would stand at less than 6000.[72]

In any case, it was possible for people to convince themselves that the new Clause IV represented little more than the updating of an archaic text. Instead of expatiating on securing 'the full fruits of their industry' for 'the workers by hand or by brain', as Webb's 1918 Clause IV did, the new version stated that Labour was 'a democratic socialist party' (mentioning the word 'socialist', which the 1918 clause had not done); spoke of the merits of 'common endeavour'; and aimed at 'a community in which power, wealth and opportunity are in the hands of the many not [sic] the few'.[73] In short, it was still possible to be a socialist in 'New Labour', although those who consoled themselves with this thought would not have been heartened by the almost complete absence of the word 'socialism' from the party's pronouncements thereafter.

Meanwhile, Blair had also been strengthening his own position through the appointment of key personnel. Mandelson, now an MP, returned to the centre of Labour politics, having played a central role in Blair's election as leader. In August 1994, Alastair Campbell, an experienced and articulate political journalist, became Blair's press secretary. Campbell was an abrasive and able figure who was to handle press relations with great care and efficiency over the coming years. His unpopularity with journalists in his new role was probably a tribute to the efficiency he brought to bear on his position.[74] With Campbell's assistance, Blair was soon courting some of Labour's traditional foes in the media, like Rupert Murdoch's News International, publisher of the *Sun*. This strategy aroused considerable Labour criticism, given Murdoch's role in 1986 in crushing newspaper trade unionism and his papers' traditional support for the Conservatives; however, its benefits were seen when both the *Sun* and its Sunday counterpart, the *News of the World*, came out for a Labour victory.[75]

A large part of the reason why they did so was the continuing difficulties of Major's government. During 1995 and 1996 the economy continued to recover strongly, interest rates and inflation remaining low while unemployment fell as low as 7.2 per cent in the final quarter of 1996. House prices also began to recover.[76] If it had been true, as many commentators had blithely asserted on many occasions in the 1980s and early 1990s, that short-term economic prospects were the key determinant of voter behaviour, then Major should have been on target for a great victory at the next election. But he was not. Throughout 1995 and 1996, the Conservatives lagged in the polls, barely reaching even 30 per cent, while Labour scarcely ever fell below 50 per cent after Blair's election to the party leadership.[77] In part, of course, the prolonged recession and Black Wednesday between them had created a mood of opinion in which favourable economic indicators did not reassure voters about the Conservatives' economic competence. But a whole host of other factors also came into play. Europe continued to split the Conservatives. As by-election after by-election was lost – often in hitherto safe Conservative seats – the potential for Euro-sceptic Conservative MPs to wreak havoc grew. In November 1994, eight rebel MPs had the whip suspended. In June 1995, Major resigned the party leadership and challenged his critics to 'put up or shut up'. The Welsh Secretary, John Redwood, resigned from the cabinet to challenge Major; although Redwood was defeated, Major's failure to secure the votes of 89 of his 327 MPs suggested that his position remained weak. Matters were not helped when the wealthy financier Sir James Goldsmith founded the anti-EU Referendum Party in November 1995. Meanwhile, against a continuing backdrop of 'sleaze' revelations, a worldwide ban on British beef in the BSE crisis alienated producers and consumers alike. Increasing taxes, including the imposition of VAT on fuel, meant that the Conservatives began to be seen as a high-tax party.

Blair and Labour were benefiting, too, from secular changes in British and world politics. The Conservative Party had remained largely united since the First World War against the threats of

Communism (both at home and abroad), Labour's socialism and militant trade unionism. But with the collapse of Communism in the late 1980s and early 1990s, the neutering of trade unionism and Labour's own effective abandonment of socialism, there was no longer a pressing imperative for the Conservatives to stick together. This in turn allowed them the luxury of fragmentation over what would once have been seen as secondary issues, such as Europe. The world of the Cold War had caused Labour great problems. It was clear that the post-Cold War world would be a much harder one for the Conservative Party.

By continuing Smith's strategy of allowing the Conservatives enough rope with which to hang themselves, Blair maximized the potential of these dilemmas. Blair also added a level of 'vision' that Smith had found elusive. No one appeared sure what a 'young country' was, for example, but it sounded good. 'New Labour' seemed to sound better than 'Labour'. There was little of substance in a lot of this. But while Labour was in opposition, and well ahead in the polls, it did not really matter very much. Blair's rhetoric added a valuable new dimension to Labour's appeal, but the continuities with earlier policies were clearly to be seen, and in view of the level of the Conservatives' problems it is hard to resist the conclusion that, even without Blair, Labour would have won a significant majority at the 1997 general election.

Having said that, Labour did move further right under Blair. In many ways this was the culmination of a long process, started as long ago as 1981–82, when the left had split and a soft-left/centre-right alliance had emerged to fight against the hard left. But under Blair the process was carried further than ever before. Blair's strategy, as stated earlier, was to ensure that the party did nothing to put off the voters who were now disappointed with the Conservative government for which they had voted in 1992. In addition, he was keen to maximize points of linkage with the Liberal Democrats. The one great fear of Labour strategists was that the party might end up as the largest party in a hung parliament. In retrospect this looks hopelessly pessimistic, but 1992 had proved a real shock: mid-term blues, crises and by-election and opinion poll setbacks had not done for the Conservatives then, and there were real fears that the process might be repeated at the next general election. Even such a bullishly optimistic scenario for a new social democratic future as Will Hutton's 1995 bestseller *The State We're In* spoke of 'Labour [taking office] alone *or in coalition with the Liberal Democrats*' [my italics].[78] This strategy was helped by the line taken by the Liberal Democrats' leader, Paddy Ashdown, in abandoning 'equidistance' between the two main parties and coming out clearly against the Conservatives. Blair held talks with Ashdown in the run-up to the 1997 election, with the aim of ensuring Liberal Democrat support for a minority Labour government, should it be necessary; Ashdown would probably, in such circumstances, have been offered a seat in the cabinet.[79] Such a line excited grumbling within both parties, but such was the common desire to see the Conservatives ousted that the grousers could not hope to prevail. The effect was striking: Blair not only neutralized potential Liberal Democrat criticism of Labour but also gained an ally against the Conservatives.

While there is no doubt that a rightward shift suited Blair, therefore, it is also clear that it was a natural corollary of the perceived political context. Electoral calculations, and the opportunity to pose as the party of probity, prudence and purpose against an ailing administration, were key elements in determining Labour Party strategy. So were 'focus groups', which were used to 'market-test' policies, especially in key marginal seats.[80] Thus most of the party's more controversial pledges were dropped. Some key commitments could not be wished away, of course. Labour in Scotland and Wales was adamantly in favour of devolution, and it was recognized in any case that failure to deliver here would lead to a surge in support for nationalist parties at Labour's expense. The unions, for their part, were strongly in favour of a national minimum wage and statutory recognition rights; any retreat on these issues might have provoked a massive backlash against the leadership. But the level of the wage remained open to negotiation, and could be kept low, satisfying shadow Chancellor Brown's commitment to financial stability. In addition, even the most convinced New Labourites were prepared to pay the price, given that the unions were prepared to reciprocate by accepting further reforms of the party that would restrict their role still more.[81] In other areas there were fewer constraints. Brown continued to reject anything that smacked of Keynesianism. Remnants of the economic policy from the 1992 manifesto were quietly jettisoned. In January 1997, indeed, Brown accepted that, should Labour win the election, it would observe Conservative spending plans for its first two years in government. Blair's successor as shadow Home Secretary, Jack Straw, soft-pedalled, or even abandoned, many of Labour's earlier policies on crime, in order to exploit Conservative failings in that area. Blair's own slogan that Labour would be 'tough on crime, tough on the causes of crime', was recycled to great effect; old civil liberties concerns were downgraded and Straw began to adopt American Democratic Party policies such as 'zero tolerance' and the idea of a 'drugs czar'. Under Blair, too, a rather more sceptical line was peddled on Europe, and House of Lords reform began to look hazier. Occasionally, Blair appeared to be striking a more radical pose, as with a series of references to 'stakeholding' early in 1996; however, although this appears to some to suggest that he was becoming receptive to Hutton's vigorous neo-Keynesianism, it was soon dropped once it became clear that it was potentially a stick with which to beat Labour.[82]

There were also changes in the party organization. While the party headquarters remained at Walworth Road in South London until 1997, a separate campaign headquarters was established in the Millbank Tower from 1995 onwards. This considerably increased Blair's control over the party machine, by effectively establishing a parallel, and in effect more powerful, headquarters which was directly under his, and not the NEC's, control. MPs were issued with pagers, a 'benefit' of new technology that would doubtless have appealed to past generations of Labour organizers and whips had it been available to them. Candidates were subjected to extensive briefings and probing questions to ensure that they were 'fit' to stand for Labour. Attacks on anything that could be perceived as leftism continued unabated. All of this became more and more possible as money flooded into the party. This did not come just from the unions. Individual membership, after years of decline, grew rapidly under Blair, from 305,000 in 1994 to 405,000 in 1997.[83] In addition, business began for the first time to back Labour on a significant scale, not least financially. By 1997 Labour's organization was light years away from the shambles of 1983 and, perhaps more significantly, considerably more professional than the decaying and virtually bankrupt Conservative machine.[84]

Major hung on for as long as he could, in the desperate hope that something would turn up to give him a chance of victory.

He ensured, too, that when he finally did announce the election, on 17 March, there would be a very long campaign, in the hope that 'New Labour' would wilt under the intense media spotlight that an election campaign provided. However, it was a desperate and, as it proved, doomed attempt; the long campaign allowed Conservative, rather than Labour, divisions to emerge, particularly over Europe. Labour cleverly scaled down expectations, its five immediate pledges – cutting class sizes for infants, speeding up legal proceedings against young offenders, reducing NHS waiting lists, moving 250,000 young people from benefits and into work and maintaining low inflation – being selected as credible, achievable and relatively uncontroversial. Apart from one rogue poll for the *Guardian* on 23 April, which put Labour's lead at only 5 per cent, no poll showed its lead over the Conservatives to be less than 10 per cent, and many showed it as being more than double that. Aside from the *Guardian* polls, none showed Labour support as less than 45 per cent; and such a level of support promised a safe Labour victory.[85]

When the results began to be declared on the night of 1–2 May, however, it rapidly became clear that Labour was on target for something more than that. In the event, it took 43.2 per cent of the votes, the Conservatives 30.7 per cent (their worst since 1832) and the Liberal Democrats 16.8 per cent. This was a substantial victory in itself, but in terms of seats, Labour won a landslide. It took 418 seats, and had a majority of 179, which was larger than Attlee had won in 1945. The Conservatives, with just 165 seats, had their worst showing since 1906; they failed to win a single seat in either Scotland or Wales. The Liberal Democrats, with 46 MPs, had the best third-party return since Lloyd George's Liberals in 1929. On the last occasion that Labour had won a general election with a decent working majority, in 1966, Tony Blair had been just 13 years old.

The scale of Labour's victory was impressive. Support for the party increased in almost all social categories, substantially so in many cases. Most spectacularly, it rose from 28 to 47 per cent among white-collar workers and from 39 to 54 per cent among skilled workers. It rose in all age groups except those 65 and over, where the fall was only marginal; significantly, it increased considerably among young and first-time voters. In 1992, 35 per cent of first-time voters had voted Conservative, and 40 per cent

Labour; now the figures were 19 and 57 per cent respectively. The gender gap closed, with 44 per cent of both men and women supporting the party.[86] Labour's support among ethnic minorities became even stronger, as it took 85 per cent of Asian and black votes (compared with 81 per cent in 1992).[87] Naturally, Labour performed very well in its core areas: in Wales, for example, 34 of the 40 seats were won; in Scotland, 56 out of 72. But Labour also made considerable progress in southern England, continuing the trend away from the old north–south divide.[88] Labour now held 58 seats outside Greater London south of the Severn–Wash line, where it had held only three at the 1983 and 1987 elections. In many of the seats won, like Exeter, Labour had been in third place as recently as 1987. There was clear evidence of an increase in tactical voting; and this was just one example of the way in which almost every aspect of the electoral system that could have worked in Labour's favour did so.[89] In fact, its share of the vote – 43.2 per cent – was lower than in all post-war elections before 1970.

Labour's return to power after 18 years in opposition was a cause for great celebration within the party and, indeed, for many outside it. In 1979, no one had expected that the return would take so long, but in the interim there had been many who had come to doubt that it would ever happen at all. The heavy defeats of 1983 and 1987 had left a great deal of ground to make up. However, determined effort over the ten years since 1987 had paid dividends. Those efforts had not been without their costs, but they had been successful. For most members of a party starved of success for so long, that was enough – at least for the time being. It remained to be seen, however, how well Blair and his colleagues would fare in government, and whether 'New Labour' would be able to live up to the hyperbole that had surrounded it in opposition.

12 New Labour in Power, 1997–2007

Labour's victory at the 1997 election saw it returned to office for the first time in 18 years. None of the ministers in Blair's new government had previously served in the cabinet; few had even held junior office. Neither Blair nor Brown had even been MPs at the time of the previous Labour government. They were not, of course, unaware of the challenges that this would pose; in some ways they were well aware of the gaps in their experience and had worked hard to compensate for them. Even so, their first months in office would represent a steep learning curve. It may be that this inexperience of office had also allowed Labour in opposition to make large claims about what the party would achieve once elected. Although the party's precise pledges had been modest, Blair's speeches in opposition had offered nothing less than the vision of 'a nation reborn'. This had clearly struck a chord with many voters, and helped to explain the scale, if not the fact, of Labour's 1997 victory; yet, as Wilson had found, attention-seeking rhetoric in opposition could raise unrealistic expectations of what might be achieved in office. It was to be Blair's misfortune that, at least in part, his decade in power would be measured by many people not by the standards of what had been feasible, but against some of the high-flown rhetoric of the early years of his leadership.

There were few surprises in Blair's first cabinet, most of its members being appointed to the ministries they had shadowed in opposition. Brown had an incontrovertible claim to the Exchequer, Blunkett had been promised Education and the claims of Cook to the Foreign Office and Straw to the Home Office were almost as strong. Prescott, who as deputy leader had been a key ally in Blair's New Labour project, was designated Deputy Prime Minister and put in charge of a new 'super-ministry', the

Department of the Environment, Transport and the Regions (DETR). Mandelson became Minister without Portfolio at the Cabinet Office, and would clearly be Blair's 'fixer'. Notably, the cabinet contained five women, far more than any of its predecessors, and a reflection of the positive discrimination policies that the party had embraced earlier in the decade. Beckett, the most senior, went to Trade and Industry, while – in one of the few appointments of a leftish figure to the cabinet – Clare Short was appointed Secretary for International Development. However, given that there were now 101 women Labour MPs, it could hardly be claimed that women were over-represented. In its first term of office, Blair's cabinet was characterized by considerable continuity at the very highest levels, with Brown, Prescott, Cook and Straw all retaining their positions. Lower down, however, only four other ministers did so – Blunkett, Short, Chris Smith (Culture) and Lord Irvine (Lord Chancellor). Even at this stage, future rivals to Brown as Blair's eventual successor were looking thin on the ground.

From the beginning, the government was very closely identified with its leader. From the first, his style had seemed to foretell a presidential approach, and New Labour was seen very much as his project. Events early in his tenure pushed him even further in that direction. Renewed trouble in the Gulf, and ethnic conflict in the Balkans, saw British forces in action twice in his first two years in office. In such circumstances, the Prime Minister was bound to play the leading role. Efforts at reconciliation in Northern Ireland, begun under Major and culminating in the 1998 Good Friday Agreement for the establishment of a power-sharing executive, also kept his profile high. So, too, did the death of Diana, Princess of Wales, in a motor accident in August 1997, when he was widely seen as sensing the national mood when he lamented the loss of 'the People's Princess'.

Blair's presidential style came across in the business of government, too. Cabinet meetings were downgraded, and rarely lasted for more than an hour. Attempts to operate an inner cabinet of the 'Big Four' – Blair, Brown, Cook and Prescott – collapsed as early as November 1997 when it became clear that they could not work together at such close quarters.[1] As with Wilson, Blair often seemed to take more notice of his 'kitchen cabinet' of close advisers, especially Mandelson, Campbell, Jonathan Powell and Anji Hunter, than he did of the cabinet proper. This would later lead to charges of an informal regime of 'sofa government' which was inimical to the best practices of transparent and accountable decision making. It was said that the most important words in government were 'Tony wants'.[2] Perhaps so; but Blair was not always able to get his own way, and could end up looking foolish, as when he publicly denounced Ken Livingstone as a candidate for London mayor and then had to look on as the latter won the election (see below). Second, Brown soon established his pre-eminence over large parts of domestic policy. How far this was the result of a 'deal' done at the time of Smith's death remained a matter of debate and gossip; but there can be no doubt that Brown's writ ran largest over whole swathes of policy, with Blair's at least tacit agreement.

Economic stability and prosperity were the rocks upon which Blair's decade in power was built. Unemployment, inflation and interest rates all remained low throughout the period. This was, to say the least, ironic, in so far as it was Brown who, as Chancellor, oversaw the economy. Labour's inheritance was extremely favourable. The economy they inherited in 1997 was recovering strongly from the recession of the early part of the decade, and many of the tough choices that had had to be made to ensure recovery had already been made by the outgoing Conservative administration. World economic trends remained favourable. Yet it would be unfair to attribute Labour's success in the area purely to luck. Other major economies did suffer high levels of unemployment in the period. Brown made two early decisions that significantly helped matters. One was to confirm the pledge made before the 1997 election: that Labour would not exceed the Conservatives' spending plans for its first two years in office. This upset many Labourites, but it further established the party's moderate credentials, particularly in relation to business.[3] Second, Brown's announcement, a few days after the election, that the Bank of England was to be given the right to set interest rates independently and without direct government intervention was a major factor in guaranteeing financial stability. For the lifetime of the 1997 parliament, the economy remained buoyant, and that in itself meant that Blair's declared aim of being the first Labour Prime Minister ever to gain a full second term looked likely to be fulfilled. Meanwhile, specific steps were taken to help the young unemployed through the New Deal programme, which was so successful that it was later extended to older workers.[4] A less positive early decision was the removal of tax relief from pension funds, which was to significantly depress the value of the funds and become a matter of controversy from the mid-2000s onwards as concerns about a future pensions crisis grew.[5]

There were fewer votes in constitutional change. This, and the fact that devolution had been a major ongoing headache for the previous Labour government, explained why Blair moved rapidly on greater self-government for Scotland and Wales. On 11 September, Scotland voted in a referendum for the establishment of a Scottish parliament with limited tax-raising powers; a week later, Wales voted by a wafer-thin majority on a low turnout to establish a National Assembly with more limited powers.[6] The resulting legislation was duly passed in 1998. In May 1999, the first elections for the two bodies showed some of the drawbacks of devolution for Labour: in neither country did it attain an overall majority, although it was the largest party in each case, forming a coalition with the Liberal Democrats in Scotland (headed by the former Scottish Secretary Donald Dewar), and a minority Labour administration in Wales (under the erstwhile Welsh Secretary Alun Michael).[7] Further problems followed in early 2000 when Michael – widely, if perhaps rather unfairly, seen as a leadership stooge – was effectively forced from office, to be replaced by Rhodri Morgan, whom Labour headquarters had worked hard to block in 1999.[8] Meanwhile, the elections for a London mayor also posed difficulties. The party leadership pulled out all the stops to prevent Livingstone from winning the Labour nomination, but in the end he stood anyway as an Independent, and won. He was expelled from the party, but the leadership would eventually feel forced to readmit him to avoid further humiliation ahead of the mayoral elections of 2004 (which he again won).

There was slower progress in most other areas of constitutional reform. Devolution to the English regions was the logical corollary of Scottish and Welsh devolution, and was especially favoured by Prescott. It was easily caricatured as creating an additional tier of government; in reality, it was more about democratizing a regional tier of administration that already existed. But there was a noticeable lack of enthusiasm for the venture. Plans announced in 2003 for referendums in the three northern English regions were scaled back, so that in November 2004 only the north-east went to the polls: when it did, more than 75 per cent of those voting opposing devolution. It was reasoned that if that region would not vote for more autonomy, no other one would, and the plans were shelved. English regional devolution was off the agenda. Although the number of Scottish MPs was reduced from 72 to 59 ahead of the 2005 general election, in reflection of the powers that the Scottish parliament had, the fact that Scottish and Welsh MPs could still vote at Westminster on purely English matters raised significant issues, particularly given that Labour historically had relied on MPs from those countries for many of its votes in parliament. It was noteworthy that, while Labour gained 286 seats to the Conservatives' 194 in England in 2005, its poll share, at 35.5 per cent, was marginally lower than the Conservatives' 35.7 per cent (the respective figures for 1997 and 2001 were 43.6 per cent to 33.7 per cent and 41.4 per cent to 35.2 per cent respectively). And, with Brown, a Scot, always the favourite to succeed Blair as Prime Minister, such concerns were not going to disappear.

While in opposition, Labour had expressed some interest in electoral reform; and when it came to power, it established a commission under Lord (Roy) Jenkins to investigate. In October 1998 the commission recommended replacing first-past-the-post with an additional member system. However, these proposals were not popular with the Labour Party at large. Talk of electoral reform had seemed appropriate when it had appeared that it might be the price of Liberal Democrat co-operation in a minority government situation, and when it had seemed possible that Labour would never again win an overall majority under the existing system. But after the 1997 landslide, neither of these considerations applied, and nothing happened. Indeed, by 2001, and still more 2005, the electoral system was so biased towards Labour that it beggared belief that the party would have tried to change it. Initially, at least, there was greater progress on House of Lords reform, with steps being taken to remove the automatic right of hereditary peers to sit in the Upper House. Even so, a number of them were then elected by their peers to serve until a final reform had been implemented; and that final reform was very slow in coming to fruition.[9] A decade later, an elected upper house seemed as far away as ever.

It had been anticipated since the late 1980s that a Labour government would move Britain closer to Europe, but in the event there was less discontinuity with the previous Conservative government than most commentators had anticipated. Brown's decision to hand over the setting of interest rates to the Bank of England was seen as a possible harbinger of British entry to the single European currency. However, Brown was becoming progressively less enthusiastic about Europe, and the Treasury's 'five tests' for entry to a single currency were stiff ones.[10] Thus when the Euro was launched in December 1998, Britain did not join. It was made clear that any such decision would be subject to a referendum, and opinion polls showed some antipathy towards the single currency. Although Blair was more enthusiastic than Brown, he was too sharp a political operator to saddle himself with an unpopular policy at this stage. His view was always that, once the single currency came fully onto the agenda, he would be able to talk voters round to it; but there was no point emerging as its champion prematurely. Instead, he occasionally made critical noises where the EU was concerned, particularly in relation to other members' failure to embrace the social market more fully.

On many issues, it was not to Europe, but to the United States, that New Labour looked for inspiration. Many of the party's initiatives – welfare to work, directly elected city mayors, drugs czars, 'zero tolerance' of petty crime and so on – were derived from the USA. Bill Clinton's New Democrats were something of an inspiration.[11] In the area of foreign policy, Blair could operate much more independently of Brown than on the domestic stage. And here, he was determined to ensure close relations with the world's only remaining superpower. Clinton was brought in, to great effect, to the resolution of the Northern Ireland problem. There were examples of joint action. However, Blair became frustrated at times with Clinton's unwillingness to take risks on the international stage. In the Kosovo crisis of 1999, for example, it was Blair who was pushing Clinton to move beyond air strikes on the Serbs and towards the deployment of ground forces, and Clinton who was resisting. There is no doubt that Blair's early experiences of armed intervention in what were seen at this stage as humanitarian crises gave him an appetite for more to come. But they offered relatively easy victories, which probably led him towards a rather over-optimistic position as to the potential of armed intervention to effect positive change quickly and effectively in other parts of the world. With hindsight, this can be seen to have crystallized in April 1999, when he outlined a full-blown philosophy of intervention in a speech at Chicago. In reference to the ongoing and successful intervention in Kosovo – which he described as 'a just war, based not on any territorial ambitions but on values' – he asserted that Britain and America had 'learned twice before in this century that appeasement does not work', and that if they 'let an evil dictator range unchallenged', they would 'have to spill infinitely more blood and treasure to stop him later'.[12] (Quite who he thought the 'evil dictator' had been in 1914 he did not make clear.) He went on to argue that there were circumstances in which intervention was justified, as against older notions of sovereignty and more restrained interpretations of the British national interest. Although, at the time, Blair was frustrated at the lack of attention that the speech received, his arguments would be heard much more in the period after the 2001 general election.[13]

For the time being, domestic matters loomed much larger. There were significant achievements in Labour's first term. The national minimum wage was introduced in April 1999. Its low level – £3.60 per hour for those over 21, and £3 for those aged 18–21 – aroused criticism, but it increased the incomes of more than two million people.[14] Conservative and employer claims that it would cost millions of jobs proved to be unfounded; and the Conservatives' acceptance of the principle in February 2000 suggested that Labour had been right to pursue it in the face of their opposition. Similarly, the working families' tax credit, a 10 per cent rate of income tax on the first part of people's earnings, and increased child benefit also brought some benefit to people traditionally seen as Labour's core supporters.[15]

Broader welfare reform posed considerable problems, however. In opposition, there had been much talk of the need for change. Labour's policies, it seemed, would promote the empowerment of those on benefits in particular, and have the useful by-product of saving money. But talk was easier than action. Labour did introduce 'welfare to work', borrowing heavily on American ideas. But wider reform made less progress. Frank Field, appointed Minister for Welfare Reform in May 1997 with a brief to conduct a radical survey of the whole subject, was dropped in the first major reshuffle (1998). Plans to restore the pensions–earnings (as opposed to prices) link, which would have led to a significant increase in the incomes of over-65s, was dropped when the tax implications became clear. Meanwhile, Labour found that the problems of the NHS, which had proved one of its most potent rallying cries through the long years of opposition, were less easily resolved than it had claimed. Its achievements in cutting waiting lists were overshadowed in the winter of 1999–2000 by increasing public attention on waiting times, where its record was far less impressive. By 2001 there would be a real sense that opportunities had been missed during the first term, and that there now needed to be a stronger steer on public service reform and the delivery of targets for improvement.

It remained very difficult, however, for Labour's critics to come up with a very convincing indictment of the party's record in government. The Conservatives struggled to come to terms with their 1997 defeat; at times, indeed, many of them still seemed unreconciled to Thatcher's departure in 1990. Following Major's resignation, they elected the former Welsh Secretary William Hague as their leader. At just 36 years of age he certainly represented change in one sense, but he was to struggle to overcome a poor public image and found it almost impossible to appeal to the voters who had abandoned the Conservatives in 1997. His party remained behind Labour in the opinion polls for the whole of 1997 parliament, with the exception of a short period of fuel price protests in September 2000. The Liberal Democrats also struggled. They had spent years attacking the Conservatives, and now found it difficult to just turn and attack Labour. This was, to some extent, the legacy of Blair's achievement in neutralizing Ashdown with talk of coalition and electoral reform in the period before 1997.[16] Even if Blair had wanted to bring Ashdown into the cabinet, the size of his majority made such a move politically unacceptable to the Labour Party. However, devolution and the establishment of the Jenkins Commission strung the Liberal Democrats along a little longer, and it was only when it became obvious that little would come of Jenkins that Ashdown finally gave up. Even so, his successor, Charles Kennedy, took time to find his feet, and was in any case on the left of the party, being a former Social Democrat.

There was no shortage of critics within the Labour Party. Some felt, justifiably enough, that there was something distasteful and wrong about New Labour's tendency to 'demonize' disadvantaged groups, such as single mothers, asylum seekers and those on disability benefit. Attacks came from those who saw it as too concerned with Labour's new friends in business and 'Middle England' and too little concerned with the party's 'core' supporters. Such critics included Lord (Roy) Hattersley, who made incisive attacks on the government's failure to help those at the very bottom of society, and who would move in 2001 towards a full-blown repudiation of the government.[17] There was some feeling that this neglect of core voters was behind some of the more startling electoral setbacks suffered by New Labour, such as the 1999 failure to gain overall majorities in the Scottish and Welsh elections and the loss of once-safe councils like Sheffield to the Liberal Democrats. How far this was really due to New Labour putting off core voters is open to question, however. One major reason for Labour's poor showing in local and devolved elections was the fact that many core Labour voters saw little reason to vote when the government at Westminster had such a commanding majority and when the party was so far ahead in the opinion polls. At most, abstention in many of these cases was borne of apathy, not hostility. And local election defeats, as in Sheffield, could be due less to New Labour than to dissatisfaction with very 'Old Labour' councils. There was also criticism from those who felt the government was too much under the control of Blair and his 'spin doctors', and there were frequent suggestions that the party had become over-disciplined. In fact, though, discipline had always been prized by Labour leaders; it was just that advances in technology allowed its enforcement to take new forms. It is also worth noting that the sheer scale of Labour's majority in 1997 presented potential problems: Labour MPs proved to be quite rebellious in both the 1997 and 2001 parliaments, wringing concessions from ministers on various issues in return for toeing the party line. In the second term the problems became greater as the issues (such as student tuition fees) became more contentious and as the ranks of the 'natural' rebels were swollen by increasing numbers of ex-ministers wielding a grudge. In short, the parliamentary party did not become the lapdog of legend.[18]

Although there were criticisms from within the party, there was also a great deal of Labour contentment. Most party members had recognized by 1997 that the key thing was to defeat the Conservatives. There was a keenness to see the government succeed and a willingness to give it an opportunity to try to do so. The government's claim that it would take time to overcome the

legacy of almost two decades of Conservative rule was taken seriously. In addition, the events of the period since the early 1980s
had weakened the left, which by now realized that it was once
again on the margins of the party, with no high-profile leadership and little sympathy in the cabinet. The election of four
members of the leftish Grassroots Alliance to the NEC in 1998
suggested a new lease of life, but came to little in the longer term.[19]
The unions, for their part, had had three main concerns in the
years immediately before 1997: to elect a Labour government, to
rebuild their membership bases and to secure particular items of
legislation, most notably the right to recognition (granted, along
with significant improvements to employees' rights, by the 2000
Employment Relations Act) and the minimum wage. However,
none of this supported the view that the unions were about to
abandon Labour, and the fact that, by 2001, Labour's alternative
sources of funding were starting to dry up also suggested that
ideas of impending divorce between party and unions were premature.[20] Indeed, between 2001 and 2005, two-thirds of Labour's
income would come from union sources.[21]

One problem with those alternative sources of money was that
they seemed to invite allegations of 'sleaze' of the kind that had
so damaged Major's Conservative government. As had been the
case then, the sexual scandals that came and went left little last-
ing stain, but hints of financial wrongdoing were more serious.
At first, Labour was given the benefit of the doubt; in 1997 and
1998, scandals over a ban on tobacco advertising in motor rac-
ing (the head of Formula One had given the party £1 million)
and cash for access to ministers soon passed.[22] The government
was even able to withstand a scandal concerning Mandelson,
seen by many as the very architect of New Labour. In December
1998, he was forced to resign as Trade and Industry Secretary
after it emerged that he had not declared a substantial private
loan from another Labour minister, Geoffrey Robinson, when
applying for a mortgage to buy an expensive new house. Initially,
Mandelson bounced back strongly, and was soon acting as Blair's
personal envoy in international negotiations, before returning to
the cabinet as Northern Ireland Secretary in October 1999. His
return proved short-lived, however, and he was forced to resign
once more in January 2001 over allegations that he had intervened to help two Indian donors to Labour Party funds get British

passports. Even at this stage, however, most people were still willing to give Blair the benefit of doubt.[23]

The government remained popular. Setbacks in the English local, Scottish and Welsh elections had to be set against a continuing commanding lead over the Conservatives in the UK opinion polls. The Conservatives tried to make a great deal of the results of the European elections in June 1999, when there was a UK swing to them of 10.4 per cent and Labour took only 28.4 per cent of the votes cast, as against their 35.8 per cent. (The effects in terms of seats were masked by the introduction of proportional representation in such elections, Labour taking 29 seats to the Conservatives' 36.) However, the most notable feature of these elections was the level of voter apathy. Given that turnout was a dismal 23 per cent – far lower than it would be at a general election – it would be fair to say that the results had little real significance.

By early 2001, with the opinion polls and economic indicators all very favourably set, it was clear that Labour strategists were planning a spring election. Labour had not lost a single seat at a by-election since 1997.[24] Polling was set for 3 May, but then delayed until 7 June due to a serious outbreak of foot-and-mouth disease in cattle, which resulted in some harrowing TV images.[25] The election, when finally under way, was unspectacular in everything but its result. Labour stood mainly on its economic record.[26] But it also pledged that the pace of public service reform would be quickened, a reflection perhaps of the frustrations that had led Blair in 1999 to complain about 'the forces of conservatism'. This had been an attack on the Conservative Party, but it had also represented a clear criticism of unions and others who were resisting change in education, the health service and elsewhere. In the election campaign, liberal use was made of negative images of the Conservatives. The Conservative campaign relied on a variety of anti-Labour and anti-EU messages, but to little effect. Labour had 'just about' realized its five pledges of 1997, and the press was even more clearly on Labour's side than it had been in 1997.[27]

When the votes were counted, Labour emerged with another commanding majority. It took 413 seats to the Conservatives' 166. After four years in opposition, the Conservatives had managed a net gain of just one seat. Labour lost only eight seats, and gained two. Once again, it was predominant in England as well as in Scotland and Wales, and results in the south held up better than many had expected. Seats that had seemed unwinnable in 1997 and unretainable once they had been won were held after all. The 'gender gap' remained closed, as in 1997.[28] Liberal Democrats made a net gain of 6 seats (to 52), but were no great threat at this stage.

It was a remarkable Labour victory, but two facts diminished talk of a second landslide. The first was the fall in Labour's poll share, from 43.2 per cent in 1997 to 40.7 in 2001. The fact that the Conservatives had only managed to rise from 30.7 to 31.7 per cent helped sweeten the pill, but the Liberal Democrats' increase from 16.8 to 18.3 per cent worried some Labourites. The second concern was the low turnout. At 59.4 per cent, it was the lowest since 1918. There has been much discussion of the reasons for this.[29] These range from societal explanations – which themselves vary between wholesale disengagement from the political process and time spent on computer games – to contingent ones such as the state of the economy, the lack of a real chance of a Conservative victory and so on. There may well be something in all these explanations, but it is hard to resist the view that more people would have voted if they had believed that the contest really had any alternative outcome. This does not mean that societal explanations were wholly bogus, however, and a series of initiatives were launched as a result of the low turnout to try and make it easier for people to vote, although some of these, like widespread postal voting, were to result in abuses of various kinds. It may be that some Labour 'core' voters were so disillusioned with the government that they abstained, but most former Labour electors had not been red-hot socialists who were now disgusted with New Labour. Nor is there much evidence that a more 'traditional' Labour approach would have brought more electors out to vote. Meanwhile, there was no joy for most of the far-left bodies, although the Scottish Socialist Party was a partial exception.[30]

Low turnout or not, Blair and New Labour had achieved what they had set out to do – win the second full term in office that had eluded all previous Labour governments. The question now, however, was whether Labour would be able to make good use of this opportunity. A major reshuffle followed the election. Some of Blair's more strident followers had dreamt that Brown might be moved elsewhere; relations between the two men had been more than usually strained during the campaign. The fact that Blair did not telephone Brown for four days after the election suggests that he was mulling the question over quite seriously.[31] But, ultimately, he seems to have decided that Brown's position was so strong that there was little chance of these fantasies being realized. Scarred by party divisions in the 1980s, he lacked the strength and resolution to rid himself of Brown if the consequence might be a period of intra-party strife. In that sense he showed himself a weak leader, because he saw the problems with Brown and yet failed to deal with them; and the Chancellor would not become easier to deal with in the years that followed. There were changes elsewhere, though. Prescott was moved: DETR had been widely seen as a failure, and so he was placed in charge of the Office of the Deputy Prime Minister (ODPM), which was to oversee certain of his pet projects. This marked the end of Prescott's role as a key executive minister, and even the ODPM would lose most of its remaining functions in 2006, in the aftermath of a sex scandal involving Prescott and a female colleague at the ODPM. That said, Prescott did retain an important role within cabinet as a guarantor of some kind of 'old' Labour values, and periodically as a private mediator between Blair and Brown. However, Cook was demoted from the Foreign Office to become Leader of the Commons, being succeeded by the more pliant Straw, who was himself succeeded as Home Secretary by the hard-line 'law and order' figure of Blunkett. Other Blairites like Clarke, Alan Milburn and John Reid gained preferment, but there was no comeback for Mandelson, who would ultimately be appointed an EU Commissioner in 2004.

Blair had always said that the second term would be time to deliver. True to his word, he now established a No. 10 Delivery Unit under Sir Michael Barber. Its job was to press for the achievement of specific high-profile targets, and while there was some criticism that it cut across departmental ties and disrupted other areas of policy, the Unit was broadly successful in improving public service performance in a number of areas.[32] There was a continuation of the spread of private sector money into the public sector through the private finance initiative (PFI). There were ideological objections from many Labourites who saw this as the private sector cashing in at the expense of the public, and PFI was, in the long run, a very expensive way of creating new buildings for schools and hospitals. But, given taxpayer resistance, it was seen as politically the easiest way to raise large sums of money, and the immediate results were often impressive: every state secondary school in a medium-sized town like Exeter was completely rebuilt, for example. Increasing levels of expenditure on health meant that waiting lists gradually became a thing of the past, and private sector health-care providers increasingly saw their future as being to supplement, rather than supplant, the state system.[33] At the same time, however, rising performance in some spheres raised expectations elsewhere, such as in secondary education, where improvements remained harder to detect despite numerous government initiatives.

Policy also remained concerned with improving the lot of those at the lower end of society. Much was made by the government's critics of the fact that the rich were getting richer, but this was not altogether unexpected given a strong economy and the continuing refusal to increase the top rate of taxation. However, a number of initiatives that had begun before 2001 began to mature after that year's election. For example, Sure Start brought together a whole range of voluntary, local authority and state activities under a single umbrella, with the aim of making life easier for families with young children. While initially the subject of criticism, it did seem by 2007 to be producing the kind of support that had been envisaged for thousands of people.[34] But in other areas there were real problems. An increasingly complex model of taxation and benefit resulted in a system of tax credits that were meant to help the worst off but which were so complicated that they simply put many people off, especially when it transpired that in some cases people had been overpaid and were then harassed to return the money. The overall shape of the initiatives could be confusing and their impact was much debated: more care could have been taken to ensure that the outcomes were correct, at the very least. At the end of the day, however, the government had taken issues of poverty and social justice far more seriously than had been anticipated in 1997, and Blair's commitment 'to eradicate child poverty in a generation' had had a significant impact, while pensioner poverty had also fallen significantly.[35]

This emphasis on public services after 2001 remained possible because economic prosperity continued. Unemployment, inflation and interest rates all remained low. Brown became bolder; at the 2001 election a pledge had been made not to increase the standard rate of income tax, but Brown's 2002 budget raised national insurance contributions, which was effectively the same thing. The reason for this was, in part, the big increase in public expenditure necessitated by the 'delivery agenda'.[36] Although the Conservatives tried to make a lot of these increases, however, they lacked credibility in the area themselves, while the Liberal Democrats had been urging increased taxation to pay for better education, and so were hardly in a position to criticize. As the British economy remained buoyant and large parts of the Eurozone economy faltered, pressure on Britain to enter the single currency eased, and it became increasingly clear that it was unlikely to take place while Brown remained Chancellor. By June 2004 he was the longest-serving Chancellor since the early nineteenth century, and in March 2005 he was able to claim to have presided over 'the longest period of sustained economic growth since records began in the year 1701'.[37] Concerns that the prosperity was based to some extent upon a credit bubble, or that the boom years were not really used to advance significant structural changes in the economy, were brushed aside. Indeed, Labour was to enter the 2005 general election once again with a strong economy to its credit, although, as will be seen, the extent to which the party's strategists wished to emphasize the point varied considerably.

Blair's government also presided over a series of measures that aimed to make Britain a more 'civilized' nation. Early changes included significant liberalization of the law regarding homosexuality, including the equalization of the age of consent at 16, the admission of gay people to the forces, and the repeal of Section 28 of the previous Conservative government's Local Government Act forbidding the 'promotion' of homosexuality by local authorities. Prejudice remained, but attitudes had changed markedly since the Thatcher–Major years, and Chris Smith and others sat effectively in cabinet without any of the condign consequences that might once have been predicted (although of course a number of gay people had already served as ministers in governments of all parties, albeit while keeping their homosexuality firmly from public view). Britain's archaic licensing laws were finally modernized, allowing pubs far more flexible opening hours, and when they came into effect media 'concerns' about wholesale urban chaos arising from '24-hour drinking' proved to have been little more than hysteria. A series of initiatives, including anti-social behaviour orders (ASBOs) were introduced to try to deal with low-level, but nonetheless problematic, criminality in local communities. However, there appeared to be no let-up in the increase in the prison population, not only the result of broader social developments but also a reflection of the government's – and Blair's – desire to be seen as 'tough on crime'.

Another aspect that worried many people was the government's tendency to favour authoritarian responses towards the perceived threat of terrorism, including plans to introduce identity cards and reduce the rights of those detained under suspicion of terrorist activities or sympathies. Government advocacy of such measures owed a lot to the events of 11 September 2001. Following that day's terrorist attacks on the World Trade Center in New York, Blair pledged his support to the United States, and in the days that followed travelled to the USA, where he was welcomed warmly by President George W. Bush (who had replaced Clinton in January 2001) and the US Congress. He then began a breathless tour of major world capitals, travelling more than 40,000 miles in eight weeks, during which he had 54 meetings with other heads of government.[38] He was instrumental in pulling together a wide coalition of powers pledged to overthrowing the Taliban government in Afghanistan, which was widely believed to be harbouring those responsible for events in New York. The Taliban were widely hated in the west, and their regime was seen as ultra-reactionary, not least in relation to the subjection of women. Concerns within the Labour Party were therefore muted as coalition forces invaded Afghanistan, taking the capital, Kabul, in November 2001.

There was also strong pressure within the US government for action to be taken against Iraq. Iraq was not especially a sponsor of terrorism, but it was a highly repressive regime, and its leader, Saddam Hussein, had long been a hate figure for the Americans. Ever since the Iraqi invasion of Kuwait in 1990–91, there had been a view that the forces then assembled should have gone on to Baghdad to overthrow Saddam and usher in a democratic regime. Such arguments tended to ignore the fact that the only clear mandate for the United Nations forces was to clear Kuwait of its invaders, however, and made some heroic assumptions about the demand for, and potential sustainability of, liberal democracy in Iraq. However, in the aftermath of 9/11 such arguments became more prevalent. American neoconservatives argued that it was a clear case of good against evil, and spoke of being engaged in 'World War IV' (the Cold War having been 'World War III'). None of this need have mattered if it had remained on the lunatic fringe of American politics, but key members of the administration were influenced by at least some of these arguments, and certainly shared the view that America should try to extend democracy in the Middle East.[39] As 2002 wore on, the Bush administration moved closer and closer towards the pursuit of war on Iraq.

This was bound to create problems for Labour. The party's preferred image of itself was as a party of peace; it had usually favoured peaceful solutions to problems, and it had always had within it a number of pacifists. On the other hand, it had never been a pacifist party as such. At various times – as in 1914 and 1939 – the majority of the party had favoured war over peace. Furthermore, the kind of interventionist liberal internationalism represented by the rather misleadingly titled 'neocons' also had resonances on the British left. Gladstone's outraged demand for action against the 'Bulgarian Horrors' in the 1870s was one example; so too was the first Labour government's support for giving the League of Nations 'teeth' by the Geneva Protocol in 1924. Labour had never wholly subscribed to the view that it was entirely up to governments of sovereign states to do whatever they liked, domestically. During the Second World War, it had been very keen to ensure positive engineering of post-war outcomes in sovereign states across Europe. And Blair's earlier forays, most notably in Kosovo, had been praised by many Labourites, and contrasted favourably with the perceived prevarication of the Major government in refusing to intervene in Bosnia. Crucially, Blair's 1999 Chicago speech had clearly envisaged armed intervention, in contravention of conventional notions of state sovereignty, and the invasion of Afghanistan had been little protested within the Labour Party.

In his thinking on Iraq, Blair appears to have been influenced by a number of factors. First, as stated above, he was drawn to notions of liberal internationalism, 'making the world safe for democracy' in the mould of First World War US President Woodrow Wilson.[40] He appears to have seen 9/11 as the perfect opportunity to remake the post-Cold War world order. Contrary to stereotypes of him as unprincipled, he was a politician who cared passionately about what he saw as right and wrong. Indeed, it was his ability to attack 'wrongs' rhetorically that had given him such a wide appeal within the party in his early years as leader. He has also been encouraged by the humanitarian interventions in Kosovo and Sierra Leone to believe that it was possible to use armed force to bring peace and stability. Neither of those operations, it is worth noting, had been under the umbrella of the United Nations, but that had not appeared to be a fatal problem; and it is clear that Blair's patience with the UN was rather thin by the early 2000s. His achievements in Northern Ireland, in addition, also gave him the belief that he had the ability to resolve really difficult problems. As seen above, all this had lulled Blair into something of a false sense of security about how straightforward such operations would be in other theatres, and also how economically they could be executed, in terms both of personnel and materials. The result was a significant underestimation of the military and logistical obstacles to success, and a failure to engage early and seriously enough with the question of cost, with the result that British forces appeared to be under-supplied and under-supported; and Blair's failure to deal with Brown gave a sense that he was often unable to force further expenditure out of his rather sceptical Chancellor. All this created significant problems, for the troops on the ground but also for the image of Labour in government.

There was also a more calculating consideration. The Bush administration had shown a strain of isolationism from the outset, in a new tough stance towards international organizations and agreements. Blair had worked hard to get close to Bush, with some success; indeed, in many ways their personal relationship was closer than the much-vaunted 'friendship' with Clinton had been. He was not Bush's poodle, but he realized that, if they wanted, the Americans could invade Iraq, and probably anywhere else, regardless of the views of other countries. The challenge therefore was not to prevent an invasion that would happen anyway, but to try and keep America within the comity of nations, rather than allowing – and indeed encouraging – it to spin off in ever more extreme directions. Instead, the challenge was to stay close to the Americans, and to work as a moderating influence on the side of 'doves' like Secretary of State Colin Powell, against the 'hawks' like Vice-President Dick Cheney and Defense Secretary Donald Rumsfeld.[41] In that way, the action against Iraq – which by mid-2002 he had convinced himself was necessary and justified – would not necessarily be the start of a series of American wars on all those parts of the world that it did not like.

To say that these arguments did not convince everyone would be an understatement. Many people believed that more could, and should, be done to find a peaceful solution: if anything, that view has grown more strongly with the passing of time. Cook, as a former Foreign Secretary, took this view, and resigned from the cabinet on 17 March 2003 in protest. His was an important resignation; but in reality he was unlikely to emerge as a serious rival to the leadership, especially since his only cabinet ally, Short, procrastinated for weeks before finally following suit.[42] A total of 139 Labour MPs, along with the Liberal Democrats, the SNP, Plaid Cymru and 15 Conservatives, voted against the government on entry into the war.[43] Outside parliament, critics were numerous, and it was claimed that up to two million people marched on a 'stop the war' demonstration in London in February 2003.[44] The invasion went ahead regardless, and at this stage opinion polls showed a clear majority in favour of it. But although military victory was, as expected, rapid, Iraq did not welcome its 'liberators' with open arms. Blairite hopes of a 'Baghdad bounce' which would boost the premier's popularity, and perhaps even allow him finally to sideline Brown, were frustrated.[45] Extensive disorder continued to characterize large parts of Iraq for years thereafter, and continuing heavy casualties, serious questions about the conduct of the occupying forces and fears that elements in the American administration intended to repeat the experience in other states that they disliked – most notably Iran – all gave cause for serious concern.

Iraq by itself would have damaged Blair and his government in the eyes of many Britons. But there was more to it than that. As stated above, Blair had probably convinced himself by mid-2002 that the invasion must go ahead. He and his government then set about establishing grounds for the invasion, in a series of events that cast them in a very poor light. Of central significance was the claim, made in a dossier published in September 2002, that Iraq not only had weapons of mass destruction (WMD) but that these could be deployed within 45 minutes of an order to do so. If true, this was deeply worrying, but evidence for it was scanty and there were claims that the 45-minute claim had been included to 'sex up' the case for war. In the furore that followed, the British weapons expert who had made the 'sexing up' claim, David Kelly, was hounded by a Commons committee and then committed suicide. When this was followed by a further dossier of 'intelligence' which turned out to be largely plagiarized from an outdated student thesis, questions about the government's integrity were asked even louder, and Blair's own credibility fell to new low levels, notwithstanding a series of inquiries that absolved him of the worst charges that were being levelled.[46]

In the midst of all this, the 1997 expectations that Labour would take Britain to the heart of the EU were very distant memories. It was true that some of the new members from eastern and central Europe were more impressed with Britain's economic policies and, in some cases at least, had sympathy with its foreign policy. But hopes that Britain would be able to rip apart the Franco-German alliance that had dominated the EU appeared to be a thing of the past. In June 2003, Brown applied the five tests for British entry into the Euro and found that only one had been met.[47] But in any case the future of the EU project itself was beginning to look murkier. To the irritation of the pro-Europeans in his cabinet, Blair announced in April 2004 that there would be a referendum on the new EU constitution, something he had previously ruled out.[48] However, the rejection of the constitution in referendums in France and the Netherlands in May–June 2005 appeared to make the necessity for British ratification remote, to say the least.

However, despite the government's difficulties, the Conservatives continued to struggle. Hague had resigned straight after the 2001 defeat, but his successor, Iain Duncan Smith, was no better, and was himself forced out in October 2003, to be succeeded by the former Home Secretary, Michael Howard. Howard was an experienced politician, and began brightly, but his fortunes soon dipped. He was unable to appeal strongly to the political centre, and his attempt to capitalize on Labour's difficulties over the war in Iraq looked unconvincing. The Conservatives remained well behind Labour in the opinion polls. Even the June 2004 European elections offered little succour – although the Conservatives took more votes than Labour, their share, at only 27 per cent, was unimpressive, and the UK Independence Party (UKIP), a potential challenger for Conservative votes, took 16 per cent. Turnout was again very low. UKIP even beat the Liberal Democrats into fourth place. Even so, the latter had reason to approach the next general election with some cheer. Their opposition to the war in Iraq played well with many Muslim voters, and helped them capture the ethnically diverse 'safe' Labour seats of Brent East in September 2003 and Leicester South in July 2004. Second, their opposition to increased fees for university students, finally passed through the House of Commons against some Labour opposition in 2004, also garnered some support. Kennedy proved a popular, if at times erratic, leader. It remained to be seen, though, how far this apparent progress could be translated into parliamentary seats.

Spring 2005 had long been pencilled in as the date of the next general election. Although the polls were not as favourable as they had been in the run-up to 2001, Howard's promising start had spluttered and a Labour victory appeared a fair bet. Initially, there were Blairite hopes that this would be the time for a 'real' New Labour agenda.[49] Such hopes reflected a remarkable recovery in Blair's fortunes. His increasing difficulties over Iraq during the course of 2003 had been compounded by personal difficulties and health problems. That September, Brown's speech to the party conference, with its strap-line 'best when we are Labour' (not 'New Labour') appears to have represented a conscious challenge for the leadership. Shortly afterwards, however, with a new and potentially more potent Conservative leader (Howard) now elected, Prescott brokered a truce between Prime Minister and Chancellor.[50] At this stage, Brown believed that Blair had promised to resign before the next general election, and such a resignation seemed likely when Blair's rather depressed mood continued into early 2004.[51] In the event, however, the Commons' passing of student fees early that year, as well as encouragement from some leading colleagues, and from Bill Clinton, that he should stay on to cement his 'legacy', buoyed him up. When that spring's local and European elections went better than expected, and the Butler Report on the decision to go to war in Iraq gave a better verdict than had been feared, Blair decided to remain.[52]

Relations with the unions had become problematic, not least because the leadership of a number of major unions had moved significantly leftwards in recent years.[53] In July 2004, however, the leadership and the major trade unions reached a modus vivendi during the NPF at Warwick, whereby the government guaranteed various extensions to workers' rights in return for more financial and other help from the unions in the run-up to the general election.[54]

In September 2004, the loyal Blairite Milburn – who had resigned from the cabinet in June 2003 after clashing with Brown over foundation hospitals – was brought back into the cabinet to run the election campaign. This had been Brown's job in 1997 and 2001, and the move suggested that Brown was being downgraded and that Blair might even try to oust him from the Treasury in the aftermath of victory.[55] Blair also announced that, while he would not fight a further general election after the coming one, he would nonetheless be looking to serve the full term of the next parliament – to stay on, in other words, until 2009 or 2010.[56]

This was all very well, but it would have meant campaigning on public service delivery and future reform, rather than on the seemingly robust economic record of Brown as Chancellor. The problem was that, for all the very real improvements that had taken place in health, education, and other public services, voters often appeared to be unimpressed, focusing much more on remaining perceived shortcomings than on the undoubted progress that there had been since 1997 (and especially since 2001). It was ironic that a government so castigated for 'spin' had actually failed to get its message across to this extent. Blair's own trustworthiness also continued to be questioned, especially in association with Iraq. As in 2001, also, Blair came to the view that Brown was simply too important within the party, and had too many allies, to be simply sidelined. When the 2005 pre-campaign began badly, the Chancellor was pulled back into the planning process, and Milburn's role was downgraded. Brown and Blair even made an election broadcast together in which they appeared to be the best of friends. The last hopes of the ultra-Blairites for a future Blair premiership unencumbered by Brown were over.

The 2005 general election was a rather sombre affair. Blair embarked on a 'masochism strategy', putting himself in TV studios to be asked difficult questions by critical audiences.[57] This did at least mark a welcome shift from the rather grandiloquent campaigns of the past. Labour campaigned on economic success and public service reform with the slogan 'Forward not Back', clearly aiming to play on residual fears of a return to the Thatcher/Major years. The problem with such tactics, of course, was that they meant less with every passing year, and this was probably the last election where they would have serious resonance. It was clear that the Conservatives would gain some seats, particularly in southern England, but they were never likely to win, while the Liberal Democrats' hopes of pursuing Labour hard in inner-city areas with high proportions of ethnic minority voters were not wholly fulfilled in a somewhat stuttering campaign.

Labour won, nonetheless. On a slightly higher turnout than in 2001 (61.2 per cent), Labour took 356 seats to the Conservatives' 198 and the Liberal Democrats' 62: with nine nationalists from Scotland and Wales and 22 others, Labour had an overall majority of 66. However, it had achieved this with only 35.2 per cent of the votes cast, as opposed to the Conservatives' 32.4 and the Liberal Democrats' 22.0. This showed the extent to which the electoral system was biased in Labour's favour. Although it had emerged as more popular than either of its main UK rivals, Labour's position was clearly weaker than it had been. For the Conservatives, there were some encouraging signs in the south-east, especially. But elsewhere their progress was far patchier. Liberal Democrat hopes of replicating Brent East across wide swathes of urban Britain were largely thwarted, although the former Labour MP George Galloway did win an ethnically mixed seat in east London for the left-wing group Respect on the basis of his anti-war and anti-Blair activities. The 2005 result was not a great one for Labour, but it was worse for its rivals, and it could be argued that, after eight years in office, and given the context of difficulties over Iraq and wider issues surrounding Blair, the attainment of a good working majority was no mean feat. It certainly did not warrant the doom-laden tones that followed from some commentators.

The result was widely seen as a negative verdict on Blair, but it was a still more negative judgement on Howard, who immediately announced plans to resign; he was eventually succeeded in December 2005 by the 39-year-old David Cameron. Cameron appeared to make some headway in terms of modernizing his party, and positive results in local elections in 2006 and 2007 suggested that his party was, for the first time in a decade, becoming a real contender for power. But local results were one thing, national ones another, and it remained to be seen whether his conscious attempt to do for his party what many believed Blair had once done for his would succeed.

In the reshuffle that followed the election, Blair again promoted some of his supporters. But Brown was able to block some of Blair's planned changes, and it was hard to see who or what would be able to stop him being Blair's successor as premier.[58] Blair started out the 2005 parliament with a radical Queen's Speech promising a whole new tranche of public service reforms.[59] He also regained some of his national stature after his robust response to the terrorist atrocities in London on 7 July 2005.[60] But he came, increasingly, to be seen as a lame duck premier. Ongoing problems in Iraq continued to damage him, as did the continuing police investigation into loans for peerages, as part of which he was himself formally questioned. Eventually, in September 2006, he announced that he would retire within a year. He remained in place to take the blame for the expectedly poor results in the 3 May 2007 Scottish parliament, Welsh assembly and English council elections; but a week later, he announced that he would stand down as soon as a successor had been elected. One of the last acts of his premiership was the restoration of devolved government to Northern Ireland. It was a remarkable achievement that he was able to leave office with the province being run by a government in which the two leading members were the veteran anti-Catholic Unionist Ian Paisley and the IRA's former chief of staff, Martin McGuinness. It was perhaps less to his credit, though, that both Scotland and Wales had fallen from Labour control in the May 2007 elections.

Blair did not leave the Labour Party itself in a particularly healthy state. Membership, which had risen in Blair's early years as leader, had fallen steadily since 1997. By 2006, it stood at just 198,000 – lower than at any point since figures were first published in 1928. It was becoming increasingly difficult to find party members prepared to stand in local government elections in some parts of the country. Many party members appear to have felt disempowered.[61] The failure of the dream of a mass party along the lines of Blair's own constituency of Sedgefield, much quoted in the pre-1997 period, meant that the party had to rely on other avenues for funding. Union money remained essential, despite earlier hopes of a radical change. This meant that the party did not fall into absolute poverty – far from it. At the 2001 general election, for example, Labour spent £12–13 million at the national level, as opposed to the Conservatives' £9 million.[62] However, there were increasingly pressing concerns about how income streams could be sustained and developed. Early in its tenure, the government had capitalized on 'Tory sleaze' by introducing strict regulations relating to individuals' political donations. Far fewer restrictions applied to loans, however, and so the party's fundraisers began to explore that avenue. However, as news of this began to leak out, questions began to be asked as to whether there was any real intention of paying these 'loans' back, and whether they were not, in fact, donations under another name; and when it became apparent that there might be a relationship between making loans and receiving peerages, a criminal investigation followed. The frequent turnover of top party officials during Labour's decade in power had hardly helped matters, and had perhaps led to a culture where essential controls were lacking.

All the same, it was easy to paint too bleak a picture, because none of these problems was irreversible. Historically, it was not surprising that a long period in government led to a decline in party membership and activism. Opposition is much easier than government for many people in this respect, because government involves taking responsibility, defending unpopular but often necessary decisions, and making compromises, when it is far easier – and emotionally more satisfying – to stand on 'principle' in opposition. It should also be noted that the fall in membership looked all the more dramatic because of the scale of the 'Blair enrolment' in 1994–97. Those new members were by no means all fickle or easily discouraged, but it does not seem unreasonable to assume that they were disproportionately responsible for falling membership after 1997. What was perhaps worth noting was the fact that the mid-1990s' membership boom followed the party's decision to put vastly increased resources into membership recruitment; and the fall had followed the failure to continue in that vein.[63] There was nothing to stop a future leader spending generously on recruitment once more.

The structures of the party had also changed. But, again, the situation was more complex than was often suggested by formulations that talked about party members losing control of their party. In fact, the Labour Party had never been a democracy in which the opinions of ordinary party members counted for very much. For most of its history, the leadership had usually got its way. Some of the reforms that had taken place under Kinnock, Smith and Blair contained the potential, at least, for party members to have more say in Labour's affairs.[64] Innovations like OMOV, by which the leadership had hoped to get its way against the activists, backfired when ordinary party members favoured candidates not approved of by headquarters, even at the height of New Labour's fortunes in the late 1990s over the Welsh leadership and the London mayoralty (see above).[65] Meanwhile, the position of women within the party had never been stronger, as a result of reforms which themselves stemmed from greater female assertiveness and the increasing proportion of trade unionists who were women.[66] Even the party conference, whose powers had been reduced significantly, was not as helpless and supine as it was often portrayed; it defeated the leadership in 2000 (on pensions), 2002 (on PFI) and 2003 (on foundation hospitals).[67]

Immediate verdicts on Blair were often harsh. It was not difficult to build up a series of charges against him. One was that he promised much more than he delivered. The 'young country' rhetoric of opposition had not been matched in government. There was a sense that, although things might have got better in some areas, overall the government had not taken a historic opportunity to change Britain massively for the better. It was easy to scour old speeches and find evidence of U-turns; pledges against student fees, for example, had been negated by New Labour in government. Blair had campaigned strongly against 'Tory sleaze' while in opposition, yet after ten years in office, it was Labour that looked sleazy, with several prime ministerial aides being under suspicion of criminal activity in the 'loans for peerages' scandal. And, of course, for many people his participation in and support for the invasion of Iraq cast him for all time as a war criminal, and as someone who had not hesitated to lie to take Britain into war at the side of America.

But it would not do to leave matters there. The raising of expectations in the period down to the 1997 election was the stuff of politics. Much of what was said was rhetoric. But the party had tried hard to deliver. Labour might not have delivered the kind of almost spiritual renewal that some of its members appear to have expected.[68] But it did bring real improvements to the lives of many people, including many of the weakest and most vulnerable in society. The minimum wage was but one example of this. Public service reform might have gone further, but here were very real gains in health and in primary and university education, although improvements at secondary level were, perhaps, less obvious. Spending per school pupil doubled between 1997 and 2005, while there was a 'huge increase' in health spending over the same period.[69] The PFI, for all its undoubted drawbacks, did see some spectacular renewal of Britain's public service infrastructure. The economy also continued to boom, something of which previous Labour premiers could only have dreamed. There had, though, been far less success in areas like housing and transport, while some of the government's more authoritarian inclinations were worrying, to say the least. In foreign policy, it seems clear that Blair did fall prey to wishful thinking over the decision to go to war with Iraq, in particular. But he appears sincerely to have believed that there was a possibility of bringing a better future to that country, and that the chance should be taken. In this he was, arguably, too easily prey to a neoconservative agenda. However, he seems also to have believed that keeping close to the Americans was the best way in which to rein them in from their wilder notions. In this he was unsuccessful, although it may be that matters might have turned out worse had he taken an alternative stance. Perhaps the best thing that can be said in Blair's defence, when he is compared with his immediate predecessors, is that between about 1950 and 1990 the Cold War had provided a reasonably predictable framework through which to operate diplomacy, and that there was no such framework for foreign policy in the early twenty-first century. But that might be too generous a verdict.

In April 1997, few people believed that Labour was on the verge of a massive landslide victory. Fewer still would have believed that the next election would bring almost a repetition of that result, or that the one after that would still see Labour returned with a very healthy parliamentary majority. Few would have expected such a long period of economic stability and growth; few would have expected so much achievement in social policy. Tony Blair was a major part of that. But he was not its sole cause. There was no reason to believe that Labour would not be able to prosper without him. Blair had not really deserved the almost sycophantic praise that had been lavished on him in his early years as Labour leader and Prime Minister. But nor did he merit the excessive criticism that met him in his last years of office. For all his faults, he had dominated the progressive side of politics in Britain, arguably to a greater extent than any politician since Gladstone. He would prove to be a very difficult act for any future Labour leader – not least his immediate successor – to follow.

13 Moving beyond Blair, 2007–15

Tony Blair had been a lucky politician. He was certainly fortunate in the timing of his departure. When he retired from front-line politics, he was able to claim that he had presided over unprecedented prosperity over a longer period than any of his predecessors.[1] It was to prove paradoxical that Gordon Brown, the architect – or, at any rate, presiding officer – of that prosperity was now to inherit the premiership at just the point when the years of easy credit and loose regulation were to catch up with western economies with a vengeance. After a bright start, Brown's premiership would be characterized by world financial crisis, severe economic recession, and a spate of political difficulties almost all of which worked against the Labour Party. In the event, they would be enough to turn Labour out of power in 2010 as Brown and his colleagues underestimated the opportunism of the Conservatives and Liberal Democrats in forming an anti-Labour Coalition. That Coalition survived its full five-year term until the general election of May 2015. Many Labourites had expected it to be an easy opponent, but Brown's successor, Ed Miliband, struggled for some time to make himself heard, and even to position himself as the obvious default beneficiary of the Coalition's difficulties. In the period after 2007 as a whole, Labour found it surprisingly difficult to find a post-Blair formula for success.

In 2007, the succession to Blair was unopposed. The media, and sections of the party, hoped for a contest, but one by one the potential challengers withdrew. Alan Johnson, the popular and populist Education Secretary, decided relatively early to concentrate on the deputy leadership.[2] Clarke and Milburn decided to establish a website, The 2020 Vision, as the guardian of the Blairite flame, rather than risk humiliation against their old adversary.[3] David Miliband, the Environment Secretary, appeared more tempted by the prospect of standing, perhaps hoping that a media bandwagon would carry him to victory (as had been the case with Cameron two years earlier in the Conservative Party), or that he would put down a marker as Brown's heir apparent. But, fearing that a hefty defeat was a more likely outcome, he declared for Brown.[4] Finally, the Home Secretary, John Reid, announced that he too would not stand, and indeed that he would not seek office in a Brown government – not that he was likely to have been offered it.[5] Meanwhile, Michael Meacher and John McDonnell, both seen as being on the left, failed to gain sufficient support from MPs to be nominated to run.[6] Brown was therefore declared leader of the party without a contest on 24 June 2007. Harriet Harman was elected deputy leader. She had not been a terribly successful minister, and indeed had been sacked from the cabinet in 1998, before returning to more junior office.[7] But the notion of a gender balance in the leadership was important, and she was Brown's preferred choice. On 27 June, Blair formally resigned the premiership and Brown was appointed in his place.

Few tears were shed for Blair. Although still only in his mid-fifties, he had seemed increasingly out of time. But Brown did not come without baggage. He had been a very successful Chancellor, and was a man of considerable intellect and political ability. But although he had spent years hinting, and more, that he would offer something different from Blair, he had been as much an architect of New Labour as the man he was replacing. He might have had a closer sense of the movement's history, but he was no more a friend of the unions or the left than Blair had been.[8] It remained to be seen whether he really was a popular figure, or whether he had only shown up as popular in polls in 2005 because he was not Blair. In particular, it was hard to see him appealing as widely across class and geographical divides as Blair had done, at least in 1997 and 2001. In addition, Brown's reputation for being a difficult colleague, and for bearing grudges, went before him. He had been able to indulge these characteristics as Chancellor, but it would be less easy for him to do so as Prime Minister. A key test of his premiership potential would be his ability to 'grow' into his new position.[9]

Once he was appointed Prime Minister, Brown lost no time in attempting to set his own stamp on the office. Most of the remaining ministers of his own generation were dropped, in an attempt to rejuvenate the government and also to remove any remaining longstanding adversaries. It was noticeable that, of Brown's first cabinet, only four other ministers beside himself had been in the cabinet at the end of 2002 (Straw, Alistair Darling, Peter Hain and Geoff Hoon). This was good in some ways, but presented the dangers of Brown being seen as old, or the team as inexperienced, or both.[10] Darling was appointed Chancellor, and David Miliband, perhaps as a tacit reward for not forcing a leadership contest, Foreign Secretary. Jacqui Smith became the first woman Home Secretary. Brown tried to inculcate a new mood of seriousness and probity, talking a lot about his 'moral compass' and becoming much more autobiographical in his public utterances, although he might have reflected that after ten years as Chancellor he really ought to have been better known by the public than he was. He tried to counter the impression that he was a more partisan figure than Blair by talking about a 'government of all the talents' and bringing in 'expert' ministers (unofficially dubbed 'goats') from outside the party, such as the former head of the CBI, (Lord) Digby Jones.[11] There was a clear attempt to stress that the new government was a new departure: references to Blair were immediately set in the past tense, and some 'errors' were admitted, in an attempt at differentiation.

At first, it seemed that this attempt at reinvention might work. Brown's assured handling of a series of crises in his first few months in office also bedded him into his new role. Attempted terrorist attacks in London and Glasgow were dealt with in a calm and assured manner. When flooding hit the country in June and July 2007, Brown's reaction was reassuring and statesmanlike. Such impressions were confirmed by his confident handling of the financial crisis which hit the Northern Rock bank that September. Labour enjoyed a substantial lead in the opinion polls.[12]

Increasingly, therefore, thoughts turned to the possibility of holding a general election. At one level, this made perfect sense: Brown had been positioning his government as something distinct from Blair's, and so the logical corollary was the need for a fresh electoral mandate. There was no constitutional need for such a mandate, but there had been significant media comment on the subject, prompted by the increasing sense since the 1970s that elections elected prime ministers and not governments. An electoral victory would be unequivocally Brown's, and would allow him a free run until 2013: if things went well, he could then seek re-election, and emulate Blair in winning an election after a full term of Labour government. And if *that* went well, he could govern until 2017 or 2018 and complete two unbroken decades in power for Labour.[13]

There were, however, two drawbacks. First, for all his talk about what he would do once the incubus of Blair had been removed, Brown had surprisingly little that was new or positive to suggest by way of policy. Of course, he had been ruinously busy as Chancellor. But few people, apart from Milburn and a few others, recognized just how little fresh strategic thinking Brown brought to the premiership.[14] One general secretary of the party came to believe that 'he totally lacked leadership skills'.[15] A more measured academic verdict would later suggest that Brown 'was not well-equipped for the highest office, in terms of ... key leadership abilities, characteristics and skills', and that although this did not doom his government from the start, it did make it 'very much harder to be successful'.[16] The second difficulty was that plans for an autumn election underestimated the Conservative Party leadership. This was, in some ways, excusable: since at least 1992, successive leaders had made life very easy for their Labour counterparts. But Brown was slow to recognize that Cameron was a more formidable opponent. Labour's determination to see Cameron and his shadow Chancellor, George Osborne, as talentless, loafing 'toffs' did them a disservice. In reality, they would prove sharp enough political operators to be able to expose Brown's flank.[17]

Talk of an election was allowed to run on apace up to and including the Labour Party conference in September 2007. However, Labour's plans to reform inheritance tax, seen as a populist measure to consolidate and even increase the party's middle-class support, exposed a possible weakness. This was, after all, Conservative territory, and it was easy to promise more as an opposition than as a government. At the Conservative Party conference the following week, Osborne announced a much more generous reform. This created consternation among Labour's leaders, but in reality they should not have been surprised. Brown was now placed in a dilemma. His people had been briefing the media extensively to the effect that there would be an autumn election. Now, however, the polls shed doubt on whether Labour could win an overall majority. The potential contents of a Brown-led Labour manifesto looked thin and unconvincing. Finally, it was decided that there would be no election.[18]

As Callaghan had found in the autumn of 1978, this might have been a justifiable decision, but it was to prove disastrous. If one of Brown's great selling points was his experience and sureness of touch, the 'election that never was' made him look panicky and indecisive.[19] Worse still, he had clearly been bested by the Conservative leaders, whose credibility grew as a result. It is not possible to be sure whether Labour would have won in the autumn of 2007, but in retrospect it seems clear that there was no subsequent point in the 2005 parliament when it would have had a better chance. Labour had never been behind the Conservatives in the polls between Brown's accession and the non-election. It would never be ahead again while Brown remained party leader.[20]

It would also prove to be the last point at which Labour could have gone to the country as a 'prosperity' government. Shortly before leaving the Treasury, Brown had spoken of a 'Golden Age' of prosperity, but financial crisis was brewing in the USA with the collapse of the subprime mortgage market.[21] This had already had significant knock-on effects in the case of Northern Rock. A wider crisis followed in 2008, with a major crisis in investment banking which included the collapse of Lehman Brothers that September.[22] Initial hopes that this crisis could be confined to the apparently esoteric worlds of investment banking and hedge funds proved false. The world financial crisis that followed manifested itself in Britain with the near-collapse of a number of the largest banks. Here, Brown played a major and positive part. His extensive experience, his political and financial contacts, and his clarity of vision in this area of policy all meant that he was able to lead a unified international response to the crisis that helped obviate a potential cataclysm. On the UK level, he was able to help the major banks avoid collapse through a series of measures, including mergers and temporary nationalization. Ironically, a major crisis helped to restore and even enhance Brown's reputation.[23]

The second result, though, was less positive for Labour. The crisis led to a significant economic recession, such that political rhetoric increasingly centred on the need for austerity and spending cuts. All governments tend to struggle in times of economic difficulty. But Labour governments have tended to do so particularly, in the sense that so much of their approach has been based on the idea of spending the fruits of a successful economy to redress what they see as social wrongs. It was especially uncomfortable for Brown because he had, of course, just spent a decade presiding over the regulatory framework that had allowed British financial institutions to come to such a sorry pass. This sense that his touch was a good deal less sure than had been thought at the time of his election was further enhanced by the fiasco over the abolition of the 10 per cent rate of income tax, which – although eventually alleviated in its effects by an emergency measure introduced by Darling – threatened to increase the tax payments of some of the poorest people in Britain.[24]

By the time of the May 2008 local elections, therefore, the electoral tide had turned against Labour: it slipped into third place in terms of poll share, and lost control of its four remaining county councils. This result, if translated to a general election, would have given the Conservatives an overall majority.[25] The two parliamentary by-elections that followed offered no consolation. In the first, at Crewe and Nantwich on 22 May, a 2005 Labour majority of over 7000 became a Conservative majority of almost 8000 on a massive swing. Two months later, the SNP snatched Glasgow East despite Labour's having had a majority of more than 13,000 there at the general election. Such reverses would not prove to be unique to 2008: in the June 2009 European elections, Labour came third behind the Conservatives and the UK Independence party (UKIP), with just 15.9 per cent of the poll (on an admittedly low turnout), and winning only 13 of the 69 seats on offer.[26]

Despite the 'coronation' of 2007, doubts about Brown had never been far below the surface. There had been no viable alternative candidate then, although some former Blairites felt let down that David Miliband had not at least given it a try.[27] Some of the misgivings about Brown came down to the bitterness and frustration felt by those whose careers he had effectively ended. But there was more to it than that. One concern, already mentioned, was the lack of a clear strategy for the government. Try as he might, Brown did not seem able to articulate a strategic vision. He was determined to steer clear of Blair, and to downplay the 'New Labour' angle, but struggled to find an alternative rhetorical device. Many of the government's policies, such as better support for Sure Start, further emphasis on tax credits and NHS reform, were worthy and important. But they were too easily seen as piecemeal and unconnected. The lack of strategy seemed, rather, to be symbolized by the development of the 'bunker' in No. 12 Downing Street, traditionally the home of the government whips but now repurposed into a war room where large numbers of staffers were joined by the Prime Minister to work away, with massive television screens at either end of the room, each showing a different 24-hour news channel. Anything less likely to foster clear and calm strategic thinking than being constantly in thrall to the knee jerks of rolling news channels would be hard to imagine.[28]

Second, there were concerns about Brown's own style and behaviour. His rants at Blair were, by now, very much in the public sphere; his antipathy towards many of his past, and even present, colleagues (and especially Mandelson), was legendary.[29] Talk of his 'moral compass' sat ill with the series of people who worked for him from a rather less moral angle: the revelation in April 2009 that his chief of staff, Damien McBride, had been urging colleagues to spread scurrilous rumours about Cameron's wife hit a new low, but seemed, to many people, to be of a piece with the previous antics of Brown's supporters.[30] Brown's response to the McBride scandal – a delayed and grudging semi-apology – seemed to sum up the problem.[31] Allegations were made in February 2010 about Brown's bullying of staff at 10 Downing Street, and while some of this appeared to be politically motivated and of dubious provenance, the fact that senior colleagues had to go on television and explain away Brown's bad temper and occasional rages was not helpful: to explain that he got frustrated and 'angry with himself' in stressful situations did not necessarily make him seem more 'normal'. Stories about his dedication to work tended to backfire when they involved him making personal calls to members of the public while they were still asleep in bed, and also contributed to a sense of someone who was struggling to cope.[32] Perhaps refreshingly, there were many people in Britain by the end of the first decade of the twenty-first century who realized that working extremely long hours was not necessarily a good, or even productive, thing. The attempt to portray Brown as a statesmanlike figure was also damaged as the 'goats' began to leave the government, frustrated at being seen as window dressing and not being taken seriously. As crises mounted, questions began to be asked as to whether Brown was suited to leadership at all.[33]

Under Brown, Labour's domestic policy was characterized by a firm belief in the importance and efficacy of state action in bringing about fairer social outcomes. Although there were innovations, many of them were cosmetic – after all, Brown had been the dominant figure in domestic policy making for a decade, which made genuinely new departures rather thin on the ground. Instead, existing initiatives, like tax credits, were re-engineered in ways that Brown hoped would lead to greater equity and fairness, but which, in too many cases, simply added further levels of complication to already complex systems and procedures. Signs of increasing taxation were eagerly seized upon by the Conservatives and, increasingly, the Liberal Democrats as tasters of the kind of 'tax and spend' politics that Brown would set out if he were to win his own electoral mandate. As the economic position worsened, Brown's clear reluctance to embrace or even countenance any serious measures of austerity earned him the respect of post-Keynesians, but aroused considerable criticism across the political spectrum, put him at odds with his Chancellor and, once again, gave Labour's opponents some easy rhetorical opportunities around its supposed wastefulness. His predecessor later went so far as to argue that this statism amounted to Brown turning away from New Labour.[34]

In terms of foreign policy, Brown was pretty well locked into continuity where Iraq and Afghanistan were concerned. He was also a confirmed Americaphile and had always believed in the importance of the Anglo-American alliance. Once again, there were some cosmetic changes: the introduction of an annual Armed Forces Day in 2009 was one such, but it had a mixed reception, and was met with considerable scepticism from many members of the forces, who believed that, as Chancellor, he had spent years starving them of resources. Brown had always been less enthusiastic than Blair about Europe. At one stage in the Blair years it had seemed a question of not whether, but when, Britain would join the single currency. This had ceased to be the case before Brown became premier, and the Eurozone crisis that followed and compounded the financial crisis of 2008 onwards left the issue dead in the water. Paradoxically, though, the crisis of the Euro seemed, to many, to make closer European integration even more necessary. Brown showed his lukewarmness to this process by refusing to join the public communal signing of the Lisbon Treaty in December 2007, signing it later in the day alone. But in some ways this got the worst of both worlds – distrust from Britain's European partners because of its style, and hostility from British Euro-sceptics because of its substance. And it played further to the narrative of a Prime Minister who was ill-mannered and indecisive.[35]

Brown was not to blame for everything that went wrong, of course. For many years, MPs' salaries had been a matter of keen public criticism, and it had become politically toxic to try to propose even the reasonable increases that would have made them comparable with the salaries of other leading professionals. One way around this had been for governments of both parties to turn a blind eye towards an increasingly liberal interpretation of what MPs could claim by way of expenses. The problem was that details of the expenses were leaked to the *Daily Telegraph*, which began publishing them in May 2009. There followed a long period of damaging revelations, dripped out over a lengthy period. Some of the expenses claims were ludicrous, and included the building of a duck house on a pond and the cleaning of a moat. Some of this might have played to the kind of 'anti-toff' approach adopted at the 2008 Crewe and Nantwich by-election, but it was clear that some Labour MPs were no cleaner than some of their Conservative counterparts. One cabinet minister, keen to spend up to the limit at the end of each financial year, was in the habit of moving into a boutique hotel for a few weeks to ensure no penny was left unspent. Ultimately, too, more Labour than Conservative MPs would be prosecuted, and indeed imprisoned, as a result of the scandal.[36] And, although all parties were affected, the fact that the regime had been presided over by Labour was damaging to the party, not just in 2009, but at the following year's general election as well.[37] It all played into a rhetoric around 'time for a change' that could not be addressed by Brown's superficial attempts at a new start. Continuing scandals over Labour Party funding added further toxicity to the mix.[38]

The result of all this was that Brown's last two years in Downing Street were characterized by a series of plots against him.[39] Although they all proved abortive, their cumulative effect was to undermine his position further. In the aftermath of the loss of Glasgow East to the SNP in summer 2008, a campaign began for a leadership election to be held. Straw, Clarke and some others worked in the background against Brown. David Miliband, the Foreign Secretary, seemed to be declaring his hand as a challenger in a newspaper article on 30 July.[40] But everyone then went on vacation: when they returned, the world was in the grip of a major economic crisis, which pushed Brown to the fore and with which he coped well. By the time of the party conference that September, Brown was reasonably re-entrenched, and was able to play heavily on the need for experience, stating mischievously that it was 'no time for a novice'.[41] But he was alarmed enough to bring Mandelson back into the government, initially as Secretary of State for Business. There was general surprise: the two men had barely spoken since Mandelson had chosen Blair over Brown in 1994, but now they made a great show of being the best of comrades.[42] Even so, unrest with Brown soon re-emerged, and in the light of Labour's abysmal local and European election results in May 2009, there was a further attempt to oust him. Here, the Blairite Work and Pensions Secretary, James Purnell, resigned and called on Brown to go. He was joined by Hazel Blears (Communities and Local Government Secretary), John Hutton (Defence), Geoff Hoon (Chief Whip) and Caroline Flint (Minister for Europe outside the cabinet). But David Miliband again refused to come out against Brown, and the plot fizzled out.[43] Mandelson benefited once again, his promotion to First Secretary and, in effect, Deputy Prime Minister following as a sop to the Blairite wing. More materially, Brown was so weakened that he was unable to carry out his plan to replace Darling with Ed Balls at the Treasury.[44] Finally, in January 2010, with a general election looming and Labour still behind in the polls, ex-ministers Patricia Hewitt and Geoff Hoon called on Brown to face a leadership election. Steve Richards has claimed that this was a real threat, with Harman and Straw, in particular, ready to wield the knife, although Straw himself disputes this. In the event, they failed to strike; and without them, Hewitt and Hoon were isolated and the plot came to nothing.[45] Any last chance of removing Brown before the general election had now disappeared.

In reality, it is hard to see how there could have been any other outcome. The party's leadership election rules were cumbersome, and did not allow for a swift change of leader unless the leader was willing to go. Brown had not spent so many years working assiduously to gain the premiership to give it up after a couple of years at the behest of people like Hewitt and Hoon. Furthermore, the only plausible alternatives in the period were probably David Miliband and Alan Johnson. But Miliband appears to have believed that he would succeed Brown anyway if he waited and showed his loyalty, and so felt that he had more to lose than he had to gain by making an early challenge, particularly if it left him leading the party into a general election which it might well be unable to win. Ultimately, this would prove a little too calculating for some people, and probably damaged him in the 2010 leadership election, but it is not hard to see why he came to that conclusion. The other alternative was Alan Johnson, who had been a popular minister under both Blair and Brown. But Johnson appears to have had serious doubts as to his own ability to do the job, and certainly did not covet it. In the end, Labour was stuck with Brown.

What was, perhaps, most notable about of all of this was Brown's tenacity in the face of hostility. It is clear that he continued to have a considerable hunger for power, and a firm belief in his own mission to create a fairer Britain. On the other hand, the Conservative leader, Cameron, had lost some of his early sheen, and Brown continued to arouse doubts about him with references to the need for experience in a crisis.

As the five-year limit for the 2005 parliament approached, therefore, Labour's position was by no means as unfavourable as many had anticipated. Brown announced on 6 April that parliament would be dissolved the following week, with polling set for 6 May. Early polls suggested that the Conservatives had a lead of between 5 and 11 percentage points over Labour, highlighting the task before the latter.[46] Labour sought to offer a new start through its manifesto, but it was hard to avoid having its policies being seen as more of the same. It was hoped that accepting television debates between the leaders for the first time would highlight Brown's strength and experience, but instead they allowed Cameron to come across well; and Clegg was exposed to a far wider audience than would otherwise have been the case.[47] This mattered, first, because it led to a bubble of Liberal Democrat poll support that perhaps raised Clegg's expectations, but also because it showed both the other party leaders trying a little too hard to appeal to the Liberal Democrat vote – suggesting, at best, that they were worried about not winning an overall majority otherwise and, at worst, that they were trying to cosy up to him in the anticipation of coalition talks after the election.[48] Brown's tendency to be accident prone took a new turn as he followed a televised conversation with a Labour supporter with a series of 'private' uncomplimentary comments about her as being a 'bigoted woman', oblivious to the fact that his microphone was still on and relaying the words to a large live TV audience.[49]

In the event, Labour emerged badly from the election. With 29.7 per cent of the vote, it won only 258 seats (90 fewer than in 2005). But the Conservatives fell short of an overall majority, their 36.9 per cent of the vote yielding 305 of the 650 seats. The Liberal Democrats polled 23.6 per cent, but although they won only 57 seats, those numbers would clearly be crucial in determining what happened next. However, even if the Liberals Democrats came in with Labour, the two parties would still be short of the 326 seats required to produce a majority. It would also need support from at least some of the MPs representing the SNP (6), Plaid Cymru (3), and Green Party (1).[50] Labour had lost the backing, disproportionately, of people of average and just above average incomes: support among social groups A and B rose slightly, but fell from 34 per cent to 28 per cent among C1s (lower middle class) and, more worryingly still, from 40 to 22 per cent among C2s (skilled working class), with support in class D (workers) falling but only from 48 to 44 per cent.[51] As in 2005, the historic gender gap was reversed, with a higher proportion of women voting Labour than of men.[52] What appeared incontrovertible was that Brown had been a major electoral liability. It may well be that he was enough to make the difference between failure and success.

For five days, the implications of the election remained in some doubt. Labour hoped to hang on to office with the help of the Liberal Democrats. A series of negotiations followed, in which impeccably moderate figures like Lords Mandelson and Adonis (himself a former Social Democrat) played a leading role.[53] At one or two points it appeared that agreement might not be too remote. But Labour clearly underestimated the extent to which the Liberal Democrats had changed their approach in recent years. The election of Clegg as their leader in succession to the patrician Menzies Campbell in December 2007 was important. Clegg was eager to continue the process, begun under Charles Kennedy, of distancing the party from Labour, and so putting a clear end to the strategy that Ashdown had pursued in the 1990s. Clegg was sympathetic to the so-called 'Orange Book' Liberals, such as David Laws, who were much more market-oriented and who believed that the extensions of state intervention represented by Brown were inimical to Liberalism. It is clear, in retrospect at least, that the Liberal Democrats were much less enthusiastic in their talks with Labour at this point than they were in the parallel negotiations that were taking place with the Conservatives. Their strategy seems to have been to gain concessions from Labour that would improve their bargaining position in relation to their preferred outcome, which was a coalition with the Conservatives. Brown eventually saw through this, and on Tuesday 11 May he told Clegg that the game was up.[54] Cameron was asked to form a government, and did so, to some surprise, by announcing a Coalition with the Liberal Democrats, a number of whose leaders, including Clegg (Deputy Prime Minister), joined the cabinet. Brown resigned immediately as leader of the party, leaving Harman to run the party pending a leadership election which would culminate at the annual conference that September.

In the event, five candidates stood for the leadership. The most obviously 'New Labour' candidate, although by now he was trying to move beyond that image, was David Miliband. As a former Foreign Secretary, he had status, and the fact that he had served under Brown while also having been clearly a Blairite suggested to some that he could be a unifying figure. But this cut both ways, and some people criticized him for having been disloyal to Brown, while others felt that he had not been disloyal enough: he had failed on three separate occasions to challenge Brown when he might have done so.[55] He was joined in the contest by his younger brother, Ed Miliband, and by Ed Balls, both of whom had worked under Brown at the Treasury and been seen as loyal retainers, but both of whom had also tried to make their own way once entering parliament in 2005 and the cabinet in 2007. Andy Burnham, the former Health Secretary, also stood, as did Diane Abbott, the first Black candidate to stand for the leadership and the only woman to put herself forward this time. The campaign for the leadership was conducted in a fairly friendly fashion, although there was considerable interest in, and a degree of friction between, the Miliband brothers. When it came to the party conference in September 2010, there were initially few surprises. Abbott (with 7.42 per cent of the electoral college vote on the first ballot), Burnham (8.68) and Balls (11.79) were eliminated in successive rounds of the alternative vote. This left David Miliband and Ed Miliband. In a very close outcome, Ed Miliband took 50.65 per cent of the electoral college, to his brother's 49.35.

Ed Miliband's victory came as something of a surprise. He had polled fewer votes than David Miliband in the sections of the electoral college representing MPs and MEPs (15.52 per cent to 17.81) and Labour Party members (15.20 to 18.13). However, he had had a lead in the section for affiliated members (overwhelmingly trade unionists), where he had taken 19.93 per cent to his brother's 13.40. While this was all within the rules, it did allow people inside and outside the party to make much of the fact that Ed Miliband owed the leadership to 'the unions', and this was further problematized when it became clear that at least some unions had backed him very vigorously indeed in their internal communications with members.[56] This, combined with the sense that he had somehow stabbed his elder brother in the back, gave Ed Miliband a rather rocky start as leader.

Miliband was only 40 (Labour's youngest leader to date), and little known in the country at large. The son of the Marxist academic (and highly critical historian of the Labour Party), Ralph Miliband, his Oxford degree had been followed by periods as a special adviser (initially to Harriet Harman) and then teaching at Harvard, before returning to work for Brown at the Treasury. He was widely regarded as a Brownite high flier, having entered the cabinet in 2007 after only two years in parliament. In October 2008, he had become Secretary of State for Energy and Climate Change, in which role he was generally seen as having acquitted himself well. But it remained to be seen how far he would be able to reunite and galvanize the party as its leader.[57]

Elections to the shadow cabinet followed. The heavyweight figures of Darling and Straw had already announced that they would not be standing; they were followed, the day after the leadership election, by David Miliband.[58] These might have all been predictable decisions, but they did represent a significant loss of experience and talent at just the point where the new leader might have welcomed, or at any rate benefited from, some seasoned guidance. Miliband tried to avoid the impression of a Brownite takeover: the obvious candidate for shadow Chancellor, Balls, was overlooked in favour of the more emollient and broadly appealing Johnson (although the beneficial effects of this were nullified when, after only three rather difficult months in the role, Johnson resigned for personal reasons, leaving Balls as the only possible replacement). Balls initially had to make do with the Home Office portfolio, while foreign affairs went to Yvette Cooper. These proved, in the event, to be the last shadow cabinet elections. The historic practice had caused problems to leaders at various points, and not least to Kinnock, who was one of Miliband's most fervent supporters among the party's grandees. In July 2011, the PLP agreed to abolish elections, leaving it to the leader to appoint the shadow cabinet.[59] This raised a little fuss, but in reality it was a piece of modernization that would have taken place some years earlier had Labour then been in opposition.

In his first speech as leader, Miliband declared that 'a new generation' was now leading the party, and renounced the war in Iraq as an error.[60] The latter statement was seen as hypocritical by many – and not least his brother – but it did serve to set him apart from Blair and, by implication, Brown, while also appealing to voters of all backgrounds who had been alienated from Labour by the war. There followed a series of initiatives designed to reposition Labour, some of them talking about the 'squeezed middle', although there was a lack of precision as to who comprised this group.[61] Miliband also sought to make capital from Coalition spending cuts. This could create difficulties as it left Labour open to charges of being dishonest and wasteful, and not facing up to economic 'realities', although there was a counter-argument, propounded by Darling, among others, that the crisis was 'a convenient excuse that provided the Conservatives with cover to make the kind of deep public spending cuts many of them were wanting to make for ideological reasons'.[62]

Beyond this, considerable thought was being given as to how to position Labour for the future. Increasing emphasis was accorded to finding a new form of radicalism that moved beyond 'Old Labour' or 'New Labour, 'left' or 'right', and Brown or Blair.[63] The Blue Labour grouping, formed in 2009 by Labour intellectual Maurice (later Lord) Glasman, was one such.[64] *The Purple Book*, published in 2011, was another, which drew on established figures like Mandelson, Milburn and Field, as well as more up-and-coming figures like Adonis, Caroline Flint, Rachel Reeves and Tristram Hunt.[65] Reeves would go on to co-edit a slim volume of essays by Labour MPs on 'One Nation' Labour in 2013.[66] There was clearly the germ of something new developing, but it was still not entirely clear, in the approach to the 2015 general election, quite what the concrete effects of any of this rethinking had been.

First reactions to the formation of the Coalition had been mixed, but many on the left had believed that it might not last too long. There was a feeling that, once the initial honeymoon wore off, Cameron and Clegg would struggle to contain their parties, the former because he had failed to win an election that many felt should have been a walkover, and the latter because his party at large would oppose him from the left. On this calculation, the introduction of cuts, as opposed to talking about them, would rend the government in two, bringing about an early realignment and possibly a general election. But Cameron was careful to bind the Liberal Democrats into a five-year deal, legislating on the date for the next election at an early stage. Both he and Clegg proved adept at keeping their parties committed to the Coalition.[67]

In fact, the survival of the Coalition may well have worked in Labour's long-term favour. By 2015, the economy would be in recovery, leaving Labour, perhaps, with another 1997 scenario – facing a government that had done much of the heavy lifting but which was poorly regarded as a result, and then able to come in to take advantage of an improving situation. More than that, the Conservatives did fulfil their pledge of a referendum on electoral reform. In May 2011, however, electors voted by a two-to-one majority to reject the chance to bring in the alternative vote. The Liberal Democrats then reacted by refusing to support Conservative plans to redistribute parliamentary constituencies, which meant that Labour's inbuilt advantage under the current boundaries would remain in 2015.[68]

One major obstacle for Labour was a continuing perception that Miliband was not up to the job. Too much could be made of this. Many Opposition leaders who have gone on to win power have trailed their parties in the polls – Thatcher in the late 1970s being one example – but this could be a dangerous argument, as Foot had found in the early 1980s. It certainly did not help that most of Miliband's shadow cabinet colleagues also seemed rather anonymous. Many of the more recognizable figures from the Blair/Brown years had retired, or were on the back benches. Darling, not perhaps the most charismatic politician but nonetheless well regarded and a guarantor of probity, was occupied with leading the campaign for a 'No' vote in the September 2014 referendum on Scottish independence. His efforts ended in success but were followed by his retirement from politics.

The period from autumn 2012 did see something of a breakthrough. At that September's party conference, Miliband appeared eager to capture the initiative, doing so particularly in terms of a more emotional and personalized rhetoric designed to make him more appealing and 'human' to voters.[69] This was followed by more tangible statements of intent. In August 2013, he made a stand on foreign policy. The Syrian civil war, raging since 2011, had taken a new and more brutal turn. Many people argued that Britain should join other countries in intervening. Cameron recalled parliament to vote in favour of a motion to pave the way for such intervention. This could have been a difficult moment for Miliband, but he stuck to the non-interventionist line he had set out over Iraq in 2010, leading Labour to vote against the government. In so doing he effectively blocked the possibility of British intervention. Other leaders might have been more easily flattered into a different course of action.

A month later, at the 2013 party conference, Miliband showed that he was prepared to intervene in the market in a way that New Labour had largely shied away from. He promised that a Labour government elected in May 2015 would freeze gas and electricity prices until the start of 2017. This aroused considerable hostile comment from the energy companies and the media, as being an unconscionable interference with the free market. But reaction among voters was much more favourable. Miliband had identified an area where very few people believed that there really was a free market, and where the companies, through byzantine pricing structures, restrictive contracts and the like, were generally felt to be holding consumers at a disadvantage. It was notable that, within months of denouncing the plans, most of the major companies were announcing their own plans to freeze prices. It was heartening for many people – many of them not, ordinarily, Labour supporters – that, for the first time in many years, a

Labour leader was proposing to use government to govern business, rather than to appease it.

Meanwhile, Miliband had also taken up the cause of Labour
Party reform. Ever since his election to the leadership, he had
been concerned about the media's 'Red Ed' image, and the fact
that he could be presented as having only won the leadership
because of union support. His first speech as leader had seen a
brief foray against 'unnecessary strikes'. When it seemed in early
2013 that there had been some local union misbehaviour over
the selection of a parliamentary candidate in the Scottish constituency of Falkirk, he declared that there needed to be a root-
and-branch reform of the party's relations with trade unions.
Many thought that this might be a mistake. But Len McCluskey,
the leader of Unite, the union involved at Falkirk, declared that
he was in favour of reform, in effect turning the issue back to
Miliband. The plans that were subsequently approved by a special
conference in March 2014 included an end to both the bloc vote
and the electoral college, and the building of a mass party with
those paying the unions' political levy being allowed to join the
party proper at a much reduced rate.[70]

It remained to be seen whether, in a context where party membership was falling right across the western world, these reforms
would succeed, but they did at least follow Gaitskell, Wilson and
others in trying to use criticism of the unions to increase a Labour
leader's prestige with the country at large. However, the disappointing results of the May 2014 local elections suggested that
Labour was by no means certain to win the May 2015 general election: its gains were real, but somewhat modest. Worse still, in the
European elections it came second to UKIP, and only marginally
ahead of the Conservatives in the popular vote (25.4 per cent, as
opposed to UKIP's 27.5 per cent and the Conservatives' 23.9).
In terms of seats, it took 20, an increase from the derisory 13 of
2009, but some way behind UKIP's 24 and only one ahead of the
Conservatives. All kinds of caveats could be entered around the
low turnout (34.2 per cent), the fact that a Westminster campaign
would show Labour to better advantage, and so on, but to make
only modest gains on the disastrous European results of 2009
did not suggest that Miliband was going to glide effortlessly into
Downing Street in May 2015. Indeed, UKIP appeared to be making some appeal to Labour's core vote, although not to the extent

alleged in the more hysterical parts of the media.[71] That said, a continuing poll lead and the pro-Labour bias now inherent in the electoral system meant that it would still be quite an achievement on Miliband's part to fail to win the premiership in 2015.

For much of the period between 1997 and 2007, Labour had looked as though it might never lose an election again. The Conservatives had been the dream opposition for Blair – usually divided and seemingly unable to make any serious appeal to contemporary Britain. But their recovery under Cameron, plus a combination of economic difficulty, poor leadership and political exhaustion, had meant that Brown had been unable to reinvent Labour or the government in the wake of Blair's years in control. Instead, he had presided over a government that seemed, for too much of its tenure, to be crawling towards its doom. From 2010 onwards, Ed Miliband's attempts to revive the party had some successes.[72] For most of the period, Labour led in the polls, but not by a margin that suggested that he had found a clear solution. The victory of the 'No' campaign in the referendum on Scottish independence in September 2014 did mean that one of Labour's strongest areas was not lost to the UK. But Miliband's role in the campaign had been unimpressive, and it remained to be seen whether his attempts at renewal would be convincing enough to oust the Coalition and bring Labour back to power, or whether the party would face a further defeat and a consequent change in leadership and direction as a consequence. But there was a lot to play for because if, as expected, the period to 2020 was likely to be characterized by economic recovery, the election of 2015 would be a very good one to win, and a particularly bad one to lose.

Conclusion

Britain has changed dramatically in the period since 1900, and the Labour Party of today is a very different body from the Labour Representation Committee that was formed in that year. The largely chronological treatment of the party's history which has formed the body of this book has aimed to tease out developments as they took place. However, such an approach risks losing some of the broad themes that characterized those developments, and so this Conclusion will try to identify some of those themes, before ending with a few comments about the unities that have made the party viable, as well as some of the divisions that have, at times, hindered it, but which have also allowed it the flexibility needed to survive as a major force in British politics.

Labour and the Electorate

There was little that was 'inevitable' about the rise of the Labour Party. Some recasting of British politics was taking place before the First World War, but its effects were not likely to be revolutionary. Had there been no war, Labour would probably have expanded over time at the expense of the Liberals, but the speed of the transformation is inexplicable without reference to the First World War. Even then, Labour did not really 'replace' the Liberals: the process was slower, messier and, certainly up to 1945, much less complete than such a formulation would allow.

Before 1914, the party put up relatively few candidates, but it is fairly clear that its main strength was concentrated in working-class areas of relatively heavy trade union density in northern England. It fared less well in the larger cities, though, while its performance in mining areas was problematic. After 1918, and still more from 1922, however, it developed a stranglehold on the coalfields, and made significant progress in many – though not all – of Britain's big cities. The more working-class areas of most

304

cities were fairly solid for Labour, helped by the shift of the majority of Catholic voters to Labour from the early 1920s onwards.
However, expansion beyond the working class was unimpressive. The 1920s were characterized by a battle between Labour,
Conservatives and Liberals for the political centre ground.
Labour did not win that battle in the 1920s, but nor did anyone
else. After 1929, however, Labour had clearly lost it, and from
1931 onwards it had equally clearly been won by the National
government. Although Labour had some middle-class support in
the 1930s, its support prior to 1939 was overwhelmingly working
class, and coming particularly from that section of the working
class which worked in the staple industries.

After 1945, things changed somewhat. Labour became rather
more effective at appealing to wider sections of the working class,
and made a stronger appeal to middle-class voters, although the
great majority the latter continued to vote Conservative. The
growing fragmentation of the middle class and the rise of white-
collar trade unionism helped Labour. There were signs as early
as 1950 that skilled workers were becoming less willing to offer
automatic support to Labour, but 1950s predictions of imminent
'embourgeoisement' were premature; 1964 can be seen, indeed,
as a peak of class voting. However, after 1966 it is quite clear that
working-class voters, particularly skilled workers, became more
critical of Labour, and the process of defection was especially
marked in 1970 and again from 1979 to 1987. In the latter period,
Thatcher's appeal seems to have struck a chord with skilled workers, especially in the south and the Midlands. On the other hand,
middle-class people employed in the public sector did, arguably,
begin to loosen their ties to Conservatism, as that sector came
under increasing attack from government; but even here the
process was not straightforward, particularly given the formation of the SDP and later the Alliance. In 1997 both lower-middle
class and skilled working-class voters swung heavily towards
Labour. This was partly because they had been alienated by the
Conservatives' performance in office, especially in relation to the
economy. But it also redounded to Blair's credit; New Labour,
at the very least, did not frighten them off, and, at most, offered
a positive appeal of a new and brighter future. Perceptions of
Conservative incompetence were then compounded, while Blair's
government, certainly in its first term, did little to repel such

voters, so that the 2001 election saw almost a re-run of 1997. By the mid-2000s, and especially once the modernizing Cameron took over from Howard, there were signs of Conservative recovery in these social groups. The decline of class voting, and of voter identification with particular parties, meant that there was greater potential for electoral volatility than in past eras, and Labour support fell away badly in 2010.

As suggested above, Labour's support has been geographically varied. Up to 1914, industrial northern England was the key area, although even it could hardly be called a heartland, and most seats would have been difficult to retain in the face of Liberal opposition. After 1918, Labour rapidly developed heartlands in the mining areas, to the extent that 16 of the 17 seats with the largest proportion of miners in their male working population remained Labour even at the 1931 election. The strongest areas of all in this respect were south Wales and the Yorks, Notts and Derby coalfield area around Sheffield. These areas remained the core of Labour's support, with the rest of industrial northern England, the Midlands (the east Midlands being more committed to Labour than the west), Scotland (the west being safer Labour territory than the east) and London all weighing in during the interwar period. After 1945, these areas generally supported Labour more consistently than they had done before the war.

However, the party's performance remained patchy in the west Midlands, particularly from 1959 onwards, and in eastern Scotland; and the east Midlands also became a problem area for Labour from 1979 onwards. More problematic still has been England south of the Severn–Wash line, outside the London region. Between the wars there were 134 seats in this area, of which Labour won 17 in 1923 and 22 in 1929. These figures were bad enough in themselves, but even more startling is that at no other election before 1945 did the party win as many as five seats in this region. In 1945 Labour won 59 of the 140 seats in the area, but its performances thereafter were less impressive, and although it recovered to win 42 of the 152 seats in 1966, it won only 15 in 1970. After a rally at the two elections of 1974, it won only 13 seats here in 1979, and its performances in the elections of 1983 and 1987 (three out of 182) and 1992 (10 out of 183), with many Labour candidates being pushed into third place behind the Alliance/Liberal Democrats, were abysmal. Labour's failure here highlights not only its weakness in rural, farming and middle-class areas but also its inability to construct large enough groups of loyal working-class voters in these areas. During the 1980s and 1990s, it seemed that Labour might never break out of this trap. But it did so in 1997, winning almost 60 seats, including eight of the 17 in Kent where it had not held a seat since 1979. However, this was the area where Labour fell back most markedly in 2005, and in 2010 it held only 10 of the 197 seats in the region, which was no better than in 1992.[1] Labour clearly needed a leader who could play as well to southern England as the early Blair had been able to do. Ironically, if Scotland had voted for independence in September 2014 it might have forced this issue – of how to make a stronger appeal to southern England – more centrally onto Labour's agenda. As it was, the sense of a solid phalanx of Scottish (and, come to that, Welsh) Labour MPs enabled the party to continue to underthink its relationship with a large part of the largest country in the United Kingdom.

For much of Labour's history, there was a significant gender differential in its support base. With the sole exception of 1987, every general election between 1918 and 1992 saw a higher proportion of men than of women vote Labour. Numerous reasons for this can be suggested: women lived longer than men and older people were, generally, more likely to vote Conservative than their younger counterparts; for most of the twentieth century, women were less exposed to trade unionism (even at the peak of union membership, 1979, only 38.8 per cent of eligible women were trade union members, as opposed to 65.6 per cent of men); Conservative governments were sometimes more willing to legislate on 'women's issues' than Labour (the 1920s being a case in point); and Conservative rhetoric of domesticity probably had a considerable appeal for much of the period, certainly when set against Labour's hesitant feminism. But the Labour Party must also be held responsible. For much of the period, its close identification with trade unions primarily representing men, and its rather 'macho' image overall, often suggested that it had less to offer women than men. However, from the early 1990s the position changed significantly. From the late 1970s onwards, women formed an increasing proportion of trade unionists. After 2002, a higher proportion of female than male employees were union members; from 2005 there were more female union members than male; and by 2012, 55 per cent of union members were women.[2] This, and the influence of feminism within the movement dating back to the 1960s, led the party to pay increasing attention to such matters. The introduction of quotas was an important step in this regard. So too was the concern of the Blair and Brown governments with issues surrounding women as workers and mothers; in policy terms, it was far more concerned than any of its predecessors with questions of equality. It is not altogether surprising that at the 2005 and 2010 general elections a higher proportion of women voted Labour than of men.

In terms of ethnicity and religion, Labour has tended to appeal to minority groups to a greater extent than the Conservatives. This was certainly the case in the first half of the twentieth century in relation to British citizens of Irish Catholic origin, a key group in many major cities whose historic links with the Liberals dissolved between 1916 and 1923, and whose support Labour was quick to seek despite the strongly Protestant bent of much of Labour's early leadership. Labour also made a strong appeal to many Jewish voters, especially the more recent immigrants among them, although here the policies of the 1929–31 and 1945–51 governments towards Palestine and, latterly, Israel were complicating factors, as was the appeal of Communism, although the latter fell away significantly once it became clear in the later 1940s that Stalin was pursuing strongly anti-Semitic policies in the USSR. From mid-century, Labour tended to draw the bulk of the support of 'New Commonwealth' immigrants from Asia and the Caribbean. Even so, the party's reluctance to upset some parts of its white voter base, shading off in some cases into sheer racism, inhibited its approach to ethnic minority voters. It seems even more remarkable in retrospect than it did at the time that Labour's first four Black or Asian MPs were only elected to parliament in 1987. Since then, the number has increased, but much remains to be done. It might well be suggested that Labour has got more from its ethnic minority supporters than vice versa.

Labour and Trade Unionism

The basic reason for the formation of the Labour Party was defensive. It was not the mark of a working class rising up to take power, but a body established to protect the rights of workers, and of trade unions in particular, at a time when they were coming under renewed threat. This is not to say that it was a 'narrowly' trade union party; for one thing, many trade unionists defined the scope of union concerns very widely indeed, to cover not just industrial relations questions but also full employment and economic policy, social welfare, and, increasingly, foreign policy. The fact that socialists were often eloquent and ready to work on such matters made them good allies for the unions. There were, of course, tensions, but these can be over-stressed, since many trade unionists were also socialists, and the generally moderate, 'businesslike' approach of most of the party's leading groups tended to chime in with union attitudes (although there were often tensions between unions and the party leadership when Labour was in government, especially in 1929–31, 1966–70 and 1977–79).

The link to trade unionism was not beneficial in all ways, however: in particular, at times when trade unionism was weak and/or unpopular, it allowed Labour to be portrayed as sectarian and/or 'unpatriotic'. At the same time, though, trade unions provided Labour with the wherewithal to set out and establish itself as an independent political party, and helped to provide a positive set of values that included a sense of community, a coherence of approach and a mode of political conduct (for example, loyalty to majority decisions). In the early days of New Labour, there was considerable talk about the possibility of a 'divorce' between the party and the unions. However, the hopes of some of the architects of New Labour that the party would somehow become financially independent of the unions were thwarted. Whether they liked it or not, ministers knew that the unions were still important to the party. Yet the other prediction often made – that the unions would cause Labour considerable trouble once in office – did not really transpire, either. In the first term, in particular, most unions were reasonably pliant, as they awaited the enactment of cherished policies such as the statutory right to recognition and the minimum wage. After that, there was more friction, as a number of unions elected new, more left-wing leaders. But the predicted 'showdown' did not materialize, and the 'Warwick agreement' of 2004 was more remarkable for the ease with which it was reached than as a symbol of endemic conflict. The union movement in the twenty-first century was, in reality, very different, and in many ways much weaker, than that of 30 or 40 years earlier, and its leaders realized that they must not over-exert, or over-assert, themselves. This in turn enabled Miliband to win approval for significant developments in the relationship in 2014. On that basis, there was no reason why the Labour–union link should not continue, to the profit of both parties.

Labour and Socialism

The Labour Party always contained socialists; from 1918, it was committed programmatically to socialism. Yet the party as a body did not, for most of its history, spend too much time thinking hard about how to produce a socialist society. This is not to argue that socialism was unimportant, however. The very vagueness of 'socialism' as a concept meant it could act as a unifying myth when all else failed. It inspired party activists to humdrum tasks like canvassing, collecting and committee work, connecting all such activities into a grander design. At the same time, it acted as a magnet to the left, which, along with the adversarial tendency of British politics fostered by the electoral system, helped to keep the party together and prevent breakaways (it was for this reason, partly, that Clause IV was adopted in 1918). However, while socialism had a valuable unifying effect, it also enabled Labour to be portrayed by its opponents as extremist and doctrinaire.

There were always radical socialists, even revolutionaries, within the Labour Party. Yet they were far from being typical. For most of its history, Labour was dominated by a much less radical view of socialism, which had more similarities with German revisionism of the late nineteenth and early twentieth centuries than with classic Marxism. This approach was predicated on the potential of capitalism to prosper in such a way as to deliver social 'goods' through increased revenues for government. This allowed Labour to be consensual, avoiding issues such as widespread redistribution of existing wealth, and chimed in with the essentially defensive nature of the trade unions' input. However, it also meant that Labour tended to fare worst in periods of economic recession, for obvious reasons. In those periods the left tended to become stronger, with its talk of the need for radical change rather than merely 'tinkering' with a failing capitalist system. But the left was always the weaker end of the party, and although in the 1930s, and again in the 1970s and early 1980s, it was strong enough to split the party, it was unable to control it for any length of time. At only one point, in the early 1970s, did the left really sit down and think hard about policy, the result being the 1973 programme. But even this was a mixed blessing: first, because the left failed spectacularly to convert the existing party leadership to its views or, failing that, to change the leadership; second, because the programme was not as coherent or robust as was usually claimed; third, because the left failed to explain its message to the electorate, relying increasingly on sloganizing; and finally because, once adopted, the policy became a touchstone of faith rather than a live programme evolving with changing circumstances. For the rest, the left was usually quite easily marginalized.

Under Blair, the word 'socialism' was rarely used at all. But this was a less dramatic change than some suggested. After all, his predecessors had not chanted the old Clause IV ritualistically in their speeches. Conversely, the 'new' Clause IV of 1995 did state boldly that Labour was 'a democratic socialist party', and despite 13 years of Blair's leadership, socialism did not wholly lose its cachet among party members. Its continuing resonance could be seen when a number of the deputy leadership candidates in 2007 used the word. Brown as Prime Minister was firmly committed to a statist approach, while Ed Miliband was not slow to stress the need for collectivist solutions to social and economic problems. Perhaps more significantly, Labour remains deeply concerned about the issues of social justice that were once taken to define people as socialists. In those senses, then, there has been more continuity with the past than is often suggested.

Labour in Government

There have been six periods of Labour government in Britain. The first five of these, before 1997, totalled just under 20 years. Those governments had very mixed fortunes. That of 1924 was intended mainly to show that Labour could govern; it was not really expected to deliver a great deal in terms of concrete changes, and nor did it. Labour was, later, unfortunate enough to win the 1929 general election: and its second government, ill prepared for reasonably stable times, let alone the economic blizzard which it did ultimately face, lurched along until it was finally crushed by the financial crisis and its own ineptitude in the summer of 1931. The third period in office, after the Second World War, was much more successful, in many ways, fulfilling a large part of the party's programme and setting the agenda for British government for a generation. The fourth period in office, between 1964 and 1970, has excited considerable debate. Since the early 1990s, the condemnatory views of years past have given way to a much more balanced, perhaps even over-sympathetic orthodoxy which stresses the extreme difficulties the government faced and the fact that, even if the government did not always have the answers, it at least asked the 'right' questions about society, the economy and the state of Britain. The Labour government of 1974–79 is still held in the popular memory as, according to taste, simply incompetent or a betrayal of all that Labour stood for. But over the past decade, historians have begun to offer a rather softer verdict: that it is hard to see how much more could have been achieved in the economic circumstances in which the government was forced to operate, and that the government did, at least after Callaghan's succession to the premiership in 1976, have some purpose and success according to its own aspirations. The Blair government, naturally, excited very mixed views. It has been suggested above that although the government did not fulfil all the hyperbolic rhetoric of the 1994–97 period, it achieved far more than many of its critics have allowed. Its work in areas like economic management, health and education can be seen as very positive. On the other hand, its performance in relation to foreign affairs (at least in relation to Iraq), housing and transport was far less so, and serious questions were also asked about the government's tone and style. Verdicts on the Brown government are unlikely to be overly favourable. It is important to give Brown credit for his handling of the world financial and economic crises, but otherwise he was unable to articulate a compelling vision for his government, which deflated slowly to defeat in 2010. It was noteworthy that, like three earlier long-suffering heirs apparent (Balfour, Chamberlain and Eden), Brown's premiership lasted only a few years before collapsing ignominiously.

Before 1997, Labour governments contributed little to constitutional reform. Between the wars, some people wanted to give greater powers to local government, but nothing was done. The Attlee governments were centralizing in their effects, but did little to reform the state machine which was taking on so many new functions. The governments of the 1960s did at least begin to look at reform, with investigations of the House of Lords, devolution and the civil service, but little came of any of these, and the devolution legislation of the 1970s owed more to political expediency than conviction (and did not come into effect in any case). There was a revival of talk of constitutional change in the 1980s. Although much of this was due to the fact that it seemed that only by changing the goalposts could Thatcher be stopped, the Blair government did implement extensive innovations. The Scottish parliament, the Welsh National Assembly, elected mayors and House of Lords reform were all radical changes. However, they brought their own problems. Labour's loss of control of both the Scottish parliament and the Welsh assembly in May 2007 showed this very well. At times, devolution seemed to sit ill with a party leadership that remained keen to control all aspects of Labour Party life from the centre. It was one thing to play the leading part in defeating Scottish independence at the 2014 referendum, but quite another to set out how a future Labour government at Westminster would relate to and work with its counterparts in Edinburgh and Cardiff: Miliband's signing up to a three-party declaration offering more extensive devolution in the event of a 'No' vote in the final stages of the campaign might have been politic, but it looked weak and suggested that Labour had too little that was positive and distinctive to offer on the subject. After all, the Blair government had soon retreated from any thought of electoral reform for the Westminster parliament, or of English regional assemblies.

Labour governments have been much more concerned with economic management, not surprisingly since they have seen a prosperous economy as the key to reform in other areas. Here their record has been mixed, although it has to be added that, in retrospect, Labour won some elections which it might have been better to have lost, such as those of 1929 and 1974. The 1929–31 ministry has to go down as the least successful, but, otherwise, Labour governments have not performed too badly. That of 1924 proved that the economy would not collapse under Labour. Attlee and his colleagues managed a sensible and effective transition of the economy from war to peace. The 1964–70 administration might not have been so heavily criticized for its economic failings had the critics known of the worse times that were to follow and had the government not pitched its aims in this area so high. The 1970s government, whatever its failings in other areas, did at least bring inflation under some degree of control. Between 1997 and 2007, Blair and Brown presided over considerable levels of economic prosperity and apparent stability. And, between 2007 and 2010, Labour avoided financial disaster on the one hand and a too-harsh series of austerity measures on the other.

Labour liked to see itself as the party that would make the economy grow faster, and hence enable government to spend more on social projects, but here its success was more limited. Labour governments were not helped by coming into office in difficult economic times, but, even after allowing for this, little progress was made. The party was often too eager to seize upon panaceas – rationalization in the 1920s, planning and nationalization in the 1940s, the 'white heat' of technology in the 1960s – and did too little to work out, when in opposition, what these things actually involved in practice. In particular, the legacy of nationalization was hardly one of which the party could be proud, other than in terms of keeping people in employment in the industries concerned. The result was that policy was often ineffective in promoting higher growth rates.

Even allowing for the fact that the economy generally remained sluggish, Labour governments did achieve much of value in social policy. Pride of place here must go to the NHS, which from a very early stage was identified positively with Labour. In housing, too, Labour governments could point to a reasonable, although not entirely unmixed, record. This was the one area of domestic policy where both the first and second Labour governments acquitted themselves well, whereas the inability to build more houses more quickly was one of the chief failings of the Attlee years. In the 1960s, quantity was less of a problem, but there were question marks about the quality and suitability of many of the housing units completed. And by 2010, there was widespread criticism of Labour's failure since 1997 to do more to promote house-building in general and the construction of affordable and social housing in particular. Less was done in education by the early governments, but both Wilson's and Blair's administrations had more success here. Overall, Labour could claim both that it was the creator of the post-war Welfare State and that, even when out of office, its presence in opposition provided a brake on any Conservative impulses to make significant cuts in provision.

In external affairs, Labour's performance was mixed. Its first two governments seemed at their most successful in this area, even if their achievements were ultimately to prove ephemeral. The Attlee government, for its part, established the parameters for British foreign policy for the Cold War; and while the fact of that 'conflict' can be regretted, once it is accepted that Britain had a problem in the late 1940s, then that government solved it by ensuring the continuing commitment of the USA to European security through NATO. In the 1960s, Wilson's government struggled to cover Britain's extensive commitments, given its limited resources: the culminating points of the process were the decisions to seek entry to the EEC and then to withdraw from east of Suez. Increasingly, by the late 1960s, the Commonwealth was being seen as an irrelevance by Labour policy makers; but this was not an intended outcome. Earlier Labour governments had been enthusiasts for greater exploitation of the colonies. British decolonization was not the result of a planned Labour assault on imperialism; the withdrawals from India in 1947 and Palestine in 1948 were intended, in part, better to enable Britain to concentrate on those areas that it could still control, rather than to launch the end of empire. In respect of Europe, meanwhile, Labour's approaches were characterized by splits throughout the 1960s and 1970s, culminating with a pledge to withdraw at the 1983 election. The party moved to a much more pro-European stance from the late 1980s onwards, and it was believed by the mid-1990s that Labour's travails on the matter were over. But this was not the case, and the Blair government was always divided on the single currency, among other matters. Indeed, under Blair and Brown, the balance of British diplomacy shifted much more towards the United States. Here, Blair's support for the Americans over Iraq may have been honestly motivated, but the methods by which Britain moved towards war seemed dishonest, and have done more than any other thing to damage his reputation, many would say deservedly so. It is hard to see a future Labour prime minister eagerly following his example. Brown withdrew forces with alacrity when he got the chance, and Miliband's opposition to intervention in Syria in 2013 was driven directly by his memories of how Blair had allowed Britain to become embroiled in Afghanistan and Iraq.

The picture of Labour in government at national level, then, is a very mixed one, with real successes countered by significant failures. Meanwhile, it must also be remembered that the national picture is not the sum total of Labour's achievements in government. Even before the formation of the LRC, 'Labour' members were being elected to local councils, school boards and so on. After 1918 there was a surge of Labour representation, particularly in the larger towns and cities. Many areas of the country, such as south Wales, or Sheffield, have been under almost constant Labour control ever since the 1920s or 1930s. Further advances were made after 1945. As local government gradually lost functions to Whitehall, the scope for local initiative was reduced (a process accelerated, it should be remembered, by Labour governments, particularly that of 1945–51). And yet it is clear that Labour local authorities have often contributed towards improving the lives of their citizens in areas like housing, sanitation and education. Labour in local government was not always good news, of course. Labour authorities were sometimes inefficient; occasionally they were corrupt. It has perhaps not been altogether healthy that, at local level, so many parts of the country have been under virtual one-party rule for so long (although until recently the same point could have been made about the vast swathes of Britain that never elected anything other than a Conservative or an 'Independent' council).

Having said all that, it must be doubted whether there would have been so much 'progress' in twentieth-century Britain without the existence of the Labour Party. Even in opposition, its presence was usually a warning to its opponents not to go too far in the other direction.

Unities and Disunities: A Final Word

What kept Labour together? First, it was committed to liberal parliamentary democracy, not even giving up on this in the early 1930s. The party was committed to the British state, although this commitment could coexist, for many, with devolution for Scotland and Wales, and sometimes for the English regions, or with a greater degree of European integration, or with a commitment to internationalism. Although not pacifist, it was a party of peace, believing that war was a catastrophe which would hit no one harder than the working people who comprised the bulk of its supporters, and seeing peace as the first prerequisite of the 'ordered progress' to which the party was committed (somewhat ironically, given the importance of the two world wars in boosting Labour's fortunes). The party was committed in policy terms to reducing the uncertainties and arbitrariness which seemed to be inherent in the unregulated market system. It advocated greater security for people, especially at work; and if full employment could not be delivered, then the unemployed had a right to benefits to alleviate their suffering. This desire for security and fairness also meant that Labour was committed to social reform on a considerable scale and, rhetorically at least (after 1918), to 'socialism', although this had perhaps more value as a unifying myth than as a guide to immediate action. The party was also, of course, committed to trade unionism, although some Labour supporters were lukewarm about it in practice, and there was debate about the exact role of the unions in the party under capitalism and in the socialist state which, it was hoped, would succeed it at some point in the future.

Here, then, was a solid basis for unity, which essentially held the party together even at times of pressure. Without understanding these forces for unity one cannot begin to comprehend why it was that, apparently despite the odds, Labour survived the First World War virtually intact (with only a few defections to Coalition Labour in 1918); why it could manage, almost uniquely among moderate left parties in Europe, to avoid a major split resulting in the formation of a strong Communist Party; why it was able to shrug off the formation of no fewer than three new parties from its ranks in a little over a year in 1931–32; and why the SDP did not draw off more Labourites than it did. Even after a decade of moves to the right, the left-wing rebellion which resulted in the formation of Scargill's Socialist Labour Party in 1996 aroused more condemnation than support from the Labour left. And Bob Crow of the National Union of Rail, Maritime and Transport Workers (RMT) might have been the best-known union leader in Britain for most of the decade up to his death in 2014, but despite leading the RMT out of the Labour Party in 2004, his calls for the establishment of a new left party had no effect at all.

At the same time, a number of things divided the party. There were splits between nationalists and internationalists, further complicated, after the Second World War, by a third group who saw the best expression of Labour's internationalism as entry into the EEC/EU. There were arguments over the role of the state: by mid-century, Labour had become a largely statist party, but this should not mask the fact that many remained committed to a greater role for local government, industrial democracy and so on. There were divergent views of the working class: should it be accepted as it was, or pushed towards more 'wholesome' habits; was it the role of the party to give 'the people' what they wanted, or to educate them into wanting something 'better'? In economic policy, there were differences between those who advocated full public control and those who felt that the market had a role to play, and much of the party's history in this area is one of an uneasy compromise. There was also the question of gender. Labour liked to claim that it was the 'women's party', yet it was often deeply divided. For some periods the claim was patently absurd, because, at least until the 1990s, Labour almost always put men first. Having said all that, these splits can be seen not as a weakness (although at times they did little to help the party's fortunes) but as a source of strength. The fact that the party often faced in more than one direction, but had a strong core of unity underlying it, meant that it was able to draw support quite widely. Being, in Wilson's phrase, a 'broad church' made it robust, not brittle.

As Labour proceeds deeper into its second century, it will need that robustness if it is to prosper. It has a fairly strong base from which to proceed. But the events of 2007–10 were enough to show how quickly political fortunes can change. Structural factors, and luck, play a part in these considerations, but politicians can, and should, also help to determine their own fortunes. If Labour is to prosper in the twenty-first century to a greater extent than it did in the twentieth, it must ensure that it embraces a politics that is sufficiently exciting to arouse its activists and members, while at the same time remaining credible and relevant enough to the wider population. The specification is easily outlined; it can prove more difficult to fulfil. Whatever the outcome, the party will, assuredly, continue to provide rich pickings for the historians of the future.

Appendix 1: Seats and Percentage of Votes Won at General Elections, 1900–2010

Year	Labour	Conservative & Allies[a]	Liberal[b, c]	Other	Total
1900	2	402	183	83	670
	1.3	50.3	45.0	3.4	100.0
1906	29	156	399	86	670
	4.8	43.4	49.4	2.4	100.0
1910 (Jan.)	40	272	274	84	670
	7.0	46.8	43.5	2.7	100.0
1910 (Dec.)	42	272	272	84	670
	6.4	46.6	44.2	2.8	100.0
1918	57	473	36	141	707
	20.8	47.1	25.6	6.5	100.0
1922	142	344	115	14	615
	29.7	38.5	28.8	3.0	100.0
1923	191	258	158	8	615
	30.7	38.0	29.7	1.6	100.0
1924	151	412	40	12	615
	33.3	46.8	17.8	2.3	100.0
1929	287	260	59	9	615
	37.1	38.1	23.5	1.3	100.0
1931	46	554	(b)	15	615
	29.3	67.2	(b)	3.5	100.0
1935	154	429	21	11	615
	38.0	53.5	6.7	1.8	100.0
1945	393	210	12	25	640
	48.0	39.6	9.0	3.4	100.0
1950	315	298	9	3	625
	46.1	43.4	9.1	1.4	100.0
1951	295	321	2	3	625
	48.8	48.0	2.6	0.6	100.0

(continued)

Continued

Year	Labour	Conservative & Allies[a]	Liberal[b, c]	Other	Total
1955	277	345	6	2	630
	46.4	49.7	2.7	1.2	100.0
1959	258	365	6	1	630
	43.8	49.4	5.9	0.9	100.0
1964	317	304	9	0	630
	44.1	43.4	11.2	1.3	100.0
1966	364	253	12	1	630
	48.0	41.9	8.5	1.6	100.0
1970	288	330	6	6	630
	43.1	46.4	7.5	3.0	100.0
1974 (Feb.)	301	297	14	23	635
	37.2	37.9	19.3	5.6	100.0
1974 (Oct.)	319	277	13	26	635
	39.2	35.8	18.3	6.7	100.0
1979	269	339	11	16	635
	36.9	43.9	13.8	5.4	100.0
1983	209	397	23	21	650
	27.6	42.4	25.4	4.6	100.0
1987	229	376	22	23	650
	30.8	42.3	22.6	4.3	100.0
1992	271	336	20	24	651
	34.4	41.9	17.8	5.9	100.0
1997	418	165	46	30	659
	43.2	30.7	16.8	9.3	100.0
2001	412	166	52	29	659
	40.7	31.7	18.3	9.3	100.0
2005	356	198	62	31	646
	35.2	32.4	22.0	10.4	100.0
2010	258	305	57	30	650
	29.0	36.1	23.0	11.9	100.0

Source: Figures for table taken from C. Rallings and M. Thrasher, *British Electoral Facts 1832–2006* (Aldershot, 2007); BBC website for 2010.

Notes

[a] Lloyd George Coalition in 1918; National government in 1931 and 1935.

[b] In 1931, a total of 72 Liberals were elected in various guises, namely 35 Liberal Nationals, who remained part of the National government and eventually joined the Conservatives; 33 official Liberals, who later withdrew support from the National government; and four others, led by Lloyd George, who opposed the government throughout.

[c] Liberal/SDP Alliance in 1983 and 1987; Liberal Democrats since 1992.

Appendix 2: Labour Party Leaders

Chairman of the Parliamentary Labour Party, 1906–22

1906–08	Keir Hardie
1908–10	Arthur Henderson
1910–11	George Barnes
1911–14	Ramsay MacDonald
1914–17	Arthur Henderson
1917–21	William Adamson
1921–22	John Clynes

Leader of the Labour Party

1922–31	Ramsay MacDonald
1931–32	Arthur Henderson
1932–35	George Lansbury
1935–55	Clement Attlee
1955–63	Hugh Gaitskell
1963–76	Harold Wilson
1976–80	James Callaghan
1980–83	Michael Foot
1983–92	Neil Kinnock
1992–94	John Smith
1994–2007	Tony Blair
2007–2010	Gordon Brown
2010–date	Edward Miliband

Appendix 3: Labour Cabinets

MacDonald's Cabinet, January to November 1924

Prime Minister and Foreign Secretary	J. R. MacDonald
Lord Chancellor	Viscount Haldane
Lord President	Lord Parmoor
Lord Privy Seal	J. R. Clynes
Chancellor of the Exchequer	P. Snowden
Home Secretary	A. Henderson
Colonial Secretary	J. H. Thomas
War Secretary	S. Walsh
Indian Secretary	Lord Olivier
Scottish Secretary	W. Adamson
Air Secretary	Lord Thomson
First Lord of Admiralty	Viscount Chelmsford
Chancellor, Duchy of Lancaster	J. Wedgwood
President, Board of Trade	S. Webb
Minister of Agriculture	N. Buxton
President, Board of Education	C. P. Trevelyan
Postmaster General	V. Hartshorn
First Commissioner of Works	F. W. Jowett
Minister of Labour	T. Shaw
Minister of Health	J. Wheatley

MacDonald's Cabinet, June 1929 to August 1931

Prime Minister	J. R. MacDonald
Lord Chancellor	Lord Sankey
Lord President	Lord Parmoor
Lord Privy Seal	J. H. Thomas (to June 1930)
	V. Hartshorn (June 1930 to March 1931)
	T. Johnston (from March 1931)

Chancellor of the Exchequer	P. Snowden
Home Secretary	J. R. Clynes
Foreign Secretary	A. Henderson
Colonial Secretary	Lord Passfield
Dominions Secretary	Lord Passfield (to June 1930)
	J. H. Thomas (from June 1930)
War Secretary	T. Shaw
Indian Secretary	W. Wedgwood Benn
Scottish Secretary	W. Adamson
Air Secretary	Lord Thomson (to October 1930)
	Lord Amulree (from October 1930)
First Lord of Admiralty	A. V. Alexander
President, Board of Trade	W. Graham
Minister of Agriculture	N. Buxton (to June 1930)
	C. Addison (from June 1930)
President, Board of Education	Sir C. P. Trevelyan (to March 1931)
	H. B. Lees-Smith (from March 1931)
First Commissioner of Works	G. Lansbury
Minister of Labour	M. Bondfield
Minister of Health	Arthur Greenwood
Minister of Transport	H. Morrison (in cabinet from March 1931)

Attlee's Cabinet, July 1945 to October 1951

Prime Minister	C. R. Attlee
Lord Chancellor	Lord Jowitt
Lord President	H. Morrison (to March 1951)
	Lord Addison (from March 1951)
Lord Privy Seal	Arthur Greenwood (to April 1947)
	Lord Inman (April to October 1947)
	Lord Addison (October 1947 to March 1951)
	E. Bevin (March to April 1951)
	R. Stokes (from April 1951)
Chancellor of the Exchequer	H. Dalton (to November 1947)
	Sir S. Cripps (November 1947 to October 1950)
	H. Gaitskell (from October 1950)

Minister of Economic Affairs	Sir S. Cripps (September to November 1947)
Home Secretary	C. Ede
Foreign Secretary	E. Bevin (to March 1951)
	H. Morrison (from March 1951)
Colonial Secretary	G. Hall (to October 1946)
	A. Creech Jones (October 1946 to February 1950)
	J. Griffiths (from February 1950)
Dominions Secretary (Commonwealth Relations from July 1947)	Lord Addison (to October 1947)
	P. Noel-Baker (October 1947 to February 1950)
	P. Gordon Walker (from February 1950)
Defence Secretary	C. R. Attlee (to December 1946)
	A. V. Alexander (December 1946 to February 1950)
	E. Shinwell (from February 1950)
War Secretary	J. Lawson (to October 1946)
Indian Secretary	Lord Pethick-Lawrence (to April 1947)
	Earl of Listowel (April to August 1947)
Scottish Secretary	J. Westwood (to October 1947)
	A. Woodburn (October 1947 to February 1950)
	H. McNeil (from February 1950)
Air Secretary	Viscount Stansgate (to October 1946)
Minister of Civil Aviation	Lord Pakenham (May 1948 to February 1950)
First Lord of Admiralty	A. V. Alexander (to October 1946)
Chancellor, Duchy of Lancaster	H. Dalton (May 1948 to February 1950)
	Viscount Alexander (from February 1950)
President, Board of Trade	Sir S. Cripps (to September 1947)
	H. Wilson (September 1947 to April 1951)
	Sir H. Shawcross (from April 1951)
Minister of Agriculture	T. Williams

Minister of Education	E. Wilkinson (to February 1947)
	G. Tomlinson (from February 1947)
Minister of Labour and National Service	G. Isaacs (to January 1951)
	A. Bevan (January to April 1951)
	A. Robens (from April 1951)
Minister of Health	A. Bevan (to January 1951)
Minister, Town & Country Planning	H. Dalton (from February 1950)
Paymaster General	Arthur Greenwood (July 1946 to March 1947)
	Viscount Addison (July 1948 to April 1949)
Minister of Fuel and Power	E. Shinwell (to October 1947)
Minister without Portfolio	A. V. Alexander (October to December 1946)
	Arthur Greenwood (April to September 1947)

Wilson's Cabinet, October 1964 to June 1970

Prime Minister	H. Wilson
First Secretary of State	G. Brown (to August 1966)
	M. Stewart (August 1966 to March 1968)
	B. Castle (from April 1968)
Lord Chancellor	Lord Gardiner
Lord President	H. Bowden (to August 1966)
	R. Crossman (August 1966 to October 1968)
	F. Peart (from October 1968)
Lord Privy Seal	Earl of Longford (to December 1965)
	Sir F. Soskice (December 1965 to April 1966)
	Earl of Longford (April 1966 to January 1968)
	Lord Shackleton (January to April 1968)
	F. Peart (April to October 1968)
	Lord Shackleton (from October 1968)

Chancellor of the Exchequer	J. Callaghan (to November 1967)
	R. Jenkins (from November 1967)
Chief Secretary to Treasury	J. Diamond (from November 1968)
Economic Affairs Secretary	G. Brown (to August 1966)
	M. Stewart (August 1966 to August 1967)
	P. Shore (August 1967 to October 1969)
Home Secretary	Sir F. Soskice (to December 1965)
	R. Jenkins (December 1965 to November 1967)
	J. Callaghan (from November 1967)
Foreign Secretary	P. Gordon Walker (to January 1965)
	M. Stewart (January 1965 to August 1966)
	G. Brown (August 1966 to March 1968)
	M. Stewart (from March 1968)
Commonwealth Secretary	A. Bottomley (to August 1966)
	H. Bowden (August 1966 to August 1967)
	G. Thomson (August 1967 to October 1968)
Scottish Secretary	W. Ross
Welsh Secretary	J. Griffiths (to April 1966)
	C. Hughes (April 1966 to April 1968)
	G. Thomas (from April 1968)
Chancellor, Duchy of Lancaster	D. Houghton (to April 1966)
	G. Thomson (from October 1969)
President, Board of Trade	D. Jay (to August 1967)
	A. Crosland (August 1967 to October 1969)
	R. Mason (from October 1969)
Minister of Technology	F. Cousins (to July 1966)
	A. Benn (from July 1966)

Minister of Agriculture	F. Peart (to April 1968)
	C. Hughes (from April 1968)
Education Secretary	M. Stewart (to January 1965)
	A. Crosland (January 1965 to August 1967)
	P. Gordon Walker (August 1967 to April 1968)
	E. Short (from April 1968)
Minister of Labour	R. Gunter (to April 1968)
Employment Secretary	B. Castle (from April 1968)
Minister, Housing & Local Govt.	R. Crossman (to August 1966)
	Anthony Greenwood (August 1966 to October 1969)
Minister, Local Govt. & Planning	A. Crosland (from October 1969)
Health and Social Security Secretary	R. Crossman (from November 1968)
Paymaster General	Lord Shackleton (April to November 1968)
	J. Hart (November 1968 to October 1969)
	H. Lever (from October 1969)
Minister of Power	F. Lee (to April 1966)
	R. Marsh (April 1966 to April 1968)
	R. Gunter (April to July 1968)
	R. Mason (July 1968 to October 1969)
Minister of Transport	T. Fraser (to December 1965)
	B. Castle (December 1965 to April 1968)
	R. Marsh (April 1968 to October 1969)
Minister without Portfolio	D. Houghton (April 1966 to January 1967)
	P. Gordon Walker (January to August 1967)
	G. Thomson (October 1968 to October 1969)
	P. Shore (from October 1969)

Wilson's and Callaghan's Cabinets, March 1974 to May 1979

Prime Minister	H. Wilson (to April 1976)
	J. Callaghan (from April 1976)
Lord Chancellor	Lord Elwyn-Jones
Lord President	E. Short (to April 1976)
	M. Foot (from April 1976)
Lord Privy Seal	Lord Shepherd (to September 1976)
	Lord Peart (from September 1976)
Chancellor of the Exchequer	D. Healey
Parl. Sec. to Treasury	R. Mellish (July 1974 to April 1976)
Chief Sec. to Treasury	J. Barnett (from February1977)
Home Secretary	R. Jenkins (to September 1976)
	M. Rees (from September 1976)
Foreign Secretary	J. Callaghan (to April 1976)
	A. Crosland (April 1976 to February 1977)
	D. Owen (from February 1977)
Minister of Overseas Development	R. Prentice (June 1975 to December 1976)
Defence Secretary	R. Mason (to September 1976)
	F. Mulley (from September 1976)
Scottish Secretary	W. Ross (to April 1976)
	B. Millan (from April 1976)
Welsh Secretary	J. Morris
Northern Ireland Secretary	M. Rees (to September 1976)
	R. Mason (from September 1976)
Chancellor, Duchy of Lancaster	H. Lever
Trade Secretary	P. Shore (to April 1976)
	E. Dell (April 1976 to November 1978)
	J. Smith (from November 1978)
Industry Secretary	A. Benn (to June 1975)
	E. Varley (from June 1975)
Minister of Agriculture	F. Peart (to September 1976)
	J. Silkin (from September 1976)
Education Secretary	R. Prentice (to June 1975)
	F. Mulley (June 1975 to September 1976)
	S. Williams (from September 1976)

Employment Secretary	M. Foot (to April 1976)
	A. Booth (from April 1976)
Environment Secretary	A. Crosland (to April 1976)
	P. Shore (from April 1976)
Minister, Planning & Local Govt.	J. Silkin (October 1974 to September 1976)
Health and Social Security Secretary	B. Castle (to April 1976)
	D. Ennals (from April 1976)
Minister of Social Security	S. Orme (from September 1976)
Minister, Prices & Consumer Protection	S. Williams (to September 1976)
	R. Hattersley (from September 1976)
Energy Secretary	E. Varley (to June 1975)
	A. Benn (from June 1975)
Minister of Transport	W. Rodgers (from September 1976)

Blair's Cabinet, May 1997 to June 2001

Prime Minister	T. Blair
Deputy PM and Secretary of State for Environment, Transport and the Regions	J. Prescott
Chancellor of the Exchequer	G. Brown
Foreign Secretary	R. Cook
Lord Chancellor	Lord Irvine
Home Secretary	J. Straw
Education and Employment Secretary	D. Blunkett
Trade and Industry Secretary	M. Beckett (to July 1998)
	P. Mandelson (July to December 1998)
	S. Byers (from December 1998)
Minister of Agriculture	J. Cunningham (to July 1998)
	N. Brown (from July 1998)
Scottish Secretary	D. Dewar (to May 1999)
	J. Reid (from May 1999)
	H. Liddell (from January 2001)
Defence Secretary	G. Robertson (to October 1999)
	G. Hoon (from October 1999)

Health Secretary	F. Dobson (to October 1999)
	A. Milburn (from October 1999)
Lord President and Leader of the Commons	A. Taylor (to July 1998)
	M. Beckett (from July 1998)
Culture Secretary	C. Smith
Social Security Secretary	H. Harman (also Minister for Women) (to July 1998)
Northern Ireland Secretary	M. Mowlam (to October 1999)
	P. Mandelson (October 1999 to January 2001)
	J. Reid (from January 2001)
Welsh Secretary	R. Davies (to October 1998)
	A. Michael (October 1998 to July 1999)
	P. Murphy (from July 1999)
International Development Secretary	C. Short
Lord Privy Seal and Leader of House of Lords	Lord Richard (to July 1998)
	Baroness Jay (also Minister for Women) (from July 1998)
Chancellor, Duchy of Lancaster	D. Clark (to July 1998)
	J. Cunningham (July 1998 to October 1999)
	M. Mowlam (from October 1999)
Minister of Transport	G. Strang (to July 1998; thereafter office not in cabinet)
Chief Secretary to Treasury	A. Darling (to July 1998)
	S. Byers (July to December 1998)
	A. Milburn (December 1998 to October 1999)
	A. Smith (from October 1999)
Parliamentary Secretary to Treasury and Chief Whip	(office not in cabinet to July 1998)
	A. Taylor (from July 1998)

Blair's Cabinet, June 2001 to May 2005

Prime Minister	T. Blair
Deputy PM	J. Prescott
Chancellor of the Exchequer	G. Brown
Foreign Secretary	J. Straw
Lord Chancellor	Lord Irvine (to June 2003)
	Lord Falconer (from June 2003)
Home Secretary	D. Blunkett (to December 2004)
	C. Clarke (from December 2004)
Education and Skills Secretary	E. Morris (to October 2002)
	C. Clarke (October 2002– December 2004)
	R. Kelly (from December 2004)
Trade and Industry Secretary	P. Hewitt (also Minister for Women and Equality)
Environment, Food and Rural Affairs Secretary	M. Beckett
Scottish Secretary	H. Liddell (to June 2003)
	A. Darling (from June 2003) (combined with Transport)
Defence Secretary	G. Hoon
Health Secretary	A. Milburn (to June 2003)
	J. Reid (from June 2003)
Lord President and Leader of the Commons	R. Cook (to March 2003)
	J. Reid (March–June 2003)
	P. Hain (from June 2003) (combined with Welsh Secretary)
Culture, Media and Sport Secretary	T. Jowell
Work and Pensions Secretary	A. Darling (to May 2002)
	A. Smith (May 2002– September 2004)
	A. Johnson (from September 2004)
Northern Ireland Secretary	J. Reid (to October 2002)
	P. Murphy (from October 2002)
Welsh Secretary	P. Murphy (to October 2002)
	P. Hain (from October 2002)

International Development   C. Short (to May 2003)
  Secretary   Baroness Amos
                            H. Benn (from October 2003)

Lord Privy Seal and Leader of   Lord Williams
  House of Lords   (to October 2003)
                                 Baroness Amos
                                   (from October 2003)

Transport, Local Government   S. Byers (to May 2002)
  and Regions Secretary   (office broken up; Local Govt.
                                 and regions go to ODPM)

Transport Secretary   (office not in cabinet)
                             A. Darling (from May 2002)

Chief Secretary to Treasury   A. Smith (to May 2002)
                               P. Boateng (from May 2002)

Parliamentary Secretary to the   H. Armstrong
  Treasury and Chief Whip

Minister without Portfolio   C. Clarke (to October 2002)
                                J. Reid (October 2002–
                                  March 2003)
                                I. McCartney (from March 2003)

Chancellor, Duchy of Lancaster   (office not in cabinet)
                                  A. Milburn
                                    (from September 2004)

Blair's Cabinet, May 2005 to June 2007

Prime Minister   T. Blair
Deputy PM   J. Prescott
Chancellor of the Exchequer G. Brown
Foreign Secretary   J. Straw (to May 2006)
                             M. Beckett (from May 2006)

Justice Secretary and   Lord Falconer
  Lord Chancellor

Home Secretary   C. Clarke (to May 2006)
                             J. Reid (from May 2006)

Education and Skills Secretary   R. Kelly (to May 2006)
                                  A. Johnson (from May 2006)

Trade and Industry Secretary   A. Johnson (to May 2006)
                                A. Darling (from May 2006)

Environment, Food and   M. Beckett (to May 2006)
  Rural Affairs Secretary   D. Miliband (from May 2006)

Transport and Scottish Secretary	A. Darling (to May 2006)
	D. Alexander (from May 2006)
Defence Secretary	J. Reid (to May 2006)
	D. Browne (from May 2006)
Health Secretary	P. Hewitt
Lord Privy Seal and Leader of the Commons	G. Hoon (to May 2006)
	J. Straw (from May 2006)
Culture, Media and Sport Secretary	T. Jowell
Work and Pensions Secretary	D. Blunkett (to November 2005)
	J. Hutton (from November 2005)
Northern Ireland and Welsh Secretary	P. Hain
International Development Secretary	H. Benn
Lord President and Leader of House of Lords	Baroness Amos
Minister/Secretary for Communities and Local Government	D. Miliband (to May 2006)
	R. Kelly (from May 2006) (also Minister for Women and Equality)
Chief Secretary to Treasury	D. Browne (to May 2006)
	S. Timms (from May 2006)
Parliamentary Secretary to the Treasury and Chief Whip	H. Armstrong (to May 2006)
	J. Smith (from May 2006)
Minister without Portfolio and Party Chair	I. McCartney (to May 2006)
	H. Blears (from May 2006)
Chancellor, Duchy of Lancaster and Minister for Cabinet Office	J. Hutton (to November 2005) (post vacant November 2005– May 2006)
	H. Armstrong (from May 2006) (also Minister for Social Exclusion)

Brown's Cabinet, June 2007 to May 2010

Prime Minister	G. Brown
Chancellor of the Exchequer	A. Darling
Foreign Secretary	D. Miliband
Justice Secretary and Lord Chancellor	J. Straw

Home Secretary	J. Smith (to June 2009)
	A. Johnson (from June 2009)
Defence Secretary	D. Browne (see below) (to October 2008)
	J. Hutton (October 2008– June 2009)
	B. Ainsworth (from June 2009)
Scottish Secretary	D. Browne (see above) (to October 2008)
	J. Murphy (from D. Browne, to October 2008)
Health Secretary	A. Johnson (to June 2009)
	A. Burnham (from June 2009)
Environment, Food and Rural Affairs Secretary	H. Benn
International Development Secretary	D. Alexander
Business, Enterprise and Regulatory Reform/Business, Innovation and Skills	J. Hutton (to October 2008) Lord Mandelson (from October 2008; also First Secretary of State from June 2009)
Lord Privy Seal, Leader of the Commons, Minister for Women, Labour Party Chair	H. Harman
Work and Pensions Secretary	P. Hain (see below) (to January 2008)
	J. Purnell (from January 2008)
	Y. Cooper (from June 2009)
Welsh Secretary	P. Hain (see above) to January 2008)
	P. Murphy (January 2008– June 2009)
	P. Hain (from June 2009)
Transport Secretary	R. Kelly (to October 2008)
	G. Hoon (October 2008– June 2009)
	Lord Adonis (from June 2009)
Communities and Local Government Secretary	H. Blears (to June 2009)
	J. Denham (from June 2009)

Parliamentary Secretary to the Treasury and Chief Whip	G. Hoon
Children, Schools and Families Secretary	E. Balls
Chancellor, Duchy of Lancaster and Minister for Cabinet Office	E. Miliband (to October 2008) (office not in cabinet)
Minister for the Cabinet Office, Minister for the Olympics and Paymaster General	(office not in cabinet) T. Jowell (from June 2009)
Culture, Media and Sport Secretary	J. Purnell (to January 2008) A. Burnham (January 2008– June 2009) B. Bradshaw (from June 2009)
Northern Ireland Secretary	S. Woodward
Lord President and Leader of House of Lords	Baroness Ashton (to October 2008) Baroness Royall (from October 2008)
Chief Secretary to Treasury	A. Burnham (to January 2008) Y. Cooper (January 2008– June 2009) L. Byrne (from June 2009)
Innovation, Universities and Skills	J. Denham (to June 2009) Lord Mandelson (see above) (from June 2009)
Energy and Climate Change	(office not in cabinet) E. Miliband (from October 2008)

Notes

Introduction

1. Labour Party, *Annual Report, 1929* (1929), pp. 150–3.
2. A. Howard, 'We are the masters now', in M. Sissons and P. French (eds), *Age of Austerity 1945–1951* (1963), p. 16.
3. H. Wilson, *A Prime Minister on Prime Ministers* (1977), p. 211.
4. B. Tillett, *Is the Parliamentary Labour Party a Failure?* (1908).
5. See, for example, G. D. H. Cole, *The People's Front* (1937), pp. 271–90.
6. M. Abrams and R. Rose, *Must Labour Lose?* (1960).
7. See, for example, B. Hindess, *The Decline of Working Class Politics* (1971); J. Hinton, *Labour and Socialism: A History of the British Labour Movement 1867–1974* (Brighton, 1983); E. Hobsbawm, 'The forward march of Labour halted?', in M. Jacques (ed.), *The Forward March of Labour Halted?* (1981).
8. See, for example, G. D. H. Cole and R. Postgate, *The Common People 1746–1946* (1946); G. D. H. Cole, *History of the Labour Party from 1914* (1948); H. Tracey (ed.), *The British Labour Party: Its History, Growth, Policy and Leaders* (3 vols., 1948); F. Williams, *Fifty Years' March: The Rise of the Labour Party* (n.d. [1949]).
9. H. Pelling, *A Short History of the Labour Party* (1961).
10. See, for example, D. Howell, *British Social Democracy: A Study in Development and Decay* (1976).
11. D. Tanner, P. Thane and N. Tiratsoo (eds), *Labour's First Century* (2000); B. Brivati and R. Heffernan (eds), *The Labour Party: A Centenary History* (2000); K. Laybourn, *A Century of Labour: A History of the Labour Party, 1900–2000* (2000).
12. See esp. R. Miliband, *Parliamentary Socialism: A Study in the Politics of Labour* (1961).
13. See esp. J. Saville, *The Labour Movement in Britain: A Commentary* (1988).
14. D. Coates, *The Labour Party and the Struggle for Socialism* (1975), *Labour in Power? A Study of the Labour Government 1974–1979* (1980), *Prolonged Labour: The Slow Birth of New Labour Britain* (Basingstoke, 2005).
15. See esp. D. Marquand, *The Progressive Dilemma* (1991).
16. Tanner, Thane and Tiratsoo, 'Introduction', in idem (eds), *Labour's First Century*, p. 2.
17. For a critique of the left in the period, see A. Mitchell, *Four Years in the Death of the Labour Party* (1983).

336

18. K. O. Morgan, *Michael Foot: A Life* (2007); R. Hattersley, 'A great man, a lousy leader', *Observer*, 11 March 2007; G. Kaufman, 'One Foot in the gravy', *Sunday Times*, 18 March 2007.
19. See R. McKibbin, *The Evolution of the Labour Party 1910–1924* (1974), pp. vii, 249.
20. See, for example, M. Worley, *Labour Inside the Gate: A History of the British Labour Party between the Wars* (2005), and review by G. Cohen, *Parliamentary History*, 25 (2006): 426–8.
21. L. M. Weir, *The Tragedy of Ramsay MacDonald* (1938).
22. See esp. Viscount Snowden, *Autobiography* (2 vols., 1934); J. R. Clynes, *Memoirs* (2 vols., 1937).
23. Lord Elton, *The Life of James Ramsay MacDonald* (1939).
24. H. Dalton, *Call Back Yesterday: Memoirs 1887–1931* (1953); M. I. Cole (ed.), *Beatrice Webb's Diaries* (2 vols., 1952–56).
25. D. Marquand, *Ramsay MacDonald* (1977).

1 Creation and Early Years, 1900–14

1. Labour Party, *Labour Party Foundation Conference and Annual Reports, 1900–1905* (1967), pp. 18, 23, 16.
2. H. Pelling, *A History of British Trade Unionism* (4th edn, 1987), p. 73.
3. D. Tanner, *Political Change and the Labour Party, 1900–1918* (1990), p. 102.
4. D. Hamer, *Liberal Politics in the Age of Gladstone and Rosebery: A Study in Leadership and Policy* (Oxford, 1972), pp. 307–8.
5. W. Lancaster, *Radicalism, Co-operation and Socialism: Leicester Working-Class Politics 1860–1906* (Leicester, 1987), p. 109.
6. J. Reid, 'The division of labour and politics in Britain, 1880–1920', in W. J. Mommsen and H. G. Husung (eds), *The Development of Trade Unionism in Great Britain and Germany, 1880–1914* (1985), p. 150.
7. J. Benson, *The Working Class in England, 1875–1914* (1985), p. 68.
8. J. Zeitlin, 'Industrial structure, employer strategy and the diffusion of job control in Britain, 1880–1920', in Mommsen and Husung (eds), *Development of Trade Unionism*, p. 325.
9. D. Blaazer, *The Popular Front and the Progressive Tradition: Socialists, Liberals and the Quest for Unity, 1884–1939* (1992), p. 47.
10. R. Price and G. S. Bain, 'The labour force', in A. H. Halsey (ed.), *British Social Trends since 1900: A Guide to the Changing Social Structure of Britain* (1988), p. 186.
11. See N. Thompson, *The Market and Its Critics: Socialist Political Economy in Nineteenth-Century Britain* (1988), esp. pp. 281–6.
12. See A. J. Reid, *The Tide of Democracy: Shipyard Workers and Social Relations in Britain, 1870–1950* (2010), pp. 149–78.
13. Labour Party, *Labour Party Foundation Conference*, p. 17.
14. Ibid., p. 20.
15. H. Pelling, *The Origins of the Labour Party, 1880–1900* (2nd edn, Oxford, 1965), p. 230.

16. D. Marquand, *Ramsay MacDonald* (1977), p. 51.
17. D. Howell, *British Workers and the Independent Labour Party 1888–1906* (1983), p. 22.
18. Labour Party, *Labour Party Foundation Conference*, p. 87.
19. Ibid., pp. 202, 210.
20. F. Bealey and H. Pelling, *Labour and Politics 1900–1906: A History of the Labour Representation Committee* (1958), p. 132.
21. F. Trentmann, *Free Trade Nation: Commerce, Consumption, and Civil Society in Modern Britain* (Oxford, 2008); E. F. Biagini, 'Popular Liberals, Gladstonian finance and the debate on taxation, 1860–1874', in E. F. Biagini and A. J. Reid (eds), *Currents of Radicalism: Popular Radicalism, Organized Labour and Party Politics in Britain, 1850–1914 (1991)*, pp. 135–6.
22. D. Tanner, 'Ideological debate in Edwardian Labour politics: radicalism, revisionism and socialism', in Biagini and Reid, *Currents of Radicalism*, p. 292.
23. Tanner, *Political Change*, pp. 22–3.
24. See, for example, F. Williams, *Fifty Years' March: The Rise of the Labour Party* (n.d. [1949]), pp. 148–58.
25. D. E. Martin, 'Ideology and composition', in K. D. Brown (ed.), *The First Labour Party, 1906–1914* (1985), pp. 17–37.
26. C. J. Wrigley, *Arthur Henderson* (1990), p. 63.
27. J. Harris, *Unemployment and Politics: A Study in English Social Policy, 1886–1914* (Oxford, 1972), pp. 242–4.
28. J. Schneer, *Ben Tillett: Portrait of a Labour Leader* (1982), pp. 133–6.
29. Author's calculations based on figures in H. Pelling, *A Short History of the Labour Party* (8th edn, 1985), p. 193.
30. J. Shepherd, 'Labour and parliament: the Lib-Labs as the first working-class MPs, 1885–1906', in Biagini and Reid (eds), *Currents of Radicalism*, pp. 187–213.
31. Howell, *British Workers*, pp. 50–1; C. Baylies, *The History of the Yorkshire Miners, 1881–1918* (1993), pp. 261, 264.
32. R. Gregory, *The Miners in British Politics, 1906–1914* (Oxford, 1968), p. 29.
33. Gregory, *Miners in British Politics*, pp. 29, 32, 188.
34. R. McKibbin, *The Evolution of the Labour Party 1910–1924* (1974), p. 1.
35. McKibbin, *Evolution*, pp. 1–2.
36. M. G. Sheppard and J. L. Halstead, 'Labour's municipal election performance in provincial England and Wales, 1901–13', *Bulletin of the Society for the Study of Labour History*, 39 (1979): 39–62.
37. McKibbin, *Evolution*, p. 72.
38. Tanner, *Political Change*, p. 321.
39. See Pelling, *British Trade Unionism*, pp. 297–8, and Pelling, *Short History*, p. 193, for these and the other figures in this and the next paragraph.
40. S. Boston, *Women Workers and the Trade Union Movement* (1980), pp. 73–8.
41. See, for example, H. Mitchell, *The Hard Way Up* (1977); C. Collette, *For Labour and For Women: The Women's Labour League, 1906–1918* (1989); P. Thane, 'The women of the British Labour Party and feminism,

1906–1945', in H. L. Smith (ed.), *British Feminism in the Twentieth Century* (1990), pp. 124–43.

42. M. Pugh, 'Labour and women's suffrage', in Brown, *First Labour Party*, pp. 233–53.
43. R. Challinor, *The Origins of British Bolshevism* (1977), p. 121; W. Kendall, *The Revolutionary Movement in Britain, 1900–1921: The Origins of British Communism* (1969), esp. pp. 28–31, 45, 63–76; M. Crick, *The History of the Social Democratic Federation* (1994), pp. 222–60.
44. J. White, 'Syndicalism in a mature industrial setting: the case of Britain', in M. van der Linden and W. Thorpe (eds), *Revolutionary Syndicalism: An International Perspective* (1990), pp. 101–18.
45. See G. D. H. Cole, *The World of Labour* (1913); A. Wright, *G. D. H. Cole and Socialist Democracy* (1979).
46. C. Howard, 'MacDonald, Henderson, and the outbreak of war, 1914', *Historical Journal*, 20 (1977): 872; McKibbin, *Evolution*, p. 76.
47. Tanner, *Political Change*, pp. 317–37.

2 The Surge to Second-Party Status, 1914–22

1. Howard, 'MacDonald, Henderson, and the outbreak of war', *passim*; J. N. Horne, *Labour at War: France and Britain, 1914–1918* (Oxford, 1991), pp. 42–5.
2. R. Harrison, 'The war emergency workers' national committee, 1914–1920', in A. Briggs and J. Saville (eds), *Essays in Labour History, 1886–1923* (1971), pp. 212–15.
3. J. Turner, *British Politics and the Great War: Coalition and Conflict, 1915–1918* (1992), pp. 70, 78–90.
4. C. J. Wrigley, *Arthur Henderson* (1990), p. 107.
5. Turner, *British Politics*, pp. 205–9.
6. D. Marquand, *Ramsay MacDonald* (1977), p. 179.
7. Harrison, 'War emergency workers' national committee', pp. 217–24.
8. B. Waites, *A Class Society at War: England, 1914–1918* (1987), pp. 190, 231–5.
9. J. M. McEwen, 'Lloyd George's Liberal supporters in December 1916: a note', *Bulletin of the Institute of Historical Research*, 53 (1980): 265–72.
10. D. Tanner, *Political Change and the Labour Party, 1900–1918* (1990), p. 427.
11. Tanner, *Political Change*, p. 382.
12. M. Pinto-Duschinsky, *British Political Finance, 1830–1980* (Washington, DC, 1981), p. 84.
13. H. C. G. Matthew, R. I. McKibbin and J. Kay, 'The franchise factor in the rise of the Labour party', *English Historical Review*, 91 (1976): 723–52.
14. D. Tanner, 'The parliamentary electoral system, the "fourth" Reform Act and the rise of Labour in England and Wales', *Bulletin of the Institute of Historical Research*, 56 (1983): 205–19.
15. H. Pelling, *A History of British Trade Unionism* (4th edn, 1987), p. 298.

16. H. Pelling, *A Short History of the Labour Party* (8th edn, 1985), p. 193.
17. R. Price, *Labour in British Society: An Interpretative History* (1986), pp. 158–9.
18. For the alternative view, see J. Hinton, *The First Shop Stewards' Movement* (1973), esp. pp. 254, 330–7.
19. S. and B. Webb, *The Consumers' Co-operative Movement* (1921), pp. 17–18.
20. A. Bonner, *British Co-operation: The History, Principles and Organisation of the British Co-operative Movement* (rev. edn, 1970), pp. 132–3; T. F. Carbery, *Consumers in Politics: A History and General Review of the Co-operative Party* (Manchester, 1969), pp. 3, 17; S. Pollard, 'The foundation of the Co-operative Party', in Briggs and Saville, *Essays in Labour History, 1886–1923*, pp. 185–210; T. Adams, 'The formation of the Co-operative party reconsidered', *International Review of Social History*, 32 (1987): 48–68.
21. J. Melling, 'Work, culture and politics on "Red Clydeside": the ILP during the First World War', in A. McKinlay and R. J. Morris (eds), *The ILP on Clydeside, 1893–1932: From Foundation to Disintegration* (1991), pp. 106–14.
22. P. E. Dewey, 'Nutrition and living standards in wartime Britain', in R. Wall and J. M. Winter (eds), *The Upheaval of War: Family, Work and Welfare in Europe, 1914–1918* (1988), pp. 201–2.
23. See, for example, L. C. Money, *The Triumph of Nationalization* (1920), esp. pp. vii–viii.
24. A. J. A. Morris, *Radicalism Against War: The Advocacy of Peace and Retrenchment* (1972), pp. 28, 204–5.
25. C. A. Cline, *Recruits to Labour: The British Labour Party 1914–1931* (1963), pp. 8–23.
26. Horne, *Labour at War*, p. 221.
27. J. M. Winter, 'Arthur Henderson, the Russian Revolution, and the reconstruction of the Labour Party', *Historical Journal*, 15 (1972), p. 755.
28. Cline, *Recruits to Labour*, pp. 20–2; M. Swartz, *The Union of Democratic Control in British Politics during the First World War* (1971), pp. 168–9.
29. Swartz, *Union of Democratic Control*, p. 199.
30. R. McKibbin, *The Evolution of the Labour Party 1910–1924* (1974), pp. 90–1.
31. G. D. H. Cole, *History of the Labour Party from 1914* (1948), pp. 47–8.
32. McKibbin, *Evolution*, p. 100.
33. A. Wright, *G. D. H. Cole and Socialist Democracy* (1979), pp. 43–7, 280; L. P. Carpenter, *G. D. H. Cole: An Intellectual Biography* (1973), pp. 71–111.
34. Cole, *History of the Labour Party*, p. 55.
35. Turner, *British Politics*, p. 318.
36. Ibid., p. 404.
37. See, for example, M. Kinnear, *The Fall of Lloyd George: The Political Crisis of 1922* (1973), p. 32.
38. J. E. Cronin, *Labour and Society in Britain 1918–1979* (1983), pp. 241–3; C. J. Wrigley, *Lloyd George and the Challenge of Labour: The Post-War Coalition 1918–1922* (1990), pp. 249–50.

39. Quoted in Cole, *History of the Labour Party*, p. 105.
40. Quoted in R. I. McKibbin, 'Arthur Henderson as Labour leader', *International Review of Social History*, 23 (1978): 93.
41. Wrigley, *Lloyd George and the Challenge of Labour*, p. 271; K. O. Morgan, *Consensus and Disunity: The Lloyd George Coalition Government, 1918–1922* (1979), p. 221.
42. D. H. Aldcroft, *The British Economy, Vol. 1: Years of Turmoil, 1920–1951* (1986), pp. 5–6.
43. P. S. Bagwell, 'The triple industrial alliance, 1913–1922', in Briggs and Saville, *Essays in Labour History 1886–1923*, pp. 117–18.
44. McKibbin, *Evolution*, pp. 124–5, 137–9, 141, 143, 213.
45. C. J. Howard, 'Expectations born to death: local Labour party expansion in the 1920s', in J. M. Winter (ed.), *The Working Class in Modern British History: Essays in Honour of Henry Pelling* (1983), pp. 77–8.
46. Howard, 'Expectations born to death', p. 71; McKibbin, *Evolution*, p. 147; K. Morgan, *Labour Legends and Russian Gold* (2006), esp. pp. 135–42.
47. McKibbin, *Evolution*, pp. 221–34; S. Koss, *The Rise and Fall of the Political Press in Britain* (paperback edn, 1990), pp. 920–1.
48. McKibbin, *Evolution*, pp. 157–78.

3 Progress and Collapse, 1922–31

1. Calculations by the author based on the 1931 *Census*.
2. P. Williamson, 'The doctrinal politics of Stanley Baldwin', in M. Bentley (ed.), *Public and Private Doctrine: Essays in British History Presented to Maurice Cowling* (1993), pp. 194–5.
3. C. Cook, *The Age of Alignment: Electoral Politics in Britain, 1922–1929* (1975), p. 149.
4. L. Radice, *Beatrice and Sidney Webb: Fabian Socialists* (1984), p. 239.
5. D. Marquand, *Ramsay MacDonald* (1977), p. 299; M. I. Cole (ed.), *Beatrice Webb's Diaries, 1924–1932* (1956), pp. 1–2, entry for 18 Jan. 1924.
6. R. W. Lyman, *The First Labour Government, 1924* (1958), p. 102; Marquand, *MacDonald*, pp. 301–3; J. Shepherd and K. Laybourn, *Britain's First Labour Government* (2006), pp. 45–67.
7. Cook, *Age of Alignment*, pp. 201–2, 216, 221–2, 265.
8. R. E. Dowse, *Left in the Centre: The Independent Labour Party, 1893–1940* (1966), pp. 102–3; Marquand, *MacDonald*, p. 297.
9. For 'economic internationalism' see R. W. D. Boyce, *British Capitalism at the Crossroads, 1919–1932: A Study in Politics, Economics and International Relations* (1987), pp. 13–18.
10. Shepherd and Laybourn, *Britain's First Labour Government*, pp. 161–80; Marquand, *MacDonald*, pp. 357–61, 364–78.
11. G. Bennett, 'A Most Extraordinary and Mysterious Business': The Zinoviev Letter of 1924* (1999).
12. Cook, *Age of Alignment*, pp. 199–201.

13. A. Thorpe, 'The industrial meaning of "gradualism": the Labour party and industry, 1918–1931', *Journal of British Studies*, 35 (1996): 84–113.

14. C. Cross, *Philip Snowden* (1966), p. 214; Marquand, *MacDonald*, pp. 391–2.

15. A. Bullock, *The Life and Times of Ernest Bevin, Vol. 1: Trade Union Leader, 1881–1940* (1960), pp. 258–60.

16. A. Morgan, *J. Ramsay MacDonald* (1987), p. 132.

17. H. A. Clegg, *A History of British Trade Unions since 1889, Vol. 2: 1911–1933* (1985), p. 381.

18. Clegg, *History of British Trade Unions*, vol. 2, pp. 422–3; P. Renshaw, 'The depression years', in B. Pimlott and C. Cook (eds), *Trade Unions in British Politics: The First 250 Years* (1991), p. 100.

19. See esp. C. J. Howard, 'Expectations born to death: local Labour party expansion in the 1920s', in J. M. Winter (ed.), *The Working Class in Modern British History: Essays in Honour of Henry Pelling* (1983), pp. 65–81.

20. H. Dewar, *Communist Politics in Britain: The CPGB from Its Origins to the Second World War* (1976), p. 38.

21. R. W. Garner, 'Ideology and electoral politics in Labour's rise to major party status, 1918–1931', unpublished PhD thesis, University of Manchester, 1988, pp. 220–1; D. Howell, *MacDonald's Party: Labour Identities and Crisis, 1922–1931* (2002), pp. 380–403.

22. P. Graves, *Labour Women: Women in British Working-Class Politics, 1918–1939* (1994), p. 223; Howell, *MacDonald's Party*, pp. 332–79.

23. J. E. Cronin, *The Politics of State Expansion: War, State and Society in Twentieth-Century Britain* (1991), p. 117.

24. Labour Party, *Annual Report, 1928* (1928), p. 212.

25. R. H. Tawney, 'The choice before the Labour Party', *Political Quarterly*, 1932, reprinted in W. A. Robson (ed.), *The Political Quarterly in the Thirties* (1971), p. 98.

26. See, for example, B. Pimlott (ed.), *The Political Diary of Hugh Dalton, 1918–1940, 1945–1960* (1986), pp. 47–8.

27. K. Laybourn, *Philip Snowden: A Biography* (1988), pp. 110–12.

28. E. Wertheimer, *Portrait of the Labour Party* (1929), pp. 177, 174.

29. Dowse, *Left in the Centre*, pp. 130–46.

30. A. Thorpe, *The British General Election of 1931* (1991), pp. 8–10.

31. Marquand, *MacDonald*, pp. 489–91.

32. See Thorpe, *1931*, pp. 49–56; P. Williamson, *National Crisis and National Government: British Politics, the Economy and Empire, 1926–1932* (1992), pp. 204–5, 207–12.

33. D. Carlton, *MacDonald versus Henderson: The Foreign Policy of the Second Labour Government* (1970), pp. 48, 98–9, 124–7; C. Wrigley, *Arthur Henderson* (1990), p. 168.

34. Thorpe, 'Industrial meaning of "gradualism"', pp. 109–10.

35. Ibid., p. 104.

36. R. Skidelsky, *Politicians and the Slump: The Labour Government of 1929–1931* (1967), pp. 171–82; R. Skidelsky, *Oswald Mosley* (1975), pp. 199–201.

37. Skidelsky, *Oswald Mosley*, pp. 201–45.

38. Skidelsky, *Politicians and the Slump*, pp. 389–92; for the counter-argument, see R. I. McKibbin, 'The economic policy of the second Labour government, 1929–31', *Past and Present*, 68 (1975): 95–123.
39. Thorpe, *1931*, pp. 61–2.
40. For fuller discussion of these issues, see A. Thorpe, *Britain in the 1930s* (1992), pp. 77–83.
41. Marquand, *MacDonald*, pp. 554–64.
42. Thorpe, *1931*, pp. 23–4.
43. F. Owen, *Tempestuous Journey: Lloyd George, His Life and Times* (1954), p. 717; Marquand, *MacDonald*, pp. 602–3; Williamson, *National Crisis*, pp. 234–42.
44. N. Riddell, *Labour in Crisis: The Second Labour Government, 1929–31* (1999), pp. 124–5.
45. For more detail on the remainder of this chapter, see Thorpe, *1931*, pp. 63–93, 127–53, 219–71.
46. See P. Williamson, 'A "bankers' ramp"? Financiers and the British political crisis of August 1931', *English Historical Review*, 99 (1984): 770–806.
47. F. W. S. Craig, *British Electoral Facts, 1832–1980* (1981), p. 162.

4 Remaking the Party? 1931–39

1. A. Thorpe, *The British General Election of 1931* (1991), pp. 270–1.
2. R. M. Y. Shackleton, 'Trade unions and the slump', in Pimlott and Cook, *Trade Unions in British Politics*, p. 112.
3. W. Knox, *James Maxton* (1987), p. 98.
4. G. Cohen, 'The Independent Labour Party, disaffiliation, revolution and standing orders', *History*, 86 (2001): 200–21.
5. R. E. Dowse, *Left in the Centre: The Independent Labour Party, 1893–1940* (1966), p. 185; J. Jupp, *The Radical Left in Britain, 1931–1941* (1982), p. 35.
6. *Jupp, Radical Left*, p. 69.
7. B. Pimlott, *Labour and the Left in the 1930s* (1977), p. 49.
8. Labour Party, NEC minutes, 10 Nov. 1931, 'Report on the General Election by the Secretary' [Henderson].
9. Labour Party, *Annual Report, 1932* (1932), pp. 204–5.
10. C. Wrigley, *Arthur Henderson* (1990), p. 180; Pimlott, *Labour and the Left*, p. 22.
11. A. Bullock, *The Life and Times of Ernest Bevin, Vol. 1: Trade Union Leader, 1881–1940* (1960), pp. 511–12.
12. G. D. H. Cole, *The Next Ten Years: In British Social and Economic Policy* (1929), pp. 37–8, 134.
13. Pimlott, *Labour and the Left*, pp. 36–40; E. Durbin, *New Jerusalems: The Labour Party and the Economics of Democratic Socialism* (1985), pp. 73–83.
14. S. Cripps, 'Can socialism come by constitutional methods?', in C. Addison et al. (eds), *Problems of a Socialist Government* (1933), pp. 35–66.

15. R. Miliband, *Parliamentary Socialism: A Study in the Politics of Labour* (2nd edn, 1972), pp. 229–30.
16. Pimlott, *Labour and the Left*, pp. 38, 54; Durbin, *New Jerusalems*, pp. 87–90; A. Booth and M. Pack, *Employment, Capital and Economic Policy: Great Britain, 1918–1939* (1985), pp. 125–33.
17. Pimlott, *Labour and the Left*, p. 49; M. Bor, *The Socialist League in the 1930s* (2005), *passim*.
18. See, for example, S. and B. Webb, *A Constitution for the Socialist Commonwealth of Great Britain* (1920), pp. 213–15.
19. See, for example, R. H. Tawney, *The Acquisitive Society* (1921), p. 48; H. Laski, *A Grammar of Politics* (5th edn, 1967; first published in 1925), p. 88; Cole, *Next Ten Years*, pp. 163–8.
20. G. D. H. Cole, *History of the Labour Party from 1914* (1948), p. 452.
21. C. R. Attlee, *The Labour Party in Perspective* (1937), pp. 31–3, 141; Durbin, *New Jerusalems*, pp. 156–7; G. Walker, *Thomas Johnston* (1988), p. 170.
22. R. H. Tawney, 'The choice before the Labour Party', *Political Quarterly*, 1932, reprinted in W. A. Robson (ed.), *The Political Quarterly in the Thirties* (1971), pp. 103–4.
23. J. E. Cronin, *Labour and Society in Britain 1918–1979* (1983), pp. 241–2.
24. Pimlott, *Labour and the Left*, p. 201.
25. P. Williamson, *National Crisis and National Government: British Politics, the Economy and Empire, 1926–1932* (1992), pp. 514–15.
26. G. Peele, 'Revolt over India', in G. Peele and C. Cook (eds), *The Politics of Reappraisal* (1975), pp. 114–45; F. Miller, 'The British unemployment assistance crisis of 1935', *Journal of Contemporary History*, 14 (1979): 329–52.
27. E. Estorick, *Stafford Cripps: A Biography* (1949), p. 141.
28. K. Harris, *Attlee* (1982), pp. 111–18; J. Swift, *Labour in Crisis: Clement Attlee and the Labour Party in Opposition, 1931–40* (2001), pp. 87–95.
29. B. Pimlott, *The Political Diary of Hugh Dalton* (1986), p. 191.
30. See Pimlott, *Labour and the Left*, pp. 73–75; Swift, *Labour in Crisis*, pp. 95–7; H. Dalton, *The Fateful Years: Memoirs, 1931–1945* (1957), pp. 79–82; Harris, *Attlee*, pp. 121–2; B. Donoughue and G. W. Jones, *Herbert Morrison: Portrait of a Politician* (1973), p. 239.
31. Cole, *History of the Labour Party*, pp. 458–9.
32. R. Toye, 'The Labour party and the economics of rearmament, 1935–39', *Twentieth Century British History*, 12 (2001): 303–26; P. Clarke, *The Cripps Version: The Life of Sir Stafford Cripps, 1889–1952* (2002), p. 64.
33. Bullock, *Bevin, vol. 1*, pp. 528, 593–4; Pimlott, *Dalton*, pp. 241–2.
34. Dalton, *Fateful Years*, p. 44.
35. Ibid., pp. 132–3; Pimlott, *Dalton*, pp. 241–2.
36. This paragraph draws heavily on T. Buchanan, *The Spanish Civil War and the British Labour Movement* (1991).
37. Pimlott, *Labour and the Left*, pp. 95–7.
38. Ibid., p. 106; Swift, *Labour in Crisis*, pp. 144–51.
39. Dalton, *Fateful Years*, p. 202.

40. I. McLean, 'Oxford and Bridgwater', in C. Cook and J. Ramsden (eds), *By-Elections in British Politics* (1973), pp. 140–64.
41. G. Tregidga, *The Liberal Party in South-West Britain since 1918* (2000), pp. 87–96.
42. D. Blaazer, *The Popular Front and the Progressive Tradition: Socialists, Liberals and the Quest for Unity, 1884–1939* (1992), pp. 187–90; P. Clarke, *The Cripps Version: The Life of Sir Stafford Cripps, 1889–1952* (2002), pp. 81–3.
43. Pimlott, *Labour and the Left*, p. 180.
44. K. Martin, *Harold Laski (1893–1950): A Biographical Memoir* (1953), p. 110.
45. Pimlott, *Labour and the Left*, pp. 134–40.
46. Durbin, *New Jerusalems*, pp. 243–8.
47. S. Brooke, *Labour's War: The Labour Party During the Second World War* (1992), p. 32.
48. E. F. M. Durbin, *The Politics of Democratic Socialism* (1940), pp. 146–7.

5 The Impact of the Second World War, 1939–45

1. S. Brooke, *Labour's War: The Labour Party During the Second World War* (1992), pp. 34–5, 75.
2. Brooke, *Labour's War*, p. 37.
3. Ibid., pp. 40–1; J. Swift, *Labour in Crisis: Clement Attlee and the Labour Party in Opposition, 1931–40* (2001), pp. 151–4.
4. Brooke, *Labour's War*, p. 43.
5. J. Campbell, *Nye Bevan and the Mirage of British Socialism* (1987), p. 84; E. Estorick, *Stafford Cripps: A Biography* (1949), p. 326.
6. W. Citrine, *My Finnish Diary* (1940), p. 5.
7. Labour Party, NEC minutes, 20 Mar. 1940.
8. Labour Party, *Annual Report, 1941* (1941), p. 20.
9. Labour Party, NEC minutes, 17 Apr. 1940.
10. Brooke, *Labour's War*, pp. 46–54; K. Jefferys, *The Churchill Coalition and Wartime Politics, 1940–1945* (1991), pp. 21–7; B. Pimlott, *The Political Diary of Hugh Dalton* (1986), pp. 271–6.
11. R. Crowcroft, *Attlee's War: World War II and the Making of a Labour Leader* (2011), *passim*.
12. A. Bullock, *The Life and Times of Ernest Bevin, Vol. 2: Minister of Labour, 1940–1945* (1967), pp. 14–15.
13. T. D. Burridge, *British Labour and Hitler's War* (1976), pp. 16, 123–4.
14. P. Addison, *The Road to 1945: British Politics and the Second World War* (1975), p. 200.
15. Addison, *Road to 1945*, pp. 206–10.
16. G. Walker, *Thomas Johnston* (1988), pp. 151–62; C. Harvie, 'Labour in Scotland during the Second World War', *Historical Journal*, 26 (1983): 929–31, 944.
17. Pimlott, *Dalton*, pp. 400–7.
18. Campbell, *Bevan*, pp. 91–145; P. Slowe, *Manny Shinwell: An Authorized Biography* (1993), pp. 188–202.

19. J. E. Cronin, *Labour and Society in Britain 1918–1979* (1983), pp. 241–2; H. Pelling, *A Short History of the Labour Party* (8th edn, 1985), pp. 193–4.

20. P. Summerfield, *Women Workers in the Second World War: Production and Patriarchy in Conflict* (1984), p. 157.

21. Bullock, *Bevin, vol. 2*, p. 22.

22. A. Thorpe, *Parties at War: Political Organization in Second World War Britain* (2009), esp. pp. 256–68.

23. R. P. Hastings, 'The Birmingham Labour movement, 1918–1945', *Midland History*, 5 (1980): 88; A. Thorpe, 'The consolidation of a Labour stronghold, 1926–1951', in C. Binfield et al. (eds), *The History of the City of Sheffield, Vol. 1: Politics* (1993), p. 110.

24. B. Pimlott (ed.), *The Second World War Diary of Hugh Dalton, 1940–1945* (1986), pp. 657–9, 725–6, 823–4, 858; D. Healey, *The Time of My Life* (1989), pp. 69–71.

25. Brooke, *Labour's War*, p. 43.

26. Ibid., pp. 108–9.

27. Jefferys, *Churchill Coalition*, pp. 117–22.

28. Brooke, *Labour's War*, pp. 260–1.

29. Quoted in Addison, *Road to 1945*, p. 256.

30. Addison, *Road to 1945*, p. 278.

31. See especially Brooke, *Labour's War, passim;* Jefferys, *Churchill Coalition, passim.*

32. W. Beveridge, *Full Employment in a Free Society* (1944), p. 128; Jefferys, *Churchill Coalition*, p. 171.

33. H. Jones, *Health and Society in Twentieth-Century Britain* (1994), pp. 108–12.

34. K. Jefferys, 'British politics and social policy during the Second World War', *Historical Journal*, 30 (1987): 140.

35. See, for example, Thorpe, 'Consolidation', pp. 148–9.

36. L. Johnman, 'The Labour party and industrial policy, 1940–1945', in N. Tiratsoo (ed.), *The Attlee Years* (1991), pp. 42, 47.

37. Quoted in G. D. H. Cole, *History of the Labour Party from 1914* (1948), p. 411; see also A. Thorpe, '"In a rather emotional state"? The Labour party and British intervention in Greece, 1944–5', *English Historical Review*, 121 (2006): 1075–1105.

38. F. Williams, *Fifty Years' March: The Rise of the Labour Party* (n.d. [1949]), p. 358.

39. See, for example, A. Marwick, *Britain in the Century of Total War: War, Peace and Social Change, 1900–1967* (1968), p. 328.

40. For more on this, see, for example, J. Lawrence, 'Popular politics and the limitations of party: Wolverhampton, 1867–1900', in Biagini and Reid, *Currents of Radicalism*, pp. 67, 84; S. Fielding, 'What did "the people" want? The meaning of the 1945 general election', *Historical Journal*, 35 (1992): 623–39.

41. S. Fielding, P. Thompson and N. Tiratsoo, *'England Arise!' The Labour Party and Popular Politics in 1940s Britain* (1995), pp. 58, 68; Hastings, 'Birmingham Labour movement', p. 87.

42. Fielding et al., *'England Arise!'*, p. 64.

6 The Attlee Governments, 1945–51

1. See, for example, D. Rubinstein, 'Socialism and the Labour party: the Labour left and domestic policy, 1945–1950', in D. E. Martin and D. Rubinstein (eds), *Ideology and the Labour Movement: Essays Presented to John Saville* (1979), pp. 226–57.
2. C. Barnett, *The Audit of War: The Illusion and Reality of Britain as a Great Nation* (1986).
3. K. O. Morgan, *Labour in Power, 1945–1951* (1984), pp. 49–50.
4. The phrase was Dalton's: see H. Dalton, *High Tide and After: Memoirs, 1945–1960* (1962), p. 187.
5. Morgan, *Labour in Power,* pp. 350–8; K. Harris, *Attlee* (1982), pp. 347–50.
6. Harris, *Attlee,* pp. 353–4; B. Pimlott, *The Political Diary of Hugh Dalton* (1986), pp. 524–48.
7. B. Donoughue and G. W. Jones, *Herbert Morrison: Portrait of a Politician* (1973), p. 369.
8. Morgan, *Labour in Power,* p. 60.
9. M. Jones, *Michael Foot* (1994), p. 135.
10. Morgan, *Labour in Power,* pp. 59–69.
11. J. Schneer, *Labour's Conscience: The Labour Left, 1945–1951* (1988), pp. 155–6.
12. D. E. Moggridge, *Maynard Keynes: An Economist's Biography* (1992), pp. 796–820.
13. K. O. Morgan, *Labour People: Leaders and Lieutenants from Hardie to Kinnock* (1987), pp. 162–3.
14. H. Pelling, *Britain and the Marshall Plan* (1988), p. 113.
15. B. Pimlott, *Harold Wilson* (1992), pp. 134–43.
16. F. W. S. Craig (ed.), *British General Election Manifestos 1900–1974* (1975), p. 127.
17. Morgan, *Labour in Power,* pp. 110–21.
18. J. Dunkerley and P. Hare, 'Nationalized industries', in N. F. R. Crafts and N. Woodward (eds), *The British Economy since 1945* (1991), p. 388.
19. H. A. Clegg, *A History of British Trade Unions since 1889, Vol. 3: 1934–1951* (1994), pp. 342–5; Schneer, *Labour's Conscience,* pp. 144–51.
20. Schneer, *Labour's Conscience,* p. 147.
21. F. Williams, *Fifty Years' March: The Rise of the Labour Party* (n.d. [1949]), p. 358.
22. Quoted in H. Mercer, 'The Labour governments of 1945–51 and private industry', in Tiratsoo, *The Attlee Years,* p. 71.
23. L. Johnman, 'The Labour Party and industrial policy, 1940–45', in Tiratsoo, *The Attlee Years,* pp. 47–8.
24. Pimlott, *Wilson,* pp. 129–30.
25. J. Tomlinson, 'Planning: debate and policy in the 1940s', *Twentieth Century British History,* 3 (1992): 154–74, but cf. S. Brooke, 'Problems of "socialist planning": Evan Durbin and the Labour government of 1945', *Historical Journal,* 34 (1991): 687–702.
26. J. Campbell, *Nye Bevan and the Mirage of British Socialism* (1987), pp. 165–85.

27. Morgan, *Labour in Power,* p. 172.
28. G. C. Peden, *British Economic and Social Policy: Lloyd George to Margaret Thatcher* (2nd edn, 1991), p. 146.
29. J. Harris, 'Did British workers want the welfare state? G. D. H. Cole's survey of 1942', in Winter, *Working Class in Modern British History,* pp. 213–14.
30. N. Tiratsoo, 'Labour and the reconstruction of Hull, 1945–51', in Tiratsoo, *The Attlee Years,* pp. 128, 135.
31. Morgan, *Labour in Power,* pp. 167, 170.
32. A. M. Carr-Saunders, D. Caradog Jones and C. A. Moser, *A Survey of Social Conditions in England and Wales* (1958), p. 40.
33. Peden, *British Economic and Social Policy,* p. 149.
34. J. Harris, 'War and social history: Britain and the home front during the Second World War', *Contemporary European History,* 1 (1992): 25; P. Thane, 'Labour and welfare', in D. Tanner, P. Thane and N. Tiratsoo (eds), *Labour's First Century* (2000), p. 102; M. Taylor, 'Labour and the constitution', in ibid., p. 164.
35. G. D. H. Cole, *Regional and Local Government* (1947), p. 47.
36. Schneer, *Labour's Conscience,* pp. 52–78.
37. Ibid., p. 75.
38. M. Gowing, 'Britain, America and the bomb', in M. Dockrill and J. W. Young (eds), *British Foreign Policy, 1945–1956* (1989), pp. 31–46.
39. R. W. D. Boyce, *British Capitalism at the Crossroads, 1919–1932* (1987), pp. 241–50.
40. J. W. Young, *Britain, France and the Unity of Europe, 1945–1951* (1984), pp. 185–6, 191.
41. A. Bullock, *Ernest Bevin, Foreign Secretary, 1945–1951* (1983), p. 348.
42. J. Gallacher, *The Decline, Revival and Fall of the British Empire* (1982), pp. 144–5.
43. Gallacher, *Decline, Revival and Fall,* p. 146.
44. J. Tomlinson, 'The Attlee government and the balance of payments, 1945–1951', *Twentieth Century British History,* 2 (1991): 63–4.
45. P. S. Gupta, 'Imperialism and the Labour government of 1945–51', in Winter, *Working Class in Modern British History,* pp. 120–3.
46. H. Pelling, *A Short History of the Labour Party* (8th edn, 1985), p. 194.
47. Craig, *British General Election Manifestos,* pp. 152–61.
48. A. Heath, R. Jowell and J. Curtice, *How Britain Votes* (1985), p. 30.
49. J. Hinton, 'Women and the Labour vote, 1945–1950', *Labour History Review,* 57 (1992): 59–66; N. Hart, 'Gender and the rise and fall of class politics', *New Left Review,* 175 (1989): 22.
50. H. G. Nicholas, *The British General Election of 1950* (1951), p. 296.
51. Harris, *Attlee,* p. 460.
52. Ibid., p. 460; Pimlott, *Wilson,* pp. 156–7; P. Ziegler, *Wilson: The Authorized Life of Lord Wilson of Rievaulx* (1993), pp. 80–2.
53. Campbell, *Bevan,* p. 246.
54. Ibid., pp. 245–50.
55. Craig, *British General Election Manifestos,* pp. 173–4.

56. C. Cook, 'Labour's electoral base', in C. Cook and I. Taylor (eds), *The Labour Party: An Introduction to Its History, Structure and Politics* (1980), p. 99.
57. Hart, 'Gender', p. 22.
58. D. E. Butler, *The British General Election of 1951* (1952), pp. 27, 271.
59. Butler, *British General Election of 1951*, p. 277.

7   Searching for a New Direction, 1951–64

1. I. Zweiniger-Bargielowska, *Austerity in Britain: Rationing, Controls, and Consumption, 1939–1955* (2000), pp. 254–5; K. Harris, *Attlee* (1982), p. 495.
2. J. Campbell, *Nye Bevan and the Mirage of British Socialism* (1987), pp. 262–3.
3. P. M. Williams, *Hugh Gaitskell: A Political Biography* (1979), pp. 302–4.
4. S. Haseler, *The Gaitskellites: Revisionism in the British Labour Party, 1951–1964* (1969), p. 23.
5. Campbell, *Bevan*, pp. 296–300; Williams, *Gaitskell*, pp. 339–47.
6. Williams, *Gaitskell*, pp. 332–3.
7. Ibid., p. 319.
8. A. Bevan, *In Place of Fear* (1952), pp. 98, 103–5.
9. Campbell, *Bevan*, p. 264.
10. R. Price and G. S. Bain, 'The labour force', in A. H. Halsey (ed.), *British Social Trends since 1900: A Guide to the Changing Social Structure of Britain* (1988), pp. 187–8, 191–2.
11. H. Pelling, *A Short History of the Labour Party* (8th edn, 1985), p. 194.
12. F. W. S. Craig (ed.), *British General Election Manifestos 1900–1974* (1975), pp. 202–8.
13. A. Heath, R. Jowell and J. Curtice, *How Britain Votes* (1985), p. 30.
14. N. Hart, 'Gender and the rise and fall of class politics', *New Left Review*, 175 (1989): 22.
15. B. Pimlott, *The Political Diary of Hugh Dalton* (1986), p. 622.
16. Harris, *Attlee*, p. 499; Williams, *Gaitskell*, p. 300.
17. Williams, *Gaitskell*, pp. 361–7.
18. Ibid., p. 304.
19. B. Donoughue and G. W. Jones, *Herbert Morrison: Portrait of a Politician* (1973), pp. 538–9.
20. Campbell, *Bevan*, p. 320.
21. J. Morgan (ed.), *The Backbench Diaries of Richard Crossman* (1981), p. 556.
22. Campbell, *Bevan*, p. 337; M. Jones, *Michael Foot* (1994), pp. 222–5; B. Castle, *Fighting all the Way* (1993), p. 256; I. Mikardo, *Back-Bencher* (1988), pp. 158–60.
23. For a rather different discussion of Bevan's motives, see Campbell, *Bevan*, pp. 339–40.
24. M. Donnelly, 'Labour politics and the affluent society, 1951–1964', unpublished PhD thesis, University of Surrey, 1995, pp. 92–125.
25. B. Pimlott, *Harold Wilson* (1992), p. 194.

26. T. Gallagher, *Glasgow, The Uneasy Peace: Religious Tension in Modern Scotland* (1987), pp. 271–2; E. Shaw, *Discipline and Discord in the Labour Party: The Politics of Managerial Control in the Labour Party, 1951–1987* (1988), pp. 78–83.
27. Shaw, *Discipline*, p. 81.
28. P. Seyd and R. Whiteley, *Labour's Grass Roots: The Politics of Party Membership* (1992), p. 18.
29. Pimlott, *Wilson*, pp. 195–6.
30. D. E. Butler and R. Rose, *The British General Election of 1959* (1960), p. 38.
31. Craig, *British General Election Manifestos*, pp. 223–32.
32. Williams, *Gaitskell*, pp. 525–9.
33. Butler and Rose, *1959*, pp. 211, 206, 216.
34. Heath et al., *How Britain Votes*, p. 30.
35. Hart, 'Gender', p. 22.
36. Butler and Rose, *1959*, p. 193.
37. M. Abrams and R. Rose, *Must Labour Lose?* (1960), p. 23.
38. Abrams and Rose, *Must Labour Lose?*, p. 63.
39. J. H. Goldthorpe et al., *The Affluent Worker: Political Attitudes and Behaviour* (1968), p. 73.
40. Goldthorpe et al., *Affluent Worker*, p. 76.
41. Heath et al., *How Britain Votes*, p. 30.
42. S. Berger and D. Broughton (eds), *The Force of Labour: The Western European Labour Movement and the Working Class in the Twentieth Century* (1995), pp. 86–8, 253–4.
43. Pimlott, *Dalton*, p. 695; B. Brivati, *Hugh Gaitskell* (1996), pp. 334–5.
44. Williams, *Gaitskell*, pp. 537–73; Haseler, *Gaitskellites*, pp. 158–77.
45. Williams, *Gaitskell*, p. 553; R. Jobson, '"Waving the banners of a bygone age": nostalgia and Labour's Clause IV controversy, 1959–60', *Contemporary British History*, 27 (2013): 123–44.
46. Pimlott, *Wilson*, p. 213.
47. Williams, *Gaitskell*, pp. 612–13.
48. Pimlott, *Wilson*, pp. 237–45.
49. Haseler, *Gaitskellites*, pp. 227–36.
50. Pimlott, *Wilson*, pp. 252–64.
51. P. Ziegler, *Wilson: The Authorized Life of Lord Wilson of Rievaulx* (1993), pp. 143–4.
52. See, for example, H. Wilson, *The New Britain: Labour's Plan* (1964), pp. 14–15.
53. Craig, *British General Election Manifestos*, pp. 255–72.
54. Heath et al., *How Britain Votes*, p. 30.
55. Ibid., p. 34.
56. Hart, 'Gender', p. 22.
57. P. Anderson, 'Problems of socialist strategy', in P. Anderson and R. Blackburn (eds), *Towards Socialism* (1965), pp. 276–8.
58. D. E. Butler and A. King, *The British General Election of 1964* (1966), pp. 291, 311.

8 Wilson in Power, 1964–70

1. Condemnatory views include P. Foot, *The Politics of Harold Wilson* (1968), C. Ponting, *Breach of Promise: Labour in Power, 1964–1970* (1989), and A. Morgan, *Harold Wilson* (1992). Among more sympathetic accounts, see especially B. Pimlott, *Harold Wilson* (1992) and P. Ziegler, *Wilson: The Authorized Life of Lord Wilson of Rievaulx* (1993).
2. Ziegler, *Wilson*, p. 245.
3. A. Heath, R. Jowell and J. Curtice, *How Britain Votes* (1985), p. 30.
4. N. Hart, 'Gender and the rise and fall of class politics', *New Left Review*, 175 (1989): 22.
5. F. W. S. Craig (ed.), *British General Election Manifestos 1900–1974* (1975), p. 259.
6. R. Coopey, 'Industrial policy in the white heat of the scientific revolution', in R. Coopey, S. Fielding and N. Tiratsoo (eds), *The Wilson Governments, 1964–1970* (1993), p. 103.
7. Pimlott, *Wilson*, p. 351.
8. J. Foreman-Peck, 'Trade and the balance of payments', in N. F. R. Crafts and N. Woodward (eds), *The British Economy since 1945* (1991), p. 161.
9. Pimlott, *Wilson*, p. 424.
10. Foreman-Peck, 'Trade', p. 168.
11. J. Tomlinson, *Public Policy and the Economy* (1990), p. 242.
12. S. Newton and D. Porter, *Modernization Frustrated: The Politics of Industrial Decline in Britain since 1900* (1985), p. 155.
13. R. Crossman, *The Diaries of a Cabinet Minister* (3 vols, 1975), I:575.
14. Pimlott, *Wilson*, p. 353.
15. N. Woodward, 'Labour's economic performance, 1964–1970', in Coopey et al., *Wilson Governments*, p. 99.
16. T. Balogh, 'The drift towards planning', in P. Anderson and R. Blackburn (eds), *Towards Socialism* (1965), p. 76.
17. D. Walker, 'The first Wilson governments, 1964–1970', in P. Hennessy and A. Seldon (eds), *Ruling Performance: British Governments from Attlee to Thatcher* (1987), p. 203.
18. S. Pollard, *The Development of the British Economy, 1914–1980* (1983), p. 345.
19. M. W. Kirby, 'Supply-side management', in Crafts and Woodward, *British Economy*, p. 246.
20. Walker, 'First Wilson governments', p. 203; Pollard, *Development*, p. 345.
21. S. N. Broadberry, 'Unemployment', in Crafts and Woodward, *British Economy*, p. 212.
22. P. Browning, *The Treasury and Economic Policy, 1964–1985* (1986), pp. 17, 358.
23. N. W. C. Woodward, 'Inflation', in Crafts and Woodward, *British Economy*, pp. 197–8; D. E. Butler and M. Pinto-Duschinsky, *The British General Election of 1970* (1971), p. 439.

24. Woodward, 'Inflation', p. 199.
25. R. Richardson, 'Trade unions and industrial policy', in Crafts and Woodward, *British Economy*, pp. 426–9.
26. J. Dunkerley and P. Hare, 'Nationalized industries', in Crafts and Woodward, *British Economy*, p. 404; Tomlinson, *Public Policy*, p. 268.
27. See, for example, Jack Jones in *Tribune*, 11 Feb. 1966, reprinted in K. Coates and A. Topham, *Industrial Democracy in Great Britain: A Book of Readings and Witnesses for Workers' Control* (1968), pp. 372–3.
28. Coopey, 'Industrial policy', p. 114.
29. N. K. Buxton, 'Introduction', in N. K. Buxton and D. H. Aldcroft (eds), *British Industry Between the Wars: Instability and Development, 1919–1939* (1979), p. 19.
30. J. G. Watkins, 'Industrial organization and competition policy', in Crafts and Woodward, *British Economy*, p. 379; Coopey, 'Industrial policy', pp. 102–22.
31. Craig, *British General Election Manifestos*, p. 261.
32. H. W. Armstrong, 'Regional problems and policies', in Crafts and Woodward, *British Economy*, p. 315.
33. N. F. R. Crafts, 'Economic growth', in Crafts and Woodward, *British Economy*, p. 261.
34. H. Perkin, *The Rise of Professional Society: England since 1880* (1989), p. 449.
35. Ponting, *Breach of Promise*, p. 133.
36. Ibid., p. 130.
37. G. Brown, *In My Way: The Political Memoirs of Lord George Brown* (Pelican edn, 1972), p. 168.
38. Ponting, *Breach of Promise*, p. 122.
39. J. Parker and C. Mirrlees, 'Housing', in A. H. Halsey (ed.), *British Social Trends* (1988), p. 384.
40. Ponting, *Breach of Promise*, p. 392.
41. Ibid., pp. 98–9.
42. J. W. Young, *The Labour Governments 1964–70*, Vol. 2: *International Policy* (2003), p. 82; see also G. Hughes, *Harold Wilson's Cold War: The Labour Government and East-West Relations, 1964–1970* (2009).
43. Ponting, *Breach of Promise*, p. 101.
44. Foot, *Politics of Harold Wilson*, *passim*; Young, *Labour Governments*, pp. 168–88, 193–212.
45. Crossman, *Diaries of a Cabinet Minister*, II:84.
46. Craig, *British General Election Manifestos*, p. 363.
47. B. Jones and M. Keating, *Labour and the British State* (1985), p. 105.
48. Ibid., p. 104; M. Keating and D. Bleiman, *Labour and Scottish Nationalism* (1979), p. 147.
49. T. Gallagher, *Glasgow, The Uneasy Peace* (1987), pp. 276–7, 326.
50. A. B. Philip, *The Welsh Question: Nationalism in Welsh Politics, 1945–1970* (1975), p. 233.
51. K. O. Morgan, *Rebirth of a Nation: Wales 1880–1980* (1981), p. 411; C. Harvie, *No Gods and Precious Few Heroes: Scotland, 1914–1980* (1981), pp. 154–5.

52. Ponting, *Breach of Promise*, p. 341.
53. See, for example, T. Nairn, *The Break-Up of Britain: Crisis and Neo-Nationalism* (1977), esp. p. 253.
54. S. Fielding, *The Labour Governments 1964–70*, Vol. 1: *Labour and Cultural Change* (2003), pp. 139–59; M. Dresser, 'The colour bar in Bristol, 1963', in R. Samuel (ed.), *Patriotism: The Making and Unmaking of British National Identity*, Vol. 1: *History and Politics* (1989), pp. 284–5, 301; Crossman, *Diaries of a Cabinet Minister*, I:149, 5 Feb. 1965.
55. P. Ratcliffe, *Racism and Reaction: A Profile of Handsworth* (1981), pp. 279–81.
56. Fielding, *Labour Governments*, p. 156.
57. C. Holmes, *John Bull's Island: Immigration and British Society, 1871–1971* (1988), p. 292.
58. Fielding, *Labour Governments*, pp. 165–86.
59. J. E. Cronin, *The Politics of State Expansion* (1991), p. 235; A. Bonner, *British Co-operation* (1970), p. 274; J. Gaffin and D. Thorns, *Caring and Sharing: The Centenary History of the Co-operative Women's Guild* (1983), p. 268.
60. Labour Party, *Annual Report, 1978* (1978), p. 90.
61. T. Forrester, *The Labour Party and the Working Class* (1976), p. 80.
62. D. Howell, *British Social Democracy: A Study in Development and Decay* (1976), p. 246.
63. D. E. Butler, *British General Elections since 1945* (1989), pp. 26–7.
64. Hart, 'Gender', p. 22; Heath et al., *How Britain Votes*, p. 30.

9 Labour in Crisis? 1970–79

1. C. A. R. Crosland, *The Conservative Enemy: A Programme of Radical Reform for the 1960s* (1962), p. 25.
2. C. A. R. Crosland, *A Social Democratic Britain* (1971), p. 8.
3. B. Pimlott, *Harold Wilson* (1992), p. 571.
4. P. Seyd, *The Rise and Fall of the Labour Left* (1987), p. 54.
5. D. Kogan and M. Kogan, *The Battle for the Labour Party* (1982), pp. 23–35.
6. L. Minkin, *The Labour Party Conference: A Study in the Politics of Intra-Party Democracy* (1978), pp. 336–7.
7. K. Middlemas, *Power, Competition and the State, Vol. 2: Threats to the Post-War Settlement, 1961–1974* (1990), p. 321; L. Minkin, *The Contentious Alliance: Trade Unions and the Labour Party* (1991), p. 118.
8. I. Mikardo, *Back-Bencher* (1988), p. 183; Minkin, *Labour Party Conference*, pp. 336–7.
9. S. Holland, *The Socialist Challenge* (1975), p. 255 and *passim*; J. Tomlinson, *The Unequal Struggle? British Socialism and the Capitalist Enterprise* (1982), pp. 99–122; G. Foote, *The Labour Party's Political Thought: A History* (2nd edn, 1986), pp. 316–23.
10. M. Hatfield, *The House the Left Built: Inside Labour Policy-Making* (1978), p. 189.
11. Labour Party, *Annual Report, 1973*, p. 167.
12. Mikardo, *Back-Bencher*, p. 187; Kogan and Kogan, *Battle for the Labour Party*, p. 23.

13. Seyd, *Rise and Fall of the Labour Left*, p. 29.
14. Pimlott, *Wilson*, pp. 580–1.
15. E. Shaw, *Discipline and Discord in the Labour Party* (1988), pp. 167, 179; J. Callaghan, *Time and Chance* (1987), p. 298; D. Owen, *Time to Declare* (1991), pp. 185–6.
16. Callaghan, *Time and Chance*, p. 299.
17. Pimlott, *Wilson*, p. 608; Callaghan, *Time and Chance*, p. 293; R. Jenkins, *A Life at the Centre* (1991), p. 365; D. Healey, *The Time of My Life* (1989), p. 370.
18. C. Cook, 'Labour's electoral base', in C. Cook and I. Taylor (eds), *The Labour Party* (1980), pp. 104–5.
19. D. Coates, *Labour in Power? A Study of the Labour Government, 1974–1979* (1980), p. 231.
20. H. Wilson, *Final Term: The Labour Government, 1974–1976* (1979), p. 107.
21. Wilson, *Final Term*, p. 109.
22. T. Benn, *Against the Tide: Diaries 1973–1976* (1990), pp. 389–95; J. Adams, *Tony Benn* (1992), pp. 371–6; for a more caustic view, see B. Donoughue, *Prime Minister: The Conduct of Policy under Harold Wilson and James Callaghan* (1987), pp. 55–6.
23. See, for example, Benn, *Against the Tide*, p. 535; B. Castle, *The Castle Diaries, 1974–1976* (1980), p. 689.
24. P. Ziegler, *Wilson: The Authorized Life of Lord Wilson of Rievaulx* (1993), p. 484; J. Haines, *Glimmers of Twilight: Harold Wilson in Decline* (2003), pp. 116–17, 201–2.
25. Callaghan, *Time and Chance*, pp. 386, 390.
26. Pimlott, *Wilson*, p. 678; Callaghan, *Time and Chance*, pp. 392–4; M. Jones, *Michael Foot* (1994), pp. 394–5; Healey, *Time of My Life*, pp. 446–7; Jenkins, *Life at the Centre*, pp. 434–6; Adams, *Benn*, pp. 379–80; S. Crosland, *Tony Crosland* (1982), pp. 311–21.
27. K. O. Morgan, *Callaghan: A Life* (1997), pp. 66–8, 72–3; P. Whitehead, 'The Labour governments, 1974–1979', in Hennessy and Seldon, *Ruling Performance*, p. 258.
28. Callaghan, *Time and Chance*, p. 444; Adams, *Benn*, p. 380.
29. M. Sawyer, 'Industrial policy', in M. Artis and D. Cobham (eds), *Labour's Economic Policies, 1974–1979* (1991), p. 160.
30. P. Whitehead, *The Writing on the Wall: Britain in the Seventies* (1985), p. 131.
31. Sawyer, 'Industrial policy', pp. 171–2; E. Dell, *A Hard Pounding: Politics and Economic Crisis, 1974–1976* (1991), pp. 89–90.
32. Wilson, *Final Term*, p. 141; Healey, *Time of My Life*, p. 459.
33. Adams, *Benn*, p. 353.
34. Sawyer, 'Industrial policy', p. 160.
35. J. Tomlinson, *Public Policy and the Economy* (1990), p. 294.
36. E. Dell, 'The Chrysler UK rescue', *Contemporary Record*, 6 (1992): 1–44; M. C. Fleming, 'Industrial policy', in W. P. J. Maunder (ed.), *The British Economy in the 1970s* (1980), p. 151; T. Forrester, 'Neutralising the industrial strategy', in K. Coates (ed.), *What Went Wrong: Explaining the Fall of the Labour Government* (1979), p. 87.

37. Tomlinson, *Public Policy*, pp. 294–5.
38. T. G. Weyman-Jones, 'The nationalised industries: changing attitudes and changing roles', in Maunder, *British Economy*, pp. 195–6.
39. J. Dunkerley and P. Hare, 'Nationalized industries', in Crafts and Woodward, *British Economy*, pp. 404–7, 415–16; K. Middlemas, *Power, Competition and the State, Vol. 3: The End of the Post-War Era, Britain since 1974* (1991).
40. P. Ormerod, 'Incomes policy', in Artis and Cobham, *Labour's Economic Policies*, p. 58.
41. Tomlinson, *Public Policy*, p. 301; T. J. Hatton and K. A. Chrystal, 'The budget and fiscal policy', in Crafts and Woodward, *British Economy*, p. 80.
42. Dell, *Hard Pounding*, p. 137.
43. Whitehead, *Writing on the Wall*, pp. 148–9; Minkin, *Contentious Alliance*, p. 168.
44. Middlemas, *Power, Competition and the State, vol. III*, pp. 94–6.
45. Ormerod, 'Incomes policy', p. 57.
46. Ibid., pp. 60–4.
47. Healey, *Time of My Life*, p. 428.
48. Callaghan, *Time and Chance*, pp. 425–7.
49. Ibid., pp. 438–9.
50. Ibid., p. 434.
51. Dell, *Hard Pounding*, pp. 237, 247–8, 254–6.
52. Ibid., p. 258; Healey, *Time of My Life*, pp. 429–30; Crosland, *Crosland*, p. 377; Adams, *Benn*, pp. 383–4.
53. Dell, *Hard Pounding*, p. 267.
54. Crosland, *Crosland*, pp. 381–2.
55. Whitehead, *Writing on the Wall*, pp. 196–7.
56. Ibid., p. 199.
57. Benn, *Against the Tide*, pp. 670–9, 682.
58. Whitehead, *Writing on the Wall*, pp. 198–9.
59. Callaghan, *Time and Chance*, pp. 439–41.
60. Healey, *Time of My Life*, p. 432.
61. Ibid., p. 433; T. Westaway, 'Stabilisation policy and fiscal reform', in Maunder, *British Economy*, p. 24.
62. Ormerod, 'Incomes policy', p. 57.
63. R. Lowe, *The Welfare State in Britain since 1945* (1993), pp. 314, 316.
64. Whitehead, *Writing on the Wall*, p. 259.
65. K. O. Morgan, *Michael Foot: A Life* (2007), pp. 349–51.
66. Whitehead, *Writing on the Wall*, p. 277.
67. K. O. Morgan, *The People's Peace: British History, 1945–1989* (1990), pp. 369–70.
68. Jones, *Foot*, p. 413.
69. W. L. Miller, *The End of British Politics? Scots and English Political Behaviour in the Seventies* (1981), p. 240.
70. Morgan, *People's Peace*, p. 410.
71. Callaghan, *Time and Chance*, p. 448; Healey, *Time of My Life*, p. 458.
72. Minkin, *Contentious Alliance*, p. 176.

73. Ormerod, 'Incomes policy', p. 57; Middlemas, *Power, Competition and the State, vol. III,* p. 161.
74. Callaghan, *Time and Chance,* pp. 514–16; Healey, *Time of My Life,* p. 462.
75. Jones, *Foot,* pp. 423–4; Callaghan, *Time and Chance,* p. 516.
76. Dell, *Hard Pounding,* p. 285.
77. Healey, *Time of My Life,* p. 463.
78. Ormerod, 'Incomes policy', pp. 70–1; M. W. Kirby, 'Supply-side management', in Crafts and Woodward, *British Economy,* p. 257.
79. Healey, *Time of My Life,* p. 463.
80. T. Benn, *Conflicts of Interest: Diaries, 1976–1980* (1990), p. 449.
81. Whitehead, *Writing on the Wall,* pp. 281–2; J. Shepherd, *Crisis? What Crisis? The Callaghan Government and the British 'Winter of Discontent'* (2013).
82. Middlemas, *Power, Competition and the State, vol. III,* pp. 163–4.
83. Benn, *Conflicts of Interest,* pp. 485–8; E. Heffer, *Never a Yes Man: The Life and Politics of an Adopted Liverpudlian* (1991), pp. 172–3.
84. D. E. Butler and D. Kavanagh, *The British General Election of October 1974* (1975), p. 278; D. E. Butler and D. Kavanagh, *The British General Election of 1979* (1980), p. 343; D. E. Butler and M. Pinto-Duschinsky, *The British General Election of 1970* (1971), p. 342.
85. P. Riddell, *The Thatcher Era and Its Legacy* (1991), pp. 233–4.

10   Down and Out? 1979–87

1. P. Whitehead, *The Writing on the Wall: Britain in the Seventies* (1985), p. 366; E. J. Hobsbawm, *The Forward March of Labour Halted?*, ed. M. Jacques (1981), esp. pp. 1–19.
2. K. Coates, 'What went wrong', in Coates, *What Went Wrong,* pp. 7–33; N. Bosanquet, 'Labour and public expenditure: an overall view', in N. Bosanquet and P. Townsend (eds), *Labour and Equality: A Fabian Study of Labour in Power, 1974–1979* (1980), p. 43.
3. D. Kogan and M. Kogan, *The Battle for the Labour Party* (1982), pp. 54–67; E. Shaw, *Discipline and Discord in the Labour Party* (1988), pp. 199–200.
4. B. Pimlott, 'Trade unions and the second coming of CND', in Pimlott and Cook, *Trade Unions in British Politics,* p. 217. L. Minkin, *The Contentious Alliance* (1991), pp. 204–5, warns against taking too 'left' a view of the unions at this time, however.
5. J. Callaghan, *Time and Chance* (1987), p. 564.
6. R. Jenkins, 'Home thoughts from abroad: the 1979 Dimbleby Lecture', in W. Kennet (ed.), *The Rebirth of Britain* (1982), pp. 9–29.
7. R. Jenkins, *A Life at the Centre* (1991), pp. 520–1.
8. N. F. R. Crafts, 'Economic growth', in Crafts and Woodward, *British Economy,* p. 285.
9. Callaghan, *Time and Chance,* p. 565; M. Jones, *Michael Foot* (1994), p. 442; D. Healey, *The Time of My Life* (1989), p. 466.
10. Labour Party, *Annual Report, 1980* (1980), pp. 157, 159.
11. Minkin, *Contentious Alliance,* pp. 204–5.
12. Kogan and Kogan, *Battle for the Labour Party,* p. 90.

13. Callaghan, *Time and Chance*, p. 565; Healey, *Time of My Life*, p. 476; I. Mikardo, *Back-Bencher* (1988), p. 201.
14. Kogan and Kogan, *Battle for the Labour Party*, p. 91; T. Benn, *The End of an Era: Diaries 1980–1990* (1992), pp. 37–8.
15. Jones, *Foot*, pp. 452–3.
16. Jenkins, *Life at the Centre*, pp. 522–3, 530.
17. Minkin, *Contentious Alliance*, pp. 123, 131, 214.
18. Healey, *Time of My Life*, p. 478; D. Owen, *Time to Declare* (1991), p. 458; Jenkins, *Life at the Centre*, p. 531; Mikardo, *Back-Bencher*, pp. 202–3.
19. Kogan and Kogan, *Battle for the Labour Party*, pp. 94–7; Jones, *Foot*, pp. 458–9.
20. Jenkins, *Life at the Centre*, pp. 534–6.
21. Minkin, *Contentious Alliance*, pp. 234–5.
22. Jones, *Foot*, p. 468.
23. A. McSmith, *John Smith: Playing the Long Game* (1993), p. 83.
24. Benn, *End of an Era*, p. 119; Jones, *Foot*, p. 467; J. Adams, *Tony Benn* (1992), p. 410; see also the milder misgivings of E. Heffer, *Never a Yes Man* (1991), pp. 177–8.
25. Benn, *End of an Era*, pp. 154–5.
26. Adams, *Benn*, p. 423.
27. See esp. D. Sanders, H. Ward and D. Marsh, 'Government popularity and the Falklands War: a reassessment', *British Journal of Political Science*, 17 (1987): 281–313.
28. M. Crick, *Militant* (1984), pp. 132, 213–14.
29. R. Heffernan and M. Marqusee, *Defeat from the Jaws of Victory: Inside Kinnock's Labour Party* (1992), p. 127.
30. Heffernan and Marqusee, *Defeat*, pp. 261–300.
31. Jones, *Foot*, p. 492.
32. Shaw, *Discipline*, pp. 225–6, 230, 235.
33. Ibid., pp. 235–6.
34. Ibid., p. 243.
35. Jones, *Foot*, p. 499; M. Foot, *Another Heart and Other Pulses: The Alternative to the Thatcher Society* (1984), pp. 20, 41.
36. R. McMullin, *The Light on the Hill: The Australian Labor Party, 1891–1991* (1991), pp. 407–9; D. E. Butler and D. Kavanagh, *The British General Election of 1983* (1984), pp. 59–60.
37. A. Mitchell, *Four Years in the Death of the Labour Party* (1983), pp. 101–2; Jones, *Foot*, pp. 505–6.
38. Healey, *Time of My Life*, pp. 499–500.
39. Foot, *Another Heart*, p. 29.
40. Butler and Kavanagh, *1983*, p. 85.
41. Labour Party, *The New Hope for Britain: Labour's Manifesto, 1983* (1983), esp. p. 8.
42. K. O. Morgan, *Michael Foot: A Life* (2007), pp. 429–34.
43. Butler and Kavanagh, *1983*, p. 119.
44. P. Dunleavy and C. T. Husbands, *British Democracy at the Crossroads: Voting and Party Competition in the 1980s* (1985), p. 123; A. Heath, R. Jowell and J. Curtice, *How Britain Votes* (1985), p. 30.

45. Jones, *Foot*, p. 517.
46. Heffernan and Marqusee, *Defeat*, pp. 40–1.
47. Labour Party, *Annual Report, 1983* (1983), p. 29 and enclosure after p. 366.
48. P. Riddell, *The Thatcher Era and Its Legacy* (1991), p. 233.
49. I. Crewe, 'Values: the crusade that failed', in D. Kavanagh and A. Seldon, *The Thatcher Effect: A Decade of Change* (1989), pp. 239–50.
50. R. Taylor, *The Trade Union Question in British Politics: Government and Trade Unions since 1945* (1993), pp. 321–5.
51. Taylor, *Trade Union Question*, p. 382; R. Price and G. S. Bain, 'The labour force', in A. H. Halsey (ed.), *British Social Trends since 1900* (1988), p. 188.
52. J. Haines, *The Politics of Power* (1977), pp. 94–111.
53. This was certainly the case in Sheffield, where the author was a Housing Repairs Clerk in 1983–84.
54. N. Ellison, *Egalitarian Thought and Labour Politics: Retreating Visions* (1994), pp. 175–8.
55. G. Goodman, *The Miners' Strike* (1985), for much of what follows.
56. Heffernan and Marqusee, *Defeat*, p. 53.
57. Ibid., p. 61.
58. Shaw, *Discipline*, pp. 256–7.
59. Minkin, *Contentious Alliance*, p. 421.
60. Labour Party, *Annual Report, 1985* (1985), p. 128. For a more sympathetic analysis of the problems facing Liverpool at the time, and how they were overcome, see D. Frost and P. North, *Militant Liverpool: A City on the Edge* (2013).
61. Shaw, *Discipline*, pp. 262–3.
62. M. Stuart, *John Smith: A Life* (2005), pp. 131–40.
63. C. Hughes and P. Wintour, *Labour Rebuilt: The New Model Party* (1990), p. 13; Heffernan and Marqusee, *Defeat*, pp. 111–13; M. Scammell, 'The phenomenon of political marketing: the Thatcher contribution', *Contemporary Record*, 8 (1994): 23–43.
64. M. J. Smith, 'The Labour party in opposition', in M. J. Smith and J. Spear (eds), *The Changing Labour Party* (1992), p. 10.
65. D. E. Butler and D. Kavanagh, *The British General Election of 1987* (1988), pp. 70–1.
66. Heffernan and Marqusee, *Defeat*, pp. 85–6.
67. D. E. Butler, *British General Elections since 1945* (1989), p. 64.
68. H. Kitschelt, 'Class structure and social democratic party strategy', *British Journal of Political Science*, 23 (1993): 299–337.
69. See, for example, D. Marquand, *The Progressive Dilemma* (1991).

11 Modernization and New Labour, 1987–97

1. M. Stuart, *John Smith: A Life* (2005), pp. 173–4.
2. V. Atkinson and J. Spear, 'The Labour party and women', in Smith and Spear, *Changing Labour Party*, pp. 165–7.
3. S. George and B. Rosamond, 'The European Community', in Smith and Spear, *Changing Labour Party*, p. 173.

4. B. Rosamond, 'The Labour party, trade unions and industrial relations', in Smith and Spear, *Changing Labour Party*, p. 92; R. Taylor, *The Trade Union Question in British Politics* (1993), p. 370; P. Riddell, *The Unfulfilled Prime Minister: Tony Blair's Quest for a Legacy* (2005), p. 2.

5. P. Alcock, 'The Labour Party and the welfare state', in Smith and Spear, *Changing Labour Party,* p. 141.

6. R. Heffernan and M. Marqusee, *Defeat from the Jaws of Victory* (1992), pp. 325–35.

7. Labour Party, *Annual Report, 1988* (1988), pp. 11, 211–21.

8. J. Adams, *Tony Benn* (1992), p. 454.

9. D. E. Butler and D. Kavanagh, *The British General Election of 1992* (1992), p. 15.

10. Ibid., p. 65.

11. Stuart, *John Smith*, pp. 208–13.

12. Butler and Kavanagh, *1992*, pp. 125–6, 237.

13. A. McSmith, *John Smith* (1993), p. 242.

14. Butler and Kavanagh, *1992*, pp. 146, 282.

15. Ibid., p. 351.

16. P. Clifford and A. Heath, 'The election campaign', in A. Heath, R. Jowell and J. Curtice (eds), *Labour's Last Chance? The 1992 Election and Beyond* (1994), p. 20.

17. M. Westlake, *Kinnock: The Biography* (2001), pp. 580–1; P. Routledge, *Mandy: The Unauthorised Biography of Peter Mandelson* (1999), p. 137.

18. McSmith, *John Smith*, p. 264.

19. Westlake, *Kinnock*, p. 584.

20. Stuart, *John Smith*, pp. 223–4.

21. McSmith, *John Smith*, p. 267.

22. L. P. Stark, *Choosing a Leader: Party Leadership Contests in Britain from Macmillan to Blair* (1996), pp. 96, 205.

23. McSmith, *John Smith*, pp. 268–9; see also B. Gould, J. Mills and S. Stewart, *A Competitive Pound* (1977) and B. Gould, *Socialism and Freedom* (1985).

24. Stark, *Choosing a Leader*, p. 94.

25. Ibid., p. 6.

26. P. Anderson and N. Mann, *Safety First: The Making of New Labour* (1997), pp. 87–8; G. Radice, *Diaries 1980–2001: From Political Disaster to Election Triumph* (2004), p. 314, 9 Feb. 1994.

27. D. Butler and D. Kavanagh, *The British General Election of 1997* (1997), p. 4.

28. L. Baston, *Sleaze: The State of Britain* (2000), pp. 180–92.

29. Routledge, *Mandy*, pp. 120, 123, 130–2, 137.

30. P. Gould, *The Unfinished Revolution: How the Modernisers Saved the Labour Party* (1998), pp. 161–2.

31. McSmith, *John Smith*, p. 326.

32. Commission on Social Justice, *Social Justice: Strategies for National Renewal* (1994), pp. i, ix–xi.

33. R. Brooks, A. Eagle and C. Short, *Quotas Now: Women in the Labour Party* (1990); M. Russell, *Building New Labour: The Politics of Party Organisation* (2005), pp. 106–8.

34. M. A. Stephenson, *The Glass Trapdoor: Women, Politics and the Media during the 1997 General Election* (1998), pp. 53–4.

35. Westlake, *Kinnock*, pp. 273–6.
36. Stuart, *John Smith*, p. 332.
37. McSmith, *John Smith*, pp. 294–5.
38. J. McIlroy, *Trade Unions in Britain Today* (2nd edn, 1995), pp. 302–3.
39. Butler and Kavanagh, *1997*, p. 188.
40. Russell, *Building New Labour*, pp. 137–9.
41. G. R. Taylor, *Labour's Renewal? The Policy Review and Beyond* (1997), pp. 64–5.
42. D. Butler, 'Elections', in P. Catterall (ed.), *Contemporary Britain: An Annual Review, 1994* (1994), pp. 50–1, and *1995* (1995), p. 59; C. Railings and M. Thrasher, *Local Elections in Britain* (1997), p. 156.
43. See, for example, *Guardian*, 13 May 1994.
44. J. Straw, *Last Man Standing: Memoirs of a Political Survivor* (2012), pp. 189–91, with quotation at p. 191; T. Blair, *A Journey* (2010), p. 37.
45. McSmith, *John Smith*, pp. 294–5; P. Routledge, *Gordon Brown: The Biography* (1998), p. 149.
46. G. Brown, *Maxton* (1986).
47. J. Sopel, *Tony Blair: The Moderniser* (rev. edn, 1995), p. 82.
48. McSmith, *John Smith*, p. 205. All four would end up leading the party, albeit, in Beckett's case, only temporarily after Smith's death in 1994.
49. Routledge, *Gordon Brown*, p. 191.
50. Ibid., pp. 169, 194.
51. Gould, *Unfinished Revolution*, pp. 192–200.
52. T. Bower, *Gordon Brown* (2004), pp. 121–2.
53. Routledge, *Gordon Brown*, pp. 171, 181.
54. Ibid., pp. 196–7; Routledge, *Mandy*, pp. 156–9.
55. Bower, *Gordon Brown*, p. 144.
56. McSmith, *John Smith*, p. 311.
57. Stark, *Choosing a Leader*, p. 6.
58. T. Blair, *New Britain: My Vision of a Young Country* (1996), pp. 3, 62–72.
59. J. McIlroy, 'The enduring alliance? Trade unions and the making of New Labour, 1994–1997', *British Journal of Industrial Relations*, 36 (1998): 537–64.
60. Ibid., p. 50.
61. Ibid., pp. 48–9.
62. T. Jones, *Remaking the Labour Party: From Gaitskell to Blair* (1996), p. 134; see also P. Riddell, 'The End of Clause IV, 1994–95', *Contemporary British History*, 11 (1997): 24–49; Straw, *Last Man Standing*, pp. 186–90.
63. Jones, *Remaking the Labour Party*, p. 139.
64. Ibid., pp. 143, 146.
65. Ibid., p. 146; Riddell, 'End of Clause IV', p. 43.
66. Butler and Kavanagh, *1997*, p. 51.
67. Anderson and Mann, *Safety First*, p. 32.
68. Gould, *Unfinished Revolution*, pp. 220–1.
69. K. Coates, *Clause IV Public Ownership and the Labour Party* (1995), p. 96.
70. Jones, *Remaking the Labour Party*, pp. 140, 146.
71. On the SLP, see R. Cross and S. Hopkins, 'The Socialist Labour Party and the general election of May 1997', *Contemporary Politics*, 4 (1998):

57–76; J. Fisher, 'Third and minor party breakthrough?', in A. Geddes and J. Tonge (eds), *Labour's Landslide: The British General Election 1997* (1997), pp. 64–5.

72. Socialist Labour Party, *Statement of Accounts for the Year Ended 31 December 2005* (Electoral Commission, 2006), p. 3.
73. *Exeter Labour News,* spring 2000.
74. For a strong critique, see N. Jones, *Sultans of Spin: The Media and the New Labour Government* (1999).
75. Butler and Kavanagh, *1997,* pp. 157–60, 172.
76. Ibid., pp. 4–5.
77. Ibid., p. 5.
78. W. Hutton, *The State We're In* (rev. edn, 1996), p. 320.
79. C. MacDonald, 'The challenge of co-operation', in B. Brivati and R. Heffernan (eds), *The Labour Party: A Centenary History* (2000), pp. 172–5.
80. Gould, *Unfinished Revolution,* pp. 326–33.
81. McIlroy, 'The enduring alliance', pp. 543, 545–6.
82. Anderson and Mann, *Safety First,* p. 39.
83. P. Seyd, 'New parties/new politics? A case study of the British Labour Party', *Party Politics,* 5 (1999): 383–405, at p. 403.
84. Butler and Kavanagh, *1997,* p. 58.
85. Ibid., p. 123.
86. Ibid., p. 246; P. Norris, 'Gender: a gender–generation gap?', in G. Evans and P. Norris (eds), *Critical Elections: British Parties and Voters in Long-Term Perspective* (1999), pp. 148–63.
87. S. Saggar and A. Heath, 'Race: towards a multicultural electorate?', ibid., pp. 102–23; S. Saggar, *The General Election 1997: Ethnic Minorities and Electoral Politics* (1998), esp. pp. 30–9.
88. J. Curtice and A. Park, 'Region: New Labour, new geography?', in Evans and Norris, *Critical Elections,* pp. 124–47, at pp. 144–6.
89. Ibid., pp. 140–4; Butler and Kavanagh, *1997,* pp. 251–2.

12 New Labour in Power, 1997–2007

1. P. Hennessy, *The Prime Minister: The Office and its Holders since 1945* (2001), p. 481.
2. Ibid., p. 486.
3. P. Toynbee and D. Walker, *Did Things get Better?* (2001), p. 232.
4. Ibid., p. 239; P. Toynbee and D. Walker, *Better or Worse? Has Labour Delivered?* (2005), pp. 60–2.
5. Toynbee and Walker, *Better or Worse?,* pp. 161–4.
6. L. McAllister, 'The Welsh devolution referendum: definitely, maybe?', and J. Mitchell, D. Denver, C. Pattie and H. Bochel, 'The 1997 devolution referendum in Scotland', *Parliamentary Affairs,* 51 (1998): 148–65, 166–81.
7. L. McAllister, 'The road to Cardiff Bay: the process of establishing the National Assembly for Wales', and J. Mitchell, 'The creation of the Scottish parliament: journey without end', *Parliamentary Affairs,* 52 (1999): 634–48 and 649–65.

8. P. Flynn, *Dragons led by Poodles: The Inside Story of a New Labour Stitch-Up* (1999).

9. P. Norton, 'Parliament', in A. Seldon (ed.), *The Blair Effect* (2001), pp. 61–2.

10. D. Smith, 'The Treasury and economic policy', in A. Seldon and D. Kavanagh (eds), *The Blair Effect 2001–5* (2005), pp. 167–8.

11. D. King and M. Wickham-Jones, 'From Clinton to Blair: the Democratic (party) origins of welfare to work', *Political Quarterly*, 70 (1999): 62–74.

12. T. Blair, speech on 'Doctrine of the International Community', Economic Club, Chicago, 24 April 1999, at http://webarchive.nationalarchives.gov.uk/+/www.number10.gov.uk/Page1297 (accessed 21 November 2014).

13. C. Hill, 'Foreign policy', in Seldon and Kavanagh, *Blair Effect*, pp. 340–2.

14. D. Metcalf, 'The British national minimum wage', *British Journal of Industrial Relations*, 37 (1999): 171–201.

15. Cm 4401, *The Government's Annual Report, 98/99* (1999), pp. 20–1, 27.

16. On this, see P. Ashdown, *The Ashdown Diaries, Vol. 2: 1997–99* (2002).

17. R. Hattersley, 'It's no longer my party', *Observer*, 24 June 2001.

18. See P. Cowley, *The Rebels: How Blair Mislaid His Majority* (2005).

19. N. Jones, *Sultans of Spin* (1999), p. 283.

20. J. McIlroy, 'The enduring alliance? Trade unions and the making of New Labour, 1994–1997', *British Journal of Industrial Relations*, 36 (1998): 559; S. Ludlam, 'New Labour and the unions: the end of the contentious alliance?', in S. Ludlam and M. J. Smith (eds), *New Labour in Government* (2001), pp. 111–29.

21. L. Baston and S. Henig, 'The Labour Party', in Seldon and Kavanagh, *Blair Effect 2001–5*, p. 118.

22. L. Baston, *Sleaze: The State of Britain* (2000), pp. 201–5.

23. Ibid., pp. 205–9; P. Routledge, *Mandy* (1999), pp. 7–12.

24. D. E. Butler and D. Kavanagh, *The British General Election of 2001* (2001), pp. 21, 36.

25. S. Fielding, '"No-one else to vote for"? Labour's campaign', in A. Geddes and J. Tonge (eds), *Labour's Second Landslide: The British General Election of 2001* (2002), pp. 28–9.

26. Ibid., pp. 30–1.

27. Toynbee and Walker, *Did Things get Better?*, p. 7; D. Wring, 'The "Tony" press: media coverage of the election campaign', in Geddes and Tonge, *Labour's Second Landslide*, p. 93.

28. Butler and Kavanagh, *2001*, p. 257.

29. For a good summary, see A. Geddes and J. Tonge 'Introduction', in idem, *Labour's Second Landslide*, pp. 4–6.

30. Fielding, '"No-one else to vote for"?', pp. 39–40.

31. A. Rawnsley, *Servants of the People: The Inside Story of New Labour* (2nd edn, 2001), p. 507; T. Bower, *Gordon Brown* (2004), p. 353.

32. See M. Barber, *Instruction to Deliver: Tony Blair, the Public Services and the Challenge of Delivery* (2007); Toynbee and Walker, *Better or Worse*, p. 209.

33. Toynbee and Walker, *Better or Worse*, p. 209; H. Glennister, 'Health and welfare', in Seldon and Kavanagh, *Blair Effect 2001–5*, p. 295.

34. P. Ormerod, 'The impact of Sure Start', *Political Quarterly*, 76 (2005): 565–7.
35. K. Stewart, 'Equality and social justice', in Seldon and Kavanagh, *Blair Effect 2001–5*, pp. 334–5; A. Seldon, 'The verdict', ibid., p. 419.
36. S. Driver and L. Martell, *Blair's Britain* (2002), pp. 226–7.
37. *The Guardian*, 17 March 2005.
38. P. Riddell, 'Europe', in Seldon and Kavanagh, *Blair Effect 2001–5*, pp. 367–8.
39. For the neoconservatives, see esp. S. Halper and J. Clarke, *America Alone: The Neo-Conservatives and the Global Order* (rev. edn, 2005; M. Freidman, *The Neoconservative Revolution: Jewish Intellectuals and the Shaping of Public Policy* (2005); N. Podhoretz, 'World War IV: how it started, what it means, and why we have to win', *Commentary*, Sept. 2004; Project for a New American Century website, at http://www.newamericancentury.org (accessed 8 June 2007).
40. J. Kampfner, *Blair's Wars* (rev. edn, 2003), pp. 123–4.
41. C. Hill, 'Foreign policy', in Seldon and Kavanagh, *Blair Effect 2001–5*, p. 406.
42. Ibid., p. 402.
43. P. Riddell, *Hug Them Close: Blair, Clinton, Bush and the 'Special Relationship'* (rev. edn, 2004), p. 263.
44. Kampfner, *Blair's Wars*, p. 272.
45. S. Fielding, 'Labour's campaign: neither forwards nor back', in A. Geddes and J. Tonge (eds), *Britain Decides: The UK General Election 2005* (2005), p. 32.
46. R. Kuhn, 'Media management', in Seldon and Kavanagh, *Blair Effect 2001–5*, pp. 99–102.
47. Kampfner, *Blair's Wars*, p. 402.
48. Bower, *Gordon Brown*, p. 426.
49. Riddell, 'Europe', pp. 374–5.
50. Fielding, 'Labour's campaign', pp. 36–7; D. Blunkett, *The Blunkett Tapes* (2006), p. 746.
51. Bower, *Gordon Brown*, pp. 430–5.
52. D. Kavanagh, 'The Blair premiership', in Seldon and Kavanagh, *Blair Effect 2001–5*, p. 3.
53. D. Kavanagh and D. E. Butler, *The British General Election of 2005* (2005), pp. 20–2.
54. See A. Murray, *A New Labour Nightmare: The Return of the Awkward Squad* (2003).
55. Baston and Henig, 'The Labour Party', p. 118.
56. P. Wintour, 'Blair's secret plan to scrap the Treasury', *Guardian*, 9 May 2007.
57. P. Riddell, *The Unfulfilled Prime Minister* (2005), p. xii.
58. Kavanagh and Butler, *2005*, p. 57.
59. Fielding, 'Labour's campaign', p. 41.
60. P. Norris, 'Elections and public opinion', in Seldon and Kavanagh, *Blair Effect 2001–5*, p. 65.
61. Riddell, *Unfulfilled Prime Minister*, pp. 207–8.

62. P. Seyd and P Whiteley, *New Labour's Grassroots: The Transformation of the Party Membership* (2002), esp. p. 109; C. Short, *An Honourable Deception? New Labour, Iraq, and the Misuse of Power* (2004), p. 280.
63. Butler and Kavanagh, *2001*, p. 259.
64. M. Russell, *Building New Labour* (2005), p. 220.
65. Ibid., pp. 282–3.
66. Ibid., pp. 89–90, 181.
67. Ibid., pp. 124, 265.
68. For much more on this see Bower, *Gordon Brown*, esp. pp. 236–7, 266, 404–5, 439.
69. See, for example, A. Giddens, 'Goodbye to the Third Way', *Parliamentary Brief*, 11, 3 (April 2007): 11–12.

13 Moving beyond Blair, 2007–15

1. T. Blair, *A Journey* (2010), pp. 636–7.
2. A. Rawnsley, *The End of the Party* (2010), pp. 434–5.
3. The 2020 Vision: http://the2020vision.org.uk (accessed 22 July 2014).
4. S. Richards, *Whatever It Takes: The Real Story of Gordon Brown and New Labour* (2010), pp. 347–8.
5. Rawnsley, *End of the Party*, pp. 435, 460.
6. C. Mullin, *Decline and Fall: Diaries, 2005–2010* (2010), pp. 170–1; P. Mandelson, *The Third Man: Life at the Heart of New Labour* (2010), pp. 431–2.
7. Rawnsley, *Servants of the People*, pp. 116–20.
8. M. Russell, *Building New Labour* (2005), pp. 205–6.
9. S. Driver and L. Martell, *New Labour* (2nd edn., 2006), pp. 213–14.
10. Rawnsley, *End of the Party*, p. 463.
11. Richards, *Whatever It Takes*, p. 268.
12. Ibid., pp. 275–7; J. Straw, *Last Man Standing* (2012), pp. 499–500.
13. A. Seldon and G. Lodge, *Brown at 10* (2010), pp. 34–53; Straw, *Last Man Standing*, pp. 508–9.
14. Mullin, *Decline and Fall*, pp. 201–2.
15. P. Watt, *Inside Out: My Story of Betrayal and Cowardice at the Heart of New Labour* (2010), p. 164.
16. K. Theakston, 'Gordon Brown as Prime Minister: political skills and leadership style', *British Politics*, 6 (2011): 98.
17. For more on this, see T. Bale, *The Conservative Party from Thatcher to Cameron* (2011), pp. 351–62.
18. Rawnsley, *End of the Party*, pp. 496–514, esp. pp. 511–12.
19. On election fever, see Mullin, *Decline and Fall*, pp. 196–201.
20. Seldon and Lodge, *Brown at 10*, pp. 474–5.
21. *Observer*, 19 October 2008.
22. A. Darling, *Back from the Brink: 1,000 Days at Number 11* (2011), pp. 110–29.
23. Rawnsley, *End of the Party*, pp. 575–97.
24. Darling, *Back from the Brink*, pp. 84–90.
25. Robert Worcester et al., *Explaining Cameron's Coalition: An Analysis of the 2010 British General Election* (2011), pp. 71–3.

26. Ibid., pp. 136–7.
27. Seldon and Lodge, *Brown at 10*, p. 140.
28. Ibid., pp. 186–7.
29. See, for example, Mullin, *Decline and Fall*, pp. 196–201. By this time, public revelations had been made in a number of places, and most notably Rawnsley, *Servants of the People* (2000), and A. Campbell, *The Blair Years: Extracts from the Alastair Campbell Diaries* (2007).
30. Rawnsley, *End of the Party*, pp. 637–9; D. McBride, *Power Trip: A Decade of Policy, Plots and Spin* (2013), esp. pp. 385–403; Mandelson, *Third Man*, pp. 461–6.
31. Seldon and Lodge, *Brown at 10*, pp. 251.
32. Rawnsley, *End of the Party*, pp. 472–3, 551–2.
33. M. Foley, 'Gordon Brown and the role of compounded crisis in the pathology of leadership decline', *British Politics*, 4 (2009).
34. Blair, *A Journey*, pp. 679–80.
35. Seldon and Lodge, *Brown at 10*, pp. 68–71.
36. Rawnsley, *End of the Party*, pp. 639–40, 645–52.
37. C. Pattie and R. Johnston, 'The electoral impact of the 2009 UK MPs' expenses scandal', *Political Studies*, 60 (2012): 730–50, esp. p. 748.
38. L. Minkin, *The Blair Supremacy: A Study in the Politics of Labour's Party Management* (2014), pp. 631–2, 740–2.
39. For a quick summary, see ibid., pp. 747–8, 752, 758.
40. Rawnsley, *End of the Party*, pp. 557–9; Richards, *Whatever It Takes*, pp. 347–9.
41. Richards, *Whatever It Takes*, pp. 367–71; Rawnsley, *End of the Party*, p. 571.
42. Rawnsley, *End of the Party*, pp. 561, 571–4; Mandelson, *Third Man*, pp. 440–1.
43. Seldon and Lodge, *Brown at 10*, pp. 273–81; Rawnsley, *End of the Party*, pp. 653–7.
44. Mandelson, *Third Man*, pp. 466–73.
45. Richards, *Whatever It Takes*, pp. 417–22; Straw, *Last Man Standing*, 521–4.
46. Worcester et al., *Explaining Cameron's Coalition*, p. 297.
47. D. Wring and S. Ward, 'The media and the 2010 campaign: the television election?', in A. Geddes and J. Tonge, *Britain Votes 2010* (2010), pp. 217–32.
48. On the bubble, see D. Cutts, 'Yet another false dawn? An examination of the Liberal Democrats' performance in the 2010 general election', *British Journal of Politics and International Relations*, 14 (2012): 96–114.
49. Worcester et al., *Explaining Cameron's Coalition*, pp. 239–42.
50. D. Denver, 'How Britain voted', in Geddes and Tonge (eds.), *Britain Votes 2010*, pp. 6–24, at p. 11.
51. S. Fielding, 'Labour's campaign: things can only get … worse?', ibid., pp. 71–84, at p. 82.
52. Worcester et al., *Explaining Cameron's Coalition*, p. 286.
53. The best account is A. Adonis, *Five Days in May: The Coalition and Beyond* (2013).
54. Ibid., p. 130.

55. Seldon and Lodge, *Brown at 10*, p. 140.
56. R. Jobson and M. Wickham-Jones, 'Reinventing the block vote? Trade unions and the 2010 Labour party leadership election', *British Politics*, 6 (2011): 317–44; Minkin, *Blair Supremacy*, pp. 763–4.
57. M. Hasan and J. Macintyre, *Ed: The Milibands and the Making of a Labour Leader* (2012).
58. Darling, *Back from the Brink*, pp. 307–8; Straw, *Last Man Standing*, pp. 532–4; *Guardian*, 29 September 2010.
59. Minkin, *Blair Supremacy*, p. 767.
60. *Guardian*, 29 September 2010.
61. *Guardian*, 26 November 2010, 14 January 2014.
62. Darling, *Back from the Brink*, p. 309.
63. R. Davis, *Tangled up in Blue: Blue Labour and the Struggle for Labour's Soul* (2011); M. Glasman et al. (eds.), *The Labour Tradition and the Politics of Paradox* (2011).
64. R. Philpott (ed.), *The Purple Book: A Progressive Future for Labour* (2011).
65. O. Smith and R. Reeves (eds.), *One Nation: Power, Hope, Community* (2013).
66. Valuable analyses of these developments include P. Diamond, 'The progressive dilemmas of British social democracy: political economy after New Labour', *British Journal of Politics and International Relations*, 15 (2013); J. Gaffney and A. Lahel, 'The morphology of the Labour party's One Nation narrative: story, plot and authorship', *Political Quarterly*, 84 (2013); and T. Bale, 'Concede and move on? One Nation Labour and the welfare state', *Political Quarterly*, 85 (2014).
67. M. d'Ancona, *In It Together: The Inside Story of the Coalition Government* (2013).
68. D. Denver and M. Garnett, *British General Elections since 1964: Diversity, Dealignment and Disillusion* (2014), pp. 196–8.
69. J. Gaffney and A. Lahel, 'Political performance and leadership persona: the UK Labour party conference of 2012', *Government and Opposition*, 48 (2013).
70. Labour Party, *The Collins Review into Labour Party Reform: Building a One Nation Labour Party* (2014), pp. 7–10.
71. For more on this, see R. Ford and M. Goodwin, *Revolt on the Right: Explaining Support for the Radical Right in Britain* (2014).
72. T. Bale, 'If Opposition is an art, is Ed Miliband an artist? A framework for evaluating Leaders of the Opposition', *Parliamentary Affairs* (2014).

Conclusion

1. *New Statesman*, 27 September 2012.
2. Department for Business, Innovation and Skills, *Trade Union Membership 2012: Statistical Bulletin* (2013), pp. 11, 22.

Bibliography

(Place of publication is London unless otherwise stated.)

General

M. Pugh, *Speak for Britain! A New History of the Labour Party* (2010) is the most recent single-volume account. The party's centenary saw a rash of publications, the best of which was D. Tanner, P. Thane and N. Tiratsoo (eds), *Labour's First Century* (Cambridge, 2000); see also B. Brivati and R. Heffernan (eds), *The Labour Party: A Centenary History* (2000) and K. Laybourn, *A Century of Labour* (Stroud, 2000). For decades, the standard short account was H. Pelling, *A Short History of the Labour Party* (1st edn 1961), which eventually ran to 11 editions in his lifetime, and which after his death went into a twelfth as A. J. Reid and H. Pelling, *A Short History of the Labour Party* (Basingstoke, 2005). Among older general accounts, see especially R. Miliband, *Parliamentary Socialism: A Study in the Politics of Labour* (2nd edn, 1972), J. Hinton, *Labour and Socialism: A History of the British Labour Movement, 1867–1974* (Brighton, 1983) and J. E. Cronin, *Labour and Society in Britain, 1918–1979* (1983). For the interwar years, see M. Worley, *Labour Inside the Gate: A History of the British Labour Party between the Wars* (2005) and G. D. H. Cole, *History of the Labour Party from 1914* (1948), which remains surprisingly useful, given its age. K. Jefferys, *The Labour Party since 1945* (1992) is a good straightforward account of post-war developments; see also E. Shaw, *The Labour Party since 1945* (Oxford, 1996). M. Pinto-Duschinsky *British Political Finance, 1830–1980* (Washington, DC, 1981) is indispensable. H. Harmer, *The Longman Companion to the Labour Party, 1900–1998* (1999) is an excellent compendium of information; see also D. Butler and G. Butler, *Twentieth Century British Political Facts* (2000).

Among books operating at a rather more profound level, see especially S. Fielding, *The Labour Party: Continuity and Change in the Making of 'New' Labour* (Basingstoke, 2003), J. Cronin, *New Labour's Pasts* (2004), T. Bale, *Sacred Cows and Common Sense: The Symbolic Statecraft and Political Culture of the British Labour Party* (1999) and R. C. Whiting, *The Labour Party and Taxation: Party Identity and Political Purpose in Twentieth-Century Britain* (Cambridge, 2001). H. M. Drucker, *Doctrine and Ethos in the Labour Party* (1979) remains important. See also D. Marquand, *The Progressive Dilemma* (1991), R. I. McKibbin, *The Ideologies of Class* (Oxford, 1990), B. Jones and M. Keating, *Labour and the British State* (Oxford, 1985) and

R. Price, *Labour in British Society: An Interpretative History* (1986). The essays in J. Lawrence and M. Taylor, *Party, State and Society: Electoral Behaviour in Britain since 1820* (Aldershot, 1997) offer stimulating insights. D. Sassoon, *One Hundred Years of Socialism: The Western European Left in the Twentieth Century* (1996) places Labour's development in an international context and is especially strong for the post-1945 period. On that European context, see also I. Favretto, *The Long Search for a Third Way: The British Labour Party and the Italian Left since 1945* (Basingstoke, 2002). Foreign policy more generally can be followed in R. Vickers, *The Labour Party and the World* (2 vols, Manchester, 2004–11), J. Callaghan, *The Labour Party and Foreign Policy: A History* (2007), P. Corthorn and J. Davis (eds), *The Labour Party and the Wider World: Domestic Politics, Internationalism and Foreign Policy* (2007) and M. Phythian, *The Labour Party, War and International Relations, 1945–2006* (2007).

For biographical details, see the indispensable *Dictionary of Labour Biography*, vols 1–10, ed. J. Bellamy and J. Saville (1972–2000), vol. 11, ed. K. Gildart, D. Howell and N. Kirk (2003), vols 12–13, ed. K. Gildart and D. Howell (2004–10); G. Rosen (ed.), *Dictionary of Labour Biography* (2001); K. O. Morgan, *Labour People: Leaders and Lieutenants from Hardie to Kinnock* (Oxford, 1987); and two volumes edited by K. Jefferys: *Leading Labour: From Keir Hardie to Tony Blair* (1999) and *Labour Forces: From Ernie Bevin to Gordon Brown* (2001). D. Weinbren, *Generating Socialism: Recollections of Life in the Labour Party* (Stroud, 1997) is an excellent collection of activists' oral testimonies.

On the trade unions, see especially A. J. Reid, *United We Stand: A History of Britain's Trade Unions* (2004), W. H. Fraser, *A History of British Trade Unionism 1700–1998* (1999), R. Martin, *TUC: The Growth of a Pressure Group, 1868–1976* (Oxford, 1980), R. Taylor, *The TUC: From the General Strike to New Unionism* (2000), S. Boston, *Women Workers and the Trade Union Movement* (1980), D. Howell, *Respectable Radicals: Studies in the Politics of Railway Trade Unionism* (Aldershot, 1999), C. J. Wrigley, *British Trade Unions since 1933* (2002) and *British Trade Unions 1945–1995* (1997), and three stimulating collection of essays: B. Pimlott and C. Cook (eds), *Trade Unions in British Politics: The First 250 Years* (2nd edn, 1991), A. Campbell, N. Fishman and D. Howell (eds), *Miners, Unions and Politics, 1910–47* (Aldershot, 1996) and A. Campbell, N. Fishman and J. McIlroy (eds), *British Trade Unions and Industrial Politics* (2 vols, Aldershot, 1999).

On ideology, see especially J. Callaghan, *Socialism in Britain since 1884* (Oxford, 1990), G. Foote, *The Labour Party's Political Thought: A History* (2nd edn, 1986), W. H. Greenleaf, *The British Political Tradition, Vol. 2: The Ideological Heritage* (1983), B. Jackson, *Equality and the British Left: A Study in Progressive Thought, 1900–64* (Manchester, 2011), N. Ellison, *Egalitarian Thought and Labour Politics: Retreating Visions* (1994), N. Thompson, *Political Economy and the Labour Party: The Economics of Democratic Socialism, 1884–1995* (1996), J. Nuttall, *Psychological Socialism: The Labour Party and Qualities of Mind and Character, 1931 to the Present* (Manchester, 2006), R. Plant, M. Beech and K. Hickson (eds), *The Struggle for Labour's Soul: Understanding Labour's Political Thought since 1945* (2004) and J. Tomlinson,

'The limits of Tawney's ethical socialism: a historical perspective on the Labour Party and the market', *Contemporary British History*, 16 (2002). There are also some very useful collections of documents, including A. Wright (ed.), *British Socialism: Socialist Thought from the 1880s to the 1960s* (1983), F. Bealey (ed.), *The Social and Political Thought of the British Labour Party* (1970) and S. Fielding (ed.), *The Labour Party: 'Socialism' and Society since 1951* (Manchester, 1997).

Debates surrounding the development of Labour politics have been enriched by local and regional studies. On Scotland, see G. Hassan (ed.), *The Scottish Labour Party: History, Institutions and Ideas* (Edinburgh, 2004), as well as I. Donnachie, C. Harvie and I. S. Wood (eds), *Forward! Labour Politics in Scotland, 1888–1988* (Edinburgh, 1988), I. McLean, *The Legend of Red Clydeside* (Edinburgh, 1980), A. McKinlay and R. J. Morris (eds), *The ILP on Clydeside, 1893–1932: From Foundation to Disintegration* (Manchester, 1990), J. Melling, 'Whatever happened to Red Clydeside', *International Review of Social History*, 35 (1990), T. Gallacher, *Glasgow, The Uneasy Peace: Religious Tension in Modern Scotland* (Manchester, 1987), J. J. Smyth, *Labour in Glasgow, 1896–1936* (2001), C. Harvie, 'Labour in Scotland during the Second World War', *Historical Journal*, 26 (1983) and G. Walker, *Thomas Johnston* (Manchester, 1988). For Wales, see the excellent centenary collection, D. Tanner, C. Williams and D. Hopkin (eds), *The Labour Party in Wales, 1900–2000* (2000), as well as K. O. Morgan, *Rebirth of a Nation: Wales, 1880–1980* (Oxford, 1981) and A. Edwards, *Labour's Crisis: Plaid Cymru, the Conservatives, and the Decline of the Labour Party in North-West Wales, 1960–74* (2011). Among a large number of studies of northern England, see especially the seminal work of M. Savage, *The Dynamics of Working-Class Politics: The Labour Movement in Preston, 1880–1940* (Cambridge, 1987). Also of value are P. J. Waller, *Democracy and Sectarianism: A Political and Social History of Liverpool, 1868–1939* (Liverpool, 1981), S. Davies, *Liverpool Labour: Social and Political Influences on the Development of the Labour Party in Liverpool, 1900–1939* (Keele, 1996), J. Smith, 'The Labour tradition in Glasgow and Liverpool', *History Workshop Journal*, 17 (1984), P. Shapely, D. Tanner and A. Walling, 'Civic culture and housing policy in Manchester, 1945–79', *Twentieth Century British History*, 15 (2004), S. Fielding and D. Tanner, 'The "rise of the left" revisited: Labour Party culture in post-war Manchester and Salford', *Labour History Review*, 71 (2006), K. Laybourn and J. Reynolds, *Liberalism and the Rise of Labour, 1880–1914* (1985), J. Reynolds and K. Laybourn, *Labour Heartland: The History of the Labour Party in West Yorkshire during the Inter-War Years, 1918–1939* (Bradford, 1987), S. Pollard, *A History of Labour in Sheffield* (Liverpool, 1959), C. Binfield, R. Harper, R. Childs, D. Hey, R. Harman, D. Martin and G. Tweedale (eds), *The History of the City of Sheffield, 1843–1993, Vol. 1: Politics* (Sheffield, 1993), T. Griffiths, *The Lancashire Working Classes, c.1880–1930* (Oxford, 2001), A. W. Purdue, 'Arthur Henderson and Liberal, Liberal-Labour and Labour politics in the north-east of England, 1892–1903', *Northern History*, 11 (1975) and M. Callcott, 'The nature and extent of political change in the inter-war years: the example of Co. Durham', *Northern History*, 16 (1980). The Midlands have also excited considerable interest: see, among other works, P. Wyncoll, *The Nottingham Labour Movement, 1880–1939* (1985), R. J. Waller, *The Dukeries Transformed: The Social and Political Development of a Twentieth-Century Coalfield* (Oxford, 1983), A. Thorpe, 'J. H. Thomas and the rise of Labour in Derby, 1880–1940', *Midland History*, 15 (1990), B. Lancaster, *Radicalism, Co-operation and Socialism: Leicester Working-Class Politics, 1860–1906* (1988), R. P. Hastings, 'The Birmingham Labour movement, 1918–45', *Midland History*, 5 (1979–80), D. Rolf, 'Birmingham Labour and the background to the 1945 general election', in A. Wright and R. M. Y. Shackleton (eds), *Worlds of Labour: Essays in Birmingham Labour History* (Birmingham, 1981), B. Lancaster and T. Mason (eds), *Life and Labour in a Twentieth-Century City: The Experience of Coventry* (Coventry, 1986), N. Tiratsoo, *Reconstruction, Affluence and Labour Politics: Coventry 1945–60* (1990) and R. C. Whiting, *The View From Cowley: The Impact of Industrialization upon Oxford, 1918–1939* (Oxford, 1983). Work on southern England is less extensive and, where it exists, is mostly about London: see P. Thompson, *Socialists, Liberals and Labour: The Struggle for London, 1885–1914* (1967), J. Marriott, *The Culture of Labourism: The East End between the Wars* (Edinburgh, 1991) and S. Goss, *Local Labour and Local Government: A Study of Changing Interests, Politics and Policy in Southwark from 1919 to 1982* (1988). However, M. Hilson, *Political Change and the Rise of Labour in Comparative Perspective: Britain and Sweden, 1890–1920* (Lund, 2006) has a good deal to say about Plymouth.

1   Creation and Early Years, 1900–14

The best place to start on the late nineteenth century 'Socialist Revival' is now M. Bevir, *The Making of British Socialism* (Princeton, 2011). The collection of essays in E. F. Biagini and A. J. Reid (eds), *Currents of Radicalism: Popular Radicalism, Organized Labour and Party Politics in Britain, 1850–1914* (Cambridge, 1991) suggests that there was considerable continuity on the British left in the late nineteenth and early twentieth centuries. J. Lawrence, *Speaking for the People: Party, Language and Popular Politics in England, 1867–1914* (Cambridge, 1998) and L. Barrow and I. Bullock, *Democratic Ideas and the British Labour Movement, 1880–1914* (Cambridge, 1996) are also important. See also M. Carter, *T. H. Green and the Development of Ethical Socialism* (2003). By contrast, H. Pelling, *The Origins of the Labour Party, 1880–1900* (Oxford, 1965) is now mainly of interest as a period piece.

On particular parties, D. Howell, *British Workers and the Independent Labour Party 1888–1906* (Manchester, 1983) is comprehensive; see also J. R. Moore, 'Progressive pioneers: Manchester Liberalism, the Independent Labour Party, and local politics in the 1890s', *Historical Journal*, 44 (2001). On the SDF, see especially M. Crick, *The History of the Social Democratic Federation* (Keele, 1994), G. Johnson, *Social Democratic Politics in Britain 1881–1911* (Lampeter, 2002), K. Hunt, *Equivocal Feminists: The Social Democratic Federation and the Woman Question, 1884–1911* (Cambridge, 1996) and D. Young, 'Social Democratic Federation membership in London',

Historical Research, 78 (2005). For the Fabians, see A. M. McBriar, *Fabian Socialism and English Politics, 1884–1918* (Cambridge, 1962), E. J. Hobsbawm, 'The Fabians reconsidered' in his *Labouring Men: Studies in the History of Labour* (1964) and R. Harrison, *The Life and Times of Sidney and Beatrice Webb: 1858–1905, The Formative Years* (2001). C. Waters, *British Socialists and the Politics of Popular Culture, 1884–1914* (Manchester, 1990) looks at broader cultural aspects.

The standard work on the Labour Party in the period between its formation and the First World War is D. Tanner, *Political Change and the Labour Party, 1900–18* (Cambridge, 1990). Also important for this and the following three sections is an excellent collection of essays: M. Worley (ed.), *The Foundations of the British Labour Party: Identities, Cultures and Perspectives, 1900–39* (Aldershot, 2009). See also K. D. Brown (ed.), *The First Labour Party, 1906–1914* (1985) and A. Chadwick, *Augmenting Democracy: Political Movements and Constitutional Reform during the Rise of Labour, 1900–24* (1999). The context in which Labour was operating is described in F. Trentmann, *Free Trade Nation: Commerce, Consumption, and Civil Society in Modern Britain* (Oxford, 2008). A number of older works remain useful, in particular F. Bealey and H. Pelling, *Labour and Politics 1900–1906: A History of the Labour Representation Committee* (1958) and P. Poirier, *The Advent of the Labour Party* (1958). J. Harris, *Unemployment and Politics: A Study in English Social Policy, 1886–1914* (Oxford, 1972) has interesting things to say about Labour's approach in that area. The Labour movement as a whole is covered by G. Phillips, 'The British Labour movement before 1914', in R. Geary (ed.), *Labour and Socialist Movements in Europe Before 1914* (Oxford, 1989). See also D. Tanner, 'The development of British socialism, 1900–1918', *Parliamentary History*, 16 (1997) and D. Powell, 'New Liberalism and the rise of Labour, 1886–1906' *Historical Journal*, 29 (1986). On the Liberal land campaign and Labour responses to it, see I. Packer, *Lloyd George, Liberalism and the Land: The Land Issue and Party Politics in England, 1906–14* (2001) and M. Tichelar, 'Socialists, Labour and the land: the response of the Labour Party to the land campaign of Lloyd George before the First World War', *Twentieth Century British History*, 8 (1997).

On international aspects, see especially P. Brigden, *The Labour Party and the Politics of War and Peace, 1900–1924* (2009), as well as D. J. Newton, *British Labour, European Socialism and the Struggle for Peace 1889–1914* (Oxford, 1985) and E. McNeilly, 'Labour and the politics of internationalism, 1906–1914', *Twentieth Century British History*, 20 (2009).

On the unions, the best place to start remains H. A. Clegg, A. Fox and A. F. Thompson, *A History of British Trade Unions since 1889, Vol. 1: 1889–1910* (Oxford, 1964). There are some useful essays in W. J. Mommsen and H. G. Husung (eds), *The Development of Trade Unionism in Great Britain and Germany, 1880–1914* (1985). Specific union histories of value include C. Baylies, *The History of the Yorkshire Miners 1881–1918* (1993), K. Coates and T. Topham, *The History of the Transport and General Workers' Union, Vol. 1: 1870–1922* (Oxford, 1991), P. S. Bagwell, *The Railwaymen: A History of the National Union of Railwaymen* (1963), R. Gregory, *The Miners and British*

Politics, 1906–14 (1963) and R. Church, 'Edwardian Labour unrest and coalfield militancy, 1890–1914', *Historical Journal*, 30 (1987). The legal problems faced by the unions in these years are dealt with by J. Saville, 'Trade unions and free labour: the background to the Taff Vale decision', in A. Briggs and J. Saville (eds), *Essays in Labour History: In Memory of G. D. H. Cole* (rev. edn, 1967), J. Thompson, 'The genesis of the 1906 Trade Disputes Act: Liberalism, trade unions, and the law', *Twentieth Century British History*, 9 (1998) and H. Pelling, 'The politics of the Osborne Judgment', *Historical Journal*, 25 (1982). For radical movements in the unions, see especially B. Holton, *British Syndicalism, 1900–14: Myths and Realities* (1976), R. Price, 'Contextualising British syndicalism, c.1907–.c.1920', *Labour History Review*, 63 (1998) and L. Mates, 'The limits and potential of syndicalist influence in the Durham coalfield before the Great War', *Labor History*, 54 (2013).

Relations between the party and the women's suffrage campaign can be followed in S. S. Holton, *Feminism and Democracy: Women's Suffrage and Reform Politics in Britain, 1900–18* (Cambridge, 1986), J. Liddington and J. Norris, *One Hand Tied Behind Us: The Rise of the Women's Suffrage Movement* (1978), C. Collette, *For Labour and For Women: The Women's Labour League, 1906–1918* (Manchester, 1989) and L. Ugolini, '"We must stand by our own bairns": ILP men and suffrage militancy, 1905–14', *Labour History Review*, 67 (2002). More broadly, see J. Hannam and K. Hunt, *Socialist Women: Britain, 1880s to 1920s* (2002) and P. Thane, 'The women of the British Labour Party and feminism, 1906–45', in H. L. Smith (ed.), *British Feminism in the Twentieth Century* (Aldershot, 1990). Also of interest here is J. Liddington, *The Life and Times of a Respectable Rebel: Selina Cooper (1864–1946)* (1984). L. Smith, *Religion and the Rise of Labour: Nonconformity and the Independent Labour Movement in Lancashire and the West Riding, 1880–1914* (Keele, 1993) looks at that aspect.

For the 'rise of Labour/decline of Liberals' debate, see especially K. Laybourn, 'The rise of Labour and the decline of Liberalism: the state of the debate', *History*, 80 (1995), P. F. Clarke, *Lancashire and the New Liberalism* (1971) and 'The electoral position of the Liberal and Labour parties, 1910–14', *English Historical Review*, 90 (1975), H. C. G. Matthew, R. I. McKibbin and J. Kay, 'The franchise factor in the rise of the Labour Party', *English Historical Review*, 91 (1976), D. Tanner, 'The parliamentary electoral system, the "fourth" Reform Act and the rise of Labour', *Institute of Historical Research Bulletin*, 56 (1983), M. Bentley, *The Climax of Liberal Politics: British Liberalism in Theory and Practice, 1868–1918* (1987), M. Childs, 'Labour grows up: the electoral system, political generations, and British politics 1890–1929', *Twentieth Century British History*, 6 (1995) and M. Dawson, 'Money and the real impact of the Fourth Reform Act', *Historical Journal*, 35 (1992).

For some of the leading figures in the early Labour Party, see K. O. Morgan, *Keir Hardie: Radical and Socialist* (1975), R. M. Martin, *The Lancashire Giant: David Shackleton, Labour Leader and Civil Servant* (2000) and P. F. Tyler, *Labour's Lost Leader: The Life and Politics of Will Crooks* (2006).

2 The Surge to Second-Party Status, 1914–22

R. I. McKibbin, *The Evolution of the Labour Party, 1910–24* (Oxford, 1974) remains the central work on the party's organization during this period. On the role of ideas, see J. M. Winter, *Socialism and the Challenge of War: Ideas and Politics in Britain, 1912–1928* (1974) and 'Arthur Henderson, the Russian Revolution and the reconstruction of the Labour party', *Historical Journal*, 15 (1972). J. Turner, *British Politics and the Great War: Coalition and Conflict, 1915–1918* (1992) has a lot to say about Labour. Other important works include C. Howard, 'MacDonald, Henderson and the outbreak of war, 1914', *Historical Journal*, 20 (1977) and R. Harrison, 'The war emergency workers' national committee, 1914–20', in A. Briggs and J. Saville (eds), *Essays in Labour History, 1886–1923* (1971). J. N. Horne, *Labour at War: France and Britain 1914–1918* (Oxford, 1991) is a good comparative study, as is S. Berger, *The British Labour Party and the German Social Democrats, 1900–1931* (Oxford, 1994). Labour's relationship with patriotism is covered in P. Ward, *Red Flag and Union Jack: Englishness, Patriotism and the British Left, 1881–1924* (1999). The international angle is well covered in C. Collette, *The International Faith: Labour's Attitudes to European Socialism, 1918–39* (Aldershot, 1998). For Labour's newspaper, see H. Richards, *The Bloody Circus: the 'Daily Herald' and the Left* (1997).

Among works on trade unionism, special notice should be paid to C. J. Wrigley, *David Lloyd George and the British Labour Movement: Peace and War* (Brighton, 1976), J. Hinton, *The First Shop Stewards' Movement* (1973), P. S. Bagwell, 'The triple industrial alliance 1913–1922', in A. Briggs and J. Saville (eds), *Essays in Labour History, 1886–1923* (1971) and, for guild socialism, A. Wright, *G. D. H. Cole and Socialist Democracy* (Oxford, 1979) and D. Blaazer, 'Guild socialists after guild socialism: the workers' control group and the House of Industry League', *Twentieth Century British History*, 11, 2000.

For the Co-operative movement, see N. Robertson, *The Co-operative Movement and Communities in Britain, 1914–1960* (Aldershot, 2010), K. Manton, 'The Labour Party and the Co-op, 1918–58', *Historical Research*, 82 (2009), T. F. Carbery, *Consumers in Politics: A History and General Review of the Co-operative Party* (Manchester, 1969) and T. Adams, 'The formation of the Co-operative Party reconsidered', *International Review of Social History*, 32 (1987).

On the UDC and related matters, see M. Swartz, *The Union of Democratic Control in British Politics during the First World War* (Oxford, 1971), P. J. Yearwood, *Guarantee of Peace: The League of Nations in British Policy, 1914–1925* (Oxford, 2009), D. Mitchell, *The Politics of Dissent: A Biography of E. D. Morel* (2014), C. A. Cline, *Recruits to Labour: The British Labour Party, 1914–1931* (Syracuse, 1963), M. Pugh, '"Class traitors": Conservative recruits to Labour, 1900–30', *English Historical Review*, 113 (1998) and P. Mulvey, *The Political Life of Josiah C. Wedgwood: Land, Liberty and Empire, 1872–1943* (2010).

For the period after 1918, Labour's electoral and political strategy is discussed in A. Thorpe, 'Labour and the frustration of the extreme left', in A. Thorpe (ed.), *The Failure of Political Extremism in Inter-War Britain*

(Exeter, 1988) and 'Reasons for "progressive" disunity: Labour and Liberal politics in Britain, 1918–45', *Socialist History,* 27 (2005), as well as in K. D. Wald, 'Advance by retreat? The formulation of Labour's electoral strategy', *Journal of British Studies,* 27 (1988). How this all related to the party's communications strategy is explained in L. Beers, *Your Britain: Media and the Making of the Labour Party* (2010). The party's approach to non-urban areas is detailed in C. V. J. Griffiths, *Labour and the Countryside: The Politics of Rural Britain, 1918–1939* (Oxford, 2007). For the immediate post-war position, see C. J. Wrigley, *Lloyd George and the Challenge of Labour: The Post-War Coalition, 1918–22* (Hemel Hempstead, 1990), K. O. Morgan, *Consensus and Disunity: The Lloyd George Coalition Government 1918–22* (Oxford, 1979) and M. Cowling, *The Impact of Labour 1920–1924: The Beginning of Modern British Politics* (Cambridge, 1971).

On women, see especially G. Braybon, *Women Workers in the First World War: The British Experience* (1981), P. Graves, *Labour Women: Women in British Working-Class Politics, 1918–39* (Cambridge, 1994), J. Alberti, *Beyond Suffrage: Women in War and Peace, 1914–28* (1989), M. Pugh, *Women and the Women's Movement in Britain 1914–59* (1992) and S. K. Kent, 'The politics of sexual difference: World War I and the demise of British feminism', *Journal of British Studies,* 27 (1988).

3   Progress and Collapse, 1922–31

The key work on this period is D. Howell, *MacDonald's Party: Labour Identities and Crisis, 1922–1931* (Oxford, 2002). M. Worley, *Labour Inside the Gate: A History of the British Labour Party between the Wars* (2005) is valuable for this section and the next. On party funding and relations with the far left, see K. Morgan, *Labour Legends and Russian Gold: Bolshevism and the British Left, Part I* (2006). For the 1924 government, J. Shepherd and K. Laybourn, *Britain's First Labour Government* (2006) is indispensable, although it can still be usefully supplemented by R. W. Lyman, *The First Labour Government, 1924* (1958). P. Williamson, *National Crisis and National Government: British Politics, the Economy and Empire, 1926–32* (Cambridge, 1992) places the second government in the wider political context of the time. That administration is discussed in stimulating fashion in R. Skidelsky, *Politicians and the Slump: The Labour Government of 1929–31* (1967), but some of the reasons why it needs to be approached with caution can be seen in R. I. McKibbin, 'The economic policy of the second Labour government', *Past and Present,* 78 (1975). N. Riddell, *Labour in Crisis: The Second Labour Government, 1929–31* (Manchester, 1999) analyses the relationship between the government and the wider Labour movement, while D. Carlton, *MacDonald versus Henderson: The Foreign Policy of the Second Labour Government* (1970) focuses on international aspects and their significance for relations between the party's leaders. J. Shepherd, J. Davis and C. Wrigley (eds.), *Britain's Second Labour Government, 1929–31: A Reappraisal* (Manchester, 2011) also repays attention.

The PLP in this period can be followed through two articles in *Twentieth Century British History*, 25 (2014): R. Toye, 'Perfectly parliamentary? The Labour Party and the House of Commons in the inter-war years', 25 (2014), and G. McClymont, 'Socialism, puritanism, hedonism: the parliamentary Labour Party's attitude to gambling, 1923–31', 19 (2008).

Different aspects of policy are covered in H. R. Winkler, *Paths Not Taken: British Labour and International Policy in the 1920s* (1994) and A. Thorpe, 'The industrial meaning of "gradualism": the Labour Party and industry, 1918–31', *Journal of British Studies*, 35 (1996). A contemporary work, E. Wertheimer, *Portrait of the Labour Party* (1929), remains valuable. The inside, official view can be seen in H. Tracey (ed.), *The Book of the Labour Party: Its History, Growth, Policy and Leaders* (3 vols, 1925). C. Howard, 'Expectations born to death: local Labour Party expansion in the 1920s', in J. M. Winter (ed.), *The Working Class in Modern British History: Essays in Honour of Henry Pelling* (Cambridge, 1983) offers a (perhaps too) gloomy of the party's development at the grassroots, and needs to be read alongside M. Worley (ed.), *Labour's Grass Roots: Essays on the Activities of Local Labour Parties and Members, 1918–45* (Aldershot, 2005). Religious aspects are dealt with in P. Catterall, 'Morality and politics: the free churches and the Labour Party between the wars', *Historical Journal*, 36 (1993) and N. Riddell, 'The Catholic Church and the Labour Party, 1918–31', *Twentieth Century British History*, 8 (1997).

The 1931 crisis is the subject of A. Thorpe, *The British General Election of 1931* (Oxford, 1991) and D. H. Close, 'The realignment of the British electorate in 1931', *History*, 67 (1982). See also P. Williamson, 'A "bankers' ramp"? Financiers and the British political crisis of August 1931', *English Historical Review*, 99 (1984), A. Thorpe, 'Arthur Henderson and the British political crisis of 1931', *Historical Journal*, 31 (1988) and '"I am in the cabinet": J. H. Thomas's decision to join the National government in 1931', *Historical Research*, 64 (1991).

For the ILP, see especially R. E. Dowse, *Left in the Centre: The Independent Labour Party, 1893–1940* (1966), R. K. Middlemas, *The Clydesiders: A Left-Wing Struggle for Parliamentary Power* (1965) and G. Brown, *Maxton* (Edinburgh, 1986). For the Communists, see A. Thorpe, *The British Communist Party and Moscow, 1920–43* (Manchester, 2000). Among notable biographies of the leaders in this period, see especially D. Marquand, *Ramsay MacDonald* (1977), K. Morgan, *Ramsay MacDonald* (2006), K. Laybourn, *Philip Snowden: A Biography* (Aldershot, 1988), C. J. Wrigley, *Arthur Henderson* (Cardiff, 1990) and R. Skidelsky *Oswald Mosley* (1975). Philip, Viscount Snowden, *An Autobiography* (2 vols, 1934) stands out among a plethora of often mediocre memoirs; see also H. Dalton, *Call Back Yesterday: Memoirs, 1887–1931* (1953) and M. I. Cole (ed.), *Beatrice Webb's Diaries, 1912–24* (1952) and *1924–32* (1956). One longstanding question about the Labour leadership in the period is dealt with in N. Owen, 'MacDonald's parties: the Labour Party and the "aristocratic embrace", 1922–31', *Twentieth Century British History*, 18 (2007).

On trade unionism, the broader context is ably portrayed in H. A. Clegg, *A History of British Trade Unions, Vol. 2: 1911–1933* (Oxford, 1985). Lord Citrine, *Men and Work: An Autobiography* (1964) and A. Bullock, *The Life and Times of Ernest Bevin, Vol. 1: Trade Union Leader, 1881–1940* (1960) are indispensable. On the events of 1926, see K. Laybourn, *The General Strike of 1926* (Manchester, 1993), K. Morgan, *Bolshevism, Syndicalism and the General Strike: The Lost Internationalist World of A. A. Purcell* (2013) and H. Barron, *The 1926 Miners' Lockout: Meanings of Community in the Durham Coalfield* (Oxford, 2010).

4   Remaking the Party? 1931–39

The best book on the party in this period remains B. Pimlott, *Labour and the Left in the 1930s* (Cambridge, 1977). J. Swift, *Labour in Crisis: Clement Attlee and the Labour Party in Opposition, 1931–40* (2001) offers a broadly positive appraisal of the party's progress in the period and argues that Attlee was more successful than is usually suggested. T. Buchanan, *The Spanish Civil War and the British Labour Movement* (Cambridge, 1992) is also important, and much broader than its title would suggest. M. Cowling, *The Impact of Hitler: British Politics and British Policy, 1933–1940* (Cambridge, 1975) places developments within the Labour Party in a wider political context. Specifically on reactions to 1931, see R. Eatwell and A. Wright, 'Labour and the lessons of 1931', *History*, 63 (1978). Two useful contemporary accounts are C. R. Attlee, *The Labour Party in Perspective* (1937) and D. E. McHenry, *The Labour Party in Transition, 1931–1938* (1938). See also M. Pugh, 'The *Daily Mirror* and the revival of Labour, 1935–45', in *Twentieth Century British History*, 9 (1998) and W. W. Knox and A. MacKinlay, 'The remaking of Scottish Labour in the 1930s', *Twentieth Century British History*, 6 (1995). On electoral politics, see T. Stannage, *Baldwin Thwarts the Opposition: The British General Election of 1935* (1980) and D. Howell, 'A faraway country: Abyssinia and the British general election of 1935', *Socialist History*, 28 (2006).

On the development of economic policy, see E. Durbin, *New Jerusalems: The Labour Party and the Economics of Democratic Socialism* (1985), A. Booth and M. Pack, *Employment, Capital and Economic Policy: Great Britain, 1918–1939* (Oxford, 1985), R. Toye, *The Labour Party and the Planned Economy, 1931–51* (2003) and D. Ritschel, *The Politics of Planning: The Debate on Economic Planning in Britain in the 1930s* (Oxford, 1997). A. Booth, 'How long are light years in British politics? The Labour Party's economic ideas in the 1930s', *Twentieth Century British History*, 7 (1996) and S. Brooke, 'Evan Durbin: reassessing a Labour "revisionist"', *Twentieth Century British History*, 7 (1996) also repay attention.

On international aspects, see J. F. Naylor, *Labour's International Policy: The Labour Party in the 1960s* (1969), B. C. Malament, 'British Labour and Roosevelt's New Deal', *Journal of British Studies*, 17 (1977–78), S. Brooke, 'Atlantic crossing? American views of capitalism and British socialist thought, 1932–1962', *Twentieth Century British History*, 2 (1991), A. Thorpe,

'Stalinism and British politics', *History*, 83 (1998), R. Toye, 'The Labour Party and the economics of rearmament, 1935–39', *Twentieth Century British History*, 12 (2001), P. Corthorn, 'The Labour Party and the League of Nations: the Socialist League's role in the sanctions crisis of 1935', *Twentieth Century British History*, 13 (2002) and 'Labour, the left, and the Stalinist purges of the late 1930s', *Historical Journal*, 48 (2005), and P. Ward, 'Preparing for the People's War: Labour and patriotism in the 1930s', *Labour History Review*, 67 (2002). H. McCarthy, *The British People and the League of Nations: Democracy, Citizenship and Internationalism, c.1918–48* (Manchester, 2011) is important for this and both earlier and later chapters. K. Morgan, *The Webbs and Soviet Communism* (2006) is broader than its title implies.

P. Seyd, 'Factionalism within the Labour Party: the Socialist League, 1932–1937', in A. Briggs and J. Saville (eds), *Essays in Labour History, 1918–1939* (1977) covers that aspect. The ILP is covered by G. Cohen, *The Failure of a Dream: The Independent Labour Party from Disaffiliation to World War II* (2007) and J. Jupp, *The Radical Left in Britain, 1931–41* (1982). See also R. Dare, 'Instinct and organisation: intellectuals and British Labour after 1931', *Historical Journal*, 26 (1983).

For the unions, see H. A. Clegg, *A History of British Trade Unions since 1889, Vol. 3: 1934–51* (Oxford, 1994), K. Middlemas, *Politics in Industrial Society: The Experience of the British System since 1911* (1979), L. P. Carpenter, 'Corporatism in Britain, 1930–45', *Journal of Contemporary History*, 11 (1976) and N. Riddell, 'Walter Citrine and the British Labour movement 1925–35', *History*, 85 (2000).

The memoirs of Hugh Dalton for this period, *The Fateful Years: Memoirs, 1931–1945* (1957) are revealing, as are B. Pimlott (ed.), *The Political Diary of Hugh Dalton, 1918–1940, 1945–1960* (1986) and B. Pimlott, *Hugh Dalton* (1985). Other notable biographies of leading figures include J. Shepherd, *George Lansbury* (Oxford, 2002), K. Harris, *Attlee* (1982), R. Pearce, *Attlee* (1997), F. Beckett, *Clem Attlee* (1997), D. Howell, *Clement Attlee* (2006), B. Donoughue and G. W. Jones, *Herbert Morrison: Portrait of a Politician* (1973), P. F. Clarke, *The Cripps Version: The Life of Sir Stafford Cripps* (2002) and I. Kramnick and B. Sheerman, *Harold Laski: A Life on the Left* (1993).

5   The Impact of the Second World War, 1939–45

The essential starting point for anyone wishing to investigate this period in greater depth is S. Brooke, *Labour's War: The Labour Party during the Second World War* (Oxford, 1992). A. Thorpe, *Parties at War: Political Organization in Second World War Britain* (Oxford, 2009) has a lot to say about Labour. See also R. Crowcroft, *Attlee's War: World War II and the Making of a Labour Leader* (2011). On the Coalition, see P. Addison, *The Road to 1945: British Politics and the Second World War* (1975), which argues for the emergence of a consensus in wartime, and K. Jefferys, *The Churchill Coalition and Wartime Politics, 1940–1945* (Manchester, 1991), which largely rejects this view. A. Bullock, *The Life and Times of Ernest Bevin, Vol. 2:*

Minister of Labour, 1940–1945 (1967) covers developments within the movement in these years in great depth. A more controversial analysis is provided by S. Fielding, P. Thompson and N. Tiratsoo, *"England Arise!" The Labour Party and Popular Politics in 1940s Britain* (Manchester, 1995). See also the important articles by S. Fielding, 'The Second World War and popular radicalism: the significance of the "movement away from party"', *History*, 80 (1995) and 'Labourism in the 1940s', *Twentieth Century British History*, 3 (1992). I. Taylor, 'Labour and the impact of war 1939–45' and T. Mason and P Thompson, '"Reflections on a revolution"? The political mood in wartime Britain', both in N. Tiratsoo (ed.), *The Attlee Years* (1991), are also important. Specifically on the 1945 election, see R. B. McCallum and A. Readman, *The British General Election of 1945* (Oxford, 1947) and S. Fielding, 'What did "the people" want? The meaning of the 1945 general election', *Historical Journal*, 35 (1992). Aspects of factionalism are covered by P. Douglas, 'No friend of democracy: the Socialist Vanguard group 1941–50', *Contemporary British History*, 16 (2002) and M. Hilson and J. Melling, 'Public gifts and political identities: Sir Richard Acland, Common Wealth and the moral politics of land owner-ship in the 1940s', *Twentieth Century British History*, 11 (2000).

Foreign policy is covered in R. M. Douglas, *The Labour Party, Nationalism and Internationalism 1939–1951* (2004) and T. D. Burridge, *British Labour and Hitler's War* (1976). See also T. Imlay, 'From villain to partner: British Labour Party leaders, France and international policy during the Phoney War, 1939–40', *Journal of Contemporary History*, 38 (2003). For the way in which such matters could both reflect and impact upon the party's mood, see A. Thorpe, '"In a rather emotional state"? The Labour Party and British intervention in Greece, 1944–45', *English Historical Review*, 121 (2006).

On economic policy, see S. Brooke, 'Revisionists and fundamentalists: the Labour Party and economic policy during the Second World War', *Historical Journal*, 32 (1989), J. Tomlinson, 'Planning: debate and policy in the 1940s', *Twentieth Century British History*, 3 (1992), L. Johnman, 'The Labour Party and industrial policy, 1940–45', in N. Tiratsoo (ed.), *The Attlee Years* (1991) and R. Toye, 'Keynes, the Labour movement, and "how to pay for the war"', *Twentieth Century British History*, 10 (1999) and 'The Labour Party's external economic policy in the 1940s', *Historical Journal*, 43 (2000).

For social policy, see J. Harris, 'War and social history: Britain and the Home Front during the Second World War', *Contemporary European History*, 1 (1992) and 'Did British workers want the Welfare State? G. D. H. Cole's survey of 1942', in J. M. Winter (ed.), *The Working Class in Modern British History: Essays in Honour of Henry Pelling* (Cambridge, 1983), as well as M. Tichelar, 'The conflict over property rights during the Second World War: the Labour Party's abandonment of land nationalization', *Twentieth Century British History*, 14 (2003).

On women, see especially P. Summerfield, *Women Workers in the Second World War: Production and Patriarchy in Conflict* (1984) and H. L. Smith, 'The problem of equal pay for equal work in Great Britain during World War II', *Journal of Modern History*, 53 (1981).

Two excellent primary sources are B. Pimlott (ed.), *The Second World War Diary of Hugh Dalton, 1940–1945* (1985) and K. Jefferys (ed.), *Labour and the Wartime Coalition: From the Diary of James Chuter Ede, 1941–1945* (1987).

6 The Attlee Governments, 1945–51

The best general history remains K. O. Morgan, *Labour in Power, 1945–1951* (Oxford, 1984), but H. Pelling, *The Labour Governments, 1945–51* (1984) and P. Hennessy, *Never Again: Britain, 1945–51* (1992) are good alternatives. M. Francis, *Ideas and Policies under Labour, 1945–1951: Building a New Britain* (Manchester, 1997) is an important book which takes the government's socialism more seriously than most. N. Tiratsoo (ed.), *The Attlee Years* (1991) and two books edited by J. Fyrth, *Labour's High Noon: The Government and the Economy 1945–1951* (1993) and *Labour's Promised Land? Culture and Society in Labour Britain, 1945–1951* (1995), are stimulating collections of essays. There is a useful collection of documents: S. Brooke (ed.), *Reform and Reconstruction: Britain after the War, 1945–1951* (Manchester, 1995). P. Hennessy, *The Prime Minister: The Office and Its Holders since 1945* (2001) offers valuable insights.

For the left, see D. Rubinstein, 'Socialism and the Labour Party: the Labour left and domestic policy, 1945–50', in D. E. Martin and D. Rubinstein (eds), *Ideology and the Labour Movement: Essays in Honour of John Saville* (1979), J. Schneer, *Labour's Conscience: The Labour Left, 1945–1951* (1988) and A. Howard, *Crossman: The Pursuit of Power* (1990).

On the unions see, as well as the works cited earlier, R. Taylor, *The Trade Union Question in British Politics: Government and Unions since 1945* (Oxford, 1993), M. Harrison, *Trade Unions and the Labour Party since 1945* (1960), K. Middlemas, *Power, Competition and the State, Vol. 1: Britain in Search of Balance, 1940–1961* (1987) and A. Taylor, *The NUM and British Politics, Vol. 1: 1944–1968* (2003).

On women, see especially J. Hinton, 'Women and the Labour vote, 1945–1950', *Labour History Review,* 57 (1992) and 'Militant housewives: the British Housewives' League and the Attlee government', *History Workshop Journal,* 38 (1994). For this and subsequent chapters, see N. Hart, 'Gender and the rise and fall of class politics', *New Left Review,* 175 (1989).

Electoral trends can be followed in H. G. Nicholas, *The British General Election of 1950* (1951) and D. E. Butler, *The British General Election of 1951* (1952). On campaigning more broadly, see M. Rosenbaum, *From Soapbox to Soundbite: Party Political Campaigning in Britain since 1945* (1997).

On the economic side, see A. Cairncross, *Years of Recovery: British Economic Policy, 1945–1951* (1985), J. Fyrth (ed.), *Labour's High Noon: The Government and the Economy, 1945–51* (1993), J. Tomlinson, *Democratic Socialism and Economic Policy: The Attlee Years 1945–1951* (Cambridge, 1997), S. Brooke, 'Problems of socialist planning: Evan Durbin and the Labour Government of 1945', *Historical Journal,* 34 (1991), R. C. Whiting, 'Income tax, the working class and party politics 1948–1952', *Twentieth Century British History,* 8 (1997), H. Irving, 'The birth of a politician: Harold Wilson and the bonfire of controls, 1948–9', *Twentieth Century British History*, 25 (2014), M. Tookey, 'Three's a crowd? Government, owners, and workers during the nationalization of the British coalmining industry 1945–47', *Twentieth Century British History*, 12 (2001) and R. Toye, 'The Attlee government, the imperial preference system and the creation of the GATT', *English Historical Review*, 118 (2003). For this and subsequent chapters, the essays in N. F. R. Crafts and N. Woodward (eds), *The British Economy since 1945* (Oxford, 1991) are of considerable value, as is J. Tomlinson, 'The Labour Party and the capitalist firm, 1950–1970', *Historical Journal*, 47 (2004).

Aspects of social policy are covered in I. Zweiniger-Bargielowska, *Austerity in Britain: Rationing, Controls and Consumption, 1939–55* (Oxford, 2000) and K. Morgan, 'The problem of the epoch? Labour and housing, 1918–51', *Twentieth Century British History*, 16 (2005). M. Roodhouse, 'The 1948 Belcher affair and Lynskey tribunal', *Twentieth Century British History*, 13 (2002) looks at how the government overcame a significant scandal.

Specifically on foreign policy, see A. Bullock, *Ernest Bevin, Foreign Secretary, 1945–1951* (Oxford, 1983), R. J. Ovendale (ed.) *The Foreign Policy of the British Labour Governments, 1945–1951* (1984), P. Weiler, *British Labour and the Cold War* (Stanford, 1988), J. Schneer, 'Hope deferred and shattered: the British Labour left and the Third Force Movement, 1945–9', *Journal of Modern History*, 56 (1984) and M. Minion, 'The Fabian Society and Europe during the 1940s: the search for a "socialist foreign policy"', *European History Quarterly*, 30 (2000). On 'fellow travellers', see D. Lilleker, *Against the Cold War: Pro-Sovietism in the British Labour Party, 1945–89* (2004) and A. Potts, *Zilliacus: A Life for Peace and Socialism* (2002). See also M. Gowing, 'Britain, America and the Bomb', in M. Dockrill and J. W. Young (eds), *British Foreign Policy, 1945–56* (1989), P. Jones, *America and the British Labour Party: The 'Special Relationship' at Work* (1997) and R. Broad, *Labour's European Dilemmas since 1945* (2001).

On the Empire/Commonwealth, see especially P. S. Gupta, *Imperialism and the British Labour Movement* (1975) and S. Howe, *Anti-Colonialism in British Politics: The Left and the End of Empire, 1918–64* (Oxford, 1993). P. S. Gupta, 'Imperialism and the Labour government of 1945–51', in J. M. Winter (ed.), *The Working Class in Modern British History: Essays in Honour of Henry Pelling* (Cambridge, 1983), R. Hyam, 'Africa and the Labour government, 1945–51', *Journal of Imperial and Commonwealth History*, 16 (1988), K. Paul, '"British subjects" and "British stock": Labour's postwar imperialism', *Journal of British Studies*, 34 (1995) and J. Kent, 'Bevin's imperialism and the idea of Euro-Africa', in M. Dockrill and J. W. Young (eds), *British Foreign Policy, 1945–56* (1989) are also useful.

7   Searching for a New Direction, 1951–64

Despite the production of some really important work in recent years, this period remains seriously under-researched at all levels of the party. The standard books on the two 'wings' of the party, creaking with age, are M. Jenkins, *Bevanism: Labour's High Tide* (Nottingham, 1979) and S. Haseler,

The Gaitskellites: Revisionism in the British Labour Party, 1951–1964 (1969).
E. Shaw, *Discipline and Discord in the Labour Party 1951–87: The Politics of
Managerial Control in the Labour Party, 1951–1987* (Manchester, 1988) is
an excellent work with both great detail and a compelling thesis, and is
valuable for this and most of the remaining chapters in the book. On the
conference from 1956 onwards see L. Minkin, *The Labour Party Conference:
A Study in the Politics of Intra-Party Democracy* (1978). See also M. Francis,
'Mr Gaitskell's Ganymede? Re-assessing Crosland's *The Future of Socialism*'
and T. Jones, '"Taking Genesis out of the Bible": Hugh Gaitskell, Clause
IV and Labour's socialist myth', both in *Contemporary British History*, 11
(1997), R. Jobson, '"Waving the banners of a bygone age": nostalgia and
Labour's Clause IV controversy, 1959–60', *Contemporary British History*, 27
(2013) and C. Ellis, 'Letting it slip: the Labour Party and the "mystical
halo" of nationalisation, 1951–64', *Contemporary British History*, 26 (2012).
For party activism, see G. Cohen et al., 'Political culture and the post-
war Labour Party: values, practices and activism in the South Lewisham
Labour Party, 1948–71', *Socialist History*, 32 (2007).

The most important works of socialist theory in this period were
A. Bevan, *In Place of Fear* (1952), R. H. S. Crossman (ed.), *New Fabian Essays*
(1952) and C. A. R. Crosland, *The Future of Socialism* (1956).

On Labour and 'affluence', see especially L. Black, *The Political Culture
of the Left in Affluent Britain, 1951–64* (2002) and '"Still at the penny-
farthing stage in a jet-propelled era": branch life in 1950s socialism',
Labour History Review, 65 (2000), and S. Fielding, 'Activists against "affluence": Labour Party culture during the "Golden Age", circa 1950–1970',
Journal of British Studies, 40 (2001). On union politics, see J. Melling ,
'Red under the collar? Clive Jenkins, white collar unionism and the
politics of the British left, 1947–65', *Twentieth Century British History*, 13
(2002). The earlier classics, M. Abrams, R. Rose and R. Hinden, *Must
Labour Lose?* (Harmondsworth, 1960) and J. H. Goldthorpe D. Lockwood,
F. Bechhofer and J. Platt, *The Affluent Worker: Political Attitudes and
Behaviour* (1968), still repay attention.

Specifically on elections, see D. E. Butler, *The British General Election of
1955* (1955), D. E. Butler and R. Rose, *The British General Election of 1959*
(1960) and D. E. Butler and A. King, *The British General Election of 1964*
(1966). See also A. Black and S. Brooke, 'The Labour Party, women, and
the problem of gender, 1951–1966', *Journal of British Studies*, 36 (1997).

Biographies help to flesh out the picture. See especially, among works
already cited, K. Harris, *Attlee*, R. Pearce, *Attlee*, B. Donoughue and
G. W. Jones, *Herbert Morrison* and B. Pimlott, *Hugh Dalton*. M. Foot, *Aneurin
Bevan: A Biography, Vol. 2: 1945–1960* (1973) must be read in conjunc-
tion with the more dispassionate J. Campbell, *Nye Bevan and the Mirage
of British Socialism* (1987). See also P. Hollis, *Jennie Lee* (Oxford, 1997).
On Gaitskell, see P. Williams, *Hugh Gaitskell: A Political Biography* (1979)
and B. Brivati, *Hugh Gaitskell* (1996). See also K. Jefferys, *Anthony Crosland*
(1999), S. Crosland, *Tony Crosland* (1982), B. Pimlott, *Harold Wilson* (1992)
and G. Goodman, *The Awkward Warrior: Frank Cousins, His Life and Times*
(Nottingham, 1984).

Three diary sources are also of particular interest: Pimlott's edition of the Dalton diaries (cited above), P. Williams (ed.), *The Diary of Hugh Gaitskell, 1945–56* (1983) and J. Morgan (ed.), *The Backbench Diaries of Richard Crossman* (1981).

8   Wilson in Power, 1964–70

There is no satisfactory single-volume treatment, although C. Ponting, *Breach of Promise: Labour in Power, 1964–1970* (1989) remains useful in many ways. Between them, the three volumes on *The Labour Governments 1964–1970* (see below) offer a much more sensitive view of the period. G. O'Hara and H. Parr (eds), *The Wilson Governments 1964–1970 Reconsidered* (2006) and R. Coopey, S. Fielding and N. Tiratsoo (eds), *The Wilson Governments, 1964–1970* (1993) are excellent collections of essays. D. Walker, 'The first Wilson governments, 1964–1970', in P. Hennessy and A. Seldon (eds), *Ruling Performance: British Governments from Attlee to Thatcher* (Oxford, 1987) is a good introduction. Minkin, *The Labour Party Conference* and Shaw, *Discipline and Discord in the Labour Party* are vital sources for Labour's internal dynamics. See also A. Blick, 'Harold Wilson, Labour and the machinery of government', *Contemporary British History*, 20 (2006). On devolution, see especially D. Tanner, 'Richard Crossman, Harold Wilson and devolution, 1966–70: the making of government policy', *Twentieth Century British History*, 17 (2006).

Social change in the period is the subject of S. Fielding, *The Labour Governments 1964–70, Vol. 1: Labour and Cultural Change* (Manchester, 2003). On various aspects of social policy, see D. Dean, 'The race relations policy of the first Wilson government', *Twentieth Century British History*, 11 (2000), R. Hansen, 'The Kenyan Asians, British politics, and the Commonwealth Immigrants Act 1968', *Historical Journal*, 42 (1999), L. Black, 'Making Britain a gayer and more cultivated country': Wilson, Lee and the creative industries in the 1960s', *Contemporary British History*, 20 (2006) and S. Thornton, 'A case of confusion and incoherence: social security under Wilson, 1964–70', *Contemporary British History*, 20 (2006).

On the economy, the standard work is now J. Tomlinson, *The Labour Governments 1964–70, Vol. 3: Economic Policy* (Manchester, 2004), but see also the essays in Crafts and Woodward, *The British Economy since 1945* and Coopey et al., *The Wilson Governments*, as well as P. Browning, *The Treasury and Economic Policy, 1964–1985* (1986), D. Edgerton, 'The "white heat" revisited: the British government and technology in the 1960s', *Twentieth Century British History*, 7 (1996), T. Bale, 'Dynamics of a non-decision: the "failure" to devalue the pound, 1964–67', *Twentieth Century British History*, 10 (1999), R. C. Whiting, 'Ideology and reform in Labour's tax strategy, 1964–70', *Historical Journal*, 41 (1998), G. O'Hara. '"Dynamic, exciting, thrilling change": the Wilson government's economic policies, 1964–70', *Contemporary British History*, 20 (2006) and 'The limits of US power: transatlantic financial diplomacy under the Johnson and Wilson administrations, October 1964–November 1968', *Contemporary European History*, 12 (2003), H. Pemberton, 'Relative decline and British economic policy in the 1960s', *Historical Journal*, 47 (2004) and 'Taxation and Labour's modernisation programme', *Contemporary British History*, 20 (2006), and R. Toye, 'The new commanding height: Labour Party policy on North Sea oil and gas, 1964–74', *Contemporary British History*, 16 (2002).

The *In Place of Strife* episode is covered, rather facetiously, by P. Jenkins in *The Battle of Downing Street* (1970); see also K. Thorpe, 'The "juggernaut method": the 1966 state of emergency and the Wilson government's response to the seamen's strike', *Twentieth Century British History*, 12 (2001) and R. Tyler, '"Victims of our history"'? Barbara Castle and *In Place of Strife*', *Contemporary British History*, 20 (2006). On industrial relations more generally, see K. Middlemas, *Power, Competition and the State, Vol. 2: Threats to the Post-War Settlement* (1990), L. Panitch, *Social Democracy and Industrial Militancy: The Labour Party, the Trade Unions and Incomes Policy, 1945–1974* (Cambridge, 1976) and two articles by J. Melling, 'Managing the white-collar union: salaried staff, trade-union leadership, and the politics of organized labour in postwar Britain, *c.*1950–1968', *International Review of Social History* (2003) and 'Leading the white-collar union: Clive Jenkins, the management of trade-union officers, and the politics of the British Labour movement, *c.*1968–1979', *International Review of Social History* (2004).

On nationalism, see T. Nairn, *The Break-Up of Britain: Crisis and Neo-Nationalism* (1977), V. Bogdanor, *Devolution* (Oxford, 1979), M. Keating and D. Bleiman, *Labour and Scottish Nationalism* (1979), K. O. Morgan, *Rebirth of a Nation: Wales, 1880–1980* (Oxford, 1981) and A. Butt Philip, *The Welsh Question: Nationalism in Welsh Politics, 1945–1970* (Cardiff, 1975). On race, see especially C. Holmes, *John Bull's Island: Immigration and British Society, 1871–1971* (1988).

The key work on external policy is J. W. Young, *The Labour Governments 1964–70, Vol. 2: International Policy* (Manchester, 2003). See also G. Hughes, *Harold Wilson's Cold War: The Labour Government and East–West Relations, 1964–1970* (2009), O. Daddow, *Harold Wilson and European Integration: Britain's Second Application to Join the EEC (2002)*, H. Parr, *Britain's Policy toward the European Community: Harold Wilson and Britain's World Role, 1964–1967* (2004), H. Parr, 'Britain, America, East of Suez and the EEC: finding a role in British foreign policy, 1964–67', *Contemporary British History*, 20 (2006) and J. Pickering, 'Politics and "Black Tuesday": shifting power in the cabinet and the decision to withdraw from east of Suez, November 1967–January 1968', *Twentieth Century British History*, 13 (2002). On the Commonwealth, see especially J. Tomlinson, 'The Commonwealth, the balance of payments and the politics of international poverty: British aid policy, 1958–1971', *Contemporary European History*, 12 (2003), P. Alexander, 'A tale of two Smiths: the transformation of Commonwealth policy, 1964–70', *Contemporary British History*, 20 (2006) and R. Coggins, 'Wilson and Rhodesia: UDI and British policy towards Africa', *Contemporary British History*, 20 (2006).

On general elections, see D. E. Butler and A. King, *The British General Election of 1966* (1966) and D. E. Butler and M. Pinto-Duschinsky, *The British General Election of 1970* (1971). For this and all following sections, see also D. Denver and M. Garnett, *British General Elections since 1964: Diversity, Dealignment and Disillusion* (Oxford, 2014).

There are three large biographies of Wilson: the broadly sympathetic
B. Pimlott, *Harold Wilson* (1992) and P. Ziegler, *Wilson: The Authorized
Life of Lord Wilson of Rievaulx* (1993) and the much less favourable
A. Morgan, *Harold Wilson: A Life* (1991). P. Routledge, *Harold Wilson* (2006)
is a slighter alternative. P. Foot, *The Politics of Harold Wilson* (1968) is a
contemporary attack on Wilson and Labour from a far-left perspective.
K. O. Morgan, *Callaghan: A Life* (Oxford, 1997) is arguably, with the excep-
tion of Marquand's book on MacDonald, the best biography of any Labour
leader thus far published. See also A. Perkins, *Red Queen: The Authorised
Biography of Barbara Castle* (2003) and J. Campbell, *Roy Jenkins* (2014).

Memoirs and published diaries are very rich for this period. Among
the former, see especially H. Wilson, *The Labour Government 1964–70:
A Personal Record* (1971), G. Brown, *In My Way: The Political Memoirs of Lord
George Brown* (1971), J. Callaghan, *Time and Chance* (1987), R. Jenkins,
A Life in the Centre (1991), D. Healey, *The Time of My Life* (1989), B. Castle,
Fighting All the Way (1993) and M. Stewart, *Life and Labour: An Autobiography*
(1980). Among the latter, see R. Crossman, *The Diaries of a Cabinet Minister*
(3 vols, 1975–77), B. Castle, *The Castle Diaries, 1964–1970* (1984) and
T. Benn, *Out of the Wilderness: Diaries, 1963–1967* (1987) and *Office Without
Power: Diaries, 1968–1972* (1988).

9   Labour in Crisis? 1970–79

A lively introduction to the period, written by someone who was a Labour
MP at the time, is P. Whitehead, *The Writing on the Wall: Britain in the
Seventies* (1985). The period up to 1974 can be followed in P. Bell, *The
Labour Party in Opposition, 1970–74* (2004) and M. Hatfield, *The House
the Left Built: Inside Labour Policy-Making 1970–1975* (1978). The 1974–79
period is covered in great detail by the essays in A. Seldon and K. Hickson
(eds), *New Labour, Old Labour: The Wilson and Callaghan Governments 1974–
79* (2004); older works which retain value include D. Coates, *Labour in
Power? A Study of the Labour Government, 1974–1979* (1980), K. Coates (ed.),
What Went Wrong: Explaining the Fall of the Labour Government (Nottingham,
1979) and M. Holmes, *The Labour Government 1974–79: Political Aims
and Economic Reality* (1985). The fall of the government is traced in
J. Shepherd, *Crisis? What Crisis? The Callaghan Government and the British
'Winter of Discontent'* (Manchester, 2013).

On developments within the party, see B. Hindess, *The Decline of Working-
Class Politics* (1971), T. Forester, *The Labour Party and the Working Class*
(1976), Minkin, *The Labour Party Conference*, Shaw, *Discipline and Discord in
the Labour Party* and P. Seyd, *The Rise and Fall of the Labour Left* (1987). The
left's policy views can be seen in S. Holland, *The Socialist Challenge* (1975).
For splits on the right, see G. Radice, *Friends and Rivals: Crosland, Jenkins
and Healey* (2002) and S. Meredith, *Labours Old and New: The Parliamentary
Right of the British Labour Party 1970–79 and the Roots of New Labour* (2008).

For general elections, see the Nuffield studies by D. E. Butler and
D. Kavanagh, *The British General Election of February 1974* (1974), *October
1974* (1975) and *1979* (1980).

Specifically on economic policy, see M. Wickham-Jones, *Economic Strategy and the Labour Party Politics and Policy-making, 1970–83* (Basingstoke, 1996), which is also valuable for the next section, M. Artis and D. Cobham (eds), *Labour's Economic Policies, 1974–1979* (Manchester, 1991) and W. P. J. Maunder (ed.), *The British Economy in the 1970s* (1980). The essays in Crafts and Woodward, *The British Economy since 1945*, are also important here. On the IMF crisis, see K. Hickson, *The IMF Crisis of 1976 and British Politics* (2005), K. Burk and A. Cairncross, *'Goodbye, Great Britain': The 1976 IMF Crisis* (1992) and D. Wass, *Decline to Fall: The Making of British Macro-economic Policy and the 1976 IMF Crisis* (Oxford, 2008). For social policy, see N. Bosanquet and P. Townsend, *Labour and Equality: A Fabian Study of Labour in Power, 1974–1979* (1980) and R. Lowe, *The Welfare State in Britain since 1945* (1993). On international policy, see K. Stoddart, 'The British Labour government and the development of Chevaline, 1974–79', *Cold War History*, 10 (2010).

See also the biographies of Wilson and Callaghan cited earlier, as well as K. O. Morgan, *Michael Foot: A Life* (2007) and D. Powell, *Tony Benn* (2001). Particularly useful memoirs include H. Wilson, *Final Term: The Labour Government, 1974–1976* (1979), Callaghan, *Time and Chance*, Healey, *The Time of My Life*, E. Dell, *A Hard Pounding: Politics and Economic Crisis, 1974–1976* (Oxford, 1991), I. Mikardo, *Back-Bencher* (1988) and two books by J. Haines, *The Politics of Power* (1977) and *Glimmers of Twilight: Harold Wilson in Decline* (2003). Three diarists stand out: T. Benn, *Against the Tide: Diaries, 1973–1976* (1989) and *Conflicts of Interest: Diaries, 1977–1980* (1990), B. Castle, *The Castle Diaries, 1974–1976* (1980) and B. Donoughue, *Downing Street Diary: With Harold Wilson in No. 10* (2005) and *Downing Street Diary: With James Callaghan in No. 10* (2008).

On the unions, see the books cited in previous sections, as well as K. Middlemas, *Power, Competition and the State, Vol. 3: The End of the Post-War Era, Britain since 1974* (1991) and P. Ferris, *The New Militants: Crisis in the Trade Unions* (1972).

10 Down and Out? 1979–87

E. Shaw, *The Labour Party since 1979: Crisis and Transformation* (1994) remains a good place to start. See also D. and M. Kogan, *The Battle for the Labour Party* (Glasgow, 1982), P. Whiteley, *The Labour Party in Crisis* (1983), L. Minkin, *The Contentious Alliance: Trade Unions and the Labour Party* (1992) and E. Shaw, *Discipline and Discord in the Labour Party*. M. Crick, *Militant* (1984) is important and was so at the time; a rather different view comes across in D. Frost and P. North, *Militant Liverpool: A City on the Edge* (Liverpool, 2013). See also J. Bloomfield, 'Labour's long haul', in S. Hall and M. Jacques (eds), *The Politics of Thatcherism* (1983) and D. Kavanagh, *Thatcherism and British Politics: The End of Consensus?* (2nd edn, Oxford, 1990).

The SDP episode is the subject of I. Crewe and A. King, *SDP: The Birth, Life and Death of the Social Democratic Party* (Oxford, 1995), as well as in W. Kennet, *The Rebirth of Britain* (1982), P. Zentner, *Social Democracy in*

Britain: Must Labour Lose? (1982), I. Bradley, *Breaking the Mould? The Birth and Prospects of the Social Democratic Party* (1981), and in the works of the 'Gang of Four': R. Jenkins, *A Life at the Centre* (1991), S. Williams, *Politics Is for People* (1981) and *Climbing the Bookshelves: The Autobiography* (2009), W. Rodgers, *The Politics of Change* (1982) and D. Owen, *Face the Future* (Oxford, 1981) and *Time to Declare* (1991).

The 'fight against the left' can be followed in J. Golding, *Hammering the Left: Defeating Tony Benn, Eric Heffer and Militant in the Battle for the Labour Left* (2003), D. Hayter, *Fightback! Labour's Traditional Right in the 1970s and 1980s* (Manchester, 2005) and N. Thomas-Symonds, 'A reinterpretation of Michael Foot's handling of the Militant Tendency', *Contemporary British History*, 19 (2005). See also, for this chapter and the next, G. Radice, *Diaries 1980–2001: From Political Disaster to Election Triumph* (2004).

On trade unionism, see G. Goodman, *The Miners' Strike* (1985), T. Lane, 'The Tories and the trade unions', in S. Hall and M. Jacques (eds), *Politics of Thatcherism* (1983), J. McIlroy, 'Trade unions and the law', in B. Jones (ed.), *Political Issues in Britain Today* (Manchester, 1985) and D. Deaton, 'The labour market and industrial relations policy of the Thatcher Government', in D. S. Bell (ed.), *The Conservative Government 1979–84: An Interim Report* (1985).

For electoral politics, see D. E. Butler and D. Kavanagh, *The British General Election of 1983* (1984), *1987* (1988) and *1992* (1992). On the debate over whether sociological trends made Labour unelectable, see B. Sarlvik and I. Crewe, *Decade of Dealignment: The Conservative Victory of 1979 and Electoral Trends in the 1970s* (Cambridge, 1983), I. McAllister and R. Rose, *The Nationwide Competition for Votes: the 1983 British Election* (1984), P. Dunleavy and C. T. Husbands, *British Democracy at the Crossroads: Voting and Party Competition in the 1980s* (Oxford, 1985) and M. N. Franklin, *The Decline of Class Voting in Britain: Changes in the Basis of Electoral Choice, 1964–1983* (Oxford, 1985). See also R. J. Johnston, *The Geography of English Politics: The 1983 General Election* (1985), A. Heath, R. Jowell and J. Curtice, *How Britain Votes* (Oxford, 1985) and (as eds), *Labour's Last Chance? The 1992 Election and Beyond* (Aldershot, 1994) and H. Kitschelt, 'Class structure and Social Democratic Party strategy', *British Journal of Political Studies*, 23 (1993).

Once again, biographies and memoirs flesh out the picture. As well as books already cited, see M. Foot, *Another Heart and Other Pulses: The Alternative to the Thatcher Society* (1984), T. Benn, *The End of an Era: Diaries, 1980–1990* (1992), M. Westlake, *Kinnock: The Biography* (2001) and E. Heffer, *Never a Yes Man: The Life and Politics of an Adopted Liverpudlian* (1991).

11   Modernization and New Labour, 1987–97

On Kinnock's attempts to revamp the party, see the quasi-official view, C. Hughes and P. Wintour, *Labour Rebuilt: The New Model Party* (1990), M. J. Smith and J. Spear (eds), *The Changing Labour Party* (1992) and the left perspective of R. Heffernan and M. Marqusee, *Defeat from the Jaws of Victory* (1992). The changing membership is analysed in P. Seyd and P. Whiteley, *Labour's Grass Roots: The Politics of Party Membership* (Oxford, 1992). Difficulties with the media are nicely contextualized in J. Thomas, *Popular Newspapers, the Labour Party and British Politics* (2005).

P. Anderson and N. Mann, *Safety First: The Making of New Labour* (1997) is a good thematic account of the party's post-1992 development. T. Jones, *Remaking the Labour Party: From Gaitskell to Blair* (1996) puts developments into a longer-term perspective. G. R. Taylor, *Labour's Renewal: The Policy Review and Beyond* (1997) links the Kinnock and Blair periods nicely. Specifically on Clause IV, see P. Riddell, 'The end of Clause IV, 1994–95', *Contemporary British History*, 11 (1997). P. Gould, *The Unfinished Revolution: How the Modernisers Saved the Labour Party* (1998) is an uncompromisingly pro-New Labour insider account.

Expectations of what it was hoped a 'New Labour' government might deliver can be gleaned from T. Blair, *New Britain: My Vision of a Young Country* (1996), P. Mandelson and R. Liddle, *The Blair Revolution: Can New Labour Deliver?* (1996), M. Perryman (ed.), *The Blair Agenda* (1996) and B. Brivati and T. Bale (eds), *New Labour in Power: Precedents and Prospects* (1997). W. Hutton, *The State We're In* (rev. edn, 1996) is still worth study.

For electoral politics, see D. E. Butler and D. Kavanagh: *The British General Election of 1992* (1992) and *The British General Election of 1997* (1997), as well as A. Geddes and J. Tonge (eds), *Labour's Landslide: The British General Election 1997* (Manchester, 1997), M. A. Stephenson, *The Glass Trapdoor: Women, Politics and the Media during the 1997 General Election* (1998) and S. Saggar, *The General Election 1997: Ethnic Minorities and Electoral Politics* (1998). For the longer view, see G. Evans and P. Norris (eds), *Critical Elections: British Parties and Voters in Long-term Perspective* (London, 1999) and A. F. Heath et al., *The Rise of New Labour: Party Policies and Voter Choices* (Oxford, 2001).

As well as Westlake's biography of Kinnock, relevant 'lives' include A. McSmith, *John Smith: A Life, 1938–1994* (1994) and M. Stuart, *John Smith: A Life* (2005). Early biographies of Blair included J. Sopel, *Tony Blair: The Moderniser* (rev. edn, 1995) and J. Rentoul, *Tony Blair* (rev. edn, 1996). For Mandelson, see P. Routledge, *Mandy: The Unauthorised Biography of Peter Mandelson* (1999) and D. Macintyre, *Peter Mandelson* (1999). A. McSmith, *Faces of Labour* (1996) and L. McKinstry, *Fit to Govern?* (1996) offer very different views of Labour's leaders and members in opposition. Relations with the Liberal Democrats can be traced in great detail in P. Ashdown, *The Ashdown Diaries, Vol. 1: 1988–97* (2001).

12   New Labour in Power, 1997–2007

Numerous works cover the performance of Labour in power, including A. Seldon (ed.), *The Blair Effect* (2001), A. Seldon and D Kavanagh (eds), *The Blair Effect 2001–5* (Cambridge, 2005), D. Coates and P. Lawler (eds), *New Labour in Power* (Manchester, 2000), S. P. Savage and R. Atkinson (eds), *Public Policy under Blair* (Basingstoke, 2001), two books edited by S. Ludlam and M. J. Smith, *New Labour in Government* (Basingstoke, 2001) and *Governing as New Labour* (Basingstoke, 2004), and two books by P. Toynbee and D. Walker, *Did Things get Better?* (2001) and *Better or Worse? Has Labour Delivered?* (2005). M. Barber, *Instruction to Deliver: Tony Blair, the Public Services and the Challenge of Delivery* (2007) offers a valuable insight into the work of the Delivery Unit established in 2001.

A considerable number of memoirs have now appeared, and they add a great deal to our understanding. They include T. Blair, *A Journey* (2010), J. Prescott, *Prezza, My Story: Pulling No Punches* (2008), J. Straw, *Last Man Standing: Memoirs of a Political Survivor* (2012), P. Mandelson, *The Third Man: Life at the Heart of New Labour* (2010) and P. Watt, *Inside Out: My Story of Betrayal and Cowardice at the Heart of New Labour* (2010). They should be supplemented by reference to A. Campbell, *The Alastair Campbell Diaries* (4 vols, 2010–12), and three volumes of diaries by C. Mullin: *A Walk-On Part, 1994–1999* (2011), *A View from the Foothills, 1999–2005* (2009) and *Decline and Fall, 2005–2010* (2010).

Relations between the leading figures in the government, and particularly between Blair and Brown, gave rise to considerable interest. Among the more significant works, see, on Blair, A. Seldon, *Blair* (2004) and P. Riddell, *The Unfulfilled Prime Minister: Tony Blair's Quest for a Legacy* (2005); on Brown, the favourable views of P. Routledge, *Gordon Brown: The Biography* (1998) and R. Peston, *Brown's Britain* (2005), as opposed to the hostile T. Bower, *Gordon Brown* (2004); and, on the partnership, J. Naughtie, *The Rivals: The Intimate Story of a Political Marriage* (rev. edn, 2002). A. Rawnsley's books, *Servants of the People: The Inside Story of New Labour* (2nd edn, 2001) and *The End of the Party: The Rise and Fall of New Labour* (2010), are also useful. Other leading figures are described in C. Brown, *Fighting Talk: The Biography of John Prescott* (1997) and J. Kampfner, *Robin Cook* (1998). D. Blunkett, *The Blunkett Tapes* (2006) and A. Campbell, *The Blair Years: Extracts from the Alastair Campbell Diaries* (2007) are important insider accounts; and see also D. Draper, *Blair's Hundred Days* (1997). P. Ashdown, *The Ashdown Diaries, Vol. 2: 1997–99* (2002) demonstrates how Blair's interest in the Liberal Democrats unravelled after the 1997 landslide.

A great deal has been made of the 'style' of the Blair government of both the country and the party, much of it derogatory. See, among other works, P. Hennessy, 'Rulers and servants of the state: the Blair style of government 1997–2004', *Parliamentary Affairs*, 58 (2005), N. Jones, *Sultans of Spin* (2000), N. Fairclough, *New Labour, New Language?* (2000), A. Seldon and D. Kavanagh, *The Powers behind the Prime Minister: The Hidden Influence of Number Ten* (2001) and D. Wring, *Politics of Marketing the Labour Party* (2004). On the substance of party organization, see the important works by L. Minkin, *The Blair Supremacy: A Study in the Politics of Labour's Party Management* (Manchester, 2014) and M. Russell, *Building New Labour: The Politics of Party Organisation* (Basingstoke, 2005). P. Seyd and P Whiteley, in *New Labour's Grassroots: The Transformation of the Party Membership* (Basingstoke, 2002), look at that aspect. Allegations of 'control freakery' enliven P. Flynn, *Dragons led by Poodles: The Inside Story of a New Labour Stitch-Up* (1999), but the extent to which Labour MPs were prepared to stand up for themselves emerges clearly from two works by P. Cowley, *Revolts and Rebellions: Parliamentary Voting under Blair* (2002) and *The Rebels: How Blair Mislaid His Majority* (2005).

The nature of 'New Labour' excited considerable discussion and debate. A. Chadwick and R Heffernan (eds), *The New Labour Reader* (2003) is a valuable collection of sources. Among the more useful interpretative works, see S. Driver and L. Martell, *New Labour: Politics after Thatcherism* (1998), A. Gamble and T. Wright (eds), *The New Social Democracy* (1999), C. Hay, *The Political Economy of New Labour: Labouring under False Pretences?* (Manchester, 1999), A. Hindmoor, *New Labour at the Centre: Constructing Political Space* (Oxford, 2004), M. Beech, *The Political Philosophy of New Labour* (2005), M. Bevir, *New Labour: A Critique* (2005), D. Coates, *Prolonged Labour: The Slow Birth of New Labour Britain* (2005), S. Driver and L. Martell, *New Labour* (2nd edn, 2006) and R. Toye, '"The smallest party in history"? New Labour in historical perspective', *Labour History Review*, 69 (2004). On electoral politics, see especially D. E. Butler and D. Kavanagh, *The British General Election of 2001* (Basingstoke, 2001), A. Geddes and J. Tonge (eds), *Labour's Second Landslide: The British General Election of 2001* (Manchester, 2002), P. Norris (ed.), *Britain Votes 2001* (Oxford, 2001), D. Kavanagh and D. E. Butler, *The British General Election of 2005* (Basingstoke, 2005) and A. Geddes and J. Tonge (eds), *Britain Decides: The UK General Election 2005* (Basingstoke, 2005).

On the trade unions, see especially J. McIlroy, 'The enduring alliance? Trade unions and the making of New Labour, 1994–97', *British Journal of Industrial Relations*, 36 (1998) and A. Murray, *A New Labour Nightmare: The Return of the Awkward Squad* (2003).

External policy is covered in R. Little and M. Wickham-Jones (eds), *New Labour's Foreign Policy: A New Moral Crusade?* (2000), J. Kampfner, *Blair's Wars* (rev. edn, 2004) and P. Riddell, *Hug them Close: Blair, Clinton, Bush and the 'Special Relationship'* (rev. edn, 2004). See also A. Doig and M. Phythian, 'The national interest and the politics of threat exaggeration: the Blair government's case for war against Iraq', *Political Quarterly*, 75 (2005). Books by the two cabinet ministers who resigned over Iraq are also revealing: see R. Cook, *The Point of Departure: Diaries from the Front Bench* (2004) and C. Short, *An Honourable Deception? New Labour, Iraq, and the Misuse of Power* (2004).

13   Moving beyond Blair, 2007–15

The Brown premiership is covered in detail by S. Richards, *Whatever It Takes: The Real Story of Gordon Brown and New Labour* (2010) and A. Seldon and G. Lodge, *Brown at 10* (2010), although attention should also be paid to Rawnsley, *End of the Party* (above). A more sympathetic account comes from W. Keegan, *'Saving the World'? Gordon Brown Reconsidered* (2012). G. Brown, *Beyond the Crash: Overcoming the First Crisis of Globalisation* (2010) gives Brown's own view of the financial crisis. Many of the memoirs cited in the section above are also relevant here; see also A. Darling, *Back from the Brink: 1,000 Days at Number 11* (2011). For the seamier side of the Brown government's operations, see D. McBride, *Power Trip: A Decade of Policy, Plots and Spin* (2013). See also M. Foley, 'Gordon Brown and the role of compounded crisis in the pathology of leadership decline', *British Politics*, 4 (2009), K. Theakston, 'Gordon Brown as Prime Minister: political skills and leadership style', *British Politics*, 6 (2011) and P. Cowley and M. Stuart, 'In the Brown stuff? Labour backbench dissent under Gordon Brown, 2007–10', *Contemporary British History*, 28 (2014).

The 2010 general election is placed in longer-term context in P. Whiteley et al., *Affluence, Austerity and Electoral Change in Brtiain* (Cambridge, 2013) and Denver and Garnett, *British General Elections since 1964* (see above). Specifically on 2010, see P. Cowley and D. Kavanagh, *The British General Election of 2010* (2010), A. Geddes and J. Tonge (eds), *Britain Votes 2010* (Oxford, 2010) and R. Worcester et al., *Explaining Cameron's Coalition: An Analysis of the 2010 British General Election* (2011). The events that followed are described in A. Adonis, *5 Days in May: The Coalition and Beyond* (2013).

The leadership election that followed is covered in P. Dorey and A. Denham, '"O, brother, where art thou?" The Labour Party leadership election of 2010', *British Politics*, 6 (2011) and R. Jobson and M. Wickham-Jones, 'Reinventing the block vote? Trade unions and the 2010 Labour Party leadership election', *British Politics*, 6 (2011). The most authoritative work on Brown's successor is M. Hasan and J. Macintyre, *Ed: The Milibands and the Making of a Labour Leader* (2012); see also J. Gaffney and A. Lahel, 'Political performance and leadership persona: the UK Labour Party conference of 2012', *Government and Opposition*, 48 (2013) and T. Bale, 'If Opposition is an art, is Ed Miliband an artist? A framework for evaluating Leaders of the Opposition', *Parliamentary Affairs* (2014). There appears, as yet, to have been little interest from biographers in any of Miliband's leading colleagues. For organizational change, see Labour Party, *The Collins Review into Labour Party Reform: Building a One Nation Labour Party* (2014). For 'Blue Labour', see R. Davis, *Tangled up in Blue: Blue Labour and the Struggle for Labour's Soul* (2011) and M. Beech and K. Hickson, 'Blue or Purple? Reflections on the future of the Labour Party', *Political Studies*, 12 (2014), as well as M. Glasman et al. (eds.), *The Labour Tradition and the Politics of Paradox* (2011) and R. Philpott (ed.), *The Purple Book: A Progressive Future for Labour* (2011). Key core texts on the 'One Nation' vision are O. Smith and R. Reeves (eds), *One Nation: Power, Hope, Community* (2013) and J. Cruddas and J. Rutherford, *One Nation: Labour's Political Renewal* (2014); the phenomenon is covered more academically in J. Gaffney and A. Lahel, 'The morphology of the Labour Party's One Nation narrative: story, plot and authorship', *Political Quarterly*, 84 (2013) and T. Bale, 'Concede and move on? One Nation Labour and the welfare state', *Political Quarterly*, 85 (2014).

Index

391